EMERGENCY AND EU LAW

Under what circumstances, if any, can the suspension of fundamental rights be considered legitimate in response to an emergency? If such suspensions were to occur within the EU legal order, which actors should bear responsibility for ensuring that the exercise of emergency powers does not undermine procedural and substantive fundamental rights: EU or national courts, the European parliament or national parliaments, or other institutions? What role should the principle of proportionality play in balancing competing rights during emergencies? Could situations labelled as an 'emergency' in one Member State be treated merely as a 'crisis' in another, and what legal consequences might follow from such divergences? Even if a shared definition of 'emergency' were agreed upon, should the migration crises, the COVID-19 pandemic, and climate change be governed by the same constitutional law approaches?

These are some of the legal dilemmas discussed in this volume by leading legal scholars in the EU and beyond.

Emergency and EU Law

The Case of Covid-19, Climate Change and Migration

Swedish Studies in European Law
Volume 21

Edited by
Sanja Bogojević
and
Xavier Groussot

•HART•
OXFORD • LONDON • NEW YORK • NEW DELHI • SYDNEY

HART PUBLISHING

Bloomsbury Publishing Plc

Kemp House, Chawley Park, Cumnor Hill, Oxford, OX2 9PH, UK

1385 Broadway, New York, NY 10018, USA

Bloomsbury Publishing Ireland Limited, 29 Earlsfort Terrace, Dublin 2, D02 AY28, Ireland

HART PUBLISHING, the Hart/Stag logo, BLOOMSBURY and the Diana logo are trademarks of Bloomsbury Publishing Plc

First published in Great Britain 2026

A catalogue record for this book is available from the British Library.

A catalogue record for this book is available from the Library of Congress.

Library of Congress Control Number: 2026931452

ISBN: HB: 978-1-50999-332-1
ePDF: 978-1-50999-334-5
ePub: 978-1-50999-333-8

Typeset by Compuscript Ltd, Shannon

For product safety related questions contact productsafety@bloomsbury.com

To find out more about our authors and books visit www.hartpublishing.co.uk. Here you will find extracts, author information, details of forthcoming events and the option to sign up for our newsletters.

Preface

THE CONCEPT FOR this edited volume emerged during a time when the world was gradually moving away from the emergency measures implemented in response to the Covid-19 pandemic. One of us spent much of the pandemic in the UK, while the other was in Sweden, each of us witnessing very different governmental responses. Having worked together in Lund during the 2015 European migration crisis that saw more than one million people seek asylum in Europe, this had not been our first encounter with emergency measures. During this period, Sweden imposed border controls and ID checks on the Öresund Bridge that connects Lund to Denmark and the rest of the European continent. Sweden was not alone in enacting emergency measures in the form of restrictions on movement within the Schengen Area – Denmark enforced similar measures at its border with Germany, and Germany did the same on its border with Austria. As EU law scholars, we were curious about the impact that emergencies have on the EU: a jurisdiction built on solidarity, free movement and the rule of law.

More precisely, we got to debating the question in which circumstances, if any, fundamental rights could legitimately be suspended in the face of an emergency. And if there were to be such a suspension, who should take responsibility for safeguarding that this exercise of power did not erode procedural and substantive fundamental rights: the EU or national courts, the EU or national parliaments, the public or a different body altogether? What role might proportionality play in balancing different rights in cases of emergency? Sitting in Sweden, which lacks formal constitutional provisions for declaring a state of emergency (except in the case of war), it quickly became apparent that a definition of what counts as an emergency is crucial: could it be that what is to be labelled an 'emergency' in one country is approached as a 'crisis' in another? What might be the legal implications of such divergencies? Even if we could rally around a common definition of what constitutes an emergency, should we approach the migration crises, the Covid-19 pandemic, and climate change the same way?

The list of legal dilemmas that we came up with in thinking about emergencies went on. It quickly became clear to us that we couldn't treat all the questions alone, and so we invited the contributors of this collection to discuss these issues at a conference in Lund. This took place in December 2023. We want to express our thanks to the Swedish Network for European Legal Studies for supporting the conference and this volume. Our work on emergency and EU law was further generously funded by the Marianne and Marcus Wallenberg Foundation, to which we remain deeply grateful.

Most of the editing of this volume was carried out at the Lund University Faculty of Law. We wish to thank all our colleagues for providing a vibrant and supportive environment that has been a constant source of inspiration for us both. Along the same lines, we want to extend our thanks to Lady Margaret Hall and the Law Faculty at the University of Oxford for supporting this collaboration. Anna Zemskova and Laurianne Allezard – our postdoctoral fellows on the Marianne and Marcus Wallenberg Foundation-funded project on emergency and EU law – deserve special mention for their enthusiasm and hard work which has inspired the same in us. Similarly, we are thankful to Ulrika Carlsson, whose immaculate editing and unwavering attention to detail has ensured that the ideas and insights shared in this book are presented with clarity and precision.

Finally, and most importantly, we would like to extend our heartfelt thanks to all the contributors, whose diverse perspectives and expertise have come together to create a dynamic and thought-provoking volume. The chapters show reasons for concern: the use of emergency measures, and therewith heightened executive power, are on the rise in the EU (and elsewhere) and the need for tight rule of law safeguards ever more in demand. The reading may be sobering, but we hope you'll enjoy it.

Sanja Bogojević
Xavier Groussot
March 2025

Contents

Preface......v
List of Contributors......ix

PART I
CONSTITUTIONAL CHALLENGES

1. *Introduction: Emergencies and Constitutional Dilemmas in EU Law*......3
Sanja Bogojević and Annika Consiglio

2. *Crisis is the 'New Black': The Constitutional Implications of the Proliferating Talk of 'Crises' in Politics*......17
Helle Krunke

3. *Emergency in Constitutional Proportionality Review: The Freedom of Judges and its Limits in Europe*......35
Laurianne Allezard

PART II
GOVERNANCE

4. *Rethinking EU Emergency Law: Towards a General Supranational Emergency Clause?*......63
Federico Casolari and Anna Pau

5. *The Emergency Models of the Nordic Countries: Four Peas in a Pod?*......81
Anna Zemskova

6. *Scaffolding an Era of Emergency: Lessons from Canada's Emergencies Act*......99
Jocelyn Stacey

PART III
MIGRATION

7. *The Constitutional Implications of Emergency Measures in European Migration and Asylum Law*......123
Salvatore Fabio Nicolosi

8. *Economic Crises and EU Migration Law: A Blast from the Past* 149
Alezini Loxa

9. *Legal Sources in Times of 'Crisis' – How Sweden's Migration Courts Responded to the 2016 Temporary Migration Law* 165
Lovisa Häckner Posse

PART IV
CLIMATE CHANGE

10. *Who Decides, and How, When Things Fall Apart? Climate Emergency, Public Participation and the Role of EU Law* 185
Chiara Armeni

11. *Climate Emergency, Vulnerability and Justice: The Ambivalent Dynamic of the European Green Deal* 207
Nathalie Hervé-Fournereau

PART V
COVID-19 PANDEMIC

12. *Discretion in the Context of the Covid-19 Pandemic and EU/EEA Law: A Study of the Precautionary and Proportionality Principles in Emergency Situations* 241
Xavier Groussot and Katharina Girbinger

13. *The Covid-19 Pandemic and Parliamentary Oversight in Finland* 263
Tuukka Brunila, Janne Salminen and Mehrnoosh Farzamfar

14. *Review of Covid-19 Measures by the European Court of Human Rights: How to Avoid the 'Fair', the 'Balance' and 'the Fair Balance'* 281
Vladislava Stoyanova

Index 301

List of Contributors

Laurianne Allezard is Postdoctoral Fellow at the Faculty of Law, Lund University.

Chiara Armeni is Professor of Environmental Law at the Faculty of Law and Criminology, Université de Bruxelles.

Sanja Bogojević is Fellow and Professor of Law at Lady Margaret Hall and the Law Faculty, University of Oxford. She was Guest Professor at the Faculty of Law, Lund University for the duration of putting this volume together.

Tuukka Brunila is Postdoctoral Researcher at the Faculty of Law, University of Turku.

Federico Casolari is Professor of European Union Law, and Head of the Department of Legal Studies, Alma Mater Studiorum, University of Bologna.

Annika Consiglio is a former LLM student at the Faculty of Law, Lund University.

Mehrnoosh Farzamfar is a postdoctoral researcher at the Faculty of Law, University of Turku.

Nathalie Hervé Fournereau is Director of Research (CNRS) at the University of Rennes.

Katharina Girbinger is a judicial clerk, Oberlandsgericht München.

Xavier Groussot is Professor of EU Law at the Faculty of Law, Lund University.

Helle Krunke is Professor of Constitutional Law at the Faculty of Law, University of Copenhagen. She is also an Honorary Doctor at the Faculty of Law, Lund University.

Alezini Loxa is a postdoctoral researcher in EU law at the Faculty of Law, Lund University.

Salvatore Fabio Nicolosi is Assistant Professor at Utrecht University Law School and Researcher at Utrecht Centre for Regulation and Enforcement in Europe (RENFORCE).

Anna Pau is Postdoctoral Research Fellow in European Union Law, Alma Mater Studiorum, University of Bologna.

Lovisa Häckner Posse is Assistant Professor at Södertörn University.

Janne Salminen is Professor of Public Law at the Law Faculty, University of Turku.

Jocelyn Stacey is Associate Professor at the Peter A. Allard School of Law, University of British Columbia.

Vladislava Stoyanova is Associate Professor of Public International Law at the Faculty of Law, Lund University.

Anna Zemskova is Postdoctoral Fellow at the Faculty of Law, Lund University.

Part I

Constitutional Challenges

1

Introduction: Emergencies and Constitutional Dilemmas in EU Law

SANJA BOGOJEVIĆ AND ANNIKA CONSIGLIO

I. INTRODUCTION

EMERGENCIES – WHETHER triggered by war, natural disaster, pandemics or any other crisis – demand quick collective decision-making.[1] This may necessitate sidestepping 'the deliberate pace of ordinary constitutional rule',[2] meaning that emergencies risk straining the delicate balance between the exercise of executive authority, on the one hand, and democratic oversight and the protection of civil liberties, on the other. Ultimately, unchecked executive decision-making poses a serious threat to the rule of law and, by extension, to the legitimacy of any legal system. It is thus easy to understand why situations of emergency are discussed in terms of 'exceptionalism' or, as Zwitter describes it: *not* 'the normal state of affairs'.[3]

At the same time, situations of emergency are becoming increasingly common. During the period of writing this volume, the world has grappled with multiple wars and an energy crisis in addition to the ongoing climate emergency. Not only are these interrelated and constitute 'a convergence of risk',[4] but they also follow on the back of a long period characterised by executive measures pertaining to the Covid-19 pandemic and multiple migration crises. There is thus no scarcity of

[1] Many such examples are found in this volume relating to migration, climate change and the Covid-19 pandemic.

[2] J Ferejohn and P Pasquino, 'The Law of the Exception: A typology of Emergency Powers' (2004) 2 *International Journal of Constitutional Law* 210, 210.

[3] Zwitter describes an emergency as 'a de facto situation, which, because of its nature, prompts the state to temporarily change some state structures so that it can more effectively and efficiently address the situation at hand. Such a situation, therefore, represents a condition which is rather different than the normal state of affairs under which the government usually operates', see A Zwitter 'The Rule of Law in Times of Crisis: A Legal Theory on the State of Emergency in the Liberal Democracy' (2012) 98 *Archives for Philosophy of Law and Social Philosophy* 95.

[4] Term borrowed from Goodman and others who, however, focus on the threat of climate change, see S Goodman et al, 'National Security and the Threat of Climate Change' (The CNA Corporation, 2007) www.cna.org/archive/CNA_Files/pdf/national%20security%20and%20the%20threat%20of%20climate%20change.pdf.

materials for examining the aptness of constitutional legal orders for dealing with emergencies. According to Ferejohn and Pasquino, 'aptness' in this regard means having a constitutional framework that can answer the following queries:[5]

> Who decides that an emergency exists and what is to be done about it? Who is entrusted with the exercise of emergency powers? What are the legal limits to the reach and intrusiveness of emergency powers? Who may review and control the exercise of emergency powers based on these legal limits? What are the procedures to terminate an emergency and restore constitutional normalcy?

This checklist is not straightforward, and for the EU legal order – the main focus of the present volume – it raises multiple constitutional dilemmas. First, there is the question about competences: whether the EU (and if so, which EU institution), or some other executive powerholder has the authority to take action in times of emergency. This raises queries about what, if any, explicit competences the EU enjoys in this regard, as well as the extent to which other general competences, and importantly, the internal market provisions, may spill over into general contingency plans.[6] Then there is the question of procedures: how the decision-making is carried out, who decides, and who exercises oversight. This also involves determining which substantive safeguards are relevant and which rights and principles guide or ought to guide decision-making, and then proceeding to rely on these in scrutinising the emergency measures when enacted. Underpinning all of this is a more fundamental conceptual dilemma: how to define what qualifies as an 'emergency', and who has the authority to declare and terminate it. It is these issues that the chapters in this volume grapple with.

In this way, the collection adds to the existing dynamic debate about how to understand the EU legal order in situations of crises.[7] In the realm of constitutional law, responses to the Covid-19 pandemic have garnered significant scholarly attention,[8] as have questions surrounding the constitutional implications of recent migration crises.[9] While the constitutional dimensions of the

[5] Ferejohn and Pasquino (n 2) 228.

[6] See, eg, European Commission, Proposal for a Regulation of the European Parliament and of the Council establishing a Single Market emergency instrument and repealing Council Regulation No (EC) 2679/98, COM(2022) 459 final.

[7] See, eg, M Cotta and P Isernia (eds), *The EU Through Multiple Crises: Representation and Cohesion Dilemmas for a 'Sui Generis' Polity* (Routledge, 2023); M Riddervold, J Trondal and A Newsome (eds), *The Palgrave Handbook of EU Crises* (Palgrave Macmillan, 2020); N Brack and S Guerkan (eds), *Theorising the Crises of the European Union* (Routledge, 2021); M Rhinard, N Nugent and WE Paterson (eds), *Crises and Challenges for the European Union* (Bloomsbury, 2023).

[8] See, eg, V Delhomme and T Hervey, 'The European Union's response to the Covid-19 crisis and (the legitimacy of) the Union's legal order' (2022) 41 *YEL* 48; and the 'Power and the COVID-19 Pandemic' symposium hosted by the *Verfassungsblog*, reported on the impact of the COVID-19 pandemic on law and legal systems in 64 countries, see verfassungsblog.de/category/debates/power-and-the-covid-19-pandemic-debates/.

[9] See, eg, A Loxa and V Stoyanova, 'Migration as a Constitutional Crisis for the European Union' in S Stijn and V Stoyanova, *Migrants' Rights, Populism and Legal Resilience in Europe* (Cambridge University Press, 2022); S Carrera, J Santos Vara and T Strik (eds), *Constitutionalising the External Dimensions of EU Migration Policies in Times of Crisis: Legality, Rule of Law and Fundamental Rights Reconsidered* (Edward Elgar, 2019).

climate emergency have also been examined,[10] they have received comparatively little attention. This volume stands out among the existing scholarship by thinking about emergencies across sectors – migration, the Covid-19 pandemic and climate change[11] – and relies on examples from the EU and its Member States as well as further afield to scrutinise the aptness of the respective constitutional frameworks for handling emergencies. While the chapters demonstrate that it is challenging to generalise about emergencies and their governance structures, they nevertheless suggest that certain forms of constitutional 'scaffolding'[12] for safeguarding the rule of law across different emergency scenarios are both feasible and desirable.

This introductory chapter draws on the insights from all the contributions to this volume. It begins by illustrating the ambiguity surrounding the concept of 'emergency' and the legal challenges that this generates. It then examines the key constitutional dilemmas explored throughout the volume and highlights how the individual chapters engage with them.

II. THE ELASTICITY OF EMERGENCY AS A CONCEPT

Calling something an emergency 'is a way of communicating the seriousness of the risks' involved.[13] The risks may be existential, as in the case of climate change and war, or, as in the case of civil unrest or economic crises, directed at a particular political and/or economic system. In some cases the cause or 'enemy' may be clearly identifiable (as in wars). But in other scenarios, often linked to health and the environment, the causes may be polycentric or (partly) unknown, making the navigation of responses particularly challenging.[14] Some emergencies have a clear end-date: a peace agreement, in the case of war, whereas the climate emergency is ongoing. Importantly, this means that the latter is 'not so much a discrete problem to be solved as it is a condition under which human beings will have to make choices about such matters as priorities for economic development and the way we govern ourselves'[15] – and do so under conditions of deep uncertainty about the future.[16] Certain emergencies have no obvious

[10] See, eg, J Stacey, *The Constitution of the Environmental Emergency* (Hart Publishing, 2018); F Gallarati, 'Is Climate Emergency a Constitutional Emergency? A Critical Appraisal' (2023) 3 *Italian Review of International and Comparative Law* 448.

[11] See also Special Issue: Public Law and the New 'Emergencies' (2023) *Edinburgh Law Review*, which similarly examines approaches to the Covid-19 pandemic and the climate emergency.

[12] J Stacey, ch 6 of this volume, 'Scaffolding an Era of Emergency: Lessons from Canada's Emergencies Act'.

[13] E Fisher, 'Climate Change and Statutory Construction: Administrative Law Expertise and "New" Emergencies' (2023) 27 *Edinburgh Law Review* 322, 324.

[14] See, eg, HM Osofsky, 'Polycentrism and Climate Change' in M Faure (ed), *Elgar Encyclopedia of Environmental Law* (Edward Elgar, 2023).

[15] S Rayner, 'Foreword' in M Hulme (ed), *Why We Disagree about Climate Change: Understanding Controversy, Inaction and Opportunity* (Cambridge University Press, 2009) xxii.

[16] Stacey (n 10) 1.

end-dates, then. Some of these differences could be taken to distinguish 'old' from 'new' types of emergencies, war exemplifying the former and climate change the latter.[17] The point here, however, is simply to show that what we count as an emergency is ultimately 'elastic'.[18]

Studying emergencies from a comparative perspective gained currency following the Covid-19 pandemic, which saw emergency measures implemented across the globe but with distinct features. Some jurisdictions imposed strict lockdowns, quarantine measures, mass testing, and border closures, whereas other countries, primarily Sweden, relied heavily on voluntary measures and social distancing upheld by social trust. Thus, even in a situation globally thought of as an emergency, countries organised themselves differently in addressing it, and the extent to which judicial, legislative and democratic oversight was granted in the process diverged widely.

Beyond Covid-19 responses, the pandemic also showed the need for further comparative analysis of how emergencies are conceptualised and governed. For instance, as of March 2025, 2,366 jurisdictions in 40 countries have declared a climate emergency.[19] This, however, has not led to the same restrictions witnessed during the pandemic where aviation and certain businesses, for example, closed down in order to limit the spread of the virus – measures which could arguably also help limit climate change.[20] If the concept is indeed elastic, and allows a wide range of responses, what power lies in the name 'emergency'?

A. Normative Pluralism and Emergency Governance

In debating the terminology of emergency, Jocelyn Stacey reminds us that 'any attempt to invoke the language of emergency should be scrutinized carefully, especially by legal scholars, in light of the long history of emergencies undermining rule-of-law and human rights commitments'.[21] The label 'emergency' thus comes with a stark warning sign. At the same time, not allowing for such legal concepts and their ability to trigger speedy responses could also jeopardise 'the lives of many citizens'.[22] Could it be that focusing on narrowly defining what qualifies as an emergency distracts us from a more important issue? While 'emergency' could simply be taken to mean a sudden, unforeseeable event demanding immediate action, what merits our attention is how

[17] N Walker and C McCorkindale, 'Public Law and the New "Emergencies": from Covid to Climate Change' (2023) 27 *Edinburgh Law Review* 249, 250.

[18] O Gross and F Ní Aoláin, *Law in Times of Crisis: Emergency Powers in Theory and Practice* (Cambridge University Press, 2006) 3.

[19] See climateemergencydeclaration.org/climate-emergency-declarations-cover-15-million-citizens.

[20] See, eg, WWF, www.worldwildlife.org/initiatives/cutting-aviation-pollution.

[21] J Stacey, 'The Public Law Paradoxes of Climate Emergency Declarations' (2022) 11 *TFEL* 291, 292.

[22] S Auer and N Scicluna, 'The Impossibility of Constitutionalizing Emergency Europe' (2021) 59 *Journal of Common Market Studies* 20, 27.

institutions, decision-makers, and individuals organise and respond during its aftermath.

The chapters in this book warn against this view. For one thing, Alezini Loxa explains, how we can legislate about emergency in the future depends first of all on how we frame it.[23] We therefore need to carefully understand it and its components. What is more, legal vagueness is its own threat to the rule of law. Thus in discussing Danish Covid-19 measures, Helle Krunke shows how, in the absence of emergency regulation, the Danish government labelled it a 'crisis', and based on this adopted executive decisions outside ordinary legislative procedures, including deciding to partly suspend the judiciary.[24] Krunke thus demonstrates how the lack of clarity regarding what constitutes an emergency, and the extent to which it encompasses 'crises', risks creating a power vacuum with limited accountability mechanisms.

To begin delimiting the concept and being mindful not to overstretch it, Joelle Grogan collects a list of common elements in provisions labelled 'state of emergency': (1) conditions for their declaration; (2) a delegation of power; (3) limitations on their use; and (4) provisions for legislative or judicial oversight.[25] Navigating situations of emergency, transparency and continued oversight of any delegation of power, even if time-restricted, is significant. But while some Member States have emergency provisions in place, either through their constitutions or ordinary and/or statutory legislation,[26] others lack a precise legal definition of emergency or fail to provide such provisions.[27] In the case of the EU, emergency measures exist at multiple levels – at times, both at the EU and the national levels – what then?

The answer arguably depends on whether a relativist or absolutist approach is adopted.[28] The former allows for the relaxation or even suspension of ordinary constitutional principles in emergency situations.[29] This is also known as the 'extra-legal measures model' where emergency powers exist outside the ordinary legal order.[30] Inspired by Carl Schmitt and the maxim that 'necessity knows

[23] A Loxa, ch 8 of this volume, 'Economic Crises and EU Migration Law: A Blast from the Past'.

[24] H Krunke, ch 2 of this volume, 'Crisis is the 'New Black': The Constitutional Implications of The Proliferating Talk of "Crises" in Politics'. Contributions beyond the chapters in this book, similarly, insist that emergency should be clearly distinct from 'crises' mode, see eg B de Witte, 'Guest Editorial: EU Emergency Law and its Impact on the EU Legal Order' (2022) 59 *CMLR* 3.

[25] J Grogan, 'States of Emergency' (*Verfassungsblog*, 26 May 2020).

[26] C Bjørnskov and S Voigt, 'The Architecture of Emergency Constitutions (2018) 16 *International Journal of Constitutional Law* 101.

[27] A Jonsson Cornell and J Salminen, 'Emergency Laws in Comparative Constitutional Law – The Case of Sweden and Finland' (2018) 19 *German Law Journal* 219. See also E Tsourdi, 'Solidarity in EU Asylum Policy: From an Emergency-driven Approach to the Fair Sharing of Responsibility' (2019) 24 *Challenge Europe*.

[28] See, eg, A Antoniadis, R Schütze and E Spaventa (eds), *The European Union and Global Emergencies: A Law and Policy Analysis* (Hart Publishing, 2011) 1.

[29] ibid.

[30] SF Nicolosi, 'Addressing a Crisis Through Law: EU Emergency Legislation and Its Limits in the Field of Asylum' (2021) 17 *Utrecht Law Review* 19.

no law', this view calls for accepting the idea that 'a state of emergency exposes the limits of law'.[31] The rationale behind this view is partly that it is difficult to define a concept that will fit emergencies that have not yet taken place.[32] As a result, the argument is that 'no constitutional shackles can wisely be imposed on the power to which the care of it is committed'.[33]

This approach challenges the assumption of constitutionality on which the absolutist approach, also known as the 'accommodations model', rests upon.[34] This model calls for the application of the constitution in all situations except those that fulfil the criteria of emergencies, in which case certain *lex specialis* may be adopted.[35] This brings situations of emergency into the legislative framework.[36] Gross and Aoláin see the latter as a group of models that 'countenance a certain degree of accommodation for the pressures exerted on the state in times of emergency', while at the same time 'maintaining normal legal principles and rules as much as possible.'[37] A similar approach that is also based on the assumption of constitutionality but goes a step further in considering the constitution as a 'law for all seasons' goes under the name 'business as usual'.[38] Here, the law that applies in normal situations does not change at all, nor does ordinary legislation consider whether there is an emergency or not.[39]

There are several other ways to describe the different systems put in place to address emergencies. Pablo Martín Rodriguez argues that different approaches may be divided into the constitutional approach and the international law approach,[40] where international law treats national emergencies as an excuse for non-compliance, while the constitutional model is[41]

> less about requiring a legal basis for reacting to the emergency [… and more] about managing the reaction, with the understanding that this reaction itself might turn into a threat for that preservation (ending in a constitutional mutation). The real issues are thus whether the legislative, the executive or a certain combination of both should rule this reaction ex ante; whether there are any uncrossable constitutional

[31] AC Dinopoulos, 'The "Legality" of Necessity in the State of Exception' (2024) 45 *Liverpool Law Rev* 255; D Dyzenhaus, *The Compulsion of Legality* (Cambridge University Press, 2008); K Loevy, 'What Is an Emergency? The Legal Politics of Defining the "Un-Definable"' (2015) 22 *ILSA Journal of International & Comparative Law* 155.

[32] Loevy, ibid.

[33] ibid.

[34] O Gross and F Ní Aoláin, *Law in Times of Crisis: Emergency Powers in Theory and Practice* (Cambridge University Press, 2006) 86–109.

[35] Nicolosi (n 30).

[36] ibid; D Dyzenhaus, 'Schmitt v. Dicey: Are States of Emergency Inside or Outside the Legal Order' (2006) 27 *Cardozo Law Review* 2005.

[37] Gross and Ní Aoláin (n 34) 17.

[38] Antoniadis, Schütze and Spaventa (n 28).

[39] Dyzenhaus, 'Schmitt v. Dicey' (n 36).

[40] P Martín Rodríguez. 'A Missing Piece of European Emergency Law: Legal Certainty and Individuals' Expectations in the EU Response to the Crisis' (2016) 12 *European Constitutional Law Review*.

[41] ibid.

> limits thereto; and what is the appropriate role for the judiciary before, during and after emergency law obtains.

This view, however, is not normative. As was also explained by Rodriguez: 'neither of the models necessarily accounts for the reality of how legal systems [*should*] deal with emergencies',[42] and there is a variety of different ways in which a jurisdiction may choose to respond to emergencies, 'particularly in the case of a multilevel setting such as the EU.'[43] Indeed, even if the narrower context of the Nordic countries, where there are many legal commonalities, Anna Zemskova finds that their constitutional design is 'not all that straightforward and allows for recourse to different emergency models in different forms and combinations during different types of extraordinary situations'.[44]

We are therefore confronted with the fluidity of what constitutes an 'emergency,' shaped by specific jurisdictions and contexts. This flexibility, however, does not imply a free-for-all. Periods of emergency show the need to carefully examine and decide on who has the authority to declare and oversee emergencies, who holds them accountable, and which legal safeguards remain in place to do so. These are, in essence, constitutional dilemmas that need to be considered to ensure that once emergencies unfold, the rule of law scaffolding is safely in place.

III. CONSTITUTIONAL DILEMMAS

Legal scholars have long grappled with the idea of emergencies, and their implication for constitutional law in particular. The key legal challenge posed by emergencies is that an unforeseen threat or disaster demands swift collective decision-making. This raises fundamental constitutional questions, including who gets to decide what counts as an emergency and trigger a state of emergency. Are the powers enjoyed by the executive without limits? If not, who scrutinises the executive branch to check whether any limits have been trespassed? What exactly can be scrutinised and on what grounds?

A. Who Decides?

Nine out of 10 countries have some type of emergency provisions recognised in their constitutions.[45] 'Emergency constitutionalism' is thus arguably the 'new

[42] ibid.
[43] ibid.
[44] A Zemskova, ch 5 of this volume, 'The Emergency Models of the Nordic Countries: Four Peas in a Pod?'.
[45] C Bjørnskov and S Voigt, 'The Architecture of Emergency Constitutions' (2018) 16 *International Journal of Constitutional Law* 101.

normal'.[46] The EU does not enjoy a general 'emergency competence' but does have a mix of specific and general legislative powers that has allowed it, especially in recent years, to legislate on what might be described as 'emergency scenarios'.[47] Such measures cover a broad field of topics, including financial assistance during the Covid-19 pandemic and the energy crises in the aftermath of Russia's invasion of Ukraine, as well as border controls during different migration crises.[48]

This body of law, as well as the competences, is what might be labelled 'EU emergency law'. According to de Witte, the EU has the power to regulate 'a horizontal balance of powers' between the Member States, and a 'vertical balance of powers' between the Member States and the EU.[49] To the former category belongs Article 42(7) TEU[50] – the clause for mutual defence first invoked by France following the 2015 terrorist attack in Paris.[51] A related 'solidarity' clause is Article 222 TFEU, which states that the EU and its Member States 'shall act jointly in a spirit of solidarity' in the case of a 'terrorist attack or the victim of a natural or man-made disaster'.[52] When it comes to the vertical balance of powers, Article 78(3) TFEU allows the Council to take action on migration 'for the benefit of the Member State(s) concerned' in the case of a 'sudden inflow of nationals of third countries'.[53] More broadly, Article 196(1) TFEU promotes 'swift, effective operational cooperation within the Union' in the case of 'natural or man-made disasters', broadly interpreted,[54] and 122 TFEU allows the Council to adopt measures in the case that 'severe difficulties arise in the supply of certain products, notably in the area of energy.' This provision is seemingly limited to 'economic situations' but it adds that the Council may also grant 'financial assistance to the Member States in case of severe difficulties caused

[46] M Belov, 'Rule of Law and Democracy in Times of Transitory Constitutionalism, Constitutional Polycrisis and Emergency Constitutionalism' in M Belov (ed), *Rule of Law in Crisis: Constitutionalism in a State of Flux* (Routledge, 2022); J Rosamond, 'The Slow-Burning Climate Emergency and the European Green Deal: Prospects and Pitfalls in the Polycrisis Era' in M Roos and D Schade (eds), *The EU under Strain?: Current Crises Shaping European Union Politics* (De Gruyter, 2023).

[47] SF Nicolosi, 'Emergency Legislation in European Union law' in T van den Brink and V Passalaqua (eds), *Balancing Unity and Diversity in EU Legislation* (Edward Elgar, 2024) 61.

[48] For an overview see, eg, M Chamon, 'The Rise of Article 122 TFEU: On Crisis Measures and the Paradigm Change' (*Verfassungsblog*, 1 February 2023).

[49] de Witte (n 24) 3.

[50] 'If a Member State is the victim of armed aggression on its territory, the other Member States shall have towards it an obligation of aid and assistance by all the means in their power, in accordance with Article 51 of the United Nations Charter. This shall not prejudice the specific character of the security and defence policy of certain Member States.'

[51] See eg House of Commons Library, 'France and Article 42(7) of the Treaty on the European Union' (Research Briefing 2015), at commonslibrary.parliament.uk/research-briefings/cbp-7390/.

[52] This is further specified in Council Decision of 24 June 2014 on the arrangements for the implementation of the Union of the solidarity clause, (COM)2014 OJ L 192/53.

[53] 'In the event of one or more Member States being confronted by an emergency situation characterised by a sudden inflow of nationals of third countries, the Council, on a proposal from the Commission, may adopt provisional measures for the benefit of the Member State(s) concerned. It shall act after consulting the European Parliament.'

[54] F Casolari and A Pau, ch 4 of this volume 'Rethinking the EU Emergency Law: Towards a General Supranational Emergency Clause?'.

by natural disasters or exceptional occurrences beyond its control'. This is indeed the provision that, as Paul Dermine notes, 'has become the cornerstone of Union action',[55] enabling the Council to decide on economic recovery plans, gas supplies to the EU, and caps on the revenues of electricity producers. The existence of these competences suggests that the EU Treaty drafters anticipated the Union's role in managing various emergency situations, although the degree to which these powers have been exercised has, as shown in this volume, sparked concerns about potential overreach with limited democratic oversight.[56]

But there is more. The EU does not necessarily need to use specific constitutional powers when confronting emergencies but may deal with these through general competences. As Fabio Nicolosi points out in this volume, the proposal to establish a Single Market Emergency Instrument to ensure the continued functioning of the internal market during times of crises[57] is an example of an emergency measure based on Article 114 TFEU and the free movement provisions.[58] This shows how Member State emergency actions that create obstacles to trade can invite the EU, which otherwise does not enjoy a *régime d'exception*, to harmonise the economic field.

In light of the foregoing, it is worth considering whether the EU Treaties should be amended to incorporate a comprehensive emergency clause into EU primary law to handle unexpected situations in a coordinated fashion across the Union rather than ex-post through internal market harmonisation. In this volume, Casolari and Pau explore the merits of introducing such a clause. On the one hand, it could help overcome the current fragmentation in EU law, where the Union relies on internal market provisions and a patchwork of 'emergency' clauses – none of which, in their view, offer a fully satisfactory legal basis for emergency governance. But on the other hand, it could be that collective decision-making power is disproportionally allotted to the executive, or the Council in the case of the EU. But as Lovisa Häckner Posse importantly remarks in this volume, the question of 'who acts' in emergencies should not be understood as implying legal voids calling for a dominant, centralised executive authority. We should envision an ongoing process involving a multiplicity of actors.[59] Given that crisis management unfolds within complex institutional environments, a detailed understanding of these environments – including their governing norms, practices, and institutional interplays – is essential for grasping the full scope of response capacities mobilised during perceived emergencies. This is important, especially in the EU context where the allocation and exercise

[55] P Dermine, 'Article 122 TFEU and the Future of the Union's Emergency Powers' (*EU Law Live*, 25 January 2024).

[56] See also ibid and de Witte (n 24).

[57] Proposal for a Regulation establishing a Single Market emergency instrument (n 6).

[58] S Nicolosi, ch 7 of this volume, 'The Constitutional Implications of Emergency Measures in European Migration and Asylum Law'.

[59] L Häckner Posse, ch 9 of this volume, 'Legal Sources in Times of "Crisis": How Sweden's Migration Courts Responded to the 2016 Temporary Migration Law'.

of competences are distributed across both EU and national levels. Any discussion of 'EU emergency law' must therefore account for the interactions between multiple actors, institutions and contexts, as well as the different mechanisms whereby such power allocation is scrutinised in an ever-complex legal system.

B. Who Scrutinises?

Judicial scrutiny serves as a fundamental safeguard for upholding the rule of law and protecting civil liberties, including in times of emergency. Several chapters in this volume show a high level of judicial deference in reviewing executive decision-making at times of emergency. This raises obvious dilemmas about the ways in which constitutional limits can be reasserted during such periods, especially if it is not done by the courts. These questions are central to Laurianne Allezard's analysis of how courts in France, Germany, the Czech Republic and Hungary review measures on climate emergency, immigration, and Covid-19.[60] She finds that while certain patterns exist, no unified theory or approach has emerged in judicial practice regarding emergencies. Her analysis shows that courts have generally aimed to limit the duration and impact of emergency measures but refrain from challenging the substance or decisions contained in the measures. As Allezard emphasises, what is ultimately at stake is the judge's freedom: their ability to act independently of restrictive legal formalism in moments of constitutional stress. This finding aligns with scholarship by David Dyzenhaus who similarly argues that legal actors must resist legitimising executive overreach by merely assuming that rule of law principles are intact. As he notes, courts should 'accept that the government and the legislature have committed themselves to ruling through the rule of law, and use that commitment as a legitimating basis for finding that the legislature must have intended real, not sham, controls'.[61]

This view is further supported by the analysis of the European Court of Human Rights (ECtHR) jurisprudence on Covid-19 measures undertaken by Vladislava Stoyanova. This chapter shows how the Court has so far refrained from developing emergency/crisis *acquis* to guide national decision-makers in reviewing (Covid-19) emergency measures. The risk of doing so is high, Stoyanova claims, concluding that 'By walking the path of avoidance, the Court risks making itself irrelevant'.[62]

Obviously, it is not just the judiciary that must secure rule of law in times of emergency. As Krunke describes things, in Denmark it was the Parliament

[60] L Allezard, ch 3 of this volume, 'Emergency in Constitutional Proportionality Review: The Freedom of Judges and Its Limits in Europe'.

[61] ibid 99. He argues that this assumption should guide judicial reasoning all the way up to the point at which the legislature clearly and explicitly states that it wants the executive to operate outside the law. See also D Dyzenhaus, *The Constitution of Law* (Cambridge University Press, 2006) 217.

[62] V Stoyanova, ch 14 of this volume 'Review of Covid-19 Measures by the European Court of Human Rights: How to Avoid the "Fair", the "Balance" and "the Fair Balance"'.

that kept the executive power in check when the latter decided to suspend or circumvent judicial oversight and at times sideline courts altogether. Likewise in Finland, as discussed by Brunila, Salminen, and Farzamfar, Parliament played a decisive role in ensuring that executive power was held accountable.[63] Notably, the Finnish Constitution and the Finnish Emergency Powers Act require parliamentary review of emergency decrees and empower it to revoke measures deemed unnecessary or disproportionate. The dilemma of who scrutinises the executive in times of emergencies was thus resolved *ex ante*.

These chapters illustrate the fact that the EU is embedded in a broader judicial and parliamentary framework where power may be scrutinised at multiple levels: at the national level, the EU level and finally before Strasbourg. Coordinating action between the various instances has its challenges, but it also shows the availability of multiple checks and balances, even if, as some contributions to this volume show, these might be strengthened.

C. On What Grounds?

This collection of chapters shows that in times of emergency, robust constitutional safeguards are essential. This includes ensuring that general principles of EU law, such as respect for fundamental rights, are embedded throughout the legislative process, from initial impact assessments of emergency measures to their implementation and oversight. Moreover, in order to prevent the erosion of legal certainty and the misuse of derogations, emergency mechanisms must be clearly defined, temporary in nature, and subject to regular, independent review. Hervé-Fournereau argues that the issue extends beyond constitutional form. When responding to climate emergencies, substantive legal protections are necessary, particularly with regard to vulnerable communities and environmental justice. Thus her chapter stresses how vital it is, in such processes, to anchor ecological transition in a model of social and environmental justice; achieve a balance among competing rights and interests; and deepen democratic processes and access to justice within the EU's legal framework.[64]

Along the same lines, Groussot and Girbinger show that principles can also serve as meaningful constraints on emergency powers. Through an analysis of case law from the Court of Justice of the European Union as well as the EFTA court, they show how these institutions have developed a model of 'controlled discretion', structured around the combined application of the precautionary principle and the principle of proportionality. While Member States are

[63] T Brunila, J Salminen and M Farzamfar, ch 13 of this volume 'The Covid-19 Pandemic and Parliamentary Oversight in Finland'.

[64] N Hervé-Fournereau, ch 11 of this volume 'Climate Emergency, Vulnerability and Justice: The Ambivalent Dynamic of the European Green Deal'.

afforded significant latitude during emergencies, this controlled discretion is bounded by substantive and procedural safeguards derived from these principles. They caution, however, that this model is not uniformly applied across different types of emergencies and so makes it difficult to speak of a unified or consistent doctrine of 'emergency discretion'.[65]

But to access courts, and partake in decision-making, procedural rights are significant, including participation rights. Chiara Armeni's contribution deals with these issues and underscores the need to enhance the legal right to participate in environmental decision-making. The obvious dilemma is that in times of emergency, there is a level of urgency that does not easily allow for wide participation. Yet Armeni convincingly argues that emergencies, and especially the climate emergency, present a test for the EU legal order – and a chance to strengthen its democratic foundations by safeguarding meaningful public involvement.[66]

This volume thus shows that there is a plethora of safeguards available to help secure the rule of law in times of emergency. These are both constitutional and legislative; rights-based and principle-focused; substantive and procedural. The point is that an emergency is not a legal vacuum but a time when citizens' rights demand continued oversight and protection.

IV. URGENCY AND THE NEED FOR CAREFUL FORESIGHT

In discussing the state of emergency following the terrorist attacks of 11 September, Burke Ackerman, a political scientist, urged EU policymakers to take proactive steps to create a legislative framework before another emergency kicks in:[67]

> In the future, it will not be enough to defeat proposals that threaten permanent damage to civil liberties. Europeans should take the lead in developing more constructive solutions. It is far wiser to consider legislation creating a sensibly limited emergency regime before, not after, London or Paris becomes the target. The overriding aim should be to enact a statute that not only contains tight temporal limits but requires increasing legislative supermajorities for further extensions. A framework law emerging from any major European state would have worldwide influence. It would help us see the 'war on terrorism' for what it is: an extravagant metaphor blocking responsible thought about a serious problem.

This is a long extract, but it is one that is important to include. It shows how times of emergency may be painful, but they are important in calling for

[65] X Groussot and K Girbinger, ch 12 of this volume 'Discretion in the Context of the Covid-19 Pandemic and EU/EEA law: A Study of the Precautionary and Proportionality Principles in Emergency Situations'.

[66] C Armeni, ch 10 of this volume 'Who Decides, and How, When Things Fall Apart? Climate Emergency, Public Participation and The Role of EU Law'.

[67] B Ackerman, 'Don't Panic', *London Review of Books* (7 February 2002).

constitutional safeguarding of our liberties. How to do this is not obvious. Ackerman hoped that a model system of emergency legislation would have emerged by now. But establishing such a framework, as Jocelyn Stacey notes, is challenging 'because the complexity of emergencies on the ground does not map onto the tidy framework for emergency management reflected in emergency legislation'. She continues:[68]

> even seemingly straight-forward emergency legislation should not try to accurately and comprehensively reflect the complexity of emergencies as they unfold in real life. Instead, legislators should strive to embed rule-of-law commitments into their emergency legislation. The result will be that such legislation will not perfectly track the reality of emergencies (as such a goal is not attainable). Instead, it will do something much more important: scaffold the rule-of-law project, which inevitably comes under strain in times of crisis.

Our scaffolding may take different forms depending on context and jurisdiction. This volume illustrates some of the legal and variations that exist. Their commonality, however, is that they are concerned with ensuring that the constitutional dilemmas outlined here are addressed and carefully navigated.

[68] J Stacey, ch 6 of this volume 'Scaffolding an Era of Emergency: Lessons from Canada's Emergencies Act'.

2

Crisis is the 'New Black': The Constitutional Implications of the Proliferating Talk of 'Crises' in Politics

HELLE KRUNKE*

I. INTRODUCTION

CRISIS RHETORIC HAS for many years been the so-called 'new black' in EU and national politics. Starting with the economic crisis in 2007, the EU and the Member States have faced a financial crisis, a migration crisis, the Brexit crisis, the Ukraine crisis,[1] a rule of law crisis, a Covid-19 crisis, an energy crisis, as well as a climate crisis. This is reflected in legal literature on crises in the EU.[2] In constitutional law literature, much of the focus has been on the notion of a state of emergency, as well as emergency legislation linked to specific crises, especially the Covid-19 pandemic.[3] In this chapter, I explore

* This chapter elaborates on a number of presentations I have delivered over the past few years, including one on the contemporary challenges faced by constitutional law, which I presented when I was awarded an honorary doctorate at Lund University (May 2023); on the Danish Mink Commission, given at the University of Bergen (2022), the IACL World Congress at the University of Johannesburg (2022), and as a Frede Castberg lecture at the University of Oslo (2023). I would like to thank Emma Marie Sejr for her research assistance in finding the relevant legal sources for this piece.

[1] Here referred to as a foreign affairs crisis for the EU starting back in 2014 with the Russian annexation of Crimea. On 24 February 2022, Russia fully invaded Ukraine, starting a war on European territory.

[2] See, eg, H Krunke, H Petersen and I Manners (eds), *Transnational Solidarity. Concept, Challenges, and Opportunities* (Cambridge University Press, 2020); M Riddervold, J Trondal and A Newsome (eds), *The Palgrave Handbook of EU Crises* (Palgrave Macmillan, 2020); N Brack and S Gürkan (eds), *Theorising the Crises of the European Union* (Routledge, 2021), and M Rhinard, N Nugent WE Paterson (eds), *Crises and challenges for the European Union* (Bloomsbury, 2023).

[3] See, eg, J Grogan 'Introduction & List of Country Reports' (*Verfassungsblog*, 6 April 2020) and JM Serna, H Krunke and IN Duy (eds), *COVID19 and Constitutional Law* (The International Association of Constitutional Law (IACL) and the Institute of Legal Research of Mexico's National University, 2020).

whether there are any constitutional law implications when decision-makers label a societal challenge a 'crisis'.

While 'state of emergency' is a familiar concept to constitutional law, the term 'crisis' seems to be less – if at all – recognised as a constitutional concept. This means that while the legal constitutional meaning, status and consequence is clear when politicians refer to a state of emergency, this is not the case when they refer to a 'crisis'. Nevertheless, politicians frequently refer to crises as reasons for rapid action where decision-making is streamlined, consultations are cut out and time efficiency takes precedent. During the Covid-19 period this became daily life in many countries but noteworthy, the crisis rhetoric did not disappear when the pandemic ended. The purpose of this chapter is not to deny that the world is currently facing many challenges of which some are intertwined. The focus is rather on how the term 'crisis' is leveraged politically to give legitimacy to policies, and the impact of this from a constitutional law perspective. More precisely, this study examines what a 'crisis' is from a constitutional law perspective: are decision-makers simply using the term as a rhetorical and political tool, or are they in fact trying to create a legal space for crises based on a 'burning platform' argument?[4] Followingly, when a societal challenge is labelled a 'crisis', it maps and assesses the constitutional law implications, including accountability measures for the government in question.

In this chapter, I rely on Denmark as a case study. I do so for several reasons. Most obviously, I am a Danish legal academic. But there is more to the case study. During the Covid-19 pandemic, the Danish government did not declare a state of emergency. However, the term 'crisis' was used extensively. What is more, following the pandemic and a general election, the new government continued to rely on a crises-rhetoric: in its 2022 political programme, for example, it relied on the term 'crisis' 22 times and 'critical' 7 times, and it has often employed a crisis rhetoric since.[5] This makes Denmark a perfect example for studying the constitutional law consequences of a crises rhetoric.

This inquiry is structured as follows. In Section II, the concepts of state of emergency and crisis are scrutinised from a constitutional law perspective. This is followed, in Section III, by an examination of these concepts during the Covid-19 in Denmark. In the subsequent part, Section IV, the focus is on the use of crisis rhetoric and its legal constitutional implications after Covid-19.

[4] A burning platform argument is an argument for (political) action based on immediate necessity.

[5] 'Ansvar for Danmark. Det politiske grundlag for Danmarks regering' (*Statsministeriet*, 14 December 2022) ('Ansvar for Danmark'). Regeringsgrundlag 2022 – Statsministeriet, available at www.stm.dk/statsministeriet/publikationer/regeringsgrundlag-2022.

This leads to a discussion of crises and accountability (Section V), followed by a conclusion (Section VI).

II. STATE OF EMERGENCY v CRISIS

The Danish Constitution has no general emergency clause. Rather, Article 23 regulates provisional laws *in case* of emergency:

> In an emergency the King [today interpreted as the government] may, when the Folketing [Parliament] cannot assemble, issue provisional laws, provided that they shall not be at variance with the Constitutional Act, and that they shall always, immediately on the assembling of the Folketing [Parliament], be submitted to it for approval or rejection.

In addition to this provision, an Act issued by the Ministry of Defence regulates the management of accidents, disasters and war:[6]

> The rescue service's task is to prevent, limit and remedy damage to persons, property and the environment in the event of accidents and disasters, including acts of terrorism and war, or imminent danger thereof.

On 29 August 2024, a new cross-sector Ministry for Emergency Situations was introduced. The Danish Emergency Management Agency ('Beredskabsstyrelsen') is tasked with prevention, preparedness and response to accidents and disasters, and with outlining a national risk profile.[7]

As mentioned, there is no general legal basis in the text of the Danish constitution for the state to deviate from the constitution if an emergency arises. However, according to the Danish constitutional law literature, the competence to deviate from the constitution during an emergency has a legal basis in an unwritten legal principle of constitutional rank.[8] One might characterise it as an unwritten constitutional principle with binding legal effect. According to this legal principle, the constitution can be deviated from if a very serious threat to the state and its institutions arises.[9] The extraordinary situation must be such as to make the deviation necessary.[10]

This unwritten legal principle has been relied upon very rarely, primarily in the context of World War II.[11] During the German occupation, an Act was adopted in Parliament banning communist associations. In 1941.1070H, a

[6] See LBK nr 314 af 03/04/2017 Bekendtgørelse af Beredskabsloven, Art 1.
[7] See the Danish Emergency Management Agency's website, www.brs.dk/en/.
[8] See eg M Sørensen, *Statsforfatningsret* (Juristforbundets forlag, 1973) 39; H Zahle, *Dansk forfatningsret 3* (DJØF, 2000) 266; and JP Christensen et al, *Dansk Statsret* (DJØF, 2020) 33ff.
[9] See eg Sørensen, ibid 39.
[10] See Christensen et al (n 8) 34.
[11] U1941.1070H and U1945.570Ø.

citizen claimed that the Act was unconstitutional because it violated Article 78 of the Danish constitution, which protects the freedom of association. According to the City Court of Copenhagen, the Act was not unconstitutional, basing its judgments on the legal principle regulating states of emergency:[12]

> Since the law in question in this case, according to the information provided to the court, has been processed and adopted under the present extraordinary circumstances and with due consideration to the principle of necessity in a fully defensible and constitutional manner, as Article 78 of the Constitution does not prevent the legislative power, under the current abnormal conditions, from establishing special rules regarding a type of detention neither directly nor indirectly mentioned or foreseen in the Constitution, when it is urgently necessary for the security of the state and its relations with foreign powers, and since the Minister of Justice's decision to maintain the detention of NN is present, and as there is no mistake regarding NN's identity or previous participation in communist activities or agitation according to the information provided.

The Supreme Court stated the following, without referring directly to that legal principle:

> As it can be agreed that the objections raised by NN against the validity of Law No. 349 of August 22, 1941, are found to be unfounded, and as [...] the conditions mentioned in Section 2, Subsection 2, of the law for lifting the implemented detention are not present.

While the notion of a state of emergency is defined in constitutional law and has been used in Danish courts in a few instances, providing a narrow legal basis for state action, 'crisis' is not defined as a legal term in constitutional literature.[13] To the extent that a crisis fulfils the definition of a state of an emergency, the situation is obviously covered by the unwritten legal principle regarding states of emergency if one is declared. However, a crisis does not in itself legitimise state action, which deviates from the Constitution. In this way, Danish constitutional law reflects the claim put forward in the beginning of this chapter well, namely that while 'state of emergency' is a concept familiar to constitutional law, the term 'crisis' seems to be less recognised as a constitutional concept – if at all. The constitutional legal meaning, status and consequences are clear when politicians refer to a state of emergency. However, when politicians speak of a 'crisis', this is not the case. Yet over the past few years, Danish governments have explicitly labelled many societal challenges 'crises', as will be seen next.

[12] See U1941.1070H, and Christensen et al (n 8) 34–35.

[13] The Danish Emergency Management Agency does not directly define what a crisis is on its website, but some guidance is provided: 'There are many factors that can trigger a crisis. Extreme weather events are set to become more frequent and severe, which could affect all of or parts of the country. The threat of man-made incidents, such as cyber attacks and sabotage, is serious due to the deteriorating security situation in Europe. Finally, accidents, technical issues or other incidents with a wide impact on society can occur', see DEMA, 'Prepared for crises', see www.brs.dk/en/prepared.

III. THE CRISIS RHETORIC AND ITS CONSTITUTIONAL IMPLICATIONS DURING THE COVID-19 PANDEMIC

No state of emergency was declared in Denmark during the Covid-19 pandemic. The government instead referred to this societal challenge as 'the Covid-19 *crisis*'. In the beginning of November 2021, the government decided to cull all Danish minks (ca. 18 million) to prevent the spread of Covid-19 from these animals to human beings, and the development of new variants of the virus in minks, which could later spread to humans. This was communicated to the public at a press conference the following day.

However, it later turned out that there was no legal basis for this decision. In 2022, Parliament introduced a Commission with the task of investigating the matter, including the question whether there had been a legal basis for culling the minks at the time of the decision and whether the principle of legality was violated. The so called 'Mink Commission' questioned almost 60 witnesses during its proceedings, one of which was the Prime Minister. The Prime Minister said she had felt a 'duty to act', but this duty was of a moral rather than legal character.[14] The Mink Commission briefly mentioned in its report that the situation did not fulfil the criteria for a state of emergency. The Commission also concluded that at the time when the decision was made, and at the press conference the following day, the Prime Minister was not aware that there was no legal basis for the decision to cull all Danish minks.

Even though no state of emergency was declared during the Covid-19, the political processes did not follow their usual course. For instance, on many occasions the ordinary legislative procedure was not followed.[15] According to the ordinary legislative procedure, a bill must be read three times in Parliament before it is passed.[16] Furthermore, the Standing Orders state:[17]

> The first reading of a Bill shall take place not earlier than 2 days after the Bill has been published on one of the Danish Parliament websites, and preferably not earlier than 5 days after it has been published on one of the Danish Parliament websites. The mover of a Bill is entitled to request that it be submitted to the first reading within 5 sitting days counting from the day on which a written request to this effect was made to the Speaker. However, the first reading shall take place not earlier than on the fourteenth sitting day after the Bill has been published on one of the Danish Parliament websites. If a Bill is introduced after April 1st, cf. section 10(3), a vote shall – if 17 Members

[14] Report of the Mink Commission, Vol 8, 10–28.

[15] See the report by the Danish Institute of Human Rights and The Danish Bar Association, 'Covid-19 tiltag i Danmark' (2020), available at menneskeret.dk/files/media/document/covid tiltag.pdf 22–23, where several examples are provided. See also the report by Parliament, 'Håndteringen af covid-19 i foråret 2020' (*Folketinget*, January 2021) 358–85, which provides a quantitative perspective on the use of the rapid legislative procedure, available at www.ft.dk//media/sites/ft/pdf/publikationer/haandtering-af-covid19-foraar-2020.pdf.

[16] Art 41 of the Constitution and Art 10, Part 4, of the Standing Orders of Parliament.

[17] Art 11, Part 1.

request it – be taken in order to decide whether a first reading can take place. Prior to such a voting, the Speaker can subject the question to a separate debate at which the rules on speaking time applying to short remarks apply. At the first reading, the Bill is debated in principle without going into too much detail. Amendments cannot be moved.

During the Covid-19 pandemic, the exception in Article 42 to the Standing Orders of Parliament was applied many times.[18] Deviations from the Standing Orders Article 42 are allowed under the following conditions:[19]

> If it is a *matter of urgency*, the rules of the Standing Orders may be disregarded at the suggestion of the Speaker or if 17 Members have suggested it in writing, provided that the rules concerned do not regard constitutional provisions or other legal provisions and in cases in which three fourths of the Members who vote accept the proposal, cf. section 33(1, 2nd clause).

Hence, the procedure was shortened so that the three readings could take place within just a few days or even 12 hours in some cases, even though the bills were complex, sometimes concerned fundamental rights, such as the right to assembly, and were very long. Hearings were also cut out in many cases. It seems implausible that the members of Parliament could read, understand and deliberate on the bills on an informed basis. According to a report from the liberal think-tank CEPOS, 19 per cent of all bills in 2019–2020 were handled according to 'rapid procedure' with a legal basis in Article 42's exception to the Standing Orders of Parliament.[20]

Interestingly, in the three years following the Covid-19 pandemic, 11.4 per cent of all bills have been handled according to the same rapid procedure grounded in Article 42. We will return to what looks like a spill-over effect from pandemic-era legislative procedure in the next section of this chapter. Applying the rapid legislative process is not a violation of the constitution. However, it is questionable how broadly 'matter of urgency' in Article 42 of the Standing Orders of Parliament can be interpreted. Furthermore, application of the rapid legislative procedure may entail a deterioration of the democratic processes and the quality of the legislation. This may also affect the courts which have to interpret legislation thus adopted, which risks being unclear and inconsistent. Not least, citizens may suffer in the application of such legislation. The rule of law, the principle of legality, and the *Rechtsstaat* are at stake.

Without going into details, it is worth noting that the political decision-making processes within the government were more centralised during

[18] See J Mchangama, 'Epidemilov vedtaget' (*Justitia*, 23 February 2021); J Herby, 'Arbejdspapir 75: En forhastet lovgivning' (CEPOS, 2023), available at cepos.dk/media/7046/arbejdspapir-75-en-forhastet-lovgivning.pdf. See also the report by Parliament, 'Håndteringen af covid-19' (n 15) 358–85; J Christoffersen and SB Jensen, 'Retsstaten og Covid-19' (*Justitia*, 23 June 2020) 82 and 85, available at justitia-int.org/wp-content/uploads/2020/06/Justitia-Retsstaten-og-Covid-19.pdf.

[19] Italics added.

[20] See eg Herby (n 18) 2.

Covid-19, and that a new Covid-19 committee, which included representatives from various ministries, was formed.[21] When power is centralised, crisis management is more efficient. At the same time, centralisation risks making political decision-making a more closed and thus less transparent process. Rushing past the normal consultation processes, decisions risk being made without all relevant arguments and knowledge. A lack of transparency may also make it difficult to hold decision-makers accountable.

When Denmark went into lockdown, the government also ordered a partial suspension of the activities of courts and took a stand on which cases the courts should continue to handle and which would have to wait (though it is not entirely clear whether this was conveyed as a request or as an order to the independent agency of court administration). Such a decision clearly falls under the competence of the president of each court. It has been discussed in legal literature and reports whether the government's actions showed sufficient respect for the separation of the judiciary and executive powers.[22] Some of the press releases from the independent agency on court administration seem to indicate that the courts were forced to act according to the orders of the government: 'we would very much like to get started in the court rooms again, as soon as it is responsible from a health perspective, *and the government gives the green light*'.[23]

Interestingly, while the government found it necessary to shut down the courts along with all other public institutions for a period in 2020, Parliament was not shut down. This was a positive deviation from the policies adopted in many other European countries. However, there was arguably a special need for the courts during Covid-19 precisely because the behaviour and rights of citizens and private companies were restricted.

In sum, while the Danish government managed to navigate through Covid-19 without introducing a state of emergency, it has been criticised for some of its actions, including culling all Danish minks – without any legal basis for it at the time when the decision was made – and how this was communicated to the public. It also adopted many bills through the rapid legislative procedure, limited the activity of the courts, and decided which cases the courts should handle. As shown above, some of this criticism concerns whether important constitutional provisions and principles were sufficiently respected and upheld, while other parts concern the Standing Orders of Parliament, and the practice related to it. Considering this, it seems that some of the political decisions based on the crisis rhetoric during Covid-19 may have had consequences of a legal constitutional character.

[21] See eg 'Håndtering af Covid-19' (n 15).

[22] See AF Nyborg et al, 'Covid-19 and emergency laws in Denmark' (2020) 10 *Svensk Juristtidning* 1098; and Christoffersen and Jensen (n 18) 95ff. These matters are regulated in Art 64, Art 3 and Art 62 of the constitution, respectively.

[23] Domstolsstyrelsens pressemeddelelse af 8. april 2020: 'Domstolene forlænger nødberedskabet', also quoted in Christoffersen and Jensen (n 18) 95 (emphasis added).

IV. THE POST-PANDEMIC CRISIS RHETORIC DURING AND AFTER THE 2022 ELECTION

While one would have expected the political crisis rhetoric to disappear after the Covid-19 pandemic, it has in fact been used extensively and spread to other fields. Before looking at examples of this, however, a note about the political landscape in Denmark after the pandemic.

Because of the debates in Parliament following the Mink Commission's critical report, published in the summer of 2022, the Danish government was politically forced to call an election. This took place on 1 November 2022; in December the same year, a new government was formed. The sitting Prime Minister remaining in that post, now presiding over a majority government, contrary to a Danish tradition of minority governments dating back to the 1970s. The new government was remarkable also in that it was formed across the political left-wing (Social Democrats), middle (Moderates) and right-wing (Liberals). By including parts of the former opposition in a majority government, the previous ruling party (Social Democrats) managed to strike a deal concerning the *Mink* case. With the new government, there was no longer majority support for having a law firm read the Commission's report and assess whether there were sufficient grounds for Parliament to pursue legal accountability (impeachment) for some of the ministers involved, including the Prime Minister.[24]

The previous government had also been plagued by its handling of an accusation against (among others) a former defence minister from the Liberals and the former head of the Military Intelligence Service for making confidential information public. Additionally, the government had been criticised for its handling of a case regarding a person thought to have been an Intelligence Service informant, later charged and imprisoned for terrorism. Recently, on 2 September 2025, the Danish Supreme Court reached the conclusion that the two Intelligence Services should confirm publicly that the mentioned individual had in fact cooperated with the Intelligence Services and received remuneration for it. The government's handling of these cases drew a great deal of criticism from Parliament as well as critical media coverage. Among other questions, Parliament debated whether the commission investigating the handling of the cases against the former defence minister and the former head of the Military Intelligence Service should be formed and run by Parliament (like the Mink Commission) or by the government. (Commissions are independent in their investigations no matter whether they are formed and run by Parliament or the Ministry of Justice.) The opposition wanted the former, while the government wanted the commission to be formed and run by the Ministry of Justice, consisting of three judges from the Western High Court, whereas a commission normally consists of a High Court judge (chairman), a university professor, and

[24] A commission investigates what happened in the case at hand, but it does not conclude whether there are grounds for impeachment against any ministers.

an attorney from a law firm.[25] The government moreover wanted the investigation, including the questioning of witnesses, to take place behind closed doors. There was also debate about the scope of the commission's task.

Following the 2022 elections, however, the new majority government had its way.[26] Contrary to standard procedure, all interviews with witnesses took place behind closed doors, and the final report by the commission is confidential. Only a short conclusion will be made publicly available. Thus, the commission's findings cannot be scrutinised and debated in Parliament, the media or by ordinary citizens. Importantly, the Supreme Court issued a verdict in the criminal case against the former Minister of Defence, concluding that there was no need for the case to take place behind closed doors.[27] However, this did not settle the matter. First of all, the prosecutor chose to annul the case against the former minister and the former head of the Military Intelligence Service in order to protect classified information from being made public.[28] Furthermore, it kept the commission's investigation behind closed doors.[29] The justification provided for all these decisions was security considerations, despite the fact that the Supreme Court had deemed such considerations insufficient in the present case to warrant a closed investigation.[30] In another verdict, the Supreme Court ruled that the indictment against the former head of the Military Intelligence Service did not have to be kept secret, contrary to what the prosecutor had argued for, again based on a security consideration.[31] Finally, the Supreme Court ruled that the case against the former minister should be brought in a jury trial.[32]

[25] See Folketingstidende 2023–24, 1. samling, tillæg A, B 87 som fremsat ('B 87'), available at www.folketingstidende.dk/samling/20231/beslutningsforslag/B87/20231_B87_som_fremsat.pdf.

[26] The government even managed to get support from a party outside the government, the Socialist People's Party (SF), in a deal that at the same time strengthened its control over the Danish Intelligence Services more generally. See 'Regeringen og SF er enige om en styrkelse af Tilsynet med Efterretningstjenesterne, udvidelse af FE-undersøgelseskommissionens mandat og undersøgelse af den såkaldte Samsam-sag' (*Justitsministeriet*, 6 December 2023) available at www.justitsministeriet.dk/pressemeddelelse/regeringen-og-sf-er-enige-om-en-styrkelse-af-tilsynet-med-efterretningstjenesterne-udvidelse-af-fe-undersoegelseskommissionens-mandat-og-undersoegelse-af-den-saakaldte-samsam-sag/.

[27] Case 94/2023, KAD001, available at domstol.dk/media/ro1nlfee/94-2023-anonym.pdf, and Case 95/2023, KAD001, available at domstol.dk/media/abqpe2gg/95-2023-anonym.pdf.

[28] See A Pedersen 'Straffesagerne mod Lars Findsen og Claus Hjort Frederiksen gennemføres ikke' (*Anklagemyndigheden*, 1 November 2023), available at anklagemyndigheden.dk/da/straffesagerne-mod-lars-findsen-og-claus-hjort-frederiksen-gennemfoeres-ikke.

[29] See 'Udtalelse fra justitsminister Peter Hummelgaard' (*Justitsministeriet*, 1 November 2023) available at www.justitsministeriet.dk/pressemeddelelse/udtalelse-fra-justitsminister-peter-hummelgaard/; see also '14. møde', *Folketinget*, (8 November 2023), available at www.ft.dk/forhandlinger/20231/20231M014_2023-11-08_1300.htm.

[30] B 87 (n 25); Folketingstidende 2023–24, tillæg A, L 133 som fremsat, in Lovforslag nr. L 133, Folketinget 2023–24, Forslag til Lov om ændring af lov om undersøgelse af beslutningen om hjemsendelse af ledende medarbejdere i Forsvarets Efterretningstjeneste (Udvidelse af undersøgelsen), eg § 4, stk. 1, 2. pkt. and § 22; and '14. møde' (n 25) available at www.folketingstidende.dk/samling/20231/lovforslag/L133/20231_L133_som_fremsat.pdf; and 'Regeringen og SF' (n 26); and EEM Henriksen, 'Regeringen afviser krav om åbenhed i FE-undersøgelse: "Vil være uansvarligt"' *DR*, (2 November 2023), available at www.dr.dk/nyheder/politik/regeringen-afviser-krav-om-aabenhed-i-fe-undersoegelse-vil-vaere-uansvarligt.

[31] Case 43/2023, KAD001, available at domstol.dk/media/3olfeoi1/43-2023-anonymiseret.pdf.

[32] Case 55/2023, KAD002, available at domstol.dk/media/4bwiujmj/55-23-anonymiseret.pdf.

Seen from a constitutional law perspective, the crisis rhetoric has led to lack of transparency in state actions, which also makes it difficult to hold decision-makers accountable. One of the two individuals prosecuted in the case is now filing a tort case against the state. On 5 November 2025, he won the case at the City Court. The case has been appealed to the High Court by the Police Intelligence Service who is represented by the public prosecutor.

Let us now return to the 2022 elections. The formation of the strengthened, majority government was justified by the many crises in Denmark and Europe. The Prime Minister ran on the promise of forming a broad coalition across the political left and right, arguing that the many crises faced by Denmark demanded this:[33]

> In the Social Democratic party, we enter into the election based on social democratic policy – as you know us. But we are open to compromises and to cooperation. Because of the difficult times we live in. With the adversity which the world faces, crises which intertwine, the time has come to try a new form of government in Denmark. A more committed political cooperation. We would like to take the lead on that. A broad government with parties from both sides of the middle of politics. A government which still supports our allies and our neighbours in Ukraine in winning the war, and solves the long-term challenges for Denmark.

These crises were listed in the government's political programme, where the term 'crisis' was used 22 times and 'critical' 7 times:[34]

> First, the pandemic hit. Then the global supply-chains became uncertain. Russia attacked Ukraine. There is now war in Europe. That has created an energy crisis, which has contributed to record-high inflation, among other things. At the same time there is a risk that the European economy will enter a recession, which will inevitably lead to growing unemployment.

The programme also mentions the 'climate crisis', 'biodiversity crisis' and 'welfare crisis'.[35]

In the years following the introduction of the government's political programme, questions were raised in public debate whether all the mentioned crises had materialised. In fact, the predicted economic crisis never became a reality: Denmark finished the fiscal year 2023 with a surplus of approximately 311 billion kroner (41.5 billion Euros).

As mentioned above, in the three years following the Covid-19 crisis, 11.4 per cent of all bills were handled according to the rapid legislative procedure with a legal basis in Article 42. That is almost four times as many bills as in the period 2000/01–2018/19.[36] We are thus seeing a development that reaches beyond Covid-19, and which could be a spill-over effect from the use of the rapid

[33] 'Pressemøde om valgudskrivelse den 5. oktober 2022' (*Statsministeriet*, 5 October 2022) available at www.stm.dk/statsministeren/taler/pressemoede-om-valgudskrivelse-den-5-oktober-2022/ (translation by author).

[34] 'Ansvar for Danmark' (n 5) (translation by author).

[35] ibid 3, 12, 17–19, 27.

[36] See Herby (n 18) 2.

legislation procedure during the pandemic. The increase is particularly great for the most rapidly handled bills – those handled within seven days (compared with the categories of bills handled within 8–14 days and 15–30 days).[37] There are examples of bills being adopted the day after they were introduced, for instance bills regarding inflation, and frozen energy bills.[38]

The Danish Parliament is aware of the development and the Select Committee on the Standing Orders published a report on this topic in 2021 where it expressed concern, defined some guidelines for the rapid treatment of bills, and emphasised that sunset clauses should always be inserted into rapidly treated legislation.[39] The Committee also emphasised that going forward, and based on the experiences from Covid-19, the principled extraordinary character of the rapid procedure should be made more explicit and formalised as a necessary exception from the Standing Orders, when Parliament vote on applying the rapid legislative procedure.[40]

The Prime Minister responded that she generally agreed with the views put forward by the Committee, and that she took note of the guidelines. However, she also pointed out that, as mentioned by the committee, whether bills were adopted by the rapid legislative procedure in any given case would depend on a political decision.[41] Whether a rapid legislative procedure is to be employed can be decided either unilaterally by the Speaker or by Parliament with a vote count of at least 17 Members (out of the total 179). The government may request a rapid procedure when sending the bill to Parliament, as it did 36 times in the parliamentary sitting of 2019–20. To be adopted by rapid procedure, a bill must receive three quarters of the votes. The Prime Minister's reference to the fact that whether the rapid legislative process is employed in any given case depends on a political decision must be seen in the context of how things have developed since then. As mentioned, the rapid procedure has been employed quite extensively in the post-Covid-19 period.[42] Although this is not a violation of the constitution, it is still problematic that a crisis rhetoric should lead to a rushed legislative process. It risks lowering the quality of the legislation and is less democratic, weakening the *Rechtsstaat* and the rule of law. The principle of legality might be violated. The mentioned development could impact the separation of powers, transferring power to the courts from the legislator, if legislation – including the preparatory works which are an important source for the interpretation of law in the Danish legal system – is not sufficiently clear.[43] All of this may adversely affect the citizens.

[37] Udvalget for Forretningsordenen, Beretning nr. 15 om hastebehandling af regeringens lovforslag, 24 March 2021 ('Beretning nr. 15') available at www.ft.dk/ripdf/samling/20201/beretningalmenart/20201_BER_15.pdf; and Herby (n 18) 4.

[38] L 212 Forslag til lov om en indefrysningsordning for høje energiregninger.

[39] Beretning nr. 15 (n 37).

[40] ibid 3.

[41] UFO alm. del – bilag 53, folketingsåret 2019-20; and Beretning nr. 15 (n 37) 2.

[42] Recall that the Prime Minister of the former government is also Prime Minister of the current government.

[43] See also RG Nielsen, '"Hastelovgivning", forarbejders retskildeværdi og magtfordeling: Essay til retskildelæren' (2023) *Juristen* 73, 73–75; and RG Nielsen, 'Politikernes hastværk baner vejen for "aktivistiske" domstole' (*Berlingske*, 16 January 2024) 16–17.

The latest example of policies based on a crisis rhetoric is the introduction of facial recognition as a tool for the Danish police when investigating serious crime such as murder, severe violence, rape, man-hunt operations and crimes against the state.[44] The initiative was taken by the government and supported by some other political parties, in September 2024. The background and context for this policy is that Denmark is increasingly affected by the gang violence that has been ravaging Sweden over the past few years. For instance, there have been several cases of very young individuals from Sweden being hired to kill Danish gang members. However, the new instrument can also be applied to offences such as rape and crimes against the state, so that the policy extends beyond the 'crisis' used to justify it. The Minister of Justice has explicitly stated that facial recognition will be introduced in the mentioned areas 'as a start'.[45] Furthermore, the Police decide in which situations they feel a need to use facial recognition in their investigation without having to request a court order first (as they would in order to conduct raids or tap phones).

This has been criticised by the Association of Danish Judges and by the Danish think-tank Justitia.[46] Even though facial recognition will be used only retrospectively, Justitia has argued that the legal basis for the use of this instrument is not sufficiently clear, and might therefore be a violation of the right to privacy enshrined in the European Convention of Human Rights and the Charter of Fundamental Rights in the European Union.[47] Justitia (and others) recommend that Parliament debate and adopt a new and more detailed Act for the regulation of facial-recognition technology.[48] The Danish Minister of Justice is aware of the criticism, and has replied that for him it is more important to provide the police with the tools they need to fight serious crime and protect the lives of citizens.[49] One might counter that this purpose can be fulfilled even if

[44] See 'Politiet får grønt lys til ansigtsgenkendelse' (*Justitsministeriet*, 5 September 2024), available at www.justitsministeriet.dk/pressemeddelelse/politiet-faar-groent-lys-til-ansigtsgenkendelse/; and P Hummelgaard, 'Orientering om politiets brug af ansigtsgenkendelsesteknologi i efterforskning' (*Justitsministeriet*, 5 September 2024), available at www.justitsministeriet.dk/wp-content/uploads/2024/09/Orientering-af-Folketingets-Retsudvalg-om-politiets-brug-af-ansigtsgenkendelse steknologi-i-efterforskning.pdf.

[45] 'Politiet får grønt lys til ansigtsgenkendelse' (n 44).

[46] See O Høj and R Uldall, 'Dommerforening vil have politiet forbi en dommer, inden de bruger ansigtsgenkendelse i efterforskningen' *DR* (26 August 2024), available at www.dr.dk/nyheder/politik/dommerforening-vil-have-politiet-forbi-en-dommer-inden-de-bruger-ansigtsgenkendelse.

[47] See, eg, BA Eiriksson, 'Ansigtsgenkendelsesteknologi: behov for regulering af politiets anvendelse' (*Justitia*, (14 March 2024), available at justitia-int.org/ansigtsgenkendelsesteknologi-behov-for-regulering-af-politiets-anvendelse/. See also a post on the website of the Danish Bar Association where privacy and data protection are discussed in relation to the introduction of facial recognition as a tool for the police, 'Ansigtsgenkendelse er et alvorligt indgreb i vores grundlæggende rettigheder' (*Advokatsamfundet*, 22 August 2024), available at www.advokatsamfundet.dk/nyheder-medier/nyheder/2024/ansigtsgenkendelse-er-et-alvorligt-indgreb-i-vores-grundlaeggende-rettigheder. Freedom of expression and freedom of assembly are mentioned as rights which might be affected in the long run.

[48] Instead, an existing legal basis, which originally regarded the use of facial recognition in cases concerning sexual abuse against children as an experiment, is used to extend the tool out to other crimes.

[49] See 'Folketinget tillader politiet brug af ansigtsgenkendelse', *Berlingske* (5 September 2024).

a court order must be obtained before using facial recognition, and if the legal basis for this use is clarified. The response then has been that in such cases, time is of the essence. Yet that must be weighed against citizens' fundamental rights, which courts are tasked with protecting. It is worth mentioning that the new AI Regulation of the European Union (2024/1689), which among other things regulates police use of facial recognition in real time, does not apply to Denmark because of the Danish opt-out on criminal law.[50] This seems to be yet another example of how a crisis rhetoric has been used by the Danish government after the Covid-19 pandemic. In this case, it even seems that the new initiative goes beyond the 'burning platform', which in this case is the fight among gangs in Copenhagen, and that important rule-of-law considerations such as the need for court orders and a clear legal basis are disregarded. Apparently, the opposition were given no more than one night to consider whether they would support the new law.[51] In this case the legal constitutional consequence for citizens of a political use of crisis rhetoric could be a violation of their right to privacy and data protection.[52]

V. CRISES AND ACCOUNTABILITY

If a government declares a state of emergency in Denmark, and the situation fulfils the criteria mentioned above, necessary and proportionate actions which violate the constitution may be taken. It could for instance be necessary to violate ordinary democratic decision-making procedures and the rights of citizens. However, the government is still responsible for its governance during a state of emergency. In other words, exceptional circumstances do not absolve the government of accountability for its exercise of power. If societal challenges are handled without declaring a state of emergency, ordinary political and legal accountability applies.[53] This means that even if Parliament has been pressured to handle and adopt, within a single day, an extensive and complex bill which will have a huge impact on ordinary citizens' lives, the legislation in question is legitimised by the involvement of Parliament in the legislative process. But in cases where Parliament has insufficient time to consider a bill, its approval of that bill becomes little more than a rubber stamp and does not represent

[50] Regulation (EU) 2024/1689 of the European Parliament and of the Council of 13 June 2024 laying down harmonised rules on artificial intelligence [2024] OJ L 2024/1689.

[51] See M Hørkilde, 'Oppositionen fik én nat til at beslutte sig om kontroversielt tiltag: "Det har været en forhastet process"' (*Berlingske*, 6 September 2024).

[52] After this chapter was written, a new example of publicly debated quite far-reaching legislation based on crisis rhetoric has been adopted, see Act on construction and civil engineering projects as well as operational activities with significant national defense purposes or significant civil emergency preparedness purposes, Act no 1097 of 15/09/2025. Article 3, Part 2, refers to "national security", other Acts and private/public rights may be derogated from according to Article 3, and the right to appeal may be restricted, Article 2.

[53] See also RG Nielsen, '"Staten er det blivende" – Troels G. Jørgensen og konstitutionel nødret: Med perspektiver til besættelsestiden og COVID-19' (2023) 136 *Tidsskrift for Rettsvitenskap* 261.

a legitimate democratic process. In reality, Parliament is put in a very difficult position because of time pressure, and may not be able to properly perform its task of controlling, scrutinising and debating legislation. During a societal challenge, the government may even misuse its position of power and force Parliament to adopt more bills than necessary through a rapid legislative process. In this way, Parliament becomes 'co-responsible' with the government. In a state of emergency where the government acts on its own, the responsibility for decisions clearly falls on the government.

What are the implications for accountability when a societal challenge is labelled a 'crisis' by the government? Since a crisis is more of a political term than a constitutional law term, calling a societal challenge a crisis may provide a government with more space for political manoeuvring – it may be a persuasive political argument. However, labelling a societal challenge a crisis does not as such remove responsibility from the government for its actions. Importantly, the constitution and fundamental legal principles must be upheld by the government also during times of serious societal challenges. In other words, calling a situation a crisis does not allow ministers to bypass the constitution or not to respect democratic decision-making processes, the rule of law, and human rights. As regards civil servants, massive time pressure may play a role in their individual responsibility for mistakes they have made. However, civil servants must not prioritise technical questions during a crisis while setting aside the duty to uphold important constitutional guarantees and principles.[54] Especially when it comes to excessively intrusive measures against citizens, which are likely to appear during a crisis, special attention should be paid to the fact that such measures require a clear legal basis.[55]

Besides creating a political space, labelling a societal challenge a crisis can also be used as a rhetorical tool. During Covid-19, the Prime Minister of Denmark effectively managed to urge the Danish citizens to uphold several Covid-19 behavioural guidelines which were supposed to prevent the spread of the virus. Since most citizens adhered to the guidelines, it was not necessary to enshrine these guidelines in official regulation. Trust in public institutions is high in Denmark – and the other Nordic countries – compared to many other countries. That makes a crisis rhetoric an effective tool.

When discussing responsibility for government actions during a societal challenge – whether referred to as a crisis or not – it is important to mention the special Danish feature of restraint courts. In general, courts in the Nordic countries are seen as rather restrained compared to courts elsewhere when it comes to constitutional review. The phenomenon has even been referred to in the literature as 'Nordic exceptionalism'.[56] Nonetheless there are differences among

[54] This was emphasised in the Mink Commission, see Minkkommissionens Beretning, Bind 2, s. 635, afsnit 8.3.4. Samlet vurdering af pressemødet den 4. november 2020.

[55] This was emphasised several times in ibid.

[56] See R Hirschl, 'The Nordic Counternarrative: Democracy, Human Development and Judicial Review' (2011) 9 *International Journal of Constitutional Law* 449.

the Nordic states as regards the degree of courts' restraint, and Danish courts belong to the more restrained ones.[57] The Danish Supreme Court has only once ruled that a piece of legislation violated the constitution.[58] Furthermore, data in the Nordic ConReason project, which analyses constitutional reasoning at the Nordic Supreme Courts, show that the Danish Supreme Court stands out in a global comparison with case law from other Supreme Courts and Constitutional Courts in the original global ConReason parent project as regards the outcomes of constitutional cases and the proportion of cases in which court findings ran counter to the political branches of government.[59] The low frequency of judgments at the Danish Supreme Court which rule that a piece of legislation violates the constitution may to some extent be explained by a traditionally sound political system which legislates in accordance with the constitution.[60] However, in times of crisis the political system may not live up to such high standards, and not maintain the same quality, safeguards, and so on. If legislation is rushed through, and constitutional provisions stretched to the limit, court restraint could be problematic. Furthermore, if courts are closed down during a crisis or only certain kinds of cases are handled during that time, the citizens may not even be able to get their cases against the state heard, at least not within a desirable time-frame, despite the fact that courts are the only way for citizens in such a situation to hold the political institutions accountable for violating their rights.

Another pertinent fact regarding the constitutional design of political and legal accountability for ministers is that in Denmark such accountability depends on political decisions. Thus, there is a close connection between legal accountability and politics. Political accountability demands that a majority in Parliament support it, as per Article 15 of the Danish constitution. This means that majority governments may enjoy protection from accountability. Political accountability may take the form of criticism, or a minister having to resign. If the Prime Minister receives a vote of no-confidence, he or she is obliged to call an election. Parliament may also choose to file an impeachment claim against one or more ministers. However, this also demands a political majority.

[57] See H Krunke and B Thorarensen, 'Concluding Thoughts' in H Krunke and B Thorarensen (eds), *The Nordic Constitutions. A Comparative and Contextual Study* (Hart Publishing, 2018) 203.

[58] U1999.841H (Tvind judgment).

[59] Data from the Nordic Conreason project places Denmark at the top regarding the outcome of the constitutional issue (together with the Supreme Court of Uruguay (R4-NO), and in second place according to the Court of Justice of the European Union for the proportion of cases in which the court's finding ran counter to the political branches of government (R4-YES)). See 'Nordic CONREASON Project: Nordic exceptionalism? Mapping constitutional reasoning in the Nordic countries' (Örebro University, 2022) and 'Nordic CONREASON kollektion av data om konstitutionellt resonemang i de nordiska högsta domstolarna' (*Svensk nationell datatjänst*, 2024), available at snd.se/sv/catalogue/dataset/2023-288. See K Krunke and M Kenno Fogde, 'Constitutional Reasoning at the Supreme Court of Denmark – In Front of and Behind the Scenes' in K Kelemen (eds), *Constitutional Reasoning in the Nordic Supreme Courts: An Empirical and Comparative Legal Perspective* (Hart Publishing, 2026).

[60] See H Krunke, 'Constitutional Identity and Equality: The Challenge of the Nordic EU Member States' (2023) 1 *Comparative Constitutional Studies* 124, 131–32.

Again, we see that a majority government may be protected against impeachment cases. Even the responsibility of civil servants will at the end of the day rely on decisions made by the ministries themselves, normally the highest ranked civil servant of the ministry. The Mink case, discussed above, illustrates the Danish accountability system very well.[61]

Another interesting case concerns a former minister, Inger Støjberg, who was accused of having illegally separated asylum seekers who were married couples, and where the wife was under 18 years old. This case shows that even members of Parliament from the same political party as the criticised minister may vote in favour of an impeachment case. In this case, the minister was put before an impeachment court and sentenced to 60 days of imprisonment.[62]

VI. CONCLUSION

Labelling a societal challenge a 'crisis' may provide a government with more political leeway within the constitutional setting, but it does not amount to more leeway legally speaking. In the case of Denmark, this has been illustrated by the fact that the government asked for the rapid legislative procedure to be employed extensively during the Covid-19 period. This procedure is an exception to the ordinary legislative procedure in the Standing Orders of Parliament and should only be applied under urgent circumstances. However, it is possible to do so without violating the constitution, which prescribes only three readings in Parliament before a bill is adopted. The government thus operates in a political rather than legal space when it can convince Parliament to apply the rapid procedure to a bill, for instance, by referring to a societal challenge as a crisis. The Danish government has even been able to convince Parliament to apply the rapid procedure to many bills after Covid-19, including bills related to some of the societal challenges (e.g. inflation and energy shortages) defined by the Prime Minister and the government as crises in its political programme.

The increased use of the rapid legislative procedure is problematic. It may lead to legislation of a lower quality, and without real democratic legitimacy. This may impact citizens and their trust in public institutions, as well as democracy as such.[63] As mentioned above, even the rule of law – the *Rechtsstaat* so

[61] While the Mink Commission report criticised 10 civil servants, most of them high-ranking, the involved ministries ended up criticising only 3 of those civil servants.

[62] See 'Rigsrettens dom afsagt mandag d. 13 december 2021' (*Rigsretten*, 2021), available at rigsretten.dk/media/of4lp4dn/rigsrettens-dom-af-13-december-2021.pdf.

[63] As mentioned above, the Nordic countries including Denmark have traditionally been characterised by a healthy political culture with respect to democracy, human rights and rule of law, as being based on good governance and transparency, and as having the world's lowest corruption rates, see H Krunke and B Thorarensen (eds), *The Nordic Constitutions: A Comparative and Contextual Study* (Hart Publishing, 2018) 204. In such a political setting, the trust of the citizens in political institutions is high. On public trust in the Nordic Countries, see: Nordisk ministerråd, 'Tillid – det nordiske guld' (*Nordisk ministerråd*, 15 June 2017), available at www.norden.org/da/publication/

called – and the principle of legality may be affected. Unclear legislation may also upset the separation of powers. It is important that politicians understand and respect this possible negative impact and not focus too heavily on the way in which a crisis rhetoric may provide them with more room for political manoeuvring. Over-use of the political space opened by crisis rhetoric may slowly erode the rule of law – a central component of the Danish legal system and society. It is also important to underline that labelling a societal challenge a crisis does *not* provide politicians with legal leeway to deviate from the constitution. The constitution sets limits on political actions even when they invoke crises. Such actions may also violate the EU Law or the European Convention of Human Rights.

tillid-det-nordiske-guld. However, if these preconditions erode, public trust may also erode, Krunke (n 61) 131–32. Interestingly, public trust in politicians in Denmark is currently decreasing. While public trust in politicians was very high in 2007, it decreased until 2015, when we saw a slight improvement, and then from 2019–2023 decreased again, Institut for vilde problemer (INVI) 'Danskerne tillid til politikerne rutsjer ned' (*INVI*) esp 2, available at static1.squarespace.com/static/64636bdcf6efc30ac84b48e1/t/651acdcf9c3d745599a06edf/1696255441297/Danskerne+tillid+til+politikerne+rutsjer+ned.pdf.

3

Emergency in Constitutional Proportionality Review: The Freedom of Judges and its Limits in Europe

LAURIANNE ALLEZARD

I. INTRODUCTION

CONSTITUTIONAL LAW IS not the law of emergency. On the contrary, it pertains to perpetuity, guaranteeing the continuity of political processes over the long term through a deliberative process that is by its nature slow.[1] Conversely, emergency situations demand rapid and extraordinary action. As characterised by Jocelyn Stacey, emergency 'requires decisions to be taken under conditions of deep uncertainty where the possibility of a catastrophe cannot be reliably eliminated in advance'.[2] Political decisions and therefore also legislative decisions are involved, both in terms of qualifying a situation as urgent and determining how to respond to it.

By its very nature, emergency is primarily a political matter, as illustrated recently by the reaction of the Swiss Council of States and Parliament, which denounced the ECtHR's decision to condemn Switzerland for lack of action in combating climate change, accusing it of setting itself up as a constitutional court.[3] Similarly, Emmanuel Macron justified his presidential discretion in drafting the law pertaining to emergency by quoting Carl Schmitt.[4] This boosted legitimacy to act in times of urgency is indeed largely inherited from Schmitt, who introduced the concept of the 'state of exception' in contrast to the 'normal situation' in which the legal order makes sense.[5] European democracies, particularly during the Covid crisis, have manifested the view that emergency requires

[1] See, eg, F Ost, *Le temps du droit* (Odile Jacob, 1999).

[2] Jo Stacey, *The Constitution of the environmental emergency* (Oxford University Press, 2018) 1.

[3] 'Pas de suite à l'arrêt de la CEDH dit le Conseil des Etats', 5 June 2024, see www.parlament.ch/fr/services/news/Pages/2024/20240605121939346194158159026_bsf073.aspx.

[4] 'Gouverner dans le chaos', 24 July 2024, *Politis*, see www.politis.fr/articles/2024/07/chronique-macron-gouverner-dans-le-chaos/.

[5] C Schmitt, *Political theology: Four Chapters on the Concept of Sovereignty* (University of Chicago Press, 2006).

granting the political decision-maker unrestricted discretion.[6] With decisions having to be made quickly about which interests to preserve and which to sacrifice, emergencies thus disrupt the balance of power and may even justify a temporary departure from the law or an exception to its normal application.[7]

International jurisdictions, such as the ECHR[8] or ITLOS,[9] as well as national administrative ones to some extent,[10] are increasingly urging states to act with regards to the climate emergency. Where do constitutional judges stand in this development?

The (sometimes unprecedented) restrictions of rights or freedoms in response to emergencies is subject to assessment by constitutional judges as to their proportionality. Although such proportionality reviews are nearly universal,[11] follow a common structure within the EU,[12] and enjoy broad appeal in comparative law doctrine, their particularities and commonalities among Member States facing emergency is an area yet to be explored. Judges' freedom is assessed by their ability to constrain the legislator. To see whether emergencies strengthen this freedom or instead leads to self-limitation, proportionality review warrants close scrutiny.[13]

According to Rivers, discretion[14] and the assessment of proportionality are closely interconnected.[15] The question of the potential activism of judges in response to emergencies such as Covid-19 or environmental crises has already been raised separately.[16] But the pandemic, the environmental emergency – in

[6] Stacey (n 2) 2.

[7] X Magnon, 'Les principes d'un droit constitutionnel jurisprudentiel d'exception. A propos des décisions du Conseil constitutionnel sur l'état d'urgence sanitaire' (2020) *Actualité juridique Droit administratif*.

[8] Grand Chamber, *Verein KlimaSeniorinnen Schweiz and others v Switzerland*, 9 April 2024.

[9] Advisory opinion, no 31, 21 May 2024.

[10] Tribunal administratif de Paris, 14 October 2021, Nos 1904967, 1904968, 1904972, 1904976/4, see T Groß, 'Why Courts will not Stop Global Warming, but Climate Litigation is Still Useful' verfassungsblog.de/why-courts-will-not-stop-global-warming-but-climate-litigation-is-still-useful/.

[11] A Stone Sweet and J Mathews, 'Proportionality Balancing and Global Constitutionalism' (2008–2009) 47(1) *Columbia Journal of Transnational Law* 192, 209.

[12] See the four steps of the review in B Sánchez Barroso, 'Beyond the Principle of Proportionality: Controlling the Restriction of Rights under Factual Uncertainty' (2022) 9(2) *Oslo Law Review* 76 or J Rivers, 'Proportionality and Variable Intensity of Review' (2006) 65(1) *Cambridge Law Journal* 174, 181 or FJ Urbina, 'A Critique of Proportionality' (2012) 57 *American Journal of Jurisprudence* 49, 49.

[13] Proportionality review in its entirety, rather than new doctrinal categorisations that show variations in control in general, such as the necessity test or balancing. This is not a study of proportionality control itself. For the implications on constitutional law of states of emergency see A Greene, *Permanent States of Emergency and the Rule of Law. Constitutions in the Age of Crisis* (Hart Publishing, 2018).

[14] See S Bogojevic and X Groussot, *Discretion in EU Public Procurement Law* (Hart Publishing, 2019).

[15] J Rivers, 'Proportionality and Discretion in International and European law' in N Tsagourias (ed), *Transnational Constitutionalism: International and European Perspective* (Cambridge University Press, 2007).

[16] See, eg, M Belov, *Courts and Judicial Activism under Crisis Conditions: Policy Making in a Time of Illiberalism and Emergency Constitutionalism* (Routledge, 2021); L Vyhnánek et al, 'The

the broad sense[17] – and the migration crisis are rarely examined together. This chapter examines them together to provide a comprehensive view of the emergency. Its ambition is to establish whether the similarities between Member States' handling of emergencies stem from a common deference to the legislator or whether emergencies are, on the contrary, the source of a new freedom for judges. This is ultimately an enquiry into judges' abilities to take on substantial roles in addressing emergencies. Do we see, in these emergencies, judges exercising the freedom of going beyond the constitutional law they are supposed to guarantee, or are they merely interpreting existing law within the bounds of usual discretion?

These questions lead us to other ones: what means does a judge have to resist the idea that handling emergencies requires giving greater discretion to the legislator? And how can constitutional constraints be reinstated even in times of emergency? More specifically, what existing or new tools are available to judges for prioritising an emergency against the initial decision of the legislator? What is the threshold that, when respected, legitimises a judge's action, and when exceeded, marks it as 'activism', going beyond their powers?

I have chosen four constitutional jurisdictions to focus my discussion on – France, Germany, the Czech Republic and Hungary – each of which has exhibited a specific and unique behaviour with regard to recent emergencies: the environment and climate change, immigration, and Covid-19. This study is qualitative rather than quantitative, based on the analysis of around 35 decisions that reflect the current issues of case law in the investigated states. I have chosen to highlight the most illustrative decisions, which also happen to be the most recent, showing variations in judicial freedom in the face of emergencies. This choice provides the opportunity for theoretical reflections on the potential short-term evolution of judicial interpretation in response to the intensification of emergencies, particularly climate-related ones.

The freedom of judges to oppose the legislator's handling of emergencies will be assessed in three ways. First, as regards their ability to utilise the rights and standards available to them in their interpretation in new and effective ways (Section II). Second, as regards their capacity to constrain the legislator with reference to factual evidence specifically pertaining to emergencies (Section III). And finally, by addressing the theoretical tensions underlying the treatment of emergencies within the constitutional framework of 'normal times' (Section IV).

Dynamics of Proportionality: Constitutional Courts and the Review of COVID-19 Regulations' (2024) *German Law Journal* 1, 21. See also N Petersen, *Proportionality and Judicial Activism: Fundamental Rights Adjudication in Canada, Germany and South Africa* (Cambridge University Press, 2017).

[17] We align with Jocelyn Stacey, who considers the environmental emergency as a whole: 'The book elaborates a concept of the "environmental emergency": the idea that all environmental issues contain the constitutive features of an emergency.' 'Like emergencies, environmental issues require decisions to be taken under conditions of deep uncertainty where the possibility of a catastrophe cannot be reliably eliminated in advance.' Stacey (n 2) 2–3.

II. A POTENTIAL FREEDOM THROUGH USUAL LEGAL TOOLS

In prioritising an emergency, a judge's freedom can be expressed through the classical means at their disposal during proportionality review. The judge can give effect to provisions that were previously devoid of it (subsection II(A)) or scrutinise the standards put forward by the legislator to justify the restriction of a freedom (subsection II(B)).

A. Possible Reinforcement of the Scope of Norms

The aim here is to see how judges might expand the proportionality review to other norms, making the law more effective in addressing certain emergencies. This would increase their competencies and thus their freedom to sustainably enforce constraint on the legislator. Two means are available to judges: (1) turning objective rights into subjective ones; and (2) recognising new principles or even granting legislative principles constitutional status. Judges have taken these two ways for long-term, recurring, and even constant emergencies: namely, environmental crises and migration. Due to their temporary nature, however, public health emergencies are better suited for integration among standards than for subjectivising a right, as we will discuss later.

Following the immigration wave of 2016, the French Constitutional Council was called upon to rule on the constitutionality of the so-called 'crime of solidarity' – which involved helping an undocumented migrant.[18] To invalidate the law, the Council elevated the 'principle of fraternity' from a symbolic value to an effective constitutional value, while also noting that the principle does not guarantee any absolute right for foreigners to settle in France and that restricting immigration may be necessary for safeguarding public order. It delegated to the legislator the future task of reconciling the principle of fraternity with public order.[19]

In the field of the environment, however, the subjectivisation of rights is a more common tool. Even if, as Lael K Weis explains, the intended effect of environmental provisions would be more 'contrajudicative'[20] – that is, serving to incentivise the political sphere to make decisions rather than being legally effective – the trend is towards the progressive strengthening of these norms. Following the democratic transition in Hungary and the Czech Republic, environmental protection and the combating of climate change were made state objectives, becoming explicit provisions in the respective constitutions, with constitutional judges giving them effectivity. In the course of a proportionality

[18] 2018-717/718 QPC, 6 July 2018.

[19] ibid §10.

[20] LK Weis, 'Environmental constitutionalism: Aspiration or transformation?' (2018) 16(3) *International Journal of Constitutional Law*.

review, Hungarian judges established that a right to a healthy environment exists which creates an obligation on the part of the state,[21] while in the Czech Republic, a healthy environment was deemed a 'public good (value)',[22] access to which is now a subjective right in the Czech Republic that individuals[23] and NGOs[24] can invoke. In Hungary, it was the elaboration of the right to life that allowed for the subjectivisation of the right to a healthy environment.[25] In the Czech Republic, however, the judge explicitly stated that, in accordance with consistent case law, the right to a favourable environment is not absolute and that other societal, economic and political obligations must be taken into account.[26] The door was thereby opened to proportionality review, giving judges the possibility to assess while preserving the role of the political decision-maker.

In the same realm of emergency, the French judge explicitly recognised the constitutional value of environmental protection in 2020,[27] yet its general scope remains uncertain.[28] While the judge acknowledged the invocability of certain provisions of the Environmental Charter located in the preamble of the Constitution,[29] not all provisions were recognised.[30] Although the precautionary principle is the most topical example of principles that have gained constitutional effectiveness through judicial interpretation[31] – explicitly or implicitly – not all environmental norms enjoy this effect. The judge's choice also depends on the developments within the EU in this area. Furthermore, the litigation remains very limited.[32] For example, no decision has changed what the Constitutional Council declared in 2012, namely that the principle of sustainable development, enshrined in Article 6 of the Environmental Charter, does not establish a right

[21] See last decision: 5/2022 (IV.4), 22 March 2022.

[22] III ÚS 70/97, 10 July 1997. See D Židek, 'Environmental protection in the constitution of the Czech Republic' (2021) 31 *Journal of Agricultural and Environmental Law*.

[23] 16/2015. (VI. 5) §85.

[24] IV. ÚS 3572/14, 13 October 2015.

[25] On the subjective interpretation of the right to the environment see J Ede Szilágyi, *Constitutional Protection of the Environment and Future Generations: Legislation and Practice in Certain Central European Countries* (CEA Publishing, 2022) 528.

[26] II ÚS 251/03, 24 March 2005.

[27] No 2019-823 QPC, 31 January 2020.

[28] See M Deffairi, 'La portée constitutionnelle des dispositions de la Charte de l'environnement' (2022) 8 *Les cahiers du Conseil constitutionnel*.

[29] The preamble has acquired constitutional value since the landmark decision known as the 'freedom of association' ruling, No 71-44 DC, 16 July 1971.

[30] Only its articles 1, 2, 3, 4, and 7 have so far been explicitly recognised as being invocable in priority preliminary rulings on constitutionality (QPC) by the Constitutional Council. See M-A Cohendet and M Fleury, 'Chronique de droit constitutionnel de l'environnement' (2018) 43(4) *RJE* 759.

[31] A Laquièze, 'L'introduction du principe de précaution dans la Constitution: sens ou non-sens ?' (2012) 76 *Revue de métaphysique et de morale*; J Bétaille, 'Le principe de précaution, un « droit » garanti par la Constitution ?' (2016) 105 *Revue française de droit constitutionnel*.

[32] Only 35 decisions concerning the Charter have been made since 2005, according to L Gay, 'Défendre l'environnement devant le Conseil constitutionnel Quelle procédure pour servir la Charte de l'environnement ?' in M Hautereau-Boutonnet and È Truilhé (eds), *Procès et environnement: quelles actions en justice pour l'environnement ?* (Aix-en-Provence: DICE Éditions, 2020).

or freedom guaranteed by the constitution.[33] Therefore, the judge made a choice regarding which provisions to make effective and which not.[34]

In a different manner, the German judge recognised a duty to protect the environment by assigning this to the state as a 'fundamental national objective'. That status means that Article 20a of the Basic Law cannot be directly invoked to bring a case before the Constitutional Court. It implies no subjective right, does not count among fundamental rights, and although the proposal to integrate a subjective right to environmental protection was discussed in parliament, it was abandoned.[35] However, as in Hungary, the Court maintains that consistent case-law has shown that subjective rights arise from the joint reading of Articles 1 and 20(1) of the Constitution, such as the 'ecological minimum standard of living' or the 'minimum standard of living consistent with human dignity'.[36]

Judges in different Member States have also not granted themselves the same freedom in recognising new constitutional principles. The Hungarian and French examples are at opposite ends on this point. In the Hungarian case, the judge ensures effectiveness of the recognised objective of environmental protection by exercising strict – though not absolute – application of the principle of 'non-derogation', which bars regression in environmental protection.[37] In France, meanwhile, the principle of non-regression – whose meaning is similar to the Hungarian one – has not reached constitutional level.[38] In the decision of October 2023, the applicants attempted to constitutionally establish this principle,[39] but the judge did not recognise it and in fact simply ignored it.[40] The subjectivisation of rights appears to be timely. Emergency provides the foundation for its justification, but without systematicity.

B. Uncontrolled Standards as Justifications of the Law

The French Constitutional Council repeats the same formula at each proportionality review: 'The limitations imposed by the legislator on the exercise of this

[33] 2012-282 QPC, 23 November 2012, *Association France Nature Environnement et autre*.

[34] See, eg, the principle of 'polluter pays' in F Bin and C Viessant, 'La prise en compte des enjeux environnementaux lors du contrôle de constitutionnalité des lois financières est-elle possible?' (2024) titre VII, Les cahiers du Conseil constitutionnel.

[35] 1 BvR 2656/18, 1 BvR 78/20, 1 BvR 96/20, 1 BvR 288/20, March 24, 2021, §112.

[36] ibid §114.

[37] Since Decision 28/1994. (V. 20.) CC [IV.1.], and increasingly in favour of the principle since 2015: Decision 16/2015. (VI.5.) CC. See F Orosz, N Suri, R Kovács and P Szöke, 'Constitutional protection of the environment with particular regard to the Hungarian, German, Italian and Belgian constitutional regulation' (2021) 16 *Journal of Agricultural and Environmental Law*.

[38] R Brett, 'Principe de non-régression' (2018) 43(3) *RJE* 631–43.

[39] Ignorance already observed in the decision no 2020-809 DC, *loi relative aux conditions de mise sur le marché de certains produits phytopharmaceutiques en cas de danger sanitaire pour les betteraves sucrières*, §9.

[40] 2023-1066 QPC, 27 October 2023, §2.

right can only be linked to constitutional requirements or justified by a reason of general interest and proportionate to the objective pursued.'[41] These justifications and requirements are translated into standards usually characterised by 'ambiguous determination' and 'limited normativity', which are uncertain, and sometimes inconsistent.[42] They include, on one hand, objectives with constitutional value, such as common interests – whether collective, general, or even state interests, depending on the state in question – which form the 'legitimate purpose' of the law. On the other hand, there are legally more uncertain standards, such as 'threats' or 'risks', which serve as the urgent reason for adopting the law immediately, or the 'particular circumstances', which are often opportunistic and without precedent.[43]

The standards serve the legislative argumentation of the law from the perspective of the legislator and can a priori serve the interpretation of the judge designated to assess this justification. The freedom of judges is assessed here on three levels: their ability to: (1) develop new objectives or interests that count in the balance; (2) invalidate the interpretation made by the legislator of these standards; and (3) constrain the legislator by giving priority to one threat over another.

As we have just seen, as early as 1994 the Hungarian judge established the right to a healthy environment is an obligation of the State, and in 1997, a Czech judge designated the environment a 'public good'[44] and later, in 2004, a 'legitimate aim'.[45] Since then, the mobilisation of these standards, and their constraint, has only increased.[46] While the French Constitutional Council has not sought to make objective rights subjective, it has developed standards through the 'discovery' of, first, 'general interest goals related to environmental protection',[47] and then, 'objectives with constitutional value' for environmental protection,[48] the 'objective of combating climate change',[49] and even the objective 'to strengthen the fight against greenhouse gas emissions'.[50] Health protection in the fight against Covid has also benefited from the mediation of 'the objective

[41] 2020-809 DC, 10 December 2020, §14; 2022-991 QPC, 13 May 2022, *Association France nature environnement et autres*, §6.

[42] P de Montalivet, 'Les objectifs de valeur constitutionnelle' (2006) 20 *Les Cahiers du Conseil Constitutionnel*.

[43] See the work of V Barbé, '"particular circumstances" before the French constitutional Council' during the workshop 'Constitution interpretation in Emergencies in Europe', 24–25 June 2024, EUI.

[44] III US 70/97, 10 July 1997.

[45] III US 482/02, 8 April 2004.

[46] See M Radvan, 'Czech Republic: Limited Constitutional Regulation of Environmental Protection Complemented by the Case Law of the Constitutional Court' in JE Szilágyi (ed), *Constitutional Protection of the Environment and Future Generations* (Central European Academic Publishing, 2022) 161–202.

[47] 2002-464 DC, 27 December 2002, cons. 57.

[48] 2016-737 DC, 4 August 2016, *Loi pour la reconquête de la biodiversité, de la nature et des paysages*, §39.

[49] 2009-599 DC, 29 December 2009, cons. 82.

[50] 2000-441 DC, 28 December 2000, cons. 35.

of constitutional value'.[51] In 2022, a French judge even strengthened the position of environmental protection in the proportionality review by declaring it to be among the fundamental interests of the nation, to be considered as much as these other interests.[52] However, the actual scope of these objectives and interests is not fixed and largely arbitrary, dependent on the assessment of the judge – and on the justification provided by the legislator in this regard.[53]

The German judge, in the face of Covid, justified a curfew in a similar manner, stating: 'Protecting life and health and maintaining the proper functioning of the healthcare system are both exceptionally significant interests of the common good in their own right, and are thus constitutionally legitimate legislative objectives.'[54] The state's duty to protect becomes compelling due to the urgent need to provide constitutional protection,[55] but such protection does not thereby become an enforceable individual right.

Once the standards are recognised as possible justifications, it is a priori up to the judge to assess how and if they are at stake in the case at hand. When faced with emergencies, judges do not have the same boldness to interfere in the concrete definition of these standards. This difference is particularly visible in the definition of 'interest'. In France, a 'banalization of the appeal of the general interest'[56] has come to mean that the standard does not require a clarification in normal and in exceptional times.[57] French judges adhere solely to the mention of the interest in the preparatory work in order to validate the procedural obligations of the legislator regarding the rationalisation of the law.[58] That is to say, if the legislator does not make any effort to justify the protection of the general interest, the judge will not highlight this omission. In contrast, the Hungarian Constitutional Court requires the legislator to prove that a measure is not contrary to the interest of the state.[59] This grants the Hungarian judge a greater discretion than the French judge.

To address long-term emergencies based on Article 20a of the Basic Law, Germany has charted another path that involves the recognition and definition of a collective interest competing with other collective interests: that of future generations versus those currently living, in accordance with the jurisprudential

[51] 2022-835 DC, 21 January 2022, *Loi renforçant les outils de gestion de la crise sanitaire et modifiant le code de la santé publique*, §7.

[52] 2022-843 DC, 12 August 2022, *Loi portant mesures d'urgence pour la protection du pouvoir d'achat*.

[53] See M Fleury and M-A Cohendet, '"Work still in progress": chronique de droit constitutionnel sur la Charte de l'environnement' (2022) 47(4) *RJE* 825, 839.

[54] 1 BvR 971/21, 19 November 2021.

[55] ibid.

[56] G Merland, 'L'intérêt général, instrument efficace de protection des droits fondamentaux?' (2004) 16 *Cahiers du Conseil constitutionnel*.

[57] See D Truchet, 'La notion d'intérêt général: le point de vue d'un professeur de droit' (2017) 58(1) *Legicom* 5, 11.

[58] 2022-843DC, 12 August 2022, *Loi portant mesures d'urgence pour la protection du pouvoir d'achat*.

[59] 16/2022 (VII.14) AB, 28 June 2022.

concept of dynamic fundamental rights protection.[60] The idea is not new:[61] the Czech constitution is part of a new generation of constitutions explicitly enshrining the rights of future generations, and its Constitutional Court made this right applicable as early as 2003 by naturally deriving it from the right to live in a healthy environment,[62] without (for the moment) deducing the same consequences as the German judge. The German judge granted the standard effectiveness by recognising the lack of accountability of the state regarding its environmental policy decisions.[63] For the first time, on 24 March 2021, by invalidating the *Climate change act* due to a lack of distribution of financial burdens on the people over time, the judge enjoined the state to do better and more. According to the Court, the duty to protect future generations must be particularly applicable when irreversible processes are unfolding. In contrast, the French Constitutional Council has also recently recognised this right of future generations, without ever deducing unconstitutionality of a law from it, without indicating its future and possible effectiveness.[64]

Finally, we come to the more explicit integration of an emergency in a proportional review that justifies the adoption of a measure at a certain moment, and by extension, the prioritisation of one interest over another. In France, 'emergency' is materially transcribed as a 'serious threat' or 'grave danger'.[65] Here again, it is sufficient for the Constitutional Council to refer to the intention of the legislator recorded in the preparatory work to validate an argument.[66] In this way, the judge was able to validate the increase in national liquefied natural gas processing capacities and the raising of the greenhouse gas emission ceiling with the justification to safeguard a fundamental interest of the nation, namely its independence and economic potential, given the serious threats to face due to the war in Ukraine.[67] The judge did not disregard the threat in favour of another, ie the environmental one. In contrast, the Hungarian judge examines the reality of the threat. For example, in the face of the Covid-19 pandemic, the Court said: 'A total prohibition of the exercise of a fundamental right cannot be justified based solely on danger; it is necessary to periodically assess whether the circumstances continue to justify the suspension of the fundamental right.'[68] The judge thus demanded an evaluation by the legislator of the danger and its changes, and opened up for their scrutiny by incorporating more realistic elements in its interpretation.[69]

[60] 1 BvR 2656/18, 1 BvR 78/20, 1 BvR 96/20, 1 BvR 288/20, 24 March 2021.
[61] See Szilágyi (n 25).
[62] IV. ÚS 254/02 28 January 2003.
[63] 1 BvR 2656/18, 1 BvR 78/20, 1 BvR 96/20, 1 BvR 288/20, March 24, 2021, §146.
[64] 2023-1066 QPC, 27 October 2023.
[65] 2020-809 DC, 10 December 2020.
[66] ibid §20.
[67] 2022-843 DC, 12 August 2022, §§11, 12, 21, 22.
[68] 23/2021 (VII.13) AB, 22 June 2021.
[69] 3537/2021, 5 October 2021.

III. A POTENTIAL FREEDOM THROUGH FACTS

Facing emergency, the judge is compelled, to some extent, to adopt consequentialism – at the very least not to ignore the reality behind the adoption of the law. Proportionality review exposes new variables that either justify the measure or are likely to hinder it. These are non-legal objects over which neither the legislator nor the judge truly has control, but which explicitly or implicitly determine whether the measure is appropriate, necessary or sufficient. The judge could seize this opportunity to constrain the legislator. In reality, however, the use of these variables is limited. These are of two kinds: one rational, the other emotional. With the common requirement for the rationalisation of the legislative process,[70] constitutional judges are required to assess the effort made by the legislator in this regard (subsection III(A)). In another domain, the judge may potentially rely on the idea of the identity in the constitution and its persuasive force (subsection III(B)).

A. A Tempting Review of Scientific Evidence

Robert Alexy has observed that balancing can be a rational procedure if based on the use of arithmetic elements.[71] However, this theoretical observation has not necessarily translated into practical application in Europe. The role scientific evidence can and should play in proportionality review is, in fact, an ongoing theoretical question,[72] and a growing challenge that has been revitalised by the Covid crisis. However, normative tools specifically based on scientific evidence exist, such as the precautionary principle, and are even used by other types of jurisdictions to justify the restriction of individual liberties. But as stated by the CJEU in the Nordic Info case,[73] the precautionary principle allows the state to take protective – and therefore restrictive – measures without waiting for scientific certainty of the risk at issue, thus offering it a certain margin of appreciation. The discretion granted to the state does not compel the legislator to act in accordance with the risk; the constitutional judge, acting in relay, does not transform this possibility into an obligation, even in cases of scientific certainty.

Once again, emergencies do not entail the same behaviour for every judge, and the weight that judges assign to scientific facts in proportionality review

[70] See D Dyzenhaus, 'Proportionality and Deference in a Culture of Justification' in G Huscroft, B Miller, and G Webber (eds), *Proportionality and Rule of Law. Rights, Justification, Reasoning* (Cambridge University Press, 2014).

[71] R Alexy, *A Theory of Legal Argumentation: The Theory of Rational Discourse as Theory of Legal Justification* (Oxford University Press, 1989); V Afonso da Silva, 'Balancing May Be Everywhere, but the Proportionality Test Is Not' (2023) *Global Constitutionalism* 1–16.

[72] FJ Urbina, *A Critique of Proportionality and Balancing* (Cambridge University Press, 2017).

[73] No C-128/22, *Nordic Info BV v Belgische Staat*, 5 December 2023, §79, 90.

varies.[74] In the face of emergency, the judge's freedom is measured by the authority he can exercise to require that the law conform to scientific evidence (1) or for the scientific reliability of the elements on which the legislator relies (2).

i. Scientific Conformity

Indeed, courts exhibit highly heterogeneous behaviour when it comes to assessing the conformity of a law to scientific facts. The degree of consideration given to scientific conformity varies by jurisdiction and can be connected to the assessment of scientific certainty. For French judges, a law's conformity to scientific knowledge is not a criterion for its evaluation. The Constitutional Council routinely assesses simply whether a measure is 'not manifestly inadequate' given the 'state of knowledge'.[75] In practice, however, this is once again merely a procedural step in the legislative process. The judge only verifies the legislator's intention to consider scientific facts in the preparatory work without delving further. Traditionally, judges self-constrain in favour of the legislator, even if the latter openly contradicts scientific consensus.[76] It was in the decision of 21 January 2022, pertaining to Covid-19, that the Constitutional Council went furthest, acknowledging the legislator's effort to act based on 'the state of scientific knowledge available to it, which is notably corroborated by the opinions of the scientific committee of December 24, 2021, and January 13, 2022'.[77] And of course, the Constitutional Council never opines on whether a measure is sufficient or whether it could go further to achieve the set objectives.[78] They do not penalise the lack of a law despite scientific certainty calling for its adoption.[79] The judge did not uphold the criticism of the plaintiffs regarding the legislator's lack of environmental ambition in the decision pertaining to the law combating climate change.

A decision by the Hungarian Constitutional Court demonstrates an active and interventionist approach to the Covid-19 crisis. In justifying the obligation for healthcare professionals to get vaccinated, the Court relied on recommendations from the World Health Organization. It deemed alternatives to mandatory vaccination 'unrealistic' and concluded that this restriction of individual freedom was necessary to prevent grave consequences.[80] The Court explicitly stated that this measure represented the best solution under the

[74] L Allezard, 'L'urgence, critère ambigu dans l'arbitrage constitutionnel entre rationalité politique et rationalité scientifique' in *Les juges constitutionnels: des juges aux yeux bandés ? Comment comprendre leur comportement dans les régimes démocratiques et autoritaires* (to be published Lextenso Editions, 2024).

[75] 2023-1066 QPC, 27 October 2023, §11.

[76] 2018-768 QPC, 21 March 2019, *M. Adama S.*

[77] 2022-835 DC, 21 January 2022, §12.

[78] 2020-881 QPC,5 February 2021; n°2020-809 DC, 10 December 2020.

[79] 2021-825 DC, 13 August 2021, §3.

[80] 3537/2021, 5 October 2021.

circumstances and scientific evidence. This approach underscores the Court's emphasis on protecting public health and mitigating the serious risks associated with the Covid-19 pandemic.

The Czech constitutional judge has adopted a philosophy diametrically opposed to that of the French, aligning instead with the realistic approach of the Hungarian court.[81] In the context of environmental[82] and health[83] emergencies, judges rely on factual scientific evidence and condition the validity of a law on its scientific rationality. For example, the Czech Court evaluates what types of information the political authority had at its disposal in making its decision, what the factual situation is, and the extent to which the legislator took this situation into account.[84] In a Covid decision, it cited scientific evidence about the rates of depression, suicide, and heart attacks in challenging the appropriateness of the legislative choice to close nearly all shops.[85] The measure, it insisted, must be based on expert recommendations and the maximum available scientific information, and take into account the context and the effects of the measure on social life in the short and medium term.[86] It thus replaced proportionality review with so-called 'rationality review'.[87] Insofar as the Court stipulates that legislation should be rational, any decision that interferes with fundamental rights must be based on sufficient documentation. Otherwise, the decision is arbitrary.[88]

In the famous *Hartz* decision of 2010, the German Constitutional Court took into account empirical studies and the legislator's propensity to use them sufficiently to finally invalidate the legislator's choice.[89] This decision constituted a paradigm shift that has not been followed in a consistent way in times of emergency.[90] The German Constitutional Court adopts a similar framework to the French model by focusing on assessing the excessiveness of the measure and applying the prohibition on excess (*Übermaßverbot*). However, it goes a step further by considering the degree of the emergency and its implications. In the decision of 19 November 2021, the Court explains that the more severely individual freedoms are restricted, the more significant the pursuit of interests related to the common good must be:[91] the restriction must be clearly proportional to

[81] The reasoning of the Czech judge is borrowed from South African doctrine on the transition from a culture of authority to a culture of justification. See E Mureinik, 'A Bridge to Where? Introducing the Interim Bill of Rights' (1994) 10 *S.A.J.H.R.* 31.

[82] Pl. ÚS 22/17-2, 26 January 2021.

[83] Pl. ÚS 106/20, 9 February 2021.

[84] ibid §75.

[85] ibid §26.

[86] ibid §77.

[87] ibid §84.

[88] ibid §83.

[89] 1 BvL 1/09, *Hartz*, 9 February 2010.

[90] K Meßerschmidt, 'Evidence-based review of legislation in Germany' (2016) 4(2) *The Theory and Practice of Legislation* 209, 235.

[91] 1 BvR 971/21, 19 November 2021.

the emergency. Following the first decision of this kind in Europe, reached by the Supreme Court of the Netherlands,[92] the German Constitutional Court invalidated the law related to reducing greenhouse gas emissions, arguing that the legislator could do more. The Court thus found that the measure was insufficient[93] in budgetary terms.[94] The Court validated that the burdens that will weigh on future generations will be too significant to ensure the future guarantee of fundamental rights and this constitute an 'emergency stop'.[95] Nevertheless, the Court reasonably took into account the scientific uncertainty regarding the measure's actual impact on climate change, considering it insufficient grounds to invalidate the measure. The judge therefore took an indirect path to reach the same result.

ii. Scientific Reliability

Perhaps more easily than with the requirement of scientific conformity or based on certainty, the judge may expect that the scientific evidence provided by the legislator, and on which the law is based, is reliable. As Matthias Klatt and Moritz Meister explain 'the unreliability of knowledge and the discretion resulting from it are important aspects in the balancing of constitutional rights'.[96] In this regard, Robert Alexy suggests adding another step to the proportionality test: whether the measure is based on sufficient scientific reliability and empirical evidences.[97] But here again, the judge's discretion is not necessarily strengthened by his ability to assess the reliability of the scientific evidence. This is first of all because reliable scientific evidence is not always attainable. And secondly, even if there is (a degree of) scientific certainty, as in the case of the current environmental emergency, the truth is that, as David L Faigman has noted, 'absolute certainty has never been a criterion for constitutional decision-making'.[98]

The French Constitutional Council stands among the most extreme in disregarding the reliability of scientific evidence upon which the legislator relies. This is evident first because it does not pay attention to the conformity of law to science, as seen earlier, and second because even when science denounce the decisions of the legislator, judges have continued to let the legislator free. This was the case in a decision rendered in 2019 regarding bone tests applied to young migrants to determine whether they were minors or not.[99] Although the test is

[92] 19/00135, *Urgenda Foundation v State of Netherlands*, 20 December 2019.
[93] 1 BvR 2656/18, 1 BvR 78/20, 1 BvR 96/20, 1 BvR 288/20, 24 March 2021.
[94] ibid §192.
[95] ibid as formulated by the complainants.
[96] M Klatt and M Meister, *The Constitutional Structure of Proportionality* (Oxford, 2012; online edn, Oxford Academic, 20 September 2012) 109.
[97] R Alexy, 'Formal principles: Some replies to critics' (2014) 12(3) *I•CON* 511–24.
[98] DL Faigman, '"Normative Constitutional Fact-Finding": Exploring the Empirical Component of Constitutional Interpretation' (1991) 193(3) *University of Pennsylvania Law Review* 607.
[99] 2018-768 QPC, 21 March 2019.

now highly contested in terms of its reliability, the Council validated the legislator's decision because it was the only solution already used to address the emergency.[100] Nor did it assess whether other scientific methods were available and presented by the complainants.

In contrast, the German Constitutional Court deduces from Article 20a of the Basic Law an obligation for the legislator to consider sufficiently reliable indicators as a basis for decisions,[101] allowing it to highlight the worst-case scenario in order to provide the most protective response.[102] The judge is therefore interested in the degree of scientific reliability of the information relied upon by the legislator. Thus in the decision of November 2021 regarding Covid-19, the research conducted by the Robert Koch Institute, to which the legislator appealed, appeared sufficiently reliable to warrant the validation of the procedural step at issue.[103] Here, the degree of uncertainty is not synonymous with complete deference to the legislator but rather encourages it to confine itself to a reliable scientific approach.

In the decision of 24 March 2021 regarding greenhouse gas emissions, the judge first emphasises the scientific uncertainty surrounding the effectiveness of legislative measures taken to achieve the objective (a certain reduction in greenhouse gas emissions by 2050). Consequently, the judge concludes that the Court cannot, on the basis given, instruct the legislator to do more.[104] However, the judge highlights another scientific fact, known with certainty: the exponential deterioration of the situation. The longer we wait, the faster climate change will accelerate and risk becoming irreversible.[105] The judge urges the legislator to act accordingly.

Scientific reliability also evolves over time, and it is up to the judge to decide whether or not to uphold the old principle of *in dubio pro libertate*,[106] ie whether to demand that the legislator constrain itself based on new scientific evidence. The Czech Constitutional Court has demanded this by reassessing scientific studies between two decisions related to Covid, as scientific knowledge had evolved in the meantime. While granting significant freedom to the legislator at the beginning of the crisis, as the emergency required rapid action before having all the factual data,[107] scientific knowledge has multiplied and gained in certainty, now implying that the legislator must act based on scientific

[100] See C Fercot, 'Données empiriques et contrôle de constitutionnalité des lois: le Conseil constitutionnel sur la réserve' (2020) 173(1) *Revue française d'administration publique* 105.

[101] 1 BvR 971/21, 19 November 2021.

[102] 1 BvR 2656/18, 1 BvR 78/20, 1 BvR 96/20, 1 BvR 288/20, 24 March 2021, §2b.

[103] 1 BvR 971/21, 19 November 2021.

[104] 1 BvR 2656/18, 1 BvR 78/20, 1 BvR 96/20, 1 BvR 288/20, 24 March 2021, §122, §142.

[105] ibid §120.

[106] P Schneider, 'In dubio pro libertate' in E von Caemnerer et al (eds), *Hundert Jahre deutsches Rechtsleben: FS zum hundertjährigen Bestehen des Deutschen Juristentages 1860–1960. Bd. 2* (Müller, 1960).

[107] Pl. ÚS 106/20, 9 February 2021, §22.

rationality.[108] Uncertainty does not, then, justify the legislator in doing nothing and only following its instincts or the pursuit of political compromise.[109]

B. An Easy Review of Identity-based Argumentation

Legitimacy based on the idea that the constitution reflects the 'real' identity of the members of the nation can now be considered a concurrent legitimacy to that derived from the will or consent of the people.[110] The case of immigration has provided an opportunity for some judges to assert a certain identity inherent in the constitution by elucidating the legal significance of its provisions. While the judge may not always be free to determine the content of the identity present in the constitutional text, they are nonetheless free to use it – whether by considering arguments raised by the parties or by invoking it themselves – or to disregard it. Explicitly or due to the underlying reason that certain provisions with an identity resonance have a strengthened binding force, the judge may thus take new liberties from the usual way to interpret the constitution – whether in alignment or opposition to the legislator, depending on the political context.

In a decision of 6 July 2018, the French Constitutional Council recognised for the first time the constitutional value and real significance of the motto of the Republic, 'liberty, equality, fraternity', enshrined in Article 2 of the Constitution and also mentioned in the Preamble and Articles 72–73, which establishes the common ideal behind these words. According to the Council, 'From the principle of fraternity arises the freedom to help others, for humanitarian purposes, without regard to the legality of their presence on the national territory.'[111] The Council argues that the principle of fraternity is not respected in the reconciliation carried out by the legislator, which condemns the assistance provided and thereby partly invalidates the law related to the 'solidarity crime'. Thus, it was the essence of the French republican ideal that alone provided a lasting response to the selfless management by individuals of this situation of individual and human emergency represented by illegal immigration.[112]

In comparison, the Hungarian example offers the possibility of the contrary use of identity. In 2016, the Hungarian Constitutional Court rendered a decision in response to the compulsory relocation of asylum seekers initiated by the European Commission in 2015, asserting Hungarian constitutional identity.[113]

[108] ibid §81.
[109] ibid §75, §93.
[110] See A Harel and A Shinar, 'Two Concepts of Constitutional Legitimacy' (2023) 12 *Global Constitutionalism* 80, 105.
[111] 2018-717/718 QPC, 6 July 2018, §7.
[112] See, eg, G Canivet, 'Conférence en l'honneur de Charles Doherty Gonthier' 20–21 May 2011, www.conseil-constitutionnel.fr/la-fraternite-dans-le-droit-constitutionnel-francais.
[113] 22/2016 (XII. 5.) AB, 30 November 2016.

After the positive referendum on 2 October 2016 was invalidated due to low participation, and a seventh constitutional amendment dedicated to the constitutional identity was aborted shortly thereafter, it was ultimately the Court that had the final say regarding the anti-migration policy pursued by the government. In validating the legislator's decision, the Court did not conduct a proportionality review in the specific case but responded to open questions posed by the ombudsman regarding the general meaning of the Fundamental Law, and particularly the clause on the EU, in light of the decision taken by the EU Council. In doing so, and following the model of the German identity review, the Court laid the groundwork for using the notion in future concrete cases.[114] However, the judge ascribed an open but discovered substance to identity,[115] considering that its mobilisation in specific cases can be effective in ensuring Hungarian linguistic, historical, and cultural traditions.[116] On one hand, the judge understands constitutional identity as a means – now a classic one in the EU – of limiting the application of European decisions, but on the other hand, it opens the way for its use within the strictly national framework.

This trend has since been confirmed. Hungary's openly Christian constitutional identity – a European exception – was incorporated into the constitutional text in May 2018, further bolstering the credibility and orientation of the Court's interpretation in this regard. However, by the end of 2021, constitutional identity alone was not sufficient for judges, as they sought justification in another type of identity, namely 'the identity of community members', to establish a new limit on the application of EU law, particularly decisions of the CJEU concerning immigration and asylum requests.[117] According to the Constitutional Court, when the joint exercise of competences with the EU is incomplete and leads to a violation of the identity of individuals living in the territory, the state must ensure the protection of this right. This assertion is notably based on the Preamble, which explicitly defines the 'natural ties, determined by birth, which shape the identity of community members' of the Hungarian people.[118] It further emphasises that this identity is unchangeable[119] and constitutes an integral part of human dignity.[120] For the judge, changes due to societal evolution can only be made insofar as they result in no significant harm to these defining elements of identity. Without the protection of the state, individuals are compelled to change this identity by force, which goes against the principle of popular sovereignty and lacks democratic legitimacy.[121] In short, the massive and permanent settlement of immigrants on Hungarian territory without democratic authorisation

[114] ibid.
[115] ibid §65.
[116] ibid §66.
[117] 32/2021, 10 December 2021, *on the joint excercise of powers.*
[118] ibid §32.
[119] ibid §34.
[120] ibid §33.
[121] ibid §35.

can violate the right to identity and self-determination of the people living in Hungary, according to the Court.[122]

So far, the Hungarian Constitutional Court has not conducted any proportionality review based on identity.[123] Just as the Hungarian judge came to the aid of the government's political project vis-à-vis the EU by 'discovering' constitutional identity, they could have chosen to use this identity to reinforce the national strategy and align with the Orbán government's discourse – as was openly done during the mandate of László Trócsányi (2014–2019), who conceptualised and built constitutional identity during his tenure as Minister of Justice.[124] In this particular context, where the Constitutional Court has been reshaped both in its composition and – especially – in its powers with the 4th amendment of the Fundamental Law in 2012, it follows its own doctrine,[125] never directly contradicting the majority's projects, thereby doubling their legitimacy. Between resistance and resilience, its freedom occupies a middle ground, in a compromise between respecting international standards and government policy, raising fears of a return to the 'red tail' – the agreement between the ruling communists and scholars who, in exchange for allegiance to Marxist ideology, enjoyed a degree of autonomy and freedom before 1990's.[126] Will the transfer of former president of the Court Tamás Sulyok (2016-2024) to the presidency of the Republic change the situation? The door is open, since for now the freedom of judges in the face of emergencies resides more in the *non*-use of identity during proportionality review.

IV. A FREEDOM LIMITED BY THEORY

The choices made by judges, facilitated by the means we have just discussed, whether in favour of or against the legislator, do not reveal the reasons behind these choices as they are not solely explained by positive law. The judge has all the means at their disposal but does not implement them to ensure that emergency is treated promptly by the legislator. Theoretical thresholds would need to be exceeded to fully respond to emergencies.

Proportionality review raises questions of reconciliation between norms as well as between theoretical conceptions. Judges are all confronted with common theoretical limits, and some have already been crossed by courts not without consequences for the constitutional paradigm. Emergency exacerbates the tensions already inherent in the judge's role in normal times, in terms of

[122] ibid §51.
[123] For example: 3/2019. (III. 7.) AB, 7 March 2019.
[124] L Trócsányi, *Constitutions nationales et intégration européenne* (Bruylant, 2015).
[125] T Sulyok, 'Universal Human Rights and National Identity», International Conference for the 25th birthday of the Slovak Constitutional Court' Košice, 10 April 2018.
[126] V Kazai 'Stop Soros Law Left on the Books – The Return of the 'Red Tail'?' (2019) verfassungsblog.de/stop-soros-law-left-on-the-books-the-return-of-the-red-tail/.

legitimacy (subsection IV(A)) and prioritisation of the individual or particular versus the collective or general (subsection IV(B)). The relative freedom of the judge is measured here by the weight of the factors prompting their self-restraint.

A. Concurrent Legitimacies

Judges are supposed to refrain from crossing the boundary into the political domain. Their legitimacy as guardians of the law does not equate to the popular legitimacy enjoyed by the legislator. However, dealing with emergency introduces considerations into their interpretations that are neither purely legal nor strictly political.

i. Interests vs Majority Will

Theoretically, the legitimacy of law derives from the will of the people as expressed through their representatives.[127] The notion of *interest* comes into play only further down the line in legal practice. The ECHR has reiterated this principle in cases related to environmental pollution, emphasising that states must maintain a 'fair balance' while considering all interests at stake.[128] Proportionality review specifically assesses whether the reconciliation of interests is fair or not.

The treatment of emergency highlights 'the interest model' over 'the trump model'.[129] In other words, rights have a relative application, depending on how interests justify restrictions where 'rights and all the public interests would compete on the same level'.[130] Scholar critics see this change in favour of interests as a normative diminution of rights.[131] In practice, emergencies eliminate the choice between models since it requires balancing interests to interpret rights. And the risk is that the context of emergency may favour the idea of interests prevailing over rights. Judges find themselves at this tipping point.

Emergency does not necessarily empower the judge to override the prioritisation made by the legislator among the interests at stake. The legitimacy that matters is the immediate political will tasked with reconciling the interests at hand – not the will of the constituent, of which the judge must be the guardian. In practice, interest still appears as a bias in the hands of the legislator, with rare exceptions. Even the Czech judge explicitly recalled, setting aside the

[127] See, eg, A Larry, *Constitutionalism: Philosophical Foundations* (Cambridge University Press, 1998) or D Dyzenhaus and M Thorburn, *Philosophical Foundations of Constitutional Law* (Oxford University Press, 2016).

[128] See, eg, ECHR, *Fadeyeva v Russia*, no 55723/00, 2005.

[129] Klatt and Meister (n 96) 17.

[130] ibid 16.

[131] See S Tsakyrakis, 'Proportionality: An assault on human rights?' (2009) 7(3) *International Journal of Constitutional Law* 489.

consideration of emergency: 'It is an ideological conflict between (especially) so-called environmentalists and businessmen, property owners, and representatives of local governments, which should be resolved in the legislator, not in the Constitutional Court.'[132]

It is not uncommon for two emergencies to coincide, and then the decision of how to rank them in importance and urgency typically falls on the legislator. This ceding of agency to the latter by the judiciary generally results in a prioritisation of short-term interests – economic mostly – that are under a serious and imminent threat over longer-term interests. In the aforementioned decision to increase the cap on greenhouse gas emissions to allow the production of more gas at the national level, the French Council recalls that 'environmental preservation must be pursued on an equal footing with other fundamental interests of the Nation and that choices intended to meet present needs must not compromise the ability of future generations to meet their own needs', except 'in the case of a serious threat to gas supply security'.[133] This implies that there is a potential hierarchy among environmental and economic threats, and that the latter, in this case, was deemed more significant because immediate, thereby justifying setting the former aside. The Council found a compromise by taking the liberty to use the Environmental Charter to, for the first time, formulate a constructive reservation limiting the measure of increasing the cap.[134] The lack of judgment of the interest itself presented as justifying the law by the legislator was a missed opportunity to prioritise emergencies and sort through them by distinguishing between the notions of threat and emergency.

Nonetheless, as seen, exceptions arise where the judiciary seizes the means offered by constitutional law to also provide a vision of how interests should be reconciled and impose it on the legislator. Generally, when judges have pronounced against the legislator on such matters, it has been to prioritise long-term interests, long-term emergencies. Future interests become binding on current interests by taking into account scientific predictions. In Germany, for example, the Court found that the environmental interest, though not absolute, faces an emergency that will intensify over time so that it must be prioritised over others.[135]

In emergencies, then, the very conception of law is being challenged: should the law serve utilitarian purposes or be derived solely from the will of the people. Faced with emergency, legitimacy drawn from will gives way to interest: constitutional norms must be reconciled through the reconciliation of interests. Yet this is something the courts generally refuse to do, as interests have a political aura. Due to this reticence, no unified and systematic approach to emergencies has emerged.

[132] Pl. ÚS 18/17-1, 25 September 2018.
[133] 2022-843 DC, 12 August 2022, §12.
[134] Fleury and Cohendet (n 53).
[135] 1 BvR 2656/18, 1 BvR 78/20, 1 BvR 96/20, 1 BvR 288/20, 24 March 2021.

ii. Truth vs Majority Will

Emergencies must be handled rationally, informed by knowledge of facts, and this invites the suggestion that courts could make their decisions by asserting 'the truth'. Generally, however, they refrain from doing so. Introducing truth as a condition for the validity of a law would bring an additional, non-legal obstacle to the people's will as embodied by elected representatives. Thus, it may be argued that the judge potentially advocates for a scientific legitimacy over which they have no control and only serve as a spokesperson in relation to the legitimacy of the representative.

As Jocelyn Stacey argues regarding the treatment of environmental emergency, 'the rule of law requirement of public justification provides a coherent theory' that illuminates the approach a judge could adopt to address emergencies.[136] However, despite a constitutional requirement for rationalisation of the law in the observed states, the resonance of this theory in Europe falls short of that in Canada, upon which Stacey's analysis is based. A notable exception, as we saw, is the Czech judge who deduced a democratic deficit from the lack of rationality in a law. The jurisdictions studied in the present chapter have instead shown a deadlock in the transformation of the political requirement of rationality into a constitutional obligation. When scientific facts might call for the legislator to act in a certain way, the judge could, as seen, assess the law's conformity with science, in addition to its constitutional conformity. This raises questions of legitimacy: between legitimacy derived from the vote, requiring judges only to make technical decisions,[137] or from truth, which would require the judge to make rational decisions because of the current reality.

The judge and the legislator stand on equal footing in terms of legitimacy regarding scientific knowledge, neither being inherently more 'scientific' in its essence than the other. With the exception of the Czech judge, the judges mentioned above delegate to the political sphere the decision whether or not to consider scientific evidence and evaluate its relevance in relation to the decisions to be made. This is a risk assumed by the political realm. It is worth noting that the Czech Constitutional Court has pushed the boundary between law and politics further by stating that it cannot judge the merits of political choices, cannot determine if there were better solutions, as long as the law is rational.[138] The Court does not wait for the legislator to adopt the best solution, especially if there is no consensus among experts and scientists.[139] However, once it deems that the legislator could have made a decision more in line with scientific

[136] Stacey (n 2) 3–4.
[137] S Salles, 'Le conséquentialisme dans la jurisprudence du Conseil constitutionnel' (2016) 53 *Nouveaux Cahiers du conseil constitutionnel*.
[138] Pl. ÚS 106/20, 9 February 2021, §87.
[139] ibid §76.

evidence, it may invalidate the resulting law. This forces the judge to engage in scientific reasoning parallel to that of the legislator.

Within the Czech Constitutional Court, however, the stance on scientific facts is not unanimous and exhibits the classic theoretical limit of a judge's action. In dissenting opinions, Judge Jaroslaw Fenyk criticised the Court for what he perceived as activist behaviour, asserting that it overstepped its authority and encroached upon the separation of powers by substituting its judgment for political decisions. He also objected to the Court's intervention in settling an epidemiological debate, arguing that it should have deferred to expert opinion. Similarly, Judge Josef Friala expressed concern about the Court's decision, believing it should have exercised self-restraint given the extraordinary circumstances, rather than nullifying provisions irresponsibly.

The transition from conformity to truth that a constitutional judge could undertake has limits given scientific uncertainties, particularly in times of new emergencies such as the Covid pandemic, but also when other uncertain parameters are at play, such as the repercussions on other interests. Scholars have proposed various remedies for this issue. Alessi Farano highlights how American judges have assessed scientific consensus when the scientific element presented in a judgment regarding the constitutionality of a law was decisive, as the Czech Court explicitly did to a certain extent. Here, however, a question arises: may a judge proceed from the consensus on a scientific paradigm – if they can even find a way to establish what the consensus is – to derive a truth sufficient to be the basis of law?[140] Here, we encounter a problem inherent to science – and to humanity – that compels us to answer this question negatively. Historical examples such as Galileo or Semmelweis serve as reminders that the scientific majority can be wrong for extended periods. Imposing a constraint on what the judge considers to be scientific truth poses a risk to the judge's legitimacy.

Indeed, the quest for scientific 'truth' by the Czech constitutional judge is ultimately comparable to the approach taken by the Hungarian judge in asserting the existence of an identity as the 'truth' of the Hungarian people – unchangeable, inherited, and to which everyone is bound in their actions, including the majority, which is itself supposed to embody this identity. The judge purports merely to capture this identity, which is not his or anybody else's creation. Identity is a factual datum akin to scientific facts and offers similar prospects for expanding the interpretative power of the constitutional judge. However, unlike scientific facts, which result from demonstration or expertise, identity is exempt from justification. There is no need to prove that identity exists to make it binding, even in the face of an emergency. The Hungarian judge indeed seemed to hesitate less in determining this 'truth' since it is constitutional and not scientific.

[140] A Farano, 'L'évaluation de la preuve scientifique' (2020) 11 *Droit & Philosophie* 49.

B. Concurrent Perspectives

The Constitution belongs to the people, the state, and the individual. But emergencies are not only individual or national but global, and thus transcend national borders. Complicating the scope of the law, emergencies confront us with the question what constitutional law should convey or accomplish, and reveals its limitations. Judges' relationship with the individual, the collective, the national and the global is challenged in emergencies.

i. National v Global

First and foremost, urgent global issues raise questions about the compartmentalisation of constitutional law in terms of geography. Territory is a natural limit to constitutional law but not to the emergencies we have witnessed. Constitutional judges sometimes limit their own action in order to encouraging the legislator in tackling the emergency because they cannot do more. While Covid-19 could be addressed through national measures, climate change cannot be addressed or controlled by individual states alone.

The German Constitutional Court has been very explicit about the latter difficulty, which threatens to render all efforts undertaken by some states in the fight against climate change obsolete. In March 2024, in highlighting the limited real impact of national measures on the global effects of climate change and the inability of individual states to remedy them alone, the Court accepted the claims of Nepalese and Bangladeshi nationals but noted that German legislation could not be expected to improve the situation for other peoples on its own. It substantiated its argument in a very pragmatic way: the state's duty to protect cannot be understood in the same way abroad because concrete 'adaptation' measures, such as new infrastructure, can only be implemented within national territory. It remains an artificial paradox: while the Court cannot overlook the question of sovereignty,[141] it validated the opposability of German objective constitutional rights for other peoples in this specific context.[142]

Faced with this dilemma, the Court had no choice but to insist on the principle of solidarity among states on this urgent environmental issue,[143] and emphasised the responsibility of northern states to take note of the real difficulties and incapacities of southern states in the fight against climate change, as well as of the younger generations worldwide who have no real say in the matter. While this evolution may not be legal in the words of the German judge, it is political. The Court provides a realistic rationale for strengthening the binding aspect of the state's duty to protect the environment. Yet the Court promotes a

[141] 1 BvR 2656/18, 1 BvR 78/20, 1 BvR 96/20, 1 BvR 288/20, March 24, 2021, §176.
[142] ibid §174.
[143] ibid §200.

change in doctrine that involves breaking down the barriers of the state, which it sees as a rational executor of a global interest for humanity and for all living beings. Furthermore, as a vehicle for this necessary change, it has, exceptionally, added French and Spanish translations to the English translation available on the Court's website.[144]

On the other hand, the state of emergency paves the way for the resurgence of the State, particularly in the current context of war, which rekindles the idea of borders and compartmentalisation. The French Constitutional Council, for its part, makes no distinction between restrictions on environmentally desirable and other needs. The short-term emergency defined by the legislator remains the yardstick. For example, it sticks to an obsolete idea of a nationally independent and self-sufficient energy system. In its decision of 12 August 2022, the Council introduces an element that seems completely outdated in light of the scientific issues at stake and France's European commitment to energy solidarity among Member States.[145] Instead it prioritises national interests over the fight against climate change.[146] It should also be noted that unlike the German Constitutional Court, the Council incompetence to review conventionality[147] and it does not help to bring the international dimension of emergency issues into its scrutiny. The two jurisdictions are thus very unequal in their capacity and willingness to constrain the legislator in weighing the global emergency against national interests.

ii. Collective v Individual

In the case of the environment and more specifically climate change, the prioritisation of the emergency entails a prioritisation of the collective. In the case of Covid, by contrast, the emergency concerns individuals relying on the collective. In the case of immigration, it is the emergency of the individual entering the collective. In general, emergencies prompt the question: for *whom* is it an emergency? The individual or the collective? Who is in danger? Who should be prioritised?

The first difficulty lies, of course, in the reconciliation of interests, and in the ability of the judge to assert which interest should be prioritised according to constitutional law. The judge does not choose between interests deemed collective. Thus the French Constitutional Council allowed the legislator to prioritise sugar beet producers over beekeepers when it temporarily permitted the use of a banned pesticide to save sugar beets at the expense of bees.[148]

[144] See J Jahn, 'Domestic courts as guarantors of international climate cooperation: Insights from the German Constitutional Court's climate decision' (2023) 21(3) *International Journal of Constitutional Law* 859–83.
[145] See in particular Regulation (EU) 2022/2576.
[146] 2022-843 DC, 12 August 2022.
[147] 74-54 DC, 15 January 1975.
[148] Tsakyrakis (n 131) 481.

Given that emergency justifies the prioritisation of one interest over others, particularly individual ones, the Council's deference to the legislator in deciding on the hierarchy of interests could be dangerous.[149] An unchecked pursuit of the general interest could establish a sort of permanent institutionalisation of emergency treatment in favour of the collective and to the detriment of the individual. However, as we know, Europe is not immune to a reversal between the individual and the collective, offering primacy to the latter. This trend has a name: illiberalism. In such a context, the justification for restrictions of fundamental rights on grounds of permanent emergency is a practice already tested, as seen in Hungary's fight against immigration through the establishment of a permanent 'mass migration emergency' state between 2016 and 2020, then prolonged with the Covid crisis, and finally since the war in Ukraine.[150]

Outside of this ideological context, the Czech Constitutional Court explicitly describes this reversal of primacy from the individual to the state in certain emergency situations – such as Covid and environmental crises – and asserts that scientific rationality justifies it.[151] Only the judge can set a limit to this inversion. But favouring the collective interest as part of emergency measures flirts with the *raison d'État*, which is inherently uncontrollable. The consideration of the collective is essential for addressing emergencies, but in a liberal regime, the role of the judge is also to safeguard the rights of the individual. The very nature of emergencies, which impact the collective, threatens the judge's role as guarantor of liberalism.

An emergency is prima facie a pivot for increasing either the freedom of judges or that of the legislator. This is an element that calls into question the boundaries between judicial authority and the powers reserved for the legislator. But unlike the legislator, judges do not obtain a specific mandate simply because there is an emergency. While it is possible for judges' interpretive discretion to be expanded, their own capacity to do so is limited. The judge remains dependent on the will of the legislator despite the means at their disposal – means both constitutional and extra-constitutional, existing and new, that are common among states which confront the same paradoxes and theoretical risks.

In the treatment of emergencies, then, no consistent, systematic behaviour is exhibited by judges across jurisdictions. Emergencies differ from one another, and while similarities exist, these have not so far led to a general consideration of the concept of emergency and how the judiciary should approach emergencies. No regime of emergency is emerging even as emergencies multiply and intensify.

[149] G Merland, 'L'intérêt général, instrument efficace de protection des droits fondamentaux ?' (2004) *Cahiers du Conseil constitutionnel*.

[150] State of emergency declared for five years on 15 September 2015. See G Meszaros, 'Rule without law in Hungary: the decade of abusive permanent state of exception' (2022) *EUI MWP*.

[151] Pl. ÚS 106/20, 9 February 2021, §94.

For the moment, judges commonly ensure that deviations from long-term emergency measures or the treatment of short-term emergencies are at least limited in time and impact. However, occasional bold actions by judges in response to emergencies highlight the opportunities provided by new constitutional tools. And it is indeed the freedom of the judge that is in question: that is, their ability to break free from a theoretical mould and not merely show discretion on a case-by-case basis.

Constitutional judges ultimately appear less free than certain administrative or international judges facing emergencies, maybe because the former are the only ones with the capacity not to condemn the legislator after the fact but to compel them to act in a certain way, in the future.

Part II

Governance

4

Rethinking EU Emergency Law: Towards a General Supranational Emergency Clause?

FEDERICO CASOLARI* AND ANNA PAU

I. INTRODUCTION

THE INCREASE IN the number and magnitude of natural and man-made emergencies the European Union (EU) and its Member States (MS) have faced in recent times has brought to light the need to define clearer structures and rules for their proper management at the EU level, including the prevention, mitigation, and response phases. Indeed, even though the supranational emergency response has proven successful in many respects, particularly regarding the implementation of the Union Civil Protection Mechanism (UCPM),[1] there is no shortage of critical elements in the current legal framework. To mention one, the Treaties – and EU secondary law as well – recognise a residual role for the European Parliament (EP) in emergencies, thus limiting the democratic control of the Union's action. On the other hand, the Council of the European Union and the Commission have seen a significant increase in their prerogatives, particularly regarding the coordination and executive powers they may exercise. In addition, the current EU legal framework for emergency response lacks uniformity, with several legal bases differing in the scope and content available according to different emergency scenarios. Moreover, the legal instruments available for addressing emergencies are tailored to specific policy areas, as the competencies established in the Treaties for crisis management differ from one policy domain to another. As a result, to borrow Bruno de Witte's words, 'EU crisis law is too fragmented along policy-specific and crisis-specific lines'.[2]

* Although the present chapter results from common and shared reflections, Federico Casolari is the author of Sections I, II and IV, while Anna Pau is the author of Section III.

[1] Explained in Section II.

[2] B de Witte, 'Guest Editorial, EU Emergency Law and Its Impact on the EU Legal Order' (2022) 59 *CMLR* 18, 16. The author considers the concept of EU crisis law to be larger than the concept of

Against this background, the present chapter will inquire into the need to introduce a 'full-fledged' emergency clause into EU primary law. Such a clause could be triggered to handle unexpected situations requiring a supranational intervention. Many countries worldwide have emergency clauses in their constitutions, which may be activated to declare a state of emergency, temporarily suspending ordinary constitutional rules and safeguards.[3] This is not the case in the actual EU constitutional framework, probably because of the implications such a clause would entail for the scope of Member States' sovereignty and the allocation of (emergency) competencies between the Member States and the European Union. In this regard, reference can be made, of course, to the famous incipit of Carl Schimtt's *Political Theology*, where the political philosopher states that 'Sovereign is he who decides on the exception',[4] meaning that the sovereignty is revealed by the decision on the state of exception (*Ausnahmezustand*).

Taking stock of the lessons learned during the Covid-19 pandemic and in light of the response elaborated by the Union on that occasion,[5] the EP recently advanced the possibility of reforming the legal framework applicable to emergency management by introducing a general emergency clause into EU primary law.[6] Building on the conclusions adopted by the Conference on the Future of Europe in 2022[7] – and also in light of the report of the Franco-German working group on EU institutional reform, which was completed in September 2023[8] – the EU institution decided in November 2023 to activate the ordinary revision procedure of EU Treaties provided for in Article 48 of the Treaty on the

EU emergency law, referring to the latter as 'the rules of primary and secondary EU law that serve to address *sudden* threats to the core values and structures of the Union and its Member States' (ibid 4). On the fragmentation of the EU instruments dealing with emergencies occurring outside the Union, see F Casolari, 'The External Dimension of the EU Disaster Response' in A de Guttry et al (eds), *International Disaster Response Law* (TMC Asser Press, 2012) 129.

[3] C Bjørnskov and S Voigt, 'The Architecture of Emergency Constitutions' (2018) 16 *International Journal of Constitutional Law* 101; M Diaz Crego and S Kotanidis, 'States of Emergency in Response to the Coronavirus Crisis: Normative Response and Parliamentary Oversight in EU Member States during the First Wave of the Pandemic', European Parliamentary Research Service, Study, PE 659.385, December 2020, www.europarl.europa.eu/. See also the Covid-19 and States of emergency debate hosted by *Verfassungs Blog*, verfassungsblog.de/.

[4] C Schmitt, *Political Theology: Four Chapters on the Concept of Sovereignty* (University of Chicago Press, 2005) 5.

[5] F Casolari, 'The EU Approach towards Disaster Management: A Critical Appraisal in the Light of the Action Put in Place to Face the COVID-19 Pandemic' (2023) 4 *Yearbook of International Disaster Law* 51.

[6] European Parliament resolution of 22 November 2023 on proposals of the European Parliament for the amendment of the Treaties, P9_TA(2023)0427.

[7] Conference on the Future of Europe, Report on the final outcome, May 2022, commission.europa.eu/. The Conference was a citizen-led forum to share ideas and proposals on the future of the European integration process.

[8] Report of the Franco-German working group on EU institutional reform, Sailing on High Seas: Reforming and Enlarging the EU for the 21st Century, Paris–Berlin, 18 September 2023, institutdelors.eu/.

European Union (TEU).[9] For present purposes, two proposals made by the EP are worth highlighting.[10]

First, the EP proposes the re-allocation of competencies between the Union and the Member States in sectors pertaining to emergency management. This is achieved by changing the nature of the Union's competence in the field of civil protection and public health, especially in cross-border health threats. Conceived as supporting competencies under Article 6 of the Treaty on the Functioning of the European Union (TFEU), these competencies should be transformed into shared ones, thus allowing a more far-reaching and effective exercise of power by the EU during emergencies.[11]

Second, the EP calls for deleting Article 122 TFEU and introducing a general emergency clause under Article 222 TFEU, which already encapsulates another emergency provision, the so-called 'solidarity clause'.[12] The new Article 222(1) TFEU would read:

> In the event of an emergency affecting the [EU] or one or more Member States, the [EP] and the Council may grant the Commission extraordinary powers, including those to enable it to mobilise all necessary instruments. In order for an emergency to be declared, the [EP] shall act by a majority of its component members and the Council shall act by a qualified majority, on a proposal from the [EP] or the Commission. That decision […] shall define the scope of the powers, the detailed governance arrangements and the period during which they apply. The [EP] or the Council, acting by a simple majority, may revoke the decision at any time. The Council and the [EP] may, in accordance with the procedure set out in the first subparagraph, review or renew the decision at any time.

At first sight, two significant innovations seem to be envisaged in the proposed clause. On the one hand, the EU could unilaterally declare the existence of a state of emergency. Such a declaration, and the consequent management of the emergency scenario, would thus be elevated to the supranational level, potentially affecting the prerogatives the Union and the Member States may exercise in similar cases. On the other hand, the EP would be directly involved in managing emergencies, thus overcoming the deficits highlighted so far in using other EU legal bases,[13] and recalibrating the institutional balance in emergency management.

These aspects will be discussed in detail in this chapter, focusing on the most significant constitutional implications of the proposal and its related

[9] On the EU Treaties' revision, see M Klamert, 'Article 48 TEU' in M Kellerbauer, et al (eds), *The EU Treaties and the Charter of Fundamental Rights: A Commentary* (Oxford University Press, 2024) 375.

[10] For a general commentary on the European Parliament's proposals, see F Fabbrini, 'The European Parliament Proposal for Treaty reforms' (*EU Law Live*, 30 November 2023) eulawlive.com/.

[11] European Parliament (n 6) para 14.

[12] See Section II.

[13] ibid.

shortcomings (Section III). To start, in Section II, the main provisions of EU primary law that today allow the activation of emergency management mechanisms in the EU are examined. This is followed by some final considerations in Section IV.

II. SETTING THE SCENE: EU LEGAL BASES FOR EMERGENCY SUPPORT WITH A GENERAL SCOPE OF APPLICATION

The current general framework for supranational emergencies is defined by three provisions of the Treaty on the Functioning of the European Union: Articles 122, 196, and 222.[14]

Article 122 TFEU is a Treaty provision that the EU legislature has frequently mobilised recently to face emergency scenarios. It contains two different legal bases.[15] Article 122(1) TFEU allows the Council to adopt 'measures appropriate to the economic situation' in case of severe difficulties arising in the supply of certain products.[16] Article 122(2) TFEU is a proper emergency legal basis, allowing the Council to grant financial assistance to Member States 'in difficulties or [...] seriously threatened with severe difficulties caused by natural disasters or exceptional occurrences'. In both cases, the role of the EP is marginal. While Article 122(1) does not mention the EP, Article 122(2) TFEU simply states that '[t]he President of the Council shall inform the European Parliament of the decision taken.'

As anticipated, Article 122 TFEU has been invoked several times in recent years. Examples of its activation include: Council Regulation (EU) 2016/369 on the provision of emergency support within the Union;[17] Council Regulation (EU) 2020/521 activating the emergency support under Regulation (EU) 2016/369, and amending its provisions taking into account the Covid-19 outbreak;[18] Council Regulation (EU) 2020/672 on the establishment of a European instrument for temporary support to mitigate unemployment risks in an emergency (SURE)

[14] Although general in nature, the humanitarian aid the Union may offer to assist people who are victims of natural or man-made disasters (Article 214 TFEU) is not mentioned here. In fact, the Union may conduct humanitarian aid operations only in support of third countries. On this legal basis, see P Van Elsuwege and J Orbie, 'The EU's Humanitarian Aid Policy after Lisbon: Implications of a New Treaty Basis' in I Govaere and S Poli (eds), *EU Management of Global Emergencies. Legal Framework for Combating Threats and Crises* (Brill Nijhoff, 2014) 21. Likewise, provisions for emergency support measures in specific EU policy areas (eg, Article 78(3) TFEU referring to situations caused by a sudden inflow of third-country nationals, or Article 194(1) mentioning the solidarity among MSs to 'ensure security of energy supply in the Union') are not considered here.

[15] L Flynn, 'Article 122 TFEU' in Kellerbauer et al (n 9) 1803.

[16] For a different reading of Article 122(1) TFEU, according to which the provision would also constitute a legal basis for non-emergency economic instruments, see M Chamon, 'The Non-Emergency Economic Policy Competence in Article 122(1) TFEU' (2024) 61 *CMLR* 1501.

[17] OJ L70, 16 March 2016, 1.

[18] OJ L117, 15 April 2020, 3.

following the Covid-19 outbreak;[19] Council Regulation (EU) 2020/2094 establishing a European Union Recovery Instrument to support the recovery in the aftermath of the Covid-19 crisis;[20] and Council Regulation (EU) 2022/2372 on a framework of measures for ensuring the supply of crisis-relevant medical countermeasures in the event of a public health emergency at Union level.[21] Although the vast majority of these instruments have significantly contributed to addressing emergency scenarios, there is no doubt that the extensive use of Article 122 TFEU has prompted a number of criticisms, not least in light of the limited transparency and democratic accountability of the decision-making process contained therein.[22]

Article 196 TFEU allows the Union to complement and support national policies 'in risk prevention, in preparing their civil-protection personnel and in responding to natural or man-made disasters within the Union'. The provision does not define the concept of 'disaster'. Such a definition is given by Decision 1313/2013/EU of the European Parliament and of the Council on a Union Civil Protection Mechanism, which constitutes the cornerstone of the activity of the Union in the civil protection domain.[23] The Decision gives a significantly broad definition, referring to 'any situation which has or may have a severe impact on people, the environment, or property, including cultural heritage.' This explains why the UCPM has been activated upon the request of MSs and third countries to give in-kind assistance in cases of natural or man-made disasters (eg, health, climate, and geohazard-related disasters), conflicts (eg, the war in Ukraine), and other humanitarian emergencies (eg, population displacement and consular support). Also significantly, the UCPM promotes the MSs' disaster prevention, further supporting them in improving their risk management.[24] In particular, it is requested that Member States provide the Commission with relevant aspects of their risk assessments and the assessment of their risk management capability focusing on key risks. They are also requested to provide information on the priority measures needed to address key risks with cross-border implications and low-probability risks with a high impact.[25]

[19] OJ L159, 20 May 2020, 1.

[20] OJ L442I, 22 December 2020, 23.

[21] OJ L314, 6 December 2022, 64.

[22] See M Chamon, 'The Use of Article 122 TFEU. Institutional Implications and Impact on Democratic Accountability', Study requested by the AFCO Committee of the European Parliament, PE 753.307, September 2023, www.europarl.europa.eu/; P Dermine, 'Article 122 TFEU and the Future of the Union's Emergency Powers' (*EU Law Live*, 30 November 2023) eulawlive.com/.

[23] OJ L771, 20 March 2019, 1. The Decision has been subject to several amendments. A consolidated text is available at eur-lex.europa.eu/. See M Gestri, 'EU Disaster Response Law: Principles and Instruments' in de Guttry et al (n 2) 105.

[24] Decision 1313/2013/EU, Article 6.

[25] The European Commission has adopted a set of guidelines to support Member States in fulfilling such reporting duties: Reporting Guidelines on Disaster Risk Management, OJ C428, 20 December 2019, 8.

Having said this, it remains that the UCPM heavily relies on the consent of affected States: indeed, the Mechanism may only be activated by that State. This solution is perfectly consistent with the MSs' prerogatives for protecting people who are subject to their jurisdiction in the event of disasters.[26] It also reflects the nature of the EU competence in question, which may only be triggered to support and coordinate MSs' action. Also significantly, under the UCPM the in-kind assistance is offered by the participant States on a voluntary basis, meaning that those States may refuse. Their only obligation is to provide a prompt answer.[27] Over time, the EU institutions have tried to reduce the voluntary nature of the UCPM. This has been done first by introducing the possibility for the States to pre-commit response capacities (the so-called 'European Civil Protection Pool'),[28] the deployment of which can be refused by the Member States that registered the response capacity concerned only in case of domestic emergencies, force majeure, or other serious reasons. More recently, the Decision has been amended to establish strategic reserves (the so-called 'RescEU capacities') that may be acquired, rented, leased, or otherwise contracted by the Member States and/or the European Commission to provide assistance in overwhelming situations.[29] Those capacities may be used for national purposes when not being used under the UCPM, and the Commission is to take the decision on their deployment and demobilisation in close coordination with the requesting Member State. Although these reforms have further enhanced the effectiveness of the UCPM,[30] and although it is rare for a request for assistance to go unheeded,[31] the fact remains that the Mechanism cannot ignore the legal constraints set by the Treaties. Only a change in these, particularly the transformation of EU civil protection policy into an area of shared competence, could overcome the current obstacles.

[26] Such a primary responsibility is well-recognised at the international level. See the Draft articles on the protection of persons in the event of disasters, adopted by the International Law Commission at its sixty-eighth session (2016), recognising 'the primary role of the State affected by a disaster in providing disaster relief assistance'. As it made clear in the Commentaries, this responsibility flows directly from the principle of State sovereignty, which 'provides the background against which the entire set of Draft articles is to be understood', cf *Yearbook of International Law Commission* (2016) vol. II, Part Two.

[27] Decision 1313/2013/EU, Article 15(4).

[28] ibid Article 11.

[29] ibid Article 12.

[30] For criticisms of the reform introducing the RescEU capacities into the UCPM, see F Casolari, 'Europe (2018)' (2020) 1 *Yearbook of International disaster Law* 346, esp. 349; F Casolari, 'Europe (2020)' (2022) 3 *Yearbook of International Disaster Law* 453, esp. 464–65.

[31] But not impossible: at the beginning of the spread of Covid-19 in Europe, Italy – the first MS to be severely affected – was refused ventilators, face masks, and medical supplies requested under the UCPM, cf DM Herszenhorn et al, 'Europe fails to help Italy in coronavirus fight' (*Politico*, 5 March 2020); C Beaucillon, 'International and European Emergency Assistance to EU Member States in the COVID-19 Crisis: Why European Solidarity Is Not Dead and What We Need to Make It Both Happen and Last' (2020) 5 *European Papers* 387.

In its actual formulation, Article 222 only enshrines the solidarity clause. Pursuant to it, '[t]he Union and its Member State shall act jointly in a spirit of solidarity if a Member State is the object of a terrorist attack or the victim of a natural or man-made disaster.' Conceived as a last resort mechanism still based on the consent of the affected State,[32] the solidarity clause imposes upon the Union and the other Member States assistance obligations.[33] However, even if it represents one of the most evident expressions of the role solidarity may play in the EU legal order,[34] the clause has never been activated so far. Arguably, the main obstacle to the activation of the clause is due to the lack of clarity about the content of the solidarity duties it entails,[35] thus making it unclear when those duties can be considered properly fulfilled. This circumstance is even more relevant considering that the implementation of the clause by the Union and its Member States may be subject to the scrutiny of the EU Court of Justice (CJEU).[36] As things stand now, the clause thus represents no more than an empty shell.

[32] According to Article 4(1) of the Council Decision 2014/415/EU of 24 June 2014 on the arrangements for the implementation by the Union of the solidarity clause (OJ L192, 1 July 2014, 53), it is for the affected State to invoke the clause if it considers, 'after having exploited the possibilities offered by existing means and tools at national and Union level,' that the crisis overwhelms its response capacities.

[33] It thus differs from the UCPM, the latter not imposing any assistance obligations upon the participant States. On the clause in general, see Gestri (n 23) 109–15.

[34] The concept of solidarity finds multiple applications in the EU Treaties: see, among others, Articles 24(2) and 42(7) TEU and Articles 78(3), 122(1) and 194(1) TFEU. Solidarity is also one of the values enshrined in Article 2 TEU and the EU Charter of Fundamental Rights, as well as an objective of the Union's external action (Article 3(5) TEU). More generally, solidarity represents 'the lifeblood of the European project': Joined Cases C-715/17, C-718/17 and C-719/17 *Commission v Poland et al* ECLI:EU:C:2019:917, Opinion AG Sharpston of 31 October 2019, para 253. For a thorough analysis of the role solidarity may play in disaster management at the EU level, see S Villani, *The Concept of Solidarity within EU Disaster Response Law: A Legal Assessment* (Bononia University Press, 2021); S Villani, 'Perspectives of Solidarity within the EU Legal Order in the Time of the COVID-19 Pandemic' (2023) 4 *Yearbook of International Disaster Law* 70. For more general reflections, see A Biondi et al (eds), *Solidarity in EU Law. Legal Principle in the Making* (Edward Elgar, 2018); E Kassoti and N Idriz (eds), *The Principle of Solidarity: International and EU Law Perspectives* (TMC Asser Press, 2023).

[35] Under the Declaration on Article 222 of the Treaty on the Functioning of the European Union (n 37), annexed to the Final Act of the Lisbon Conference (OJ C202, 7 June 2016, 349), 'none of the provisions of Article 222 is intended to affect the right of another Member State to choose the most appropriate means to comply with its own solidarity obligations toward [the affected] Member State'. According to Marco Gestri, the interpretation of Article 222 TFEU in light of that Declaration should imply that Member States 'maintain the right to choose, in good faith, the concrete modalities of assistance'; cf Gestri (n 23) 114. However, it remains unclear whether such modalities must reach a minimum threshold.

[36] In light of the foregoing, it does not come as a surprise that the decision adopted by France right after the terrorist attacks in Paris on 13 November 2015 relied on Article 42(7) TEU (the so-called 'mutual assistance clause') instead of triggering Article 222 to obtain the other Member States' support. Unlike Article 222 TFEU, the enforcement of Article 42(7) TEU is not subject to the judicial scrutiny of the Luxembourg judges. See NIM Nováky, 'The Invocation of the European Union's Mutual Assistance Clause: A Call for Enforced Solidarity' (2017) 22 *European Foreign Affairs Review* 357.

III. CONSTITUTIONAL ISSUES ARISING FROM THE INTRODUCTION OF A GENERAL EMERGENCY CLAUSE IN THE EU TREATIES

The previous Section lays out the legal constraints and shortcomings of existing general emergency legal bases available at the EU level. The EP's proposed reform of the EU emergency legal framework has the potential to expand the EU prerogatives in this key area, with a stronger EU oversight of national policies. Indeed, the clause would be the first and only example of a legal basis allowing the Union to declare a general state of emergency, granting extraordinary powers to the European Commission. As far as the EU is concerned, a relevant binding precedent is the mechanism leading to the recognition of public health emergencies at the EU level under Article 23 of Regulation (EU) 2022/2371 of the European Parliament and of the Council on serious cross-border threats to health.[37] In this case, however, the decision, which the Commission is to take after consulting expert opinion, may only deal with threats that might endanger 'public health at Union level.'[38] As opposed to this provision, the clause proposed by the EP is general in scope, echoing the emergency mechanisms that are available in the municipal legal orders of many Member States.[39] Also importantly, if the Security Council's power under Article 39 of the United Nations Charter is excluded, that clause would represent the first case of a general emergency clause that an international organisation may adopt, thus constituting a significant innovation in the context of the law of international organisations.[40] The World Health Organization (WHO) Director General can indeed adopt declarations proclaiming a public health emergency of international importance (PHEIC),

[37] OJ L314, 6 December 2022, 26. A purely symbolic precedent may be found in the declaration of a climate and environment emergency adopted by the European Parliament ahead of the UN COP25 Climate Change in Madrid; cf European Parliament resolution of 28 November 2019 on the climate and environment emergency, P9_TA(2019)0078. According to C Kreuder-Sonnen, the Council's recommendation establishing an excessive imbalance (pursuant to Article 7 of the Regulation (EU) No 1176/2011 of the European Parliament and of the Council of 16 November 2011 on the prevention and correction of macroeconomic imbalances, OJ L306, 23 November 2011, 25) could also be an example of an emergency power of the Union introduced 'by means of *legislative acts*': C Kreuder-Sonnen, *Emergency Powers of International Organizations: Between Normalization and Containment* (Oxford University Press, 2019) 34.

[38] Regulation (EU) 2022/2371, Article 23(1). The Commission also determines when a public health emergency has come to an end (Article 29(2)). Equally interesting, and 'on duly justified imperative grounds of urgency related to the severity of a serious cross-border threat to health or to the rapidity of its spread among Member States', the Commission may declare a public health emergency at the Union level through immediately applicable implementing acts (Article 23(4)).

[39] For a comparative assessment of the EU emergency clause in light of emergency laws available in the Member States, see G Bellenghi, 'The European Parliament's Proposal for an EU State of Emergency Clause: A Comparative and Constitutional Analysis' (2024) 20 *Croatian Yearbook of European Law and Policy* (advance access). According to the author, 'the state of emergency clause proposed by the Parliament largely follows EU Member States' common constitutional traditions with regard to the powers to declare and end an emergency' (ibid 25).

[40] Kreuder-Sonnen (37) 33.

requiring the establishment of an Emergency Committee.[41] However, leaving aside any reasoning on the 'specialness' of the Union vis-à-vis other international organisations,[42] it cannot but be emphasised that, unlike the prerogative (which could be) attributed to the Union according to the EP's reform, that of the WHO is, in any case, a narrowly defined power that does not confer extraordinary powers on its institutions.[43]

Next, the main constitutional implications of the proposed general emergency clause for the EU legal order are highlighted.[44]

A. Circumstances Justifying the Activation of the General Emergency Clause

First, however, it is necessary to consider the situations in which EU intervention would be legitimate under the clause at issue. The EP's proposal does not clarify which situations can be the basis for emergencies that trigger the clause, suggesting that the threat's origin is irrelevant per se. It merely clarifies that an EU state of emergency may be declared in all cases where an emergency 'affect[s] the European Union or one or more Member States'. This has rightly been criticised in doctrine.[45] This circumstance, however, does not entirely rule out the possibility of attempting to reconstruct its contours.

Even if a literal interpretation of the clause's wording does not exclude the possibility of activating it in the case of an emergency affecting a single Member State,[46] a more articulated reading seems to be preferred, according to which – and in line with the classical paradigm of the scope of application of EU law – this clause requires the existence of a supranational emergency, having a cross-border relevance as well as possible spill-over effects. A clear illustration of a similar emergency is represented by the Covid-19 pandemic, which posed serious cross-border threats to the Union and its Member States. However, this does not mean that the clause may be activated only when all Member States are

[41] 2005 International Health Regulations (IHR), Article 12.

[42] P Palchetti and RA Wessel, 'Our Love for the European Union. But Is It an International Organization?' (2024) 21 *International Organizations Law Review* 499.

[43] In the case of a declaration that a public health emergency of international concern is occurring, the WHO Director General is to issue temporary recommendations to be implemented by the State Party experiencing the emergency or by other State Parties (IHR, Article 12). The inadequacy of the IHR mechanisms to face severe health emergencies is stressed, among others, by GL Burci and S Negri, 'Governing the Global Fight Against Pandemics: The WHO, the International Health Regulations, and the Fragmentation of International Law' (2021) 53 *New York University Journal of International Law and Politics* 501.

[44] See also Bellenghi (n 39); M Chamon, 'The EU's Dormant Economic Policy Competence: Reliance on Article 122 TFEU and Parliament's Misguided Proposal for Treaty Revision' (2024) 49 *ELR* 166, esp. 183–87; A Pau, 'Verso la dichiarazione di uno "stato di emergenza sovranazionale"? Clausola di solidarietà e prospettive di riforma dei Trattati' (2024) 4 *Quaderni AISDUE*, Special Issue n 3, 105.

[45] Bellenghi (n 39) 6–7; Chamon (44) 185.

[46] Bellenghi (n 39) 7.

affected simultaneously by the emergency at issue: emergencies affecting a single MS may eventually have repercussions for the rest of the Union.

Moreover, given the extraordinary nature of the resulting measures, the clause must necessarily refer to emergencies of a magnitude that cannot be effectively addressed by the other emergency instruments at the disposal of the Union and its Member States. It thus seems logical to infer that, just like the solidarity clause, the emergency clause should be activated as a last-resort mechanism.[47]

To properly realise the underlying objective of the reformed proposal, ie to give the Union a more decisive role in emergency management, the clause should be activated unilaterally at the Union level. This means that the Council and the EP should enjoy a certain degree of discretion in qualifying an event or a series of events as an emergency according to the understanding of the proposed clause. However, as clarified below,[48] this does not mean that the two institutions should be unbound by EU law in realising such a qualification.

This latter circumstance, together with the relevant notion of emergency, should help draw a line between the scope of the emergency clause and that of the solidarity clause. Indeed, in all cases where an emergency directly affects one Member State without posing a threat to others and/or the Union as a whole, the affected State would still be able to invoke the 'spirit of solidarity' under the current Article 222 TFEU. Consequently, the affected State's principle[49] would continue to apply where the EU intervenes directly in support of a Member State facing a (merely) *internal* emergency. In all cases where the emergency takes on a supranational dimension, the Union legislature should be able to intervene unilaterally to preserve the latter's interests.

B. Centralised Emergency Management and Member States' Prerogatives in the National Security Domain

To get a sense of the constitutional implications the new clause may have, it is useful to consider first its implications for the allocation of competences between the Union and its Member States. In this respect, it is apt to start by recalling the prerogatives enjoyed by the Member States in public order and national security. As is well-known, Article 4(2) TEU includes maintaining national security among the essential functions of the MSs, which the EU is obliged to respect. More precisely, Article 4(2) TEU specifies that 'national security remains the sole responsibility of each Member State', thus constituting an exclusive competence of the latter.[50] Considering that emergency

[47] ibid.

[48] See Section III(C).

[49] Section II.

[50] See G Di Federico, *L'identità nazionale degli Stati membri nel diritto dell'Unione europea. Natura e portata dell'art. 4, par. 2, TUE* (Editoriale Scientifica, 2017) 65; M Dobbs, 'Sovereignty, Article 4(2) TEU and the Respect of National Identities: Swinging the Balance of Power in Favour of the Member States?' (2014) 33 *YEL* 298; M Klamert, 'Article 4 TEU' in Kellerbauer et al (n 9) 47.

scenarios are likely to present security implications for the affected States, one could conclude that a proper interpretation of Article 4(2) TEU should prevent the Union from interfering with States' emergency management, particularly when such event(s) may have a significant impact on the affected countries. This reading perfectly aligns with the understanding of the solidarity clause, the activation of which is based on the consent of the affected State.

As stressed elsewhere,[51] however, the fact that Member States enjoy a prerogative for maintaining their national security does not imply that they can invoke it to set aside EU law. Indeed, it cannot be ignored that Article 4(2) is supposed to be read in conjunction with Article 4(3) TEU, which codifies the principle of sincere cooperation and the related Member State duties. In particular, the negative duties flowing from Article 4(3) TEU, prohibiting States from acting if such action risks undermining the EU's objectives and interests, have contributed to the affirmation of what AG Pikämae has named the 'framing of powers theory'.[52] That theory urges Member States to exercise their prerogatives with due regard to EU law, which means that possible negative consequences for Union interests must be considered. Applying this in an emergency scenario could reshape (or prevent) a State's intervention, even in cases where such intervention could be justified for national security reasons.

Significantly, the EP's proposal to introduce a general emergency clause in EU primary law reinforces such a reading, contributing to the 'passion' for security that the Union has recently emphasised.[53] The rationale behind the EP's reform is clear in this respect. The idea it promotes is that an EU intervention to manage an emergency having cross-border implications pursues a clear supranational interest: maintaining the essential functions of the Union in the event of a vast emergency. The unprecedented challenges posed by the spread of the Covid-19 pandemic illustrated how cross-border emergencies – and unilateral actions taken by Member States to deal with them – risk undermining key areas of EU integration, such as the internal market and the Schengen area. This is why introducing a centralised emergency management mechanism could help preserve that supranational interest better.

To be clear, we are not claiming, to mention Schmitt's incipit again, that the introduction of such a clause would certify that the Union has achieved its own sovereignty, even though this is an objective assigned to it by the heads of state or government of the MSs at their informal meeting in Versailles a few days after

[51] F Casolari, 'Supranational Security and National Security in Light of the EU Strategic Autonomy Doctrine: The EU-Member States Security Nexus Revisited' (2023) 28 *European Foreign Affairs Review* 323.

[52] Case C-457/18 *Republic of Slovenia v Republic of Croatia*, ECLI:EU:C:2020:1067, Opinion AG Pikämae of 11 December 2020, para 138.

[53] Reference is made in particular to the growing interest shown by the Union, also in light of the strategic autonomy doctrine, in securing its fundamental interests and values. See Editorial Comments, 'The Passion for Security in European Societies' (2024) 61 *CMRL* 283.

the invasion of Ukraine by Russian armed forces.[54] What we want to argue is that the introduction of a general emergency clause, which entrusts the Union institutions with the power to declare the existence of a state of emergency and the related extraordinary powers of management, requires, in light of the theory of the framing of powers, that the MSs work in close coordination with the Union to ensure that the exercise of their prerogatives does not hinder or render less effective supranational intervention. Therefore, in the hypothetical scenario in which both the Union and one or more Member States decided to declare a state of emergency, close coordination between them and the Commission would have to be put in place, with a centralised role headed by the Commission.[55] Member States could thus continue to manage the emergency complementary to the Union, ensuring that they do not undermine the centralised management. A fortiori, similar reasoning should apply in relation to the derogation clauses the EU Treaties incorporate for situations affecting law and order or public security, starting from the 'wholly exceptional' derogation clause enshrined in Article 347 TFEU.[56] As was made clear by the CJEU's Grand Chamber:[57]

> It cannot be inferred that the FEU Treaty contains an inherent general exception excluding all measures taken [by MSs] for reasons of law and order or public security from the scope of European Union law.

C. EU Emergency Powers in the Context of the Supranational Constitutional Framework

Having clarified the interaction between the Union's and Member States' prerogatives, the next issue that deserves to be addressed is that of the role played by the EU institutions in the context of the emergency clause and, in particular, the nature and limits of the Commission's extraordinary powers. As seen, the

[54] cf Informal meeting of the Heads of State or Government, Versailles Declaration, 10 and 11 March 2022, para 7: 'Confronted with growing instability, strategic competition and security threats, we decided to take more responsibility for our security and take further decisive steps towards building our European sovereignty, reducing our dependencies and designing a new growth and investment model for 2023'. Text available at www.consilium.europa.eu/. See also T Verellen, 'European Sovereignty Now? A Reflection on What It Means to Speak of "European Sovereignty"' (2020) 5 *European Papers* 307.

[55] See also Bellenghi (n 39) 24, who rightly underlines that 'the current Treaty design reflects the EU's lack of independent enforcement capacities'.

[56] 'Member States shall consult each other with a view to taking together the steps needed to prevent the functioning of the internal market being affected by measures which a Member State may be called upon to take in the event of serious internal disturbances affecting the maintenance of law and order, in the event of war, serious international tension constituting a threat of war, or in order to carry out obligations it has accepted for the purpose of maintaining peace and international security.' The 'wholly exceptional nature' of Article 347 TFEU was first recognised in Case 222/84 *Johnston*, ECLI:EU:C:1986:206, para 27. On this clause, see P Koutrakos, 'Is Article 297 EC a "Reserve of Sovereignty"?' (2000) 37 *CMRL* 1339.

[57] Case C-808/18 *European Commission v Hungary*, ECLI:EU:C:2020:1029, para 214.

EP's proposal entrusts the Parliament and the Council with the decision on the severity of the emergency and the EU's ability to manage it. The operational management of extreme events is left to the Commission, which can use the extraordinary powers granted by the legislature. Such powers may be revoked, renewed, or reviewed at any time by the legislature.

While echoing the solutions adopted at the state level for declaring a state of emergency, this proposal is at odds with the conventional approach concerning the end of the emergency: contrary to the vast majority of such laws, the EP's proposed clause does not predetermine the maximum duration of the state of emergency, which is established by the legislature.[58] A similar conclusion could also be reached at first sight with reference to the nature and limits of the extraordinary powers the Commission may exercise in the context of a supranational emergency, considering the 'minimalistic' formulation of the clause compared to state emergency laws.[59]

At closer inspection, however, it is logical to argue that the EU legislature, in declaring a state of emergency, should also contextualise the powers attributed to the Commission and the limits they may encounter (both procedural and in content). Pursuant to the EP's proposal, indeed, the decision taken by the legislature 'shall define the scope of the powers, the detailed governance arrangements and the period during which they apply.' In this sense, the clause seems to refer by analogy to the provisions of Article 290 TFEU on legislative delegation.[60] The Treaty Article, as is well known, expressly requires that the legislative act containing the delegation also define 'the objectives, content, scope and delegation of power'. Viewed from this perspective, the extraordinary nature of the powers attributed to the Commission must essentially be assessed in comparison to the ordinary powers the institution may exercise in an emergency scenario. In other words, it does not seem acceptable to read the clause as allowing the EU legislature to confer powers on the Commission that it itself does not possess. Not only would this reading legitimise a sort of super competent Commission, which is inconsistent with the principle of conferral. It would also dramatically impair the institutional balance of the Union. That the emergency clause constitutes a special case of delegation of powers also seems to be confirmed by the fact that the Parliament and the Council would retain the possibility of amending, revoking, or renewing these powers at any time. And in an organisation still governed by the structural principle of conferral, how could the legislature dispose of them without first possessing them?

[58] Bellenghi (n 39) 9.

[59] ibid 11.

[60] cf Chamon (44) 184, arguing that the Parliament's clause leads to 'an atypical institutional balance' compared to the legislative procedure provided for in Article 290 TFEU. Bellenghi (n 39) 10, maintains that 'the limits to the granting of powers provided for in Article 222(1) TFEU would be less stringent than those set by the main paradigm of delegation under EU law, namely Article 290 TFEU'. For a general overview of the Article 290 TFEU procedure, see B Driessen, 'Delegated Legislation after the Treaty of Lisbon: An Analysis of Article 290 TFEU' (2010) 35 *ELR* 837.

In this respect, it also seems possible to conclude that the clause dictates the involvement of the EU legislature in emergency management, as the Parliament and the Council should carefully define the scope of the powers delegated to the Commission.[61] In so doing, the clause contributes to recalibrating the institutional balance in emergency situations by strengthening the parliamentary role, in line with the supranational value of democracy[62] and the supremacy of the legislature, which is stressed, inter alia, in the *Rule of Law Checklist* that the Venice Commission also elaborated for the exceptions to the principle of legality in emergency situations.[63]

Although not expressly mentioned in the clause, there are structural limits to the EU institutions' action to be taken into consideration. They may be inferred from a systematic interpretation of the clause in light of the EU constitutional framework. First, both the decision adopted by the legislature and the powers exercised by the Commission must not exceed what is necessary for tackling the ongoing emergency. This is what the principle of proportionality governing the exercise of all the EU competencies requires. Moreover, considering that the clause is not an expression of exclusive competence of the Union and that it should be activated only as a last-resort mechanism, the EU institutions should also be guided by the principle of subsidiarity. Another constitutional limit should be represented by the need to preserve the 'very identity of the European Union as a common legal order',[64] namely its fundamental values – respect for human dignity, freedom, democracy, equality, the rule of law and respect for human rights, including the rights of persons belonging to minorities. In *Kadi and Al Barakaat International Foundation*, the Grand Chamber of the EU Court of Justice stated that Treaty provisions allowing MSs to derogate from EU law for security reasons (eg, Article 347 TFEU) 'cannot be understood [...] to authorise any derogation from the principles of liberty, democracy and respect for human rights and fundamental freedoms enshrined in Article [... 2 TEU] as a foundation of the Union'.[65] It would frankly be difficult to argue that this is possible for the EU institutions once the emergency clause has been activated!

Nor can it be ignored that the EU Charter of Fundamental Rights binds the institutions, organs, and bodies of the Union, as well as the Member States, to the extent that they implement EU law (Article 51(1)) so that 'situations

[61] Significantly, the Parliament shares the power of proposal with the European Commission.

[62] See K Lenaerts, 'The Principle of Democracy in the Case Law of the European Court of Justice' (2013) 62 *International and Comparative Law Quarterly* 271; cf also Case C-814/21 *European Commission v Republic of Poland* ECLI:EU:C:2024:963, para 112.

[63] European Commission for Democracy through Law (Venice Commission), Rule of Law Checklist, CDL-AD(2016)007, 18 March 2016, www.venice.coe.int/.

[64] Case C-156/21 *Hungary v European Parliament and Council of the European Union* ECLI:EU:C:2022:97, para 127.

[65] Joined Cases C-402/05 P and C-415/05 P *Kadi and Al Barakaat International Foundation* ECLI:EU:C:2008:461, para 303.

cannot exist which are covered in that way by European Union law without those fundamental rights being applicable'.[66] Moreover, the EU Charter does not contain a general derogation clause that could limit its application in times of emergency, in contrast with many national constitutions and the European Convention on Human Rights.[67] This means that implementing the emergency clause cannot undermine the essence of fundamental rights.[68] The position of the President of the EU Court of Justice is clear in this respect: 'the essence of fundamental right is the most fundamental bastion of liberty that the CJEU will never give up.'[69]

This last remark leads us to briefly consider the controls and remedies that could be available if the clause is improperly implemented. Besides the political control mechanisms that the EU legislature could incorporate in the 'detailed governance arrangements' mentioned in the decision on the EU state of emergency, judicial control by the Court of Justice can be envisaged. However, if the matter is justiciable, it is also clear that the Court could encounter some difficulties in assessing the action taken by the EU institutions in similar exceptional circumstances. In particular, the fact that neither the clause nor other primary EU law provisions contain a well-established notion of 'supranational emergency' could limit the scope of the judicial review.[70] It is difficult not to recall here the remarks made by Advocate General Jacobs in the case against Greece, alleging misuse of power under Article 347 TFEU, to justify the unilateral measures adopted prohibiting trade in products with the former Yugoslav Republic of Macedonia. While referring to a different kind of emergency, namely a situation of war or international tension constituting a threat of war, the Advocate General emphasised, recalling the words of an English judge, that 'there are … no judicial or manageable standards by which to judge these matters, or to adopt another phrase … the court would find itself in a judicial no-man's land.'[71] The fact remains that even in this uncharted land, the Court should demonstrate its ability to protect the 'bastion of liberty' of the EU legal order.[72]

[66] C-617/10 *Åkerberg Fransson* ECLI:EU:C:2013:105, para 21.

[67] de Witte (n 2) 5.

[68] Article 52(1): 'Any limitations on the exercise of the rights and freedoms recognized by this Charter must be provided for by law and *respect the essence of those rights and freedoms*.' Emphasis added. See de Witte (n 2) 3.

[69] K Lenaerts, 'Limits on Limitations: The Essence of Fundamental Rights in the EU' (2019) 20 *German Law Journal* 779, 793.

[70] Bellenghi (n 39) 19–21.

[71] Case C-120/94 *Commission of the European Communities v Hellenic Republic* ECLI:EU:C:1995:109, Opinion AG Jacobs of 6 April 1995, para 50. The Court could not adjudicate on the merit of the case.

[72] N Alivizatos et al, 'Respect for Democracy, Human Rights and the Rule of Law During States of Emergency: Reflections', Venice Commission Report, CDL-AD(2020)014, 19 June 2020, para 86: 'Judicial control of the declaration of state of emergency may be limited to the control of the procedural aspects of the declaration. If, however, emergency measures involve derogations from human rights, the substantive grounds for the state of emergency shall be subject to judicial review as well.'

IV. CONCLUSION

In her 2020 State of the Union address, the President of the European Commission, Ursula von der Leyen, made the following statement:[73]

> In the last six months, our health systems and workers have produced miracles. Every country has worked to do its best for its citizens. And Europe has done more together than ever before. When Member States closed borders, we created green lanes for goods. When more than 600,000 European citizens were stranded all over the world, the EU brought them home. When some countries introduced export bans for critical medical goods, we stopped that and ensured that critical medical supply could go where it was needed. We worked with European industry to increase the production of masks, gloves, tests and ventilators. Our Civil Protection Mechanism ensured that doctors from Romania could treat patients in Italy or that Latvia could send masks to its Baltic neighbours. *And we achieved this without having full competences.*

Undoubtedly, the Covid-19 pandemic showed how relevant a supranational response is when extraordinary emergencies occur – and how difficult it is to prepare such a response with the existing instruments of EU emergency law. It is no coincidence that during the pandemic emergency or immediately after it, ordinary EU legal bases, like Article 114 TFEU, were reinterpreted creatively to find other possible solutions.[74] That said, it is difficult to deny that the piecemeal approach resulting from the available set of tools undermined the effectiveness of EU action. Moreover, the institutional imbalance cannot be underestimated, with the European Parliament scarcely being involved in activating the relevant tools.

From this point of view, and even though it is highly unlikely to be implemented anytime soon, the EP's proposal to introduce a general emergency clause into EU primary law – while at the same time strengthening the EU's competencies in the context of civil protection and health – has the merit of opening an institutional debate on the need to find general solutions to the emergencies of our time without underestimating the role of the legislature. Despite its evident flaws[75] – first and foremost, the lack of a definition of emergency – the clause, if properly read in the context of the EU constitutional framework and subject to some necessary amendments, could contribute to creating a more uniform supranational emergency law.

Given the difficulty of revising the EU Treaties again, one may wonder whether some of the suggestions invoked by the clause could be implemented differently. For instance, as already mentioned by former AG Tesauro in a piece

[73] State of the Union Address by President von der Leyen at the European Parliament Plenary, Building the world we want to live in: A Union of vitality in a world of fragility, 16 September 2020 ec.europa.eu/. Emphasis added.

[74] For a general overview on the normative creativity showed by the EU institutions, see Casolari (n 5) and F Casolari, 'Europe (2023)' (2025) 6 *Yearbook of International Disaster Law*, forthcoming.

[75] Bellenghi (n 39) 25; Chamon (n 44) 185.

written in the middle of the first wave of the Covid-19 pandemic, the possibility of adopting an EU Emergencies Act – 'un atto dell'Unione sulle emergenze in generale' in Tesauro's words – to (try to) overcome the existing legal fragmentation could be considered.[76] Another available way could be reactivating the flexibility clause enshrined in Article 352 TFEU to introduce an emergency mechanism similar to that envisaged by the Parliament (ie, a mechanism where the EU legislature may delegate emergency powers to the European Commission). In the last decades, the relevance of the flexibility clause has significantly diminished due to the Treaties reforms introduced in the meantime. As rightly noted, 'the small number of proposed measures under Article 352 TFEU demonstrates that very little can go under the Treaty's once catch-all provision'.[77] However, this provision has not completely lost its role in filling the gaps in primary EU law. This is a circumstance that should not be forgotten.

[76] G Tesauro, 'Senza Europa nessun Paese andrà lontano', Dibattito "Coronavirus e diritto dell'Unione", n 3, 18 April 2020, 16, www.aisdue.eu/.

[77] T Konstadinides, 'Drawing the Line between Circumvention and Gap-Filling: An Exploration of the Conceptual Limits of the Treaty's Flexibility Clause' (2012) 31 *YEL* 227, 261.

5

The Emergency Models of the Nordic Countries: Four Peas in a Pod?

ANNA ZEMSKOVA

I. INTRODUCTION

LITTLE DID ANYONE know, at the beginning of 2020, that in just a couple of weeks the world would be submerged in a global public health emergency,[1] which would trigger state of emergency regimes (of various sorts) in most countries across the world,[2] and that the emergency powers of states would soon come under the spotlight of both public, political and academic debates.

The emergency law frameworks of the Nordic countries have not been exceptional in this regard – while they had attracted some attention before the pandemic,[3] they came under close scrutiny once the worldwide public health emergency was at full speed. One might have assumed that Sweden, Denmark, Finland and Norway, belonging to the 'Scandinavian law' group,[4] might take similar political and legal approaches to emergencies. This assumption was soon dispelled as Sweden was seen taking a radically differentiating path.[5] This

[1] The WHO declared the Covid-19 outbreak a global health emergency on 30 January 2020 (WHO, Statement on the second meeting of the International Health Regulations (2005) Emergency Committee regarding the outbreak of novel coronavirus (2019-nCoV), 30 January 2020, available at www.who.int/news/item/30-01-2020-statement-on-the-second-meeting-of-the-international-health-regulations-(2005)-emergency-committee-regarding-the-outbreak-of-novel-coronavirus-(2019-ncov)) and then a pandemic on 11 March 2020, WHO Director General's opening remarks at the media briefing on COVID-19–11 March 2020, available at www.who.int/director-general/speeches/detail/who-director-general-s-opening-remarks-at-the-media-briefing-on-covid-19---11-march-2020.

[2] See the extensive work of the 'COVID-19 and States of Emergency' symposium, hosted by Verfassungsblog and Democracy Reporting International and coordinated by Joelle Grogan; J Grogan, 'Introduction & List of Country Reports' (*Verfassungsblog: On Matters Constitutional*, 2020) intr2dok.vifa-recht.de/receive/mir_mods_00008563.

[3] See, for instance, A Jonsson Cornell and J Salminen, 'Emergency Laws in Comparative Constitutional Law – The Case of Sweden and Finland' (2018) 19 *German Law Journal* 219.

[4] U Bernitz, 'What Is Scandinavian Law – Concept, Characteristics, Future' (2007) 50 *Scandinavian Studies in Law* 13.

[5] I Cameron and A Jonsson Cornell, 'Dealing with COVID-19 in Sweden' in J Grogan and A Donald, *Routledge Handbook of Law and the COVID-19 Pandemic*, 1st edn (Routledge, 2022).

chapter will investigate the emergency law frameworks of Sweden, Denmark, Finland and Norway through the prism of emergency models with the aim of providing a better understanding of the emergency regimes envisaged by the constitutional frameworks of those countries, and highlight the risks associated with the models, especially in the context of recent global challenges such as the Covid-19 pandemic and climate change.[6] While it is generally easy for public health emergencies to qualify as emergencies, the categorisation of climate change as an emergency in a legal sense is problematic due to its protracted development. Indeed, climate change might be better understood as posing a constitutional crisis rather than a constitutional emergency.[7] This categorisation, however, does not eliminate the need to act urgently in addressing climate change,[8] as is also required in emergencies, and to take notice of and evaluate the legal approaches adopted for combatting the Covid-19 pandemic. After all, climate change and the pandemic project a 'symmetric shock' whose impact is both polycentric[9] and transgressive in nature.[10]

This chapter focuses on elucidating the typology of emergency models (Section II) and clarifying the models of the selected Nordic countries in general, while weaving some examples of responses to the pandemic into the discussion (Section III). Section IV, which contains some reflections on the analysis carried out, concludes the chapter.

II. A QUICK GLIMPSE INTO THE THEORETICAL FRAMEWORKS OF EMERGENCY MODELS

The academic discussion of emergency powers employs various doctrinal formulations.[11] While some of these formulations might be very nuanced and

[6] The European Parliament declared a climate and environment emergency in its resolution back in 2019, European Parliament, Resolution on the Climate and Environment Emergency, 28 November 2019, 2019/2930(RSP) www.europarl.europa.eu/doceo/document/TA-9-2019-0078_EN.html.

[7] B De Witte, 'Guest Editorial: EU Emergency Law and Its Impact on the EU Legal Order' (2022) *Common Market Law Review* 3, 4; F Gallarati, 'Is Climate Emergency a Constitutional Emergency?: A Critical Appraisal' (2023) 3 *The Italian Review of International and Comparative Law* 448, 467.

[8] A positive development in this regard is one of the most recent ECtHR judgments *Verein Klimaseniorinnen Schweiz and Others v Switzerland* [2024] Application no. 53600/20, where the ECtHR in its Grand Chamber formation held that Switzerland had failed to fulfil its obligations under the ECHR in regard to combatting climate change.

[9] L Fisher, 'Public Law, Law Jobs, and New Emergencies', presentation at 'Constitutional Dimensions of Emergencies in EU Law: the Case of Covid-19, Climate and Migration', SNELS/Lund University, Lund, Sweden, 15 December 2023.

[10] Referred to as 'the evolving nature of crises', A Greene, 'Questioning Executive Supremacy in an Economic State of Emergency' (2015) 35 *Legal Studies* 594, 609.

[11] E Posner and A Vermuele use the expression 'doctrinal formulations' while discussing the strict enforcement view and the accommodation view in their work, EA Posner and An Vermeule, 'Accommodating Emergencies' (2003) 56 *Stanford Law Review* 605; for mappings of various doctrinal formulations see, for instance, fn 19 in K Loevy, *Emergencies in Public Law: The Legal Politics of Containment* (Cambridge University Press, 2016) 24.

not fully overlap with other conceptualisations, it is possible to schematically distinguish a few distinct types of emergency models.[12]

The first cluster of emergency models can be generally captured by the umbrella term 'extra-legal',[13] and are based on a combination of such premises as the unpredictable nature of emergencies and the law's unsuitability for accommodating them.[14] This in its turn prompts placing accommodation of emergencies outside of the legal order and results in the executive branch exercising broad extraordinary powers. The most notorious proponent of the extra-legal model is of course Carl Schmitt.[15] Oren Gross has proposed an extra-legal measures model (ELM) of emergency powers that differs from the extra-legal model of an emergency regime, and is rooted in political realism and guided by maxims like 'necessity knows no law'.[16] The ELM entails the possibility for public officials to act outside the law in emergency scenarios, where the nature of such actions needs to be openly and publicly acknowledged by public officials.[17] Mark Tushnet, while rejecting the idea that law can determine the conditions for suspending legality, which is 'almost inevitable' in the case of emergencies, speaks of 'extra-constitutional emergency powers' that are neither legal nor illegal.[18]

The second type of emergency model is variously referred to as a the 'business-as-usual',[19] 'legality',[20] or 'absolutist'[21] model, and is an antipode to the above-mentioned variations of an extra-legal model. It rests upon the idea that law represents a suitable tool for dealing with emergencies and, what is more, can be designed in such a way as to accommodate any type of emergency. This model perceives existing law as a perfect construction[22] that does not need to be set aside or overridden by new norms even during emergencies. The

[12] This chapter builds upon the categorisation of emergency models put forward by O Gross and F Ní Aoláin in *Law in Times of Crisis: Emergency Powers in Theory and Practice* (Cambridge University Press, 2006). Note, however, that the analysis conducted in this chapter explicitly excludes any evaluation of the potential use of interpretative accommodation, which would have involved an extensive analysis of the role of the judiciary in the chosen states.

[13] ibid 110–71; K Lane Scheppele, 'Legal and Extralegal Emergencies' in GA Caldeira, R Daniel Kelemen and KE Whittington (eds), *The Oxford Handbook of Law and Politics*, 1st edn (Oxford University Press, 2009) 165; Loevy (n 11) 25–28.

[14] This idea is rooted in Locke's theory of prerogative, J Locke and P Laslett, *Locke: Two Treatises of Government Student Edition* (Cambridge University Press, 1988) ss 159–60; Loevy (n 11) 25–28; A Zemskova, *The Rule of Law in Economic Emergency in the European Union* (Lunds universitet. ed, Lund University, Faculty of Law, 2023) 113.

[15] C Schmitt, *Political Theology: Four Chapters on the Concept of Sovereignty* (University of Chicago Press, 2005).

[16] O Gross, 'Chaos and Rules: Should Responses to Violent Crises Always Be Constitutional?' (2003) 112 *The Yale Law Journal* 1011, 1096–1134; Gross and Ní Aoláin (n 12) 110–71.

[17] Gross and Ní Aoláin (n 12) 110–11.

[18] M Tushnet and M Tushnet (eds), 'Emergencies and the Idea of Constitutionalism' (2005) 1 *Constitution in Wartime: Beyond Alarmism and Complacency* 39, 45–46.

[19] This term is used, for instance, by Gross and Ní Aoláin (n 12); Gross (n 16).

[20] Loevy uses the term 'legality model', Loevy (n 11) 28–29.

[21] Jules Lobel employs such categories as 'absolutist', 'relativist' and 'liberal' frameworks, J Lobel, 'Emergency Power and the Decline of Liberalism' (1989) 98 *The Yale Law Journal* 1385, 1386–92.

[22] Gross and Ní Aoláin (n 12) 87.

existing legal framework already possesses the necessary legal instruments to address any type of extraordinary occurrences. The other side of the coin of this idea of 'legal perfection' is its strict refusal of recourse to any new, extraordinary or complementary tools, and its unconditional (at least in theory)[23] adherence to the legal framework in place,[24] which in practice can be extremely difficult to fully maintain.

The last cluster of emergency models is a so-called 'accommodation view'[25] or models of accommodation,[26] that calls for adopting a flexible and more relaxed approach regarding adherence to the constitutional legal framework (in contrast with the above-mentioned business-as-usual/legality/absolutist model), and allows for deviation from the law or even partial suspension of it if an emergency at hand so requires.[27] This model arguably represents the golden mean between the two previously mentioned clusters of emergency models, as on the one hand it contains *legal* tools that can be directly employed in case of an emergency, where the emergency responses are positioned within the legal order, but on the other hand allows for adjusting the constitutional framework. Gross and Ní Aoláin distinguish three categories of models of accommodation: constitutional,[28] legislative[29] and interpretive.[30] The model of constitutional accommodation encapsulates the presence of constitutional arrangements that constitute a legal framework and can be used in emergencies, in either constitutional documents themselves[31] or within the general constitutional structure of the state.[32] When it comes to the latter case, the doctrine/principle of constitutional necessity deserves special attention due to its ambiguous and blurry nature. This doctrine represents a tricky conundrum: on the one hand, the doctrine can constitute a constitutional principle or practice within the legal order that, while being either an independent source of constitutional law or a 'meta-rule of constitutional construction',[33] can justify emergency responses that conflict with the ordinary legal framework. In such a case the doctrine/principle of constitutional necessity would act as a 'philosopher's stone' for bringing the actions that otherwise would have been deemed unlawful into the ambit of

[23] The criticism of the business-as-usual model is often directed towards its maximalist, unrealistic expectations from law (referred to as 'naïve' at best) and potential hypocrisy that can manifest itself in turning a blind eye or simply refusing to acknowledge recourse to extraordinary tools employed to cope with extraordinary exigencies, Loevy (n 11) 28; Gross and Ní Aoláin (n 12) 94–98.

[24] Hence the conceptualisation of the model as the 'legality' model; Eric Posner and Adrian Vermeule refer to this model as 'the strict enforcement view', Posner and Vermeule (n 11) 608.

[25] ibid 606–609.

[26] Gross and Ní Aoláin (n 12) 17–86; Gross (n 16) 1058.

[27] Posner and Vermeule (n 11) 606; Gross and Ní Aoláin (n 12) 17.

[28] Gross and Ní Aoláin (n 12) 35–66.

[29] ibid 66–72.

[30] ibid 72–86.

[31] I suggest using the term 'textual' model of constitutional accommodation in such a case.

[32] Gross and Ní Aoláin (n 13) 46–47. I suggest using the term 'structural' model of constitutional accommodation in such a case.

[33] ibid.

legality. In this regard, when it is an acknowledged but unwritten constitutional principle that in itself encapsulates a rule, the doctrine/principle of constitutional necessity is embedded within the general constitutional structure and resorting to it constitutes a legal response, to be contrasted with responses situated outside the legal realm (as in the extra-legal model). On the other hand, however, constitutional necessity can be seen as an artificial construction whose contours are blurry and in which necessity can be politically operationalised for justifying actions that contradict the established legal order,[34] in practical terms bringing the responses, adopted on the basis of the doctrine of constitutional necessity, within the ambit of the extra-legal model. Hampered by this tension, the doctrine/principle of constitutional necessity represents an instrument whose invocation is associated with great unease and whose application has been extremely limited. The model of legislative accommodation allows for adapting the constitutional framework to an emergency by either introducing amendments into the existing legislation or adopting completely new legislation, which might be either temporary or permanent,[35] whereas in the model of interpretive accommodation, the judicial branch employs emergency-sensitive,[36] flexible or innovative interpretations of the existing provisions of law to cope with an extraordinary situation.[37]

In summing up, it should be mentioned, however, that states' constitutional legal frameworks rarely employ only one particular type of emergency model: in practice they tend to take recourse to a combination of models,[38] depending on different factors such as the lack or presence of emergency regimes in the constitution, the typology of emergencies adopted in constitutional orders, and the design of existing emergency provisions.

III. THE EMERGENCY MODELS OF THE NORDIC COUNTRIES

A. Sweden

The typology of emergencies bears a substantial impact not only in the context of academic debates but also in practice: different types of emergencies require different kinds of governmental responses and hence powers.[39] Sweden serves

[34] See three problematic approaches that Oren Gross and Fionnuala Ní Aoláin outline in their work, ibid 47.

[35] For a discussion on the pros and cons of the model of legislative model see J Ferejohn and P Pasquino, 'The Law of the Exception: A Typology of Emergency Powers' (2004) 2 *International Journal of Constitutional Law* 210, 216–21.

[36] Gross (n 16) 1059–64; Gross and Ní Aoláin (n 12) 72–86.

[37] On the application of the resourceful interpretation in the context of economic emergency in the EU see Zemskova (n 14) 122, fn 6.

[38] See s 3.5.3, for instance, where the author argues that the EU adopted a hybrid emergency model in regard to the economic emergency, exemplified by the Great Crisis of 2007–2008 and the European sovereign debt crisis, Zemskova (n 14).

[39] Gross and Ní Aoláin (n 12) 45.

as a perfect example in this regard, demonstrating the seminal importance of categorising emergencies for their regulation.

The Swedish constitution consists of four fundamental laws (*grundlagar*): the Instrument of Government (*Regeringsformen* or RF), the 1810 Act of Succession (*Successionsordningen* or SO), the 1949 Freedom of the Press Act (*Tryckfrihetsförordningen* or TF) and the 1991 Fundamental Law on Freedom of Expression (*Yttrandefrihetsgrundlagen* or YGL). The RF contains an explicitly unexpressed separation between war emergencies[40] and peacetime crisis situations,[41] where the former ones are constitutionally regulated in Chapter 15[42] and the latter ones are not specifically governed by the RF,[43] representing a case of 'constitutional silence'.[44] This separation in its turn reveals that in the context of war-related emergencies, the Swedish constitutional framework resorts to the textual model of constitutional accommodation, where the contours of emergency powers in a particular type of emergency are explicitly enshrined in the constitution, and there is legislation that further develops the elements associated with the invocation of this emergency regime.[45]

One ambiguous and unclear position on the issue of the doctrine of constitutional necessity in Sweden requires some extra attention. It has been expressed on several occasions that the doctrine of constitutional necessity is not considered to be a feasible alternative in emergencies and should not constitute a basis for adopting measures under extraordinary circumstances.[46] Yet a deviation from this

[40] 'War and the threat of war', Chapter 15 of the RF.

[41] The notion of 'peacetime crisis situations', that encompasses situations that 'deviate from normality, affect many people, large parts of society or threaten fundamental values, entail a serios disruption or imminent risk of such a disruption of vital societal funstcions, and require coordinated and urgent actors by multiple actors', is now provided in § 6 (1) in the new Ordinance (2022:524) on State Authorities' Preparedness (the Preparedness Ordinance). Please note that the pandemic acted as a trigger for both reviving a discussion regarding the existing legal framework on emergencies (see Swedish Government Official Reports 'Sweden during the pandemic' Volume 1 and 2, SOU 2022:10, 'Strengthening constitutional preparedness' SOU 2023:75) and launching a structural reform of crisis preparedness and civil defence that entered into force on the 1st of October 2022.

[42] Chapter 15 of the RF. Its English translation is available here, https://www.riksdagen.se/globalassets/05.-sa-fungerar-riksdagen/demokrati/the-instrument-of-government-2023-eng.pdf accessed 17 April 2024.

[43] Interestingly enough the RF contains a reference to such a peacetime crisis situation as an epidemic in the context of justifiable restrictions of freedom of assembly and freedom to demonstrate in Chapter 2, Article 24, first paragraph. The RF also mentions a possibility to delegate some powers to the Riksbank in peacetime crisis situations in Chapter 8, Article 13, first paragraph, but these are the instances where peacetime crisis situations are mentioned only in passing.

[44] Cornell and Salminen (n 3); please note that introducing the regulation of peacetime crisis situations into the RF has been raised on several occasions before the COVID-19 pandemic, Tormod Otter Johansen, *Krisjuridik: Rättsliga Befogenheter Från Olycka till Höjd Beredskap* (Upplaga 1, Norstedts Juridik 2024) 258 and after it, see Swedish Government Official Report 'Strengthening constitutional preparedness' SOU 2023:75.

[45] See eg the 1992 Act on Total Defence and High Preparedness (1992:1403). For a discussion on other rules contained in ordinary laws and ordinances that can be invoked in war-related emergencies see M Ericson and O Wilske, 'Covid-19 i Sverige : rättsliga perspektiv på krisberedskap och de åtgärder som vidtagits för att hantera pandemin' (2020) 105 *Svensk Juristtidning* 1080, 1086.

[46] Swedish Government Official Report 'Our preparedness after 11 September', Part 1, SOU 2003:32, 96; 'A reformed constitution', part 1, SOU 2008:125, 512. Note however that in the

stance occurred in the context of some extraordinary domestic situations during the 1970s.[47] Recourse was taken to emergency practices without the responsible actors strictly speaking having a legal basis for adopting them, or without taking into account the laws in place, but their actions were nonetheless subsequently approved by the Committee on the Constitution.[48] In light of this, it has unsurprisingly been noted that the doctrine of constitutional necessity is not unknown to the Swedish constitutional framework,[49] although its status remains unclear.[50]

When it comes to peacetime crisis situations, two models are available: the business-as-usual model and the model of legislative accommodation. The Swedish crisis management strategy, namely anticipatory statutorification (*författningsberedskap*),[51] suggests as a first recourse the business-as-usual model but then, in case more tailored measures are required, using the model of legislative accommodation. Indeed, while examples of the application of each model could be identified in the crisis management of the pandemic, legislative accommodation was employed more often.[52] For instance, the prohibition on public gatherings and events was actualised on the basis of existing provisions in the Public Order Act,[53] whereas the 2004 Communicable Diseases Act,[54] whose scope was expanded to include Covid-19,[55] was temporarily complemented

same report it is stated that 'In certain emergencies, it may be possible to take decisions contrary to the provisions of the Constitution on the basis of constitutional emergency law', Swedish Government Official Report 'A reformed constitution', part 1, SOU 2008:125, 525; 'Structure for increased resilience' SOU 2021:25, 155; 'Strengthening constitutional preparedness', SOU 2023:75, see point 4.1, in regard to the latter see also Johansen (n 43) 254.

[47] The hijacking at Bulltofta in 1972, the Norrmalmstorg robbery in 1973 and West German Embassy siege in Stockholm in 1975; see s 3.2 in J Hirschfeldt, 'Svensk krishantering i fredstid – de konstitutionella aspekterna och en framåtblick', (2020) 105 *Svensk Juristtidning* 1148, 1152–53, Cornell and Salminen refer to them as 'internal emergencies' in Cornell and Salminen (n 3).

[48] Reports of the Committee on the Constitution on the review of the performance of the duties of ministers and the handling of government business KU 1974:22, KU 1975:12 and KU 1975/76:50.

[49] H Jermsten, *Konstitutionell Nödrätt* (Gotab) 86–87; E Wennerström 'Inget undantag utan regel – den konstitutionella nödrätten och Sverige' in S Heckscher and J Hirschfeldt, *Vänbok till Sten Heckscher* (Iustus, 2012) 371; Anna Jonsson Cornell and Janne Salminen refer to it as a 'supra-legal state of emergency', when discussing emergency laws in Sweden and Finland through Ernst-Wolfgang Böckenförde's theoretical lens Cornell and Salminen (n 3). I Cameron and A Jonsson Cornell, 'Fredstida kriser i en konstitutionell kontext – en komparativ analys och en försiktig framåtblick för Sveriges del' (2020) 105 *Svensk Juristtidning* 1172, 1176.

[50] Report of the Committee on the Constitution on the Government's emergency preparedness and response to the 2004 tsunami disaster 2005/06:KU8; Swedish Government Official Report 'Strengthening constitutional preparedness', SOU 2023:75, 83.

[51] Cameron and Cornell (n 48) 1177. A Jonsson Cornell, 'Författningsberedskap i praktiken – en kommentar med anledning av lagen om ändring i smittskyddslagen' (2020) *Svensk Juristtidning* 377, 377.

[52] The Covid-19 pandemic represented a clear example of a peacetime crisis situation, falling outside the ambit of ch 15 of the RF.

[53] Ch 2, section 15, the 1993 Public Order Act (Ordningslag (1993:1617), www.riksdagen.se/sv/dokument-och-lagar/dokument/svensk-forfattningssamling/ordningslag-19931617_sfs-1993-1617/.

[54] The 2004 Communicable Diseases Act (Smittskyddslag (2004:168), available at www.riksdagen.se/sv/dokument-och-lagar/dokument/svensk-forfattningssamling/smittskyddslag-2004168_sfs-2004-168/#K9.

[55] This classification was in force between 1 February 2020 and 1 April 2022.

with provisions that would allow the government to issue regulations affecting personal and financial aspects of the lives of individuals.[56] Of the newly adopted measures put into practice, some were temporary and others permanent: for instance, while the highly debated Covid-19 Act[57] was expressly temporary[58] and indeed cancelled after 16 months,[59] the Act on Temporary Closure of Activities within the Field of Education during Extraordinary Events in Peacetime[60] continues to exist. The Swedish Corona Commission, however, reached the conclusion that the legal tools in place were insufficient to address a peacetime crisis situation of such a scale, and that the current legal design needs to be reconsidered.[61]

B. Denmark

Denmark has chosen a different approach to regulating emergencies on the constitutional level. Thus the Constitutional Act of Denmark (*Grundloven*), while encompassing some provisions mentioning extraordinary circumstances,[62] intentionally does not outline any state of emergency regimes, whether in relation to war or peacetime emergencies.[63] Instead, the Danish constitutional framework relies heavily on the doctrine of constitutional necessity, which constitutes an unwritten part of the Danish constitution[64] and recognises the possibility of derogating from the ordinary legal framework, including the constitution itself. In order to do so, however, the emergency at hand must unequivocally qualify as 'a really serious danger to the state and

[56] The Act (2020:241) amending the Infection Control Act (Lagen (2020:241) om ändring i smittskyddslagen), available at svenskforfattningssamling.se/sites/default/files/sfs/2020-04/SFS2020-241.pdf, also called the Autorisation Act (bemyndigandelagen), see Swedish Government Official Reports 'Sweden during the pandemic' Volume 2, SOU 2022:10, 452.

[57] For more details on the Covid-19 Act see T Mattsson, A Nordberg and M Axmin, 'Sweden: Legal Response to Covid-19' in T Mattsson, A Nordberg and M Axmin, *The Oxford Compendium of National Legal Responses to Covid-19* (Oxford University Press, 2021).

[58] Lag (2021:4) om särskilda begränsningar för att förhindra spridning av sjukdomen covid-19, available at www.riksdagen.se/sv/dokument-och-lagar/dokument/svensk-forfattningssamling/lag-20214-om-sarskilda-begransningar-for-att_sfs-2021-4/.

[59] Lag (2022:214) om upphävande av lagen (2021:4) om särskilda begränsningar för att förhindra spridning av sjukdomen covid-19, svenskforfattningssamling.se/sites/default/files/sfs/2022-03/SFS2022-214.pdf.

[60] Lag (2020:148) om tillfällig stängning av verksamheter på skolområdet vid extraordinära händelser i fredstid, available at www.riksdagen.se/sv/dokument-och-lagar/dokument/svensk-forfattningssamling/lag-2020148-om-tillfallig-stangning-av_sfs-2020-148/.

[61] Swedish Government Official Report 'Sweden during the pandemic' Volume 2, SOU 2022:10, 665–67.

[62] Sections 23, 37, 42(7) and 79(3) of the Constitutional Act of Denmark. See also H Zahle, *Danmarks Riges Grundlov Med Kommentarer* (Jurist- og Ökonomforbundets Forl, 1999) 143.

[63] K Cedervall Lauta, 'Something is Forgotten in the State of Denmark: Denmark's Response to the COVID-19 Pandemic' (Verfassungsblog: On Matters Constitutional, 4 May 2020).

[64] A Mette Fallentin Nyborg, S Klinge, H Krunke and J Elo Rytter, 'Covid-19 and Emergency Laws in Denmark' (2020) 105 *Svensk Juristtidning* 1098, 1098; J Elo Rytter, *Individets Grundlæggende Rettigheder* (Karnov Group, 2024) 115.

its institutions',[65] and any measures must fulfil the criteria of necessity and proportionality.[66] If, however, an extraordinary situation falls short of these criteria, either the model of legislative accommodation or/and the business-as-usual model will likely be employed.

The Danish management of the pandemic demonstrated, however, that in an unprecedented emergency the business-as-usual model might not be enough, and the model of legislative accommodation might then take the lead. Even though the Emergency Act was in place long before the pandemic,[67] it had to be amended to address the Covid-19 outbreak,[68] and was then replaced by the new Epidemic Act,[69] which was also modified afterwards.[70] Moreover, while deviations from the Standing Orders of the Danish Parliament were invoked to speed up the legislative process,[71] the emergency measures were adopted by means of either adjusting the existing laws to the pandemic,[72] or introducing new laws.[73] It is worth mentioning that even though the Danish authorities did not invoke

[65] M Sørensen, *Statsforfatningsret* (Juristförbundet, 1973) 39; H Zahle, *Dansk Forfatningsret* (Ejler, 2003) 286; it is also suggested that deviations from the Constitution can be justified if 'a really serious danger of extensive loss of human life' obtains, J Peter Christensen, J Albæk Jensen and M Hansen Jensen, *Dansk Statsret* (Jurist- og Økonomforbundet, 2020) 34; Annemette Fallentin Nyborg put forward a following definition: 'a situation that requires an extraordinary response and where the state and its critical institutions or functions are in serious, present or imminent danger', A Fallentin Nyborg 'Fravigelse af menneskerettigheder i nødsituationer' (2023) 6(2) *Retskraft – Copenhagen Journal of Legal Studies* 4, 24, Rytter (n 63) 115.

[66] For a more detailed discussion of these aspects see Nyborg (n 64) 24.

[67] Lov nr 114 af 21/03/1979 was adopted in 1979 and came into force on 1 January 1980, available at www.retsinformation.dk/eli/lta/1979/114.

[68] Lov nr 208 af 17/03/2020 Lov om ændring af lov om foranstaltninger mod smitsomme og andre overførbare sygdomme, available at www.retsinformation.dk/eli/lta/2020/208. The operational functionality of the revised Epidemic Act was limited by a sunset clause (Section 2 (2)). The amendments introduced a transfer of the competences, originally vested in regional epidemic commissions, into the Minister of Health and the Elderly (Section 1(2)), where other public authorities, such as local police, aviation, environmental and food authorities, the customs and tax administration, the emergency services and even the Danish Defence authority, among others, were obliged to assist the Minister in the exercise of their duties and powers under the modified Epidemic Act (Section 1(3)). Moreover, sections 15 and 16 regarding the modification of section 12 allowed the Minister to adopt the rules that might derogate from other legislation.

[69] Lov nr 285 af 27/02/2021 Lov om epidemier m.v. (epidemiloven), available at www.retsinformation.dk/eli/lta/2021/285.

[70] Lov nr 1441 af 29/06/2021 Lov om ændring af epidemiloven, available at www.retsinformation.dk/eli/lta/2021/1441.

[71] Section 42 of Ch XVI permits disregarding the rules of the Standing Orders in a situation of urgency, see the Standing Orders of the Danish Parliament (*Forretningsorden for Folketinget*). On the use of the expedited procedure see Nyborg, Klinge, Krunke and Rytter (n 63) 1100–01.

[72] 2020: L133, L135, L142, L143, L144, L145, L154, L157, L169, L171, L172, L181, L190, L191, L192, L195, L198, L199, L200, L202, L203, L204, L205, L207, L211; 2020-2021: L4, L27, LL30, L75, L76, L82, L83, L110, L114, L122, L123, L125, L135, L136, L140, L152, L153, L161, L162, L164, L165, L166, L186, L192, L193, L197, L206, L208, L211, L218, L219, L225, L231, L235, L234, L235, L237; 2021-2022: L8, L9, L35, L36, L50, L51, L61, L66, L71, L81, L87, L89, L98, L101, L102, L144, L147, L168, L175, L179, L180. Available at www.ft.dk/aktuelt/tema/historisk_folketinget-og-coronasituationen#1850ACC313F94DBFAECB6042EC7BC837.

[73] 2020: L134, L140, L141, L153, L161, L168, L168A, L168B, L175, L201, L208, L212; 2020-2021: L77, L102, L139, L144, L145, L146; 2021-2022: L26, L94. Available at www.ft.dk/aktuelt/tema/historisk_folketinget-og-coronasituationen#1850ACC313F94DBFAECB6042EC7BC837.

the doctrine of constitutional necessity,[74] there was one instance where the measures adopted by the government recalled the doctrine's underlying modus operandi: the infamous Minkgate, where the Danish government ordered the cull of roughly 17 million minks on 4 November 2020,[75] without having any legal basis for doing so. While this legal conundrum was solved post-factum by the adoption of a law six weeks later,[76] the mink slaughter was subjected to scrutiny by a special Commission of Inquiry, the Mink Commission, appointed by the Danish Parliament to investigate this matter. The Mink Commission, having confirmed the lack of a legal basis for the mink cull at the time of the government's announcement, harshly criticised its mode of action.[77]

C. Finland

The Finnish emergency legal framework represents a synergy of several emergency models that coexist and may be used to complement each other in case one provides a more preferable solution to the challenges posed by the emergency at hand. Whereas the Constitution of Finland (*Suomen perustuslaki*) (*Finlands grundlag*) contains a provision circumscribing the contours of potential limitations on the basic rights and liberties in situations of emergency[78] – a provision that pays respect to Finland's international obligations[79] – the in-depth regulation of emergencies is actually enshrined in the Emergency Powers Act,[80] adopted on the basis of section 73 of the Constitution as an exceptive enactment.[81] While section 23 of the Constitution explicitly mentions the possibility of an armed attack against Finland, its scope is not limited to that type of emergency. It also includes other emergency situations that are to be defined by an Act of the Parliament, which at the same time needs to respect the conceptual framework of emergencies contained in international treaties.[82]

[74] Nyborg, Klinge, Krunke and Rytter (n 63) 1099.

[75] Press conference on 4 Novermber 2020, available at www.stm.dk/presse/pressemoedearkiv/pressemoede-den-4-november-2020/.

[76] Lov nr 2185 af 29/12/2020 (Act on the culling and temporary ban on keeping mink), available at www.retsinformation.dk/eli/lta/2020/2185.

[77] The Commission of Inquiry's report on the mink culling case, available at www.ft.dk/samling/20211/almdel/GRA/bilag/46/index.htm.

[78] The Constitution of Finland, section 23 of Ch 2.

[79] See a correlation between section 23 of Ch 2 of the Constitution of Finland and Art 15 of the ECHR. A strong interplay between the Constitution of Finland and Finland's international obligations is a distinctive feature of Finnish constitutional law, Cornell and Salminen (n 3) 237; J Husa, *The Constitution of Finland: A Contextual Analysis* (Hart Publishing, 2011) 172–73.

[80] Valmiuslaki or Beredskapslag (1552/2011), www.finlex.fi/sv/laki/ajantasa/2011/20111552.

[81] The doctrine of exceptive enactment permits materially altering the Constitution without changing its text. For a discussion of this legal phenomenon and the challenges associated with it, see Cornell and Salminen (n 3) 237–40; Husa (n 78) 227–32; A Jyränki and J Husa, *Konstitutionell rätt* (Sten Palmgren tr, [1 uppl], Talentum, 2015) 60–61, 248–53.

[82] At first glance this requirement does not appear to cause any problems; however, in the long run the conceptual framework of international treaties acts as a limitation on determining the existence

The Emergency Powers Act now contains six categories of emergency[83] that can serve as factual grounds for imposing the rights limitations in accordance with section 23 of the Constitution of Finland,[84] and identifies the guiding principles[85] and the powers to be granted to authorities in the respective types of emergency.[86] This Finnish emergency regulation, provided in the Constitution of Finland and further developed in the Emergency Powers Act, suggests a possibility of the application of the textual model of constitutional accommodation, which reflects an aspiration of the legal framework to be as prepared for emergencies as possible, regulating unforeseeable exigencies in advance.[87] However, at a closer look it becomes clear that the conditions contained in section 23 presuppose emergencies of massive magnitude. The conditions are difficult to fulfil, which makes it necessary to resort to alternative ways of addressing extraordinary situations of a lesser magnitude and severity.

While Finland is the only one among the four selected Nordic states that does not acknowledge the doctrine of constitutional necessity,[88] the country can be expected to use the business-as-usual model and the model of legislative accommodation in cases where recourse to the model of constitutional accommodation is fraught with difficulties or when emergencies can be dealt with using the ordinary powers vested in authorities. In this regard, Finnish crisis management has also absorbed the principle of anticipatory statutorification,[89] which stipulates that the ordinary legal framework should contain rules capable of coping with emergencies of lesser impact and according to the principle of normalcy.[90] The Emergency Powers Act should be invoked only if an emergency situation cannot be contained with the help of ordinary powers.[91]

of an emergency situation and can constitute a potential hurdle in practice. This is vividly demonstrated by para 41 of the Siracusa Principles on the Limitation and Derogation Provisions in the International covenant on Civil and Political Rights (1 July 1984), which stipulates that 'economic difficulties per se cannot justify derogation measures', creating obstacles for acknowledging the existence of economic emergency situations, Cornell and Salminen (n 3) 245; Jyränki and Husa (n 80) 427–28. This is of particular importance in the context where Art 4 of the ICCPR constitutes the basis for Art 15 of the ECHR (I (2), Guide on Article 15 of the ECHR, ECtHR, available at ks.echr.coe.int/documents/d/echr-ks/guide_art_15_eng), which is an international human rights instrument that has been incorporated into Finnish constitutional law. This adds another layer to a problematic acknowledgement of both the existence of economic emergencies and their potential regulation in the constitutional legal frameworks in states or polities in general, as argued in Zemskova (n 14).

[83] As a result of the changes introduced in 2022 by Laki valmiuslain muuttamisesta or Lag om ändring av beredskapslagen (706/2022), available at www.finlex.fi/sv/laki/alkup/2022/20220706; for a critical analysis of the introduced amendments see M Scheinin, 'Is Finland Joining the Backsliding Trend in Europe?' [2022] *Verfassungsblog: On Matters Constitutional.*

[84] 3§, Valmiuslaki or Beredskapslag (1552/2011).

[85] 4§, Valmiuslaki or Beredskapslag (1552/2011).

[86] Section II, Valmiuslaki or Beredskapslag (1552/2011).

[87] J Salminen, 'Finsk krishantering i fredstid – beredskapslagen tillämpas för första gången' (2020) 105 *Svensk Juristtidning* 1116, 1116.

[88] Cameron and Cornell (n 48) 1177.

[89] Cornell and Salminen (n 3) 238–239.

[90] Normalitetsprincipen, Janne Salminen (n 86) 1119.

[91] Para 2 in 4§, Valmiuslaki or Beredskapslag (1552/2011); the Constitutional Law Committee has also highlighted this line of thought in their statements, P Johanna Neuvonen, 'The COVID-19

The Finnish management of the Covid-19 pandemic exhibited all of the three emergency models. The nature of the emergency made it possible to trigger for the first time both the Emergency Powers Act[92] and section 23 of the Constitution.[93] A state of emergency was declared twice, on 16 March 2020[94] and on 1 March 2021,[95] both times under the Emergency Powers Act. As a result, several decrees based on that Act and Acts of Parliament restricting the rights of property and free conduct of business via the temporary closure of restaurants, adopted on the basis of section 23 of the Constitution,[96] were adopted.[97] While the provision of the existing Border Guard Act was used to close the borders at the outbreak of the pandemic,[98] the Communicable Diseases Act,[99] which

Policymaking under the Auspices of Parliamentary Constitutional Review: The Case of Finland and Its Implications' (2020) 6 *European Policy Analysis* 226, 229–31 see also the report 'First Wave of the COVID-19 Pandemic in Finland in 2020' (P2020–01), Safety Investigation Authority, 77.

[92] Salminen (n 86) 1116.

[93] Please note that the invocation of both instruments required some explanations, which were provided by the Constitutional Law Committee, T Kotkas et al, 'Finland: Legal Response to Covid-19' in T Kotkas et al, *The Oxford Compendium of National Legal Responses to Covid-19* (Oxford University Press, 2022) point 6.

[94] 'Government, in cooperation with the President of the Republic, declares a state of emergency in Finland over coronavirus outbreak', Press Release, 16 March 2020, Government Communications Department Ministry of Education and Culture Ministry of Social Affairs and Health, available at valtioneuvosto.fi/en/-//10616/hallitus-totesi-suomen-olevan-poikkeusoloissa-koronavirustilanteen-vuoksi#:~:text=On%2016%20March%202020%2C%20the,force%20until%2013%20April%202020. Note that even though two emergencies were declared (one pertaining to health and one economic), no measures were adopted with reference to the economic one, whereas the application of emergency powers was solely based on the provision of the Emergency Powers Act, referring to a pandemic (3§5), see 'Coronavirus COVID-19 outbreak in the EU Fundamental Rights Implications', Institute for Human Rights, Åbo Akademi University, 23 March 2020. While some scholars consider the declaration of the economic emergency to have been hasty (Salminen (n 86) 1124), I consider such a development to be in line with the general reluctance to acknowledge the existence of an economic emergency and the weaknesses associated with that, as argued in Zemskova (n 14), together with a deep connection of Finnish constitutional law with the international instruments, which do not employ such a category as economic emergencies.

[95] 'Finland declares a state of emergency', Press Release, 1 March 2021, Government Communications Department, available at valtioneuvosto.fi/en/-//10616/finland-declares-a-state-of-emergency. Note that this time, only a health emergency was declared.

[96] Laki majoitus- ja ravitsemistoiminnasta annetun lain väliaikaisesta muuttamisesta or Lag om temporär ändring av lagen om inkvarterings- och förplägnadsverksamhet (153/2020) and Laki majoitus- ja ravitsemistoiminnasta annetun lain väliaikaisesta muuttamisesta or Lag om temporär ändring av lagen om inkvarterings- och förplägnadsverksamhet (184/2021). Note that a legislative proposal (39/2021) for another Act, based on section 23 of the Constitution of Finland, restricting the freedom of movement, was submitted to the Finnish Parliament, but was subsequently withdrawn after the negative review of the Constitutional Law Committee of the Parliament, M Dahlberg, 'Finland – ex ante constitutionality review of laws relating to the COVID-19 pandemic – the ultimate protector of the rule of law or losing a sense of rationality?' (2021) Public law: the constitutional and administrative law of the commonwealth, (4), 819–822, Kotkas et al (n 92) point 71.

[97] Kotkas et al (n 92) point 11.

[98] Section 16, Rajavartiolaki or Gränsbevakningslag ((578/2005). Note that section 16 was amended in 2022 by Laki rajavartiolain muuttamisesta or Lag om ändring av gränsbevakningslagen (698/2022).

[99] Tartuntatautilaki or Lag om smittsamma sjukdomar (1227/2016).

was in place before the pandemic, constituted the primary basis for the measures adopted during the pandemic, quite aside from the instruments mentioned above.[100] Nevertheless, the Act had to undergo numerous modifications in the context of the emergency at hand.[101] Moreover, tackling the negative impact on the economy required not only the introduction of temporary amendments into existing legislation,[102] but also the adoption of the new temporary legislation.[103]

While all three emergency models were utilised in the course of the pandemic, it was evident that although recourse to the textual model of constitutional accommodation was possible, it was limited due to the high threshold for invoking it. At the same time, the pandemic highlighted the drawbacks of the business-as-usual model which made it necessary to resort to the model of legislative accommodation, which allows adjusting the legal framework to a present exigency.

D. Norway

Like the Constitutional Act of Denmark, the Constitution of the Kingdom of Norway (*Grunnlov*) – the world's second-oldest written constitution[104] – does not contain a separate state of emergency regime,[105] but instead has a couple of provisions that mention extraordinary circumstances as qualifiers for deviating from the ordinary legal framework.[106] This is not incidental but based on the

[100] M Scheinin, *Finland's Success in Combatting COVID-19: Mastery, Miracle or Mirage?* (Taylor and Francis, 2022) 132.

[101] J Salminen and M Farzamfar, 'The Supervision of Legality by the Finnish Parliamentary Ombudsman during the COVID-19 Pandemic' (2022) 99 *Nordisk Administrativt Tidsskrift*; Kotkas et al (n 92) point 16.

[102] See, eg, amendments to the Unemployment Security Act, the Sickness Insurance Act, the Value Added Tax Act, Kotkas et al (n 92) points 132–138.

[103] The Act on the Temporary Assistance to Persons Who Are Absent from Work without Pay (297/2020) and the Act on a Temporary Epidemic Allowance (687/2020), ibid points 127 and 128.

[104] M Langford and BK Berge, 'Norway's Constitution in a Comparative Perspective' (2019) 6 *Oslo Law Review* 198; H Eirik, H Benedikte Moltumyr and EC Conrad, 'Norway: Legal Response to Covid-19' in H Eirik, H Benedikte Moltumyr and EC Conrad, *The Oxford Compendium of National Legal Responses to Covid-19* (Oxford University Press, 2021) point 1. The Norwegian Constitution was amended in May 2024 concerning the functioning of the judicial branch, see the Announcement of the Storting's decision of 21 May 2024 on amendments to the Norwegian Constitution, available at lovdata.no/dokument/LTI/forskrift/2024-06-07-928.

[105] O Rambjör Heide, *Konstitusjonell Nødrett: Sett i Lys Av Den Europeiske Menneskerettighetskonvensjon Artikkel 15* (Tano Aschehoug, 1998) 19; While suggestions to introduce derogations clauses into the Norwegian Constitution were put forward, they were never actualised, E Holmøyvik, 'Grunnlovsfesting Av Menneskerettane' [2010] Tidsskrift for rettsvitenskap Report of the Human Rights Committee on Human Rights in the Constitution of the Kingdom of Norway, submitted on the 19th of December 2011, 91, available at www.stortinget.no/globalassets/pdf/dokumentserien/2011-2012/dok16-201112.pdf.

[106] Art 12 of the Constitution of the Kingdom of Norway allows the King to summon Norwegian citizens that are not members of the Norwegian Parliament to take a seat in the Council of State; Arts 25 and 26 concern the use of military forces, Art 54 contains the rules on elections to the Norwegian Parliament in case of extraordinary events; Art 68, which determines the seat of the

idea that a constitution should be a long-living legal instrument, applicable both in times of normalcy and exception.[107]

Mirroring the Danish approach to emergency regulation, the Norwegian constitutional framework acknowledges the unwritten doctrine of constitutional necessity,[108] which, as in Denmark, was extensively used during World War II.[109] Despite its acknowledgement and use, the doctrine's conceptualisation and substance remain blurry and undefined.[110] At the same time, the imperative to be true to the foundational values of Norwegian society, both during and after states of emergency, is highlighted.[111] Scholars and regulators nonetheless seem to agree that some definite prerequisites exist for a valid invocation of the doctrine of constitutional necessity: the emergency must be of such a magnitude as to jeopardise vital societal interests,[112] and the chosen responses must be temporary[113] and fulfil the requirements of proportionality and necessity.[114] Whereas a war, the risk of war, and major natural disasters are typically regarded as serious emergencies that could justify recourse to the doctrine of constitutional necessity, other emergency situations, including terrorist attacks,[115] are unlikely to be qualified as such.[116] Other than that, the regulation of different emergencies can be found either in laws specifically

Parliament, is the only one that explicitly mentions the examples of extraordinary circumstances – hostile invasion or infectious disease. The Constitution of the Kingdom of Norway (*Grunnlov*), available at lovdata.no/dokument/NLE/lov/1814-05-17. Note that Art 17 of the Constitution of the Kingdom of Norway also implies the existence of such an extraordinary situation when the Norwegian Parliament is, for some reason, not assembled, BM Høgberg, 'Lockdown og kriseregulering i Norge' (2020) 105 *Svensk Juristtidning* 1132, 1132.

[107] D Michalsen, *Unntakstilstand Og Forfatning: Brudd Og Kontinuitet i Konstitusjonell Rett* (Pax, 2013) 11–12; D Michalsen, 'Frede Castberg and the Invention of State of Emergency in Norwegian Constitutional Law in the Twentieth Century' in O Mäenpää et al (eds), *Oikeuden historiasta tulevaisuuden Eurooppaan: Pia Letto-Vanamo 60 vuotta* (Suomalainen Lakimiesyhdistys, 2014) 202–203.

[108] Heide (n 104) 20.

[109] State of emergency practices also took place before that, eg in 1905 when the union with Sweden was dissolved, Michalsen (n 106) 27–31; Michalsen in Mäenpää et al (n 106) 203–204; and in 1926–1927 when the impeachment proceedings against Norwegian prime minister Abraham Berge were initiated, Report of the Human Rights Committee on Human Rights in the Constitution of the Kingdom of Norway, submitted on 19 December 2011, 91, F Castberg, *Norges Statsforfatning* (Universitetsforlaget, 1964); Heide (n 104) 19–20, 103–105.

[110] Report of the Human Rights Committee on Human Rights in the Constitution of the Kingdom of Norway, submitted on 19 December 2011, 91, Høgberg (n 105) 1132.

[111] Heide (n 104) 41.

[112] Report of the Human Rights Committee on Human Rights in the Constitution of the Kingdom of Norway, submitted on 19 December 2011, 91.

[113] ibid 92.

[114] JA Stubberud, 'Hva er unntakstilstand?' in Michalsen (n 106) 84.

[115] D Michalsen, 'Frede Castberg and the Invention of State of Emergency in Norwegian Constitutional Law in the Twentieth Century' in Mäenpää et al (n 106) 211–12.

[116] Report of the Human Rights Committee on Human Rights in the Constitution of the Kingdom of Norway, submitted on 19 December 2011, 91. The Covid-19 pandemic also did not fall within the category of emergencies that could be addressed with the help of the doctrine of constitutional necessity, Høgberg (n 105) 1132.

devoted to such emergencies or preparedness for them,[117] or in the sectoral legislation,[118] which contains provisions for vesting the government with broad powers during exigencies. As in Denmark, if recourse to the doctrine of constitutional necessity is not possible, it is to be expected that a combination of the model of legislative accommodation and the business-as-usual model will be employed.

In the context of the Covid-19 pandemic, which did not fall within the category of emergencies that could be addressed with the help of the doctrine of constitutional necessity,[119] the 1994 Infection Control Act and the 2000 Health Preparedness Act, both predating this public health emergency, were the primary source for the measures adopted.[120] Both Acts allow for deviations from the existing legal framework,[121] yet they required further amendment in order to be able to effectively address the pandemic. In its first report, the government-appointed Norwegian Corona Commission would later conclude that the 1994 Infection Control Act, while having been instrumental in combatting the Covid-19 pandemic, needed to be altered.[122] Moreover, the pandemic triggered the adoption of some new legislation, among which was the temporary 2020 Corona Act,[123] which provided the government with powers to adopt regulations supplementing, amending or deviating from the statutes that were listed in the Act.[124] As can be seen, while

[117] Such as the 1950 Preparedness Act (Lov om særlige rådgjerder under krig, krigsfare og liknende forhold (beredskapsloven)), containing the rules applicable in war-related emergencies, available at lovdata.no/dokument/NL/lov/1950-12-15-7; the 1994 Infection Control Act (Lov om vern mot smittsomme sykdommer (smittevernloven)), available at lovdata.no/dokument/NL/lov/1994-08-05-55?q=smittevernloven; the 2000 Health Preparedness Act (Lov om helsemessig og sosial beredskap (helseberedskapsloven)), available at lovdata.no/dokument/NL/lov/2000-06-23-56; the 2011 Act on Business and Industry Preparedness (Lov om næringsberedskap (næringsberedskapsloven)), available at lovdata.no/dokument/NLE/lov/2011-12-16-65; the 2010 Act on Municipal Emergency Preparedness, Civil Protection Measures and the Civil Defense Lov om kommunal beredskapsplikt, sivile beskyttelsestiltak og Sivilforsvaret (sivilbeskyttelsesloven), available at lovdata.no/dokument/LTI/lov/2010-06-25-45.

[118] The 2000 Act on Radiation Protection and Use of Radiation (Lov om strålevern og bruk av stråling (strålevernloven)), available at dsa.no/en/legislation/Act%20and%20Regulations%20on%20Radiation%20Protection%20and%20Use%20of%20Radiation.pdf; the 1990 Energy Act (Lov om produksjon, omforming, overføring, omsetning, fordeling og bruk av energi m.m. (energiloven)), available at lovdata.no/dokument/NL/lov/1990-06-29-50?q=energiloven.

[119] Høgberg (n 105) 1132.

[120] Holmøyvik, Høgberg and Conrad (n 103) points 12 and 14.

[121] Sections 7–12 and 6–2 respectively.

[122] *Myndighetenes håndtering av koronapandemien rapport fra Koronakommisjonen: oppnevnt ved kongelig resolusjon 24. april 2020 for å gjennomgå og trekke lærdom fra covid-19-utbruddet i Norge, avgitt til statsministeren 14. april 2021* (Departementenes sikkerhets- og serviceorganisasjon, Teknisk redaksjon, 2021).

[123] Midlertidig lov om forskriftshjemmel for å avhjelpe konsekvenser av utbrudd av Covid-19 mv. (koronaloven), available at lovdata.no/dokument/LTI/lov/2020-03-27-17.

[124] Section 2, ibid. Note, that such regulations could not contradict the rules enshrined in the Constitution; at the same time they could contain restrictions of the rights. The problematic aspects associated with the adoption and use of the Act can be found in Holmøyvik, Høgberg and Conrad (n 103); H Petter Graver, 'Fighting the Virus and the Rule of Law – A Country Report on Norway'

the Norwegian legal framework, striving for the use of the Business-as-Usual Model, contained legal acts that could be used in the emergency at hand, the existing legal framework had to be either amended or complemented with the new legislation.

IV. REFLECTIONS

The constitutional design of the Nordic states is not all that straightforward and allows for recourse to different emergency models in different forms and combinations during different types of extraordinary situations. The possibility of taking recourse to each emergency model can be schematically presented in the following way:

	Business-as-Usual Model	**Model of Constitutional Accommodation: Textual**	**Model of Constitutional Accommodation: Structural**	**Model of Legislative Accommodation**
Sweden	+	+	*[125]	+
Denmark	+	–	+	+
Finland	+	+	–	+
Norway	+	–	+	+

There are several important aspects to be mentioned in this regard. Firstly, the model of constitutional accommodation comes with a high threshold, making its potential use quite limited. Both Sweden and Finland can take recourse to the textual model of constitutional accommodation, namely emergency provisions enshrined in their constitutions, but the scope of these provisions differs. While Sweden can employ the model in war-related emergencies, the scope of the application of this model in Finland is broader since the Finnish constitution contains the conditions for limitations of human rights in emergencies in general, allowing for the opportunity to invoke this provision in an emergency that fulfils the stipulated conditions. The probability of either country invoking the textual model of constitutional accommodation is low, however. In the case of Sweden, only a particular emergency can permit recourse to the model; in Finland, despite broad potential of the emergency provision in the constitution, the high threshold built into it makes it difficult to apply any section 23 in practice. The same goes for the doctrine of constitutional necessity in Denmark and Norway: while both states explicitly recognise the possibility

(*Verfassungsblog*, 13 April 2020), available at verfassungsblog.de/fighting-the-virus-and-the-rule-of-law-a-country-report-on-norway/, H Petter Graver, *Baselining COVID-19: How Do We Assess the Success or Failure of the Responses of Governments to the Pandemic?* (Taylor and Francis, 2022).

[125] '*' reflects the ambivalent position of the doctrine of constitutional necessity in Sweden, see section 3.1.

of its application,[126] this goes only for extraordinary occurrences of a grave nature, where unwritten conditions are fulfilled. The Covid-19 pandemic, for instance, was not considered an emergency that could justify the invocation of the doctrine of constitutional necessity.[127]

Second, while the Nordic states might be striving to prepare their ordinary legal frameworks for accommodating different emergencies, reflecting the business-as-usual model, these practices demonstrate the weaknesses of the model in terms of its limited ability to create a full-fledged system that can cope with any exigency without needing alterations. The obvious alternative, used in all four states in the context of the pandemic, is the model of legislative accommodation, which allows for adapting the existing legal framework to an extraordinary situation at hand.[128] The business-as-usual model should not, however, be disregarded as unfeasible; it should rather be conceived as a 'solution concept'[129] – something that, while it does not by itself resolve the problem, sets out a direction for addressing it.[130]

Third, and most importantly, the general lack of textual constitutional accommodation for peacetime emergencies in all the countries examined except Finland, whose section 23 of the Constitution provides for a possibility to invoke this provision in other than war-induced emergencies, results in the management of peacetime emergencies primarily via the model of legislative accommodation, which represents an ad hoc solution employed in contexts where time for deliberating over the best course of action is limited and where the urgency of the situation might lead to the adoption of legally flawed solutions. Of course, the unforseeability of peacetime emergencies makes it difficult to textually accommodate them in a constitution; however, the recent example of the pandemic should provide a ground for discussions on the recalibration of the emergency law frameworks of the four states towards the types of emergency that are

[126] As for Sweden, it is caught between not recognising the doctrine as an appropriate tool and at the same time admitting the possibility of a limited application, a possibility substantiated by the fact that the country has in practice resorted to it on several occasions.

[127] In fact, none of the states that recognise constitutional necessity invoked it in the context of the pandemic, Cameron and Cornell (n 48) 1176.

[128] In the context of addressing climate change, all the Nordic states introduced ordinary laws on climate change that incorporate strategies aimed at combatting this exigency into their legal frameworks. Quite often these legal instruments require subsequent adjustments: while both Denmark and Finland adopted new laws (the 2020 Climate Act, modified in 2021, and the 2022 Climate Act, amended in 2023, respectively, replacing the previous laws on climate change from 2014 and 2015 respectively), Norway introduced a minor correction to the 2017 Climate Change Act in 2023. The Swedish Climate Act of 2017 remains unchanged as of now since its adoption.

[129] See an analogy with the solution concept of the rule of law, J Waldron, 'Is the Rule of Law an Essentially Contested Concept (In Florida)?' (2002) 21 *Law and Philosophy* 137, 158; J Waldron, 'The Rule of Law as an Essentially Contested Concept' in J Meierhenrich and M Loughlin (eds), *The Cambridge Companion to the Rule of Law* (Cambridge University Press, 2021) 133; Zemskova (n 14) 66.

[130] A similar view is expressed by Tormod Otter Johansen while discussing emergency models in the context of Sweden, Johansen (n 43) 260.

becoming more frequent.[131] Exploring the possibilities of such a recalibration should not, however, take into account only the willingness to make the existing emergency law frameworks more tailored to the current state of affairs, but also ensure that the principle of the rule of law and respect for fundamental rights are properly safeguarded in such emergencies.

[131] See the discussions in the context of Sweden, for instance, in Swedish Government Official Report 'Strengthening constitutional preparedness' SOU 2023:75.

6

Scaffolding an Era of Emergency: Lessons from Canada's Emergencies Act

JOCELYN STACEY*

I. INTRODUCTION

IN THE WINTER of 2022, a protest movement descended upon Ottawa, Canada's national capital. Sparked by a relatively minor Covid-19 pandemic measure (vaccination requirements for cross-border commercial truckers), the 'Freedom Convoy' was unlike any protest movement previously experienced in the country. It resulted in the first-ever use of Canada's centralised emergency legislation: the Emergencies Act.[1] The Convoy occupied the national capital with more than ten thousand demonstrators and hundreds of big rig semi-trucks.[2] Some protesters represented the minority of unvaccinated truckers whose livelihoods were directly impacted by the addition of a new pandemic measure. Many more were Canadians unsettled by the pandemic and who perceived pandemic response measures as governmental overreach and an abuse of power. Some demonstrators blasted air horns day and night, seeming to 'enjoy the harm that the noise was causing.'[3] Some demonstrators vandalised statues and property; some threatened local communities; and some expressed racist, antisemitic and extremist views. In general, '[t]here was a breakdown of order

* I served as a member of the Public Order Emergency Commission's Research Council. While I draw on my experience working on the Council, I write in my capacity as a scholar on emergencies and the law. Thanks to Nomi Claire Lazar for many conversations about the Emergencies Act and emergency powers, which have informed this chapter. Thanks also to Sanja Bogojevic for her comments which greatly improved the clarity of this chapter.

[1] RSC 1985, c 22 (4th Supp).

[2] Public Order Emergency Commission, *Report of the Public Inquiry into the 2022 Public Order Emergency Volume 2: Analysis (Part 1)* (2022) 137, publicorderemergencycommission.ca/files/documents/Final-Report/Vol-2-Report-of-the-Public-Inquiry-into-the-2022-Public-Order-Emergency.pdf (POEC Report Vol 2).

[3] ibid 53.

and social norms' and the perception of 'lawlessness in the downtown area'.[4] Businesses in Ottawa had to close. Those residents who could evacuated the downtown core. In addition, the movement targeted border crossings around the country, impeding the flow of essential goods and services across the Canada–United-States border. Across the country, '[t]housands of supporters cheered them on [and m]illions of dollars were donated to support their cause.'[5]

Many, perhaps most, of the protesters sought to air their grievances with government through protest – a vital part of democratic life and (at least initially) an exercise of constitutionally-protected freedoms of expression and peaceful assembly. Some of the participants, however, had more ambitious intentions, such as overthrowing the government unless all COVID-19 measures were repealed. Law enforcement agencies were visibly unprepared and, in the case of the Ottawa Police Service, 'became overwhelmed' within the first 24 hours of the Convoy's arrival.[6] There was speculation that law enforcement officials were too sympathetic to the protesters and their aims.[7] And then two weeks into the events, a large cache of firearms was discovered at one of the roadblocks, alarming almost everyone, including many protesters.

Just over two weeks after the Convoy arrived in the national capital, the federal government invoked the Emergencies Act for the first time in the Act's 35-year lifespan. It declared a 'public order emergency' and imposed emergency measures that deemed unlawful the Convoy gatherings, froze the financial assets of anyone participating in these unlawful gatherings, and enabled coordinated enforcement.[8] In nine days, without injury or violence, the capital and border crossings were cleared and the state of emergency lifted.[9]

This first use of the Emergencies Act presents a useful case for examining the role of centralised emergency legislation. As explained below, Canada's Emergencies Act is a distinctive emergency statute. It was thoroughly deliberated upon during a time of calm, responsive to the concerns of those most impacted by past uses and abuses of emergency powers, enacted with multi-party support, and intentionally drafted to maintain the rule of law, even through crisis. The Convoy was not an especially difficult set of circumstances, as emergencies go. Organisers telegraphed their intentions well in advance, protest activities were

[4] ibid 53.

[5] Public Order Emergency Commission, *Report of the Public Inquiry into the 2022 Public Order Emergency Volume 1: Overview* (2022) 14, publicorderemergencycommission.ca/files/documents/Final-Report/Vol-1-Report-of-the-Public-Inquiry-into-the-2022-Public-Order-Emergency.pdf (POEC Report Vol 1).

[6] ibid 50.

[7] Public Order Emergency Commission, *Report of the Public Inquiry into the 2022 Public Order Emergency Volume 3: Analysis Part 2* (2022) 190, publicorderemergencycommission.ca/files/documents/Final-Report/Vol-3-Report-of-the-Public-Inquiry-into-the-2022-Public-Order-Emergency.pdf.

[8] SOR/2022-20; SOR/2022-22; SOR/2022-21.

[9] SOR/2022-26.

confined to specific geographic locations, the most disruptive activities lasted only one month, the federal state of emergency lasted only nine days, and the circumstances were addressed domestically without resort to international resources or intervention.[10] And yet it can be seen as a harbinger of an era of emergency: a warning sign of the confluence of political, economic and ecological instability that is now upon us.

This chapter argues that emergency legislation can and should scaffold the commitment to the rule of law through times of crisis. In emergencies, the rule of law comes under strain, with some claiming that it is luxury society cannot afford when the executive must act swiftly to respond to a perceived threat.[11] But the first use of the Emergencies Act demonstrates that it is possible and desirable for emergency legislation to hold government officials to account for the use of emergency powers; it is possible, in other words, to demand that public officials adhere to the fundamental rule-of-law requirement of public justification.

This chapter is structured as follows. Section II contrasts conventional emergency powers with the unique features of Canada's Emergencies Act. It describes the Act's triple-layer definition of 'emergency'; the permissible emergency powers; its requirements of interjurisdictional coordination; and its layered accountability mechanisms. Despite its careful design, however, many limitations and imperfections were apparent when the Emergencies Act confronted the social reality of the Convoy. Section III turns to these limitations and imperfections. Drawing on interdisciplinary disaster studies scholarship, Section III argues that these limitations are inevitable and unavoidable features of emergency legislation; emergency legislation cannot match the complexity and nuance of emergencies as they unfold in real life. This sets the stage for the argument in Section IV: what emergency legislation *can* do well is scaffold the rule of law. By this I mean that emergency legislation can and should supply a framework that structures decision-making that is publicly justified on the basis of fundamental, constitutional principles which in turn sustains – even through emergency – a culture of justification. Section V concludes.

[10] The federal state of emergency under the Emergencies Act was declared on 14 February 2022 and lifted on 23 February 2022. The provincial state of emergency under Ontario's Emergency Management and Civil Protection Act, RSO 1990, c E.9 was in force from 11 February 2022 to 23 February 2022. Local states of emergency, which under Ontario law do not permit the use of expanded and exceptional powers, were issued in Ottawa (6–24 February 2022) and Windsor (14–24 February 2022).

[11] See eg O Gross, 'Chaos and Rules: Should Responses to Violent Crises Always be Constitutional?' (2003) 112 *Yale LJ* 1011. See also the discussion of models for emergency powers that either weaken or temporarily step outside the constitutional order in O Gross and F Ní Aoláin, *Law in Times of Crisis: Emergency Powers in Theory and Practice* (Cambridge University Press, 2006) and in J Ferejohn and P Pasquino, 'The Law of the Exception: A Typology of Emergency Powers' (2004) 2 *Int J of Constitutional Law* 210.

II. CANADA'S DISTINCTIVE EMERGENCIES ACT

In 1988, the Parliament of Canada enacted the Emergencies Act, a centralised code for the use of exceptional federal measures to respond to perceived emergencies. In many ways the Act is everything that emergencies law is thought not to be: specific and transparent, accountable, and explicitly subject to ordinary constitutional law requirements. In this part, I highlight four unique features of the Emergencies Act, which distinguish it from conventional emergency legislation.

A core challenge for lawmakers in crafting emergency legislation is the inability to know in advance all particular types of extreme events that may occur and the specific types of measures that will be necessary in response to them.[12] Accordingly, most constitutions contain provisions that address the specific challenges of emergencies by allocating more power to the executive during times of crisis.[13] Emergency legislation in countries around the world and at the subnational level in Canada make sweeping delegations of authority to the executive to declare emergencies and take any measures necessary to respond.[14] For example, Canada's historic War Measures Act (1914) empowered the government to proclaim an emergency for any 'war, invasion, or insurrection, real or apprehended' and, having made such a proclamation, to govern by decree bypassing the legislative branch of the state.[15]

Such an approach is rife with potential for governmental abuses of power. Emergency legislation often authorises types of measures that would otherwise be considered unacceptable. For instance the War Measures Act was used to intern Canadian citizens on the basis of race, to suppress speech, and to confiscate property, amongst other things.[16] Moreover, the Act was controversially invoked in peacetime in response to domestic terrorism, resulting in over four hundred detentions without charges being brought.[17] Also, courts have historically been either unwilling or unable to subject these exercises of executive power to rigorous judicial review.[18]

[12] The relationship between law and emergency powers is a perennial subject of political and legal theory. For thoughtful syntheses of these debates see K Loevy, *Emergencies in Public Law: The Legal Politics of Containment* (Cambridge University Press, 2016); NC Lazar, *States of Emergency in Liberal Democracies* (Cambridge University Press, 2009); Gross and Aoláin, *Law in Times of Crisis* (n 11).

[13] C Bjørnskov and S Voigt, 'The Architecture of Emergency Constitutions' (2018) 16 *Int J of Constitutional Law* 101, 125. According to the analysis by Bjørnskov and Voigt, 90% of constitutions worldwide provide for emergencies and, across these constitutions, the long-term trend has been to 'allocate more, rather than less, powers to the executive during times of emergency'.

[14] Ferejohn and Pasquino (n 11).

[15] War Measures Act, RSC 1927, c 206, s 3.

[16] P Peppin, 'Emergency Legislation and Rights in Canada: The War Measures Act and Civil Liberties' (1993) 18 *Queen's LJ* 129.

[17] ibid.

[18] For Canadian examples see *Reference re Wartime Leasehold Regulations*, [1950] SCR 124; *Fort Frances Pulp and Paper Co. v Manitoba Free Press Co.*, [1923] 3 DLR 629 (UK JCPC). In the

Even modern emergency legislation replicates this dynamic. For instance, British Columbia's 2023 modernised legislation that implements the Sendai Framework on Disaster Risk Reduction preserves the structure that an emergency is whatever the executive says it is.[19] Long-debated legislative reforms in Aotearoa, New Zealand, similarly intended to reflect the complexity and frequency of emergencies, would have retained subjective and open-ended requirements allowing the Minister to declare an emergency if 'it appears' to the Minister that an emergency has occurred or may occur and is likely to be of such extent that its handling is beyond local capacity.[20]

Canada's Emergencies Act, in contrast, is emergency legislation designed with the rule of law in mind.[21] Influenced by the advocacy of those most affected by past uses and abuses of emergency powers,[22] legislators crafted the Emergencies Act to not repeat mistakes of emergency powers of the past.[23] The Act has four distinctive characteristics.

The first feature is the Act's definition of emergency. It sets a high bar for declaring an emergency through a triple-layer definition. A situation must pass through all three layers to rise to the level of emergency. The first layer is that the situation must fit within one of four specific categories of emergency. There is no catch-all category. The Act recognises four kinds of emergency:

- Public welfare emergency: a real or imminent event, such as a fire, flood, earthquake, disease or accident, that poses a 'danger to life or property,

United States and United Kingdom this pattern of judicial deference to emergency measures was observed by scholars in the aftermath of the 9/11 and 7/7 terrorist attacks: eg D Cole, 'Judging the Next Emergency: Judicial Review and Individual Rights in Times of Crisis' (2003) 101 *Mich L Rev* 2565; TR Hickman, 'Between Human Rights and the Rule of Law: Indefinite Detention and the Derogation Model of Constitutionalism' (2005) 68 *The Modern Law Review* 655.

[19] Emergency and Disaster Management Act, SBC 2023, c 37. See J Stacey, 'Confronting Modern Disaster? British Columbia's New Emergency and Disaster Management Act' (2024) 57 *UBC Law Rev* 615.

[20] Emergency Management Bill 2023 (225–1), cl 81 (NZ). The new government announced in May 2024 that it would not bring forward this bill, shelving years of law reform work. See Office of the Minister for Emergency Management and Recovery, *Discharging the Emergency Management Bill* (2024) www.civildefence.govt.nz/assets/Uploads/documents/proactive-release/Release-version-Documents-relating-to-the-Governments-decision-to-not-proceed-with-the-Emergency-Management-Bill.pdf.

[21] NC Lazar and J Stacey, 'Introduction' (2023) 46 *Manitoba Law Journal* 9.

[22] Particularly, the advocacy of Japanese Canadians seeking protections to ensure that human rights violations – such as the internment and dispossession of Japanese Canadians during and after World War II – are not repeated. See Canada HC Deb 25 April 1988, vol 12, 14765, 14769, 14770.

[23] ibid, 14763-4. Speaking in favour of the bill, Mr Bud Bradley (Parliamentary Secretary to the Minister of National Defence and the bill's sponsor) stated: 'Since 1970 all Parties of the House have been on record as favouring new legislation to replace that archaic and abhorrent act [the War Measures Act]. Nearly 18 years have elapsed since Canadians were promised a more enlightened approach for dealing with safety and security during national emergencies … It is time to ensure that the abuses of civil liberties committed against Japanese Canadians in World War II, and against Quebecers during the 1970 October crisis, will never happen again. Bill C-77 [the Emergencies Act] does this, and more. … As a political device the War Measures Act was tremendously effective. As an instrument for dispensing justice, it was not effective at all.'

social disruption or a breakdown in the flow of essential goods, services or resources' (section 5).

- Public order emergency: a threat to the security of Canada, including terrorism, i.e. the use (or threat thereof) of serious violence against persons or property for achieving political, religious or ideological objective (section 16).[24]
- International emergency: an emergency involving Canada and one or more other countries that arises from acts of intimidation or coercion or the real or imminent use of serious force or violence (section 27).
- War emergency: a war or other armed conflict, real or imminent, involving Canada or any of its allies (section 37).

Simply falling within one of these categories is not enough, however, for qualifying as an emergency under the Act. The second layer stipulates a threshold for emergency – additional criteria that make the event rise to the level of *national emergency*. The situation must be urgent, critical and temporary, and cannot be effectively dealt with under any other law of Canada. In addition, it must either be one that seriously threatens Canada's ability to preserve its sovereignty, security and territorial integrity; or it must be one that seriously endangers life, health, and safety, and exceeds the capacity or authority of the affected province(s).[25]

The third definitional layer is evidentiary. The decision-maker must have reasonable grounds to believe that the events meet the definitional requirements.[26] It is an objective, not simply a subjective evidentiary threshold.[27]

The second distinctive feature of the Act is its tailored scope of emergency powers. Unlike much emergency legislation, which empowers the executive to take all measures believed necessary to respond to the emergency,[28] the Emergencies Act sets out fixed types of measures that are matched to the type of emergency declared. For instance, in a public order emergency – such as the Convoy events – the government can make orders regulating and restricting gatherings, but it cannot make orders authorising the entry, search

[24] One complicated feature of the Emergencies Act is that its definition of public order emergency incorporates by reference the definition of 'threats to the security of Canada' from the Canadian Security Intelligence Service Act, RSC 1985, c C-23, an act with the very different purpose of governing the gathering of intelligence.

[25] Emergencies Act, RSC 1985, c 22 (4th Supp), s 3.

[26] ibid ss 6, 17, 28, 38.

[27] Canada HC Deb 25 April 1988, vol 12, 14765. Legislators described this as 'perhaps the most important' change because it 'means that all important decisions made by the Governor in Council relating to the invocation and use of the emergency power will be challengeable in the courts'.

[28] As one example of the norm in provincial legislation across Canada, in the Alberta Emergency Management Act, RSA 2000, c E-6.8, sections 19(1) and 19(1.1) empower the Minister to 'do all acts and take all necessary proceedings'; and '[i]n addition to any other orders the Minister is authorized to make … the Minister may make my order necessary, in the Minister's opinion, to lessen the impact of the emergency.'

and/or seizure of property (something it can do for international emergencies).[29] Moreover, the Emergencies Act takes some types of emergency action off the table. The Act explicitly prohibits the use of emergency powers to amend the Act;[30] to detain, imprison, or intern Canadian citizens or permanent residents on the 'basis of race, national or ethnic origin, colour, religion, sex, age or mental or physical disability';[31] to censure, suppress or control publication or communication of information during an international emergency;[32] or to order conscription during a war emergency.[33] While Parliament is supreme and could enact different legislation to authorise these types of emergency measures, the explicit prohibition in the Emergencies Act makes such legislative action politically infeasible.

The third distinctive feature is the Act's attention to interjurisdictional accountability and coordination, reflecting the constitutional division of powers between the provincial and federal governments. The federal government cannot act unilaterally in declaring an emergency. Rather, it must first consult with the provinces, with the nature of that consultation varying depending on the type of emergency.[34] Further, the Emergencies Act requires that the federal government coordinate its emergency measures, so as to 'not unduly impair' provincial action and to act in concert with the provinces to the extent possible.[35] Finally, the Emergencies Act prohibits the federal government from using emergency powers to take control of provincial or municipal policing, further reinforcing – and not deviating from – the ordinary constitutional division of powers.[36]

The fourth distinctive feature of the Act is that it clearly and proactively subjects the executive to both legal and political mechanisms of accountability for any use of emergency powers. When a government considers the use of emergency powers under the Act, it knows in advance that it will be called to account in a number of fora. In principle, this structure incentivises prudent emergency decision-making. The Emergencies Act sets out a clear role for Parliament in ratifying or vetoing any declaration of emergency,[37] and for ongoing oversight of emergency measures through a mandatory parliamentary committee.[38] In addition, the Act requires an after-the-fact inquiry into the circumstances that prompted the use of the Act and the measures that were taken for dealing with the emergency.[39] Finally, the Emergency Act envisions robust judicial oversight

[29] For the set categories of emergency measures that can be issued in a public order emergency, see Emergencies Act, RSC 1985, c 22 (4th Supp), s 19(1).

[30] ibid s 4(a).

[31] Emergencies Act, RSC 1985, c 22 (4th Supp), s 4(b).

[32] ibid s 30(2)(b).

[33] ibid s 40(2).

[34] ibid s 14, 25, 35, 44.

[35] ibid s 8(3), 19(3), 30(2), 40(4).

[36] ibid s 9(1), 20(1), 31(1).

[37] ibid s 58-60.

[38] ibid s 62.

[39] Emergencies Act, RSC 1985, c 22 (4th Supp), s 63.

as indicated by its reference to the use of the Act being subject to the Charter of Rights and Freedoms, Canada's constitutional bill of rights.[40]

While understood as a tool of last resort, the Emergencies Act nonetheless stands as an example of how to govern emergencies in accordance with 'normal' law. It was enacted through full parliamentary process; its invocation is subject to constitutional limits of federalism and Charter rights; and it delegates a constrained set of powers to the executive, all of which are subject to multiple forms of accountability. In contrast to typical emergency legislation, the Emergencies Act is intended to sustain – and not depart from – the ongoing project to govern in accordance with the rule of law.

III. INHERENT LIMITS AND IMPERFECTIONS OF EMERGENCY LEGISLATION

When confronted with the messy reality of the Convoy, however, the well-thought-out Emergencies Act seemed to fall short. It is this mismatch between well-conceived legislation and actual emergency response that opens space for deeper analysis of the proper role of emergency legislation. One immediate objection might be that Canada's Emergencies Act is simply out of date and out of touch. It was enacted in the early days of the country's Charter of Rights and Freedoms, long before the impacts of climate change began to ripple across the country, and during a period of relative political stability. And the Convoy events, while unexpected, was surely not the kind of complex, intractable emergency that governments worldwide repeatedly face. As I set out in this part, however, the Convoy emergency presents a nicely contained example of the unavoidable limits and imperfections of codified responses to emergency. These features of emergency legislation hold important lessons for legislating in an era of complex, compounding and cascading emergencies.

This part turns to interdisciplinary scholarship on disaster studies. Consistent with parliamentarians' intentions to govern emergencies through 'normal' law, decades of disaster studies and emergency management research similarly emphasises the normality of emergency; that is, as an endemic feature of society and not an outlier or exception. In this part, we see that disaster studies scholarship raises critical challenges to even well-thought-out emergency legislation, challenges that are illustrated even by the case of the Convoy. This part identifies four basic lessons from the first use of the Emergencies Act:

[40] Canada HC Deb 25 April 1988, vol 12, 14765-6. Again, from the Parliamentary debates: 'I cannot emphasize too strongly how important this new approach is to the assurance of full protection of fundamental rights and freedoms. The continued application of the Charter, which is also assured by the Bill, coupled with the accountability of the Governor in Council inherent in this new wording, ensures that the fundamental freedoms of Canadians will be preserved as long as the nation, its institutions and its constitution are preserved.'

(i) legislators govern based on the past, not the future; (ii) legislation overestimates institutional competence and capacity; (iii) what counts as an emergency is inevitably contested; and (iv) the emergency management cycle acts as a closed loop that reinforces the status quo.

A. Legislating for the Future

The first limitation of emergency legislation is that legislators tend to legislate for the previous emergency.[41] It is much easier for legislators to consider how better legislation could have prevented prior emergencies, than to anticipate unknown future ones. While legislation should be informed by past experience, it is future-oriented and thus is a form of predictive decision-making about how events will transpire going forward. Regulatory scholars, such as Sheila Jasanoff, emphasise the well-known tendency of '[p]redictive methods [to] focus on the known at the expense of the unknown, producing overconfidence in the accuracy and completeness of the pictures they produce'.[42] Put differently, it is very challenging to imagine a state of affairs that does not yet exist. Even in an era of repeated wildfires, floods, heat-waves and storms, these events rarely unfold in the same way twice, sometimes making it difficult to predict the types of responses that will be needed in future cases.[43] This is especially true in the context of climate change and its many interlocking ecological crises. The United Nations' 2019 Global Assessment on Disaster Risk Reduction exclaimed that 'surprise is the new normal' as social and environmental changes accelerate and outpace predictions based on past patterns.[44]

Canada's Emergencies Act demonstrates the limitations of past experiences of emergency in governing future events. The Act contains four soundly considered categories for emergencies, each tailored to reflect emergency experiences in the preceding decades.[45] But legislators did not consider the role that threats to economic security might play in triggering a public order emergency. It is clear from the legislative history and statutory language that economic emergencies (like a financial crisis) are not intended to be covered by the Emergencies Act.[46]

[41] See eg S Park, 'Role of the Sovereign State in 21st Century Disasters' (2022) 31 *Environmental Politics* 8, 19.

[42] S Jasanoff, 'Technologies of Humility' (2007) 41 *Minerva* 223, 239.

[43] GJ Schenk, 'Learning from History?' in F Krüger, G Bankoff, T Cannon, B Orlowski and ELF Shipper (eds), *Cultures and Disasters: Understanding Cultural Framings in Disaster Risk Reduction* (Routledge, 2015).

[44] United Nations, *2019 Global Assessment on Disaster Risk Reduction* (2019) 3, gar.undrr.org/sites/default/files/gar19distilled.pdf.

[45] J Lindsay, 'Canada's Fractured Emergency Management System' (2023) 46 *Manitoba Law Journal* 163, 167–68.

[46] Emergency Preparedness Canada, *Bill C-77: An Act to Provide for Safety and Security in Emergencies: Working Paper* (Emergency Preparedness Canada 1987) 4, 26 www.publicsafety.gc.ca/lbrr/archives/ke%205460%20b55%201987-eng.pdf.

But it was not clear, before its invocation, whether economic impacts ought to factor into a decision to declare a public order emergency.

Legislators in the 1980s also did not consider the cumulative impacts of a global pandemic, a looming war in Ukraine, and fragile global supply-chains when imagining what kind of emergency-level threats and disruption might be caused by a public order event. Accordingly, the definition of public order emergency in the Emergencies Act did not address this situation – nor could it have. The Convoy tapped into changed global dynamics that were not foreseen in the 1980s and may not even have been foreseen immediately prior to the Covid-19 pandemic.[47] Thus, even with a relatively uncomplicated emergency such as the Convoy, we can see how emergent, context-specific dynamics reveal limitations and ambiguity in legislative definitions. Emergencies may not be wholly unforeseeable, but they often have unforeseeable elements to them, meaning that legislation will inevitably fall short in its responses to these events.

B. Institutional Competence and Capacity cannot be Assumed

The first limitation is linked to the second one: past practice at managing emergencies can lead to overconfidence in the ability to manage future events. As regulatory scholars and organisational theorists emphasise: our systems fail all the time. Charles Perrow notably describes how 'failures are inevitable' within organisations.[48] Under common conditions, small failures interact in unexpected ways, causing 'normal accidents' (eg, train derailment or nuclear meltdown). Perrow's insight that 'small failures abound in big systems'[49] is relevant not only to technical fields of regulation, but also to the field of emergency management.[50] What if the emergency response does not go as anticipated and, in fact, generates another emergency?

But emergency legislation does not typically reflect this interaction between the triggering event and the system's ability to respond. Emergency legislation presumes that the government can and will respond effectively: that it has the

[47] There were indicators for careful observers, such as criticism by experts that the intelligence community has been slow to recognise the violence of far-right extremism. See Kent Roach, 'The February Emergency: Intelligence, Policing and Governance Failures and the Future of Charter-Proofed Emergencies' (2022) 70 *Criminal Law Quarterly* 195, 199–200.

[48] C Perrow, *Normal Accidents: Living With High Risk Technologies* (Princeton University Press, 1984) 5.

[49] ibid 9.

[50] Leading disaster studies scholar Terry Cannon notes that the social systems of disaster-risk reduction and emergency management are themselves understudied. See T Cannon, 'Disasters, Climate Change and the Significance of "Culture"' in F Krüger, G Bankoff, T Cannon, B Orlowski and ELF Shipper (eds), *Cultures and Disasters: Understanding Cultural Framings in Disaster Risk Reduction* (Routledge, 2015) 88–89.

capacity, competency and willingness to do so.[51] In other words, emergency legislation does not typically take into account the possibility that the governmental response might contributing to the emergency itself.

Canada's Emergencies Act is a striking illustration of a legislative presumption of institutional competence and capacity. Under the Act, the federal government's ability to implement an emergency response is generally limited to circumstances in which the events 'exceed the capacity or authority' of the affected provinces to deal with it.[52] As noted above, the Act requires consultation, coordination and complementarity with the provinces. In other words, the Act seems premised on an assumption that the provinces will competently and expeditiously address the emergency.

Messy political and social reality played out differently in the case of the Convoy. Political leadership in Ontario was absent until very late in the timeline of response.[53] Some police were sympathetic to the demonstrators.[54] The Ottawa police oversight body was dysfunctional, embroiled in interpersonal dynamics.[55] The situation seemed to raise questions of competence and willingness rather than the Emergencies Act's threshold requirements of a lack of resource capacity or jurisdictional authority.

To be sure, it is possible to reform the threshold requirements of the Emergencies Act to shift away from this calculation of provincial response. But what is not possible is the codification of all emergent dynamics of emergency management: eg, the choices that need to be made when resources are scarce, and the impacts of weak leadership or organisational conflict. Emergency legislation is inherently limited because it cannot anticipate all the contingencies and uncertainties of the myriad interactions between the dozens of government officials across multiple jurisdictions and their interactions with particular triggering events.

C. Definitions are Contested

The third limitation of emergency legislation is that it must draw a line between emergency and normalcy and thus privilege one understanding of emergency over others. However, as disaster scholars have written for decades, emergencies and disasters are not self-defining: their definitions are often contested.[56]

[51] K Loevy, 'The Problem of Threshold in the Emergencies Act – A Triple Incapacity Model' (2023) 46 *Manitoba Law Journal* 175, 184.

[52] Emergencies Act, RSC 1985, c 22 (4th Supp), s 3(a).

[53] POEC Report Vol 1 (n 5) 175.

[54] Public Order Emergency Commission, 'Public Hearing Volume 15' (2022) 80, publicorderemergencycommission.ca/files/documents/Transcripts/POEC-Public-Hearings-Volume-15-November-2-2022.pdf.

[55] POEC Report Vol 2 (n 2) 249 ff.

[56] Loevy (n 12) ch 3.

Different communities will have different understandings and experiences of what counts as an emergency. What registers as an emergency in a particular community may not register as an emergency for the purpose of meeting a legislative threshold, or vice versa.[57] Whether and which particular circumstances are deemed emergencies in law has important implications for shaping the response.

Under the Emergencies Act, the Convoy, with its border blockades and unlawful occupation of the national capital, was considered a public order emergency. The emergency ended when the occupation and blockades ended. But in fact, the emergency was not so self-contained. The Convoy public order emergency was embedded within a public health emergency. The protests galvanised around a particular pandemic response measure, channelling broader resentment about perceived governmental overreach through pandemic response. The Convoy emergency was thus one smaller piece of the debate and contestation about a health emergency and its appropriate emergency response. For some Canadians, the pandemic was the emergency that necessitated governmental response, while for others it was the governmental response itself that presented the emergency.

The public order emergency was also embedded in the much broader climate emergency. The Convoy is part of a pattern of right-wing populist movements characterised by economic marginalisation, social anxiety and distrust in political institutions.[58] Specifically, in the case of the Convoy, its origins are closely linked to federal climate mitigation laws. The main organisers of the Convoy were a domestic off-shoot of the international Yellow Vest Movement, who previously organised a national trucker protest against federal greenhouse gas reduction measures.[59] The Convoy movement remains active in relation to climate-amplified events. In the summer of 2023, a branch of the Convoy showed up to a wildfire evacuation zone to protect property, in conflict with law enforcement.[60] For this group, the climate emergency is not the warming climate, but rather the accompanying governmental overreach that threatens their identities and the economic status quo.

Even a seemingly straight-forward and contained emergency – the occupation of Ottawa and border blockades – raises important questions about how to define emergencies. A key objective of legislation is to create social order, which is achieved in part by fixing concepts through definitions. Emergency legislation must necessarily narrow our understanding of emergencies in order to mobilise a special, coordinated response. And yet what counts as an emergency is inevitably contested and dependent on a constellation of interacting social, economic,

[57] Rachel Luft writes that for marginalised communities a 'disaster' is more a matter of degree rather than the 'on-off switch' that is usually perceived by government decision-makers. See R Luft, 'Beyond Disaster Exceptionalism' (2009) 61 *American Quarterly* 499, 506–507.

[58] POEC Report Vol 2 (n 2) 73–77.

[59] ibid 81–82.

[60] J McElroy, 'Convoy protest highlights the different levels of disagreement in Shuswap wildfire' (*CBC News*, 24 August 2023) www.cbc.ca/news/canada/british-columbia/shuswap-convoy-negotiations-analysis-1.6947228.

health-, and environmental forces. These complex dynamics cannot be fully captured in a legislative definition.

D. Emergency Management is not a Closed Loop

The final limitation of emergency legislation again flows from the above, since the way an emergency is framed affects the framing of its response. Both emergency legislation and emergency management, more generally, conceive of emergency as an exceptional, discrete, time-bound, external event (a hazard, threat or triggering incident). Emergency management practice consists of a continuous pattern of governance activities from prevention, to preparedness, to response, to recovery, and back again to prevention.[61] Emergency legislation, generally speaking, encodes this cycle (or a version of it), looping around the extreme event as aberration and focusing on how to prepare for this event, how to respond to it, how to recover from it and how to mitigate future damage from a similar event.

As critical scholars have observed, the emergency management cycle functions as a self-contained loop, pivoting around the emergency event and its most immediate causes and effects.[62] This cycle does not provoke assessment of conditions that have been accepted as normal or the deeper drivers that produced the emergency. Terry Cannon observes that this narrow margin of practice for emergency managers is likely 'because it is difficult to change power systems that are largely responsible for people being vulnerable [and so] organisations have "mental models" (cultures) that enable them to operate without attempting to make fundamental changes'.[63] Framed as the external event and managed through a closed-loop emergency management practice, there is no opening to address challenges that arise outside of this model.[64] This is despite the fact that decades of disaster research has emphasised the deeper factors generating conditions of vulnerability: e.g. the social systems that create and sustain economic inequality, or the racial and gender discrimination that puts different groups of people at risk.[65] Yet these are the background conditions that, from within the emergency management cycle, are generally accepted as normal. … and thus not within the remit of emergency management law and practice.

[61] See, eg, DM Neal, 'Reconsidering the Phases of Disaster' (1997) 15 *Intl J Mass Emergencies & Disasters* 239.

[62] S Bandopadhyay, *All is Well: Catastrophe and the Making of the Normal State* (Oxford University Press, 2022) 28.

[63] T Cannon, 'Disasters, Climate Change and the Significance of "Culture"' in F Krüger, G Bankoff, T Cannon, B Orlowski and ELF Shipper (eds), *Cultures and Disasters: Understanding Cultural Framings in Disaster Risk Reduction* (Routledge, 2015) 101, relying on and adapting: B Ramalingam, *Aid on the Edge of Chaos: Rethinking International Cooperation in a Complex World* (Oxford University Press, 2013).

[64] Jasanoff (n 42) 239.

[65] T Cannon, 'What Must be Done to Rescue the Concept of Vulnerability?' in G Bankoff and D Hilhorst (eds), *Why Vulnerability Still Matters* (Routledge, 2022) 69 (and sources cited therein).

By way of example, official discourse around the use of the Emergencies Act has largely focused on the Convoy's blockades and occupation as the extreme event and problem to be managed. Unsurprisingly, then, analysis of the event understood in these terms produces specific answers: reform to policing practices,[66] better protocols for governments consulting each other when a threat is building or unfolding,[67] or perhaps broader reforms such as redrawing police jurisdictions in the national capital.[68] But the emergency management cycle does not admit analysis of deeper, systemic issues, such as experiences of economic insecurity and deep mistrust of government institutions, or whether the constitutional status quo of Canadian federalism is up to the task of addressing the multi-jurisdictional phenomenon of emergencies.

In sum, emergency legislation is inherently limited and imperfect. Such legislation addresses previous emergencies and not the unknown future; it presumes institutional capacity and competence to address emergencies; it attempts to reduce the complexity and contestation of what constitutes an emergency; and it narrows our analytical gaze to discrete, isolated events and not the underlying systemic conditions that we have accepted as normal. All of these are features, not flaws, of emergency legislation.

Jurists and scholars must be aware of this mismatch between legal framing and social reality, but we must not learn the wrong lessons. When faced with this misalignment, one response might be to champion the conventional approach to emergency law, one that grants sweeping discretion to the executive branch to deal with the unpredictability, complexity, vagueness of definition, and underlying drivers of emergencies. Another response might be to try to match emergency complexity with legislative complexity.

But these, I argue, are not the lessons we should take from the 2022 invocation of the Canadian Emergencies Act. Instead, I argue that our attention to the inevitable limitations and imperfections of emergency legislation requires jurists and scholars to understand the role of emergency legislation differently. Emergency legislation can and should scaffold the rule-of-law project.

IV. SCAFFOLDING EMERGENCY: RESILIENCE AND THE RULE OF LAW

To recap, Section II showed that deliberate, measured emergency legislation is possible and that Canada's Emergencies Act is perhaps an exemplary approach. Section III illustrated, however, that even seemingly straight-forward emergencies pose real challenges for such detailed emergency legislation because the

[66] Roach (n 47); R Diab, 'The Real Lesson of the Freedom Convoy "Emergency": Canada Needs a Public Order Policing Act' (2022) 70 *Criminal Law Quarterly* 230.

[67] D Newman, 'Constitutional Dimensions of the Consultation and Accountability Systems within Canada's Emergencies Act' (2023) 46 *Manitoba Law Journal* 101, 106–107.

[68] Roach (n 47) 205–207.

complexity of emergencies on the ground does not map onto the tidy framework for emergency management reflected in emergency legislation. This section argues that emergency legislation should not try to accurately and comprehensively reflect the complexity of emergencies as they unfold in real life. Instead, legislators should strive to embed rule-of-law commitments into their emergency legislation. The result will be that such legislation will not perfectly track the reality of emergencies (as such a goal is not attainable). Instead, it will do something much more important: scaffold the rule-of-law project, which inevitably comes under strain in times of crisis.

A. Rule of Law as Public Justification

Many scholars and jurists take emergency powers to be subject to less-than fulsome rule-of-law requirements.[69] Indeed for some, the role of emergency legislation is precisely to release the executive from rule-of-law obligations in order to enable a swift and effective response to the threat. Civil liberties may be temporarily curtailed in order to allow for necessary emergency measures. While scholars readily contest when resort to such exceptional emergency powers is necessary, most accept that – in principle – some situations will warrant the use of this type of exceptional power.

In contrast, David Dyzenhaus argues that we should understand emergency powers as part of the same rule-of-law project as all exercises of public power in a democratic society. While emergencies may require special measures, he argues that these should never be exempt from everyday rule-of-law protections, such as the right to due process and access to independent judges for review of executive action.[70] He reasons that, even in emergencies, public officials will feel compelled to claim they act with legal authority (e.g. redefining an act as something other than torture). So the question, then, is whether this claim to legal authority comes with substantive rule-of-law protections or whether it is, in the words of Justice Sullivan, only a 'thin veneer of legality',[71] meaning that although there are legal requirements, 'these are not substantive enough to give the affected individuals any real protection'.[72] For instance, emergency legislation that delegates to the executive the power to take all measures believed necessary to respond to the emergency risks creating a veneer of legality. A court or tribunal, upon review, could uphold a measure as legal merely because the

[69] They often blend empirical rationales (eg, historical practice) with normative arguments. See eg Gross and Aoláin (n 11).

[70] D Dyzenhaus, *The Constitution of Law: Legality in a Time of Emergency* (Cambridge University Press, 2006). See p 13 for a fuller description of the concept of the rule of law he has in mind.

[71] D Dyzenhaus, 'Preventive Justice and the Rule of Law Project' in A Ashworth, L Zedner and P Tomlin (eds), *Prevention and the Limits of Criminal Law* (Oxford University Press, 2013) 98.

[72] ibid 99.

executive subjectively held the belief that a measure was necessary, contrary to evidence. Such a finding reveals the veneer: the executive is validated as acting with legal authority (and thus granted a form of legitimacy) even as that legality offers no real protection for those affected by the executive action.

Dyzenhaus argues that, when faced with such a situation, jurists must resist the temptation to give the executive this veneer. Instead, they must make good on the executive's claim to act with legal authority, by upholding substantive rule-of-law constraints. As he writes, jurists should 'accept that the government and the legislature have committed themselves to ruling through the rule of law, and use that commitment as a legitimating basis for finding that the legislature must have intended real, not sham, controls'.[73] Even in a common law system that lacks a constitutionalised bill of rights, jurists have access to rule-of-law resources to give to these controls. These are the fundamental principles that make law *law* (rather than something else, like an order or command), often expressed, at least in part, through administrative law requirements of fair process, reasonableness, and equality before the law. On this view, the judge described in the scenario above should quash the emergency measure because the executive's determination was not a reasonable one, supported by the evidentiary record.[74]

This substantive conception of the rule of law goes hand-in-hand with what many have called a 'culture of justification'.[75] A culture of justification is one in which the exercise of political power is justified on the basis of fundamental, constitutional principles. On this view, the rule of law is not a system of commands, but rather an ongoing requirement to publicly justifying the exercise of public authority as fulfilling fundamental constitutional principles. These principles are constitutional in the sense that they are constitutive of legal authority.[76] This understanding of the rule of law as public justification is both aspiration and reality – a constant work-in-progress. Its reality is reflected in the Supreme Court of Canada's endorsement of a culture of justification as an essential part of upholding the rule of law through substantive review of administrative action.[77] It is aspirational in the sense that it is an ongoing commitment to a political project and there is always more work to be done to make public decision-making – from the quotidian to the existential – more fair, reasoned and equitable.

[73] ibid 99. He argues that this assumption should guide judicial reasoning all the way up to the point in which the legislature clearly and explicitly states that it wants the executive to operate outside the law. See also Dyzenhaus, *The Constitution of Law* (n 70) 217.

[74] D Dyzenhaus, 'Law as Justification: Etienne Mureinik's Conception of Legal Culture' (1998) 14 *South African Journal on Human Rights* 11, 18.

[75] Originating with E Mureinik, 'A Bridge to Where: Introducing the Interim Bill of Rights' (1994) 10 *South African Journal on Human Rights* 31.

[76] Dyzenhaus, *The Constitution of Law* (n 70) 218. For an elaboration of this conception of legality and its implications in the environmental context, see J Stacey, *The Constitution of the Environmental Emergency* (Hart Publishing, 2018).

[77] *Canada (Minister of Citizenship and Immigration) v Vavilov*, 2019 SCC 65 at para 14.

Dyzenhaus's argument has merit in the context of emergencies. That compliance with fundamental principles – and the requirement of public justification – is non-derogable flows, in Dyzenhaus's words, from 'the constitutional nature of the democratic state with its inherent commitment to the rule of law'.[78] Unlike specific constitutional or legislative protections, which are vulnerable to suspension or amendment in the face of emergency, compliance with the rule of law, on this view, cannot be suspended or circumvented. This is because to derogate from the requirement to publicly justify the exercise of public powers on the basis of core commitments is to cede the claim to act with legal authority.

This might appear to be a theory that sidelines legislative or even constitutional text because it does not make constitutional commitments contingent on specific constitutional or legislative provisions. But this is not the case. In fact, Dyzenhaus emphasises that this is a theory of legislation and not adjudication.[79] He describes the 'surplus value' that legislation creates by translating public policy into public, general, prospective standards that guide executive action.[80] While legislation can certainly be better or worse at promoting a culture of justification, it is this act of translation that brings into being the possibility of rule-of-law protections described above. Yet Dyzenhaus cautions that 'it is a mistake to suppose that the culture of justification kicks in after a statute has been enacted. A wise parliament is a reason-demanding institution, one which does not delegate entirely the task of making a legal regime human-rights- and rule-of-law-compliant to courts'.[81]

For Dyzenhaus, the legislature plays a crucial role in generating the kind of institutional creativity that is needed to sustain the rule-of-law project in complex societies. Within this theoretical framing, specialised tribunals, innovative oversight bodies, and human-rights-promoting parliamentary institutions, as examples, all play essential roles in promoting a culture of justification. Indeed, this institutional creativity, he argues, is essential to upholding the culture of justification through emergencies because of the judiciary's long-standing record of undue deference to the executive in times of crisis.[82] It is the legislature which plays the principal role in designing and rearranging public institutions that can hold one another to account by compelling public justification even when faced with secrecy, urgency, complexity and other barriers to meaningful judicial oversight.

[78] D Dyzenhaus, 'Deference, Security and Human Rights' in B Goold and L Lazarus (eds), *Security and Human Rights* (Hart Publishing, 2007) 125, 127.

[79] Dyzenhaus, 'Law as Justification' (n 74) 21.

[80] Dyzenhaus, 'Preventive Justice and the Rule of Law Project' (n 71) 96. Here the reference to Fuller's King Rex parable is apparent, if not explicit. See LL Fuller, *The Morality of Law: Revised Edition* (Yale University Press, 1969) ch 2.

[81] Dyzenhaus, 'Preventive Justice and the Rule of Law Project' (n 71) 112.

[82] Dyzenhaus, 'Deference, Security and Human Rights' (n 78).

B. Scaffolding the Rule of Law

With this understanding of the rule of law in mind, I argue that we must regard emergency legislation as a kind of scaffolding for sustaining a culture of justification in an age of emergencies. The metaphor of scaffolding extends the notion of cathedral thinking often used in advocacy around the climate emergency. As described by Friberg,[83]

> [t]he concept of cathedral thinking traditionally refers to the far-reaching visions of architects and builders in the Middle Ages who would commence work fully aware that they would not live to see the project's completion … The concept thus signals the need for extensive visions and a commitment to long-term implementation.

In her powerful remarks to the European Parliament in 2019, climate activist Greta Thunberg made this connection.[84] For her, cathedral thinking represents the need for a collective effort in which every person has a role to play – in decarbonising society as in building a cathedral. And it also represents the fact that work must begin 'to lay the foundation' for a just transition without necessarily having a clear plan for 'how to build the ceiling' (or achieve climate justice).[85]

Extending on Thunberg's metaphor, it is the rule-of-law project – understood as the requirement of public justification – that is the cathedral. Within this rule-of-law project, the legislature's role is to put in place the scaffolding – the framework that supports and sustains the building and maintenance of the culture of justification and its fundamental rule-of-law requirement of public justification. Where there are gaps or frailties in the scaffolding, it is the role of every public official (every tribunal, every judge) to make the most of the scaffolding that does exist and not let that part of the cathedral crumble. The scaffolding (the legislation) is essential to building the cathedral, but it is secondary to the main objective: a constitutional system in which public power is exercised with democratic and legal authority.

Here is where, despite its limitations, the Emergencies Act offers an important positive example of emergency legislation as scaffolding for the rule-of-law project. Its combination of specific legislative standards in conjunction with layered forms of accountability promotes – rather than undermines – public justification for the use of emergency powers.

[83] A Friberg, 'On the need for (con) temporary utopias: Temporal reflections on the climate rhetoric of environmental youth movements' (2022) 31 *Time & Society* 48, citing to JE Rogers, 'Environmental leadership in a boundary-less world' (1994) 4 *Environmental Quality Management* 4, 1.

[84] G Thunberg, 'You Did Not Act in Time: Greta Thunberg's Full Speech to MPs' *The Guardian* (23 April 2019) www.theguardian.com/environment/2019/apr/23/greta-thunberg-full-speech-to-mps-you-did-not-act-in-time.

[85] ibid.

First, the triple-layer definition of emergency, described in Section 2, provides the sturdy structure of the scaffolding. The Act's definition means that the executive must be specific about the threats motivating the declaration of emergency. The federal government must publicly provide reasons for the declaration and have reasonable grounds for making it and for believing that the particular emergency measures are, in fact, necessary.[86]

Because the Emergencies Act definitions are specific – albeit imperfect – it could then be debated whether the reasons provided by the government (largely economic concerns) were both lawful and adequate for invoking the Emergencies Act. The ultimate tests for political and legal accountability for these public decisions – a federal election and the outcome of judicial review – have, at the time of writing not yet come to pass. When they do, the outcomes will be better informed by the contestation, debate and deliberation all set in motion by legislation that required public, reasoned decisions for invoking emergency measures.

Like scaffolding, the Emergencies Act contains many layers of accountability. As with scaffolding, having multiple layers proved important: not all of these mechanisms worked well – but some did. First, the required parliamentary vote to ratify the declaration of public order emergency brought some level of transparency to the declaration (which in many jurisdictions would be a closed-door executive decision, protected by rules of privilege). But it was not a free vote, and members of parliament were subject to party discipline if they did not vote along party lines.[87] While there was some measure of publicity and debate, this did not constitute oversight in the parliament's full representative democratic form.[88]

The Act requires further parliamentary oversight in the form of a mandatory parliamentary committee to review the 'exercise of powers and the performance of duties and functions pursuant to a declaration of emergency'.[89] The language of the provision suggests that the committee's intended role was to meet for the duration of any emergency in order to debate and suggest amendments to the specific emergency measures while they were in effect.[90] In this case, the Parliamentary Review Committee was slow to get moving,[91] confused about its

[86] SOR/2022-20. Scaffolding can always be improved. See NC Lazar, 'What's "Necessary" Under the Emergencies Act' (2023) 46 *Manitoba Law Journal* 53 and H Kong 'Thresholds, Powers and Accountability in the Emergencies Act' (2023) 46 *Manitoba Law Journal* 41 for specific reforms that would strengthen these requirements.

[87] Canada HC Deb 21 February 2022, vol 151, 2882–83.

[88] Newman (n 67) 108.

[89] Emergencies Act, RSC 1985, c 22 (4th Supp), s 62.

[90] See discussion by the Parliamentary Committee on the scope of its role, and specifically the comments by Mr Philippe Hallée (Law Clerk and Parliamentary Counsel for the Senate): Special Joint Committee on the Declaration of Emergency, 'Evidence' (Parliament of Canada, 29 March 2022) 1840 www.parl.ca/documentviewer/en/44-1/DEDC/meeting-3/evidence.

[91] Its first meeting was 14 March 2022, four weeks after the emergency declaration was revoked. Parliament of Canada, 'Special Joint Committee on the Declaration of Emergency: Meetings' www.parl.ca/Committees/en/DEDC/Meetings.

role,[92] and prone to partisanship.[93] More than two years after the emergency orders were lifted, the committee had yet to issue a public report.

Further, the Emergencies Act requires an inquiry 'into the circumstances that led to the declaration being issued and the measures taken for dealing with the emergency',[94] which must yield a report within a year of the emergency's end. This was a requirement that was thrown into the Emergencies Act late in the legislative process and with no clearly articulated purpose in the legislative record.[95] And yet, the inquiry was public, independent and timely.[96] The federal government fully complied – even going beyond what was strictly required by the legislation.[97] Ottawa residents and business owners felt heard. Moreover, the Convoy organisers – folks with extreme political views and deep mistrust of government – also participated fully, seemingly feeling that this was a process they could trust. While the inquiry faced some criticism that it was too soft on the federal government, its work was generally well received.[98]

The inquiry resulted in a comprehensive and public accounting of the events and an initial assessment of government response. It found shortcomings on the part of nearly all government actors. It concluded that given how the events unfolded, the use of the Emergencies Act was justified – though not overwhelmingly so[99] – and that some of the measures were not well tailored to the needs of the situation.[100] Furthermore, the inquiry circled the closed loop of emergency management; that is, it focused its recommendations on immediate reforms to policing and emergency response.[101] But there were also hints at systemic issues, such as failed federalism,[102] factors driving right-wing populism,[103] and the need to grapple with mis- and disinformation.[104] In this way, the inquiry sowed seeds

[92] Special Joint Committee on the Declaration of Emergency, 'Evidence' (n 90).

[93] S Wright Allen, '"Get cracking': joint committee reviewing emergency powers should not get 'bogged down' debating scope, experts say' *The Hill Times* (1 April 2022) www.hilltimes.com/story/2022/04/01/get-cracking-joint-committee-reviewing-emergency-powers-should-not-get-bogged-down-debating-scope-experts-say/230096/.

[94] Emergencies Act, RSC 1985, c 22 (4th Supp), s 63.

[95] Canada HC Deb 25 April 1988, vol 151, 14766.

[96] The inquiry was given the scope and powers available under the federal *Inquiries Act*, which was not explicitly required by the Emergencies Act, but was important to the inquiry's legitimacy: PC 2022-392, (2022) C Gaz II.

[97] According to the inquiry this was only the fourth time out of 371 federal inquiries that cabinet confidence was waived: POEC Report Vol 1 (n 5) 17.

[98] See eg B Lilley, 'Lilley Unleashed: Emergencies Act was justified according to commission' *Toronto Sun* (17 February 2023) torontosun.com/news/lilley-unleashed-emergencies-act-was-justified-according-to-commission.

[99] POEC Report Vol 1 (n 5) 217 (stating the threshold was met), and in his public statement on the release of the report, Rouleau stated, 'I do not consider the factual basis for it to be overwhelming': Public Order Emergency Commission, 'Webcast of Commissioner's Public Statement' publicorderemergencycommission.ca.

[100] POEC Report Vol 1 (n 5) 233-4 (designation of protected places), 236–37 (border measures).

[101] ibid 251–60 (Recommendations # 1-27).

[102] ibid 175.

[103] POEC Report Vol 2 (n 2) 74–77.

[104] ibid 77-80; POEC Report Vol 1 (n 5) 265 (Recommendation #53).

for a wider conversation, rather than closing the book on this use of emergency powers.

Review by independent judges plays an essential (though insufficient) role in sustaining the rule-of-law project. The scaffolding provided by the Emergencies Act facilitates robust judicial review, which in the Convoy case ensured that the executive complied with the statutory mandate and the principles of legality. Protesters and civil liberty organisations challenged the declaration of emergency and emergency orders on the basis that they did not comply with the Emergencies Act and were unconstitutional. The Federal Court agreed, ruling that the declaration was unreasonable and that some of the emergency measures unjustifiably infringed on constitutionally protected rights.[105] At the time of writing, the case is before the Court of Appeal.

Like scaffolding, these layers of accountability seem to support one another by ratcheting up expectations for public justification. The Federal Court delayed its hearing so that the Court and the parties would benefit from the process and results of the inquiry. Considerable evidence from the inquiry was submitted to the Federal Court and, ultimately, relied upon by the judge.[106] The judge noted that, from the perspective of judicial review, the exercise of emergency powers under the Act 'attracts no special deference beyond that set out in *Vavilov*'.[107] Applying the ordinary and robust standard of review from *Vavilov* was only possible because of the features of the Act that required publicity, reason-giving and evidence-gathering through the inquiry. This is the kind of institutional cooperation in service of the rule-of-law project that Dyzenhaus and others have theorised. When put to the first test, the scaffolding of the Emergencies Act has proven to be quite strong.

V. CONCLUSION

This chapter has argued that Canada's first use of its central emergency legislation holds important lessons on the role of law in governing the use of emergency powers. The Act's distinctive approach demonstrates the vital role that emergency legislation can play in scaffolding the rule-of-law project even through crisis.

[105] *Canadian Frontline Nurses v Canada (Attorney General)* (2024) FC 42.

[106] *Canadian Frontline Nurses* (n 105) paras 80–82, 89 (for admission of evidence), paras 269, 290–291 (for the judge's reliance on portions of this evidence), though the reliance on this evidence is notably selective, particularly in the discussion of the evidence of threats of serious violence of which there was considerable testimony before the inquiry.

[107] ibid para 210. Though there are many indications in the judgment that this judge subscribed to a 'culture of authority' rather than a 'culture of justification', since there is little focus on the executive's justification; an emphasis on the judge's interpretation of the legislative text; and repeated statements that he would have honoured any 'unconstrained' discretion had it been granted by the legislation (eg paras 209 and 296).

As we confront an era of emergencies, jurists and legal scholars must attend to important insights from critical scholars who understand emergencies and disasters not as aberrations, but as features of society. Emergencies and disasters are complex phenomena stemming from deep-rooted causes and with disparate and disproportionate impacts across society. This chapter has argued that emergency legislation cannot and should not try to comprehensively and accurately map the social reality of emergencies.

Instead, emergency legislation can and should scaffold the rule-of-law project. In emergencies, the commitment to the rule of law comes under strain. But emergency legislation need not and should not be enacted in times of emergencies. It can be considered and deliberated upon without the pressure of an extreme and urgent threat. Under such 'normal' circumstances it can be designed to scaffold the commitment to the rule of law: to require publicly justified exercises of emergency power and to create the institutions needed to sustain a culture of justification even (and perhaps especially) through the era of emergencies that we may now well be facing. As governments around the world consider how to govern through this era of emergencies, they would do well to follow the lead of Canada's Emergencies Act.

Part III

Migration

7

The Constitutional Implications of Emergency Measures in European Migration and Asylum Law

SALVATORE FABIO NICOLOSI

I. INTRODUCTION

THE CONCEPT OF 'emergency' has surfaced as a *leitmotif* in European Union (EU) law and policies, prompting academic attempts to sketch the contours of 'EU emergency law' as an expanding scholarly field. As highlighted by Bruno De Witte, this refers 'to the rules of primary and secondary EU law that serve to address *sudden* threats to the core values and structures of the Union and its Member States'.[1] Scholars have also mapped a growing process of 'crisification' of EU policy-making aimed at identifying appropriate fora and mechanisms as well as ad hoc procedures for managing the effects of an emergency or a crisis in the EU.[2] This has contributed to a view of the EU polity as operating 'in crisis mode permanently'.[3]

The EU Treaties do not provide an unequivocal definition of crisis or emergency.[4] On the contrary, the EU legal framework contains 'a complex and disparate set of rules found in many different parts of primary and secondary law, supplemented by institutional practice and judicial interpretations'.[5] A common feature of this set of rules is the goal of addressing unforeseen situations of necessity for which

[1] B de Witte, 'Guest Editorial: EU emergency law and its impact on the EU legal order' (2022) 59 *Common Market Law Review* 3.

[2] M Rhinard, 'The Crisification of Policy-making in the European Union' (2019) 57 *Journal of Common Market Studies* 616.

[3] F Schimmelfennig, 'European integration (theory) in times of crisis. A comparison of the euro and Schengen crises' (2018) 25 *Journal of European Public Policy* 969.

[4] The terms 'crisis' and 'emergency' will be used interchangeably, as they both convey the idea of an urgent need to take action, see Oxford Advanced Learner's Dictionary, www.oxfordlearnersdictionaries.com/.

[5] De Witte (n 1) 5. For an analysis of the 'emergency constitution' of the EU, see SF Nicolosi, 'Emergency Legislation in European Union Law' in T van den Brink and V Passalacqua (eds), *Balancing Unity and Diversity in EU Legislation* (Edward Elgar, 2024) 61.

no adequate legal response exists.[6] Hence, as has been argued, 'situations of emergency under EU law have to be read through the diversified system of Union competences around which all policy areas are organised'.[7]

The EU's growing role in crisis management is confirmed by the plethora of mechanisms and legislative frameworks that have been devised over the past years to address emergencies in various areas subject to EU competence. These mechanisms include a sophisticated toolbox of legislation and soft law measures that have been adopted in response to various situations of emergency. Without any claim to exhaustiveness, more recent examples of these mechanisms include the proposal to establish a Single Market Emergency Instrument (SMEI)[8] or the contingency plan for ensuring food supply and food security in times of crisis.[9] These initiatives complement existing frameworks, including the EU Civil Protection Mechanism,[10] the Emergency Support Instrument (ESI),[11] the EU Solidarity Fund[12] and the EU Integrated Political Crisis Response Arrangements.[13] Most of these mechanisms are emergency tools rooted in ordinary legal bases rather than in dedicated emergency treaty provisions. This can be explained by the fact that the EU Treaties contain relatively few explicit references to emergency procedures. An example is offered by the safeguard clauses in Articles 122 and 222 of the Treaty on the Functioning of the European Union (TFEU),[14] which allow for coordinated responses in cases of severe difficulties or terrorism. However, the proliferation of these mechanisms in secondary legislation confirms that the EU often resorts to its general competences and ordinary legislative procedures to create emergency response measures. This is evident in areas like market stability and public health, where instruments, such as the SMEI, rely on Article 114 TFEU as one of the common legal bases for the Single Market. In other words, the scarcity of treaty-based emergency provisions

[6] In this regard see PM Rodríguez, 'A Missing Piece of European Emergency Law: Legal Certainty and Individuals' Expectations in the EU Response to the Crisis' (2016) 12 *European Constitutional Law Review* 265, 268.

[7] Nicolosi (n 5) 64.

[8] European Commission, Proposal for a Regulation of the European Parliament and of the Council establishing a Single Market emergency instrument and repealing Council Regulation No (EC) 2679/98, COM(2022) 459, 19 September 2022.

[9] European Commission, Communication to the European Parliament, the Council, the European Economic and Social Committee and the Committee of the Regions, 'Contingency plan for ensuring food supply and food security in times of crisis' COM(2021) 689 final, 12 November 2021.

[10] Regulation (EU) 2021/836 of the European Parliament and of the Council of 20 May 2021 amending Decision No 1313/2013/EU on a Union Civil Protection Mechanism [2021] OJ L185/1–22.

[11] Council Regulation 2016/369 of 15 March 2016 on the provision of emergency support within the Union [2016] OJ L70/1–6.

[12] Regulation (EU) No 661/2014 of the European Parliament and of the Council of 15 May 2014 amending Council Regulation (EC) No 2012/2002 establishing the European Union Solidarity Fund [2014] OJ L189/143–154.

[13] Council Implementing Decision (EU) 2018/1993 of 11 December 2018 on the EU Integrated Political Crisis Response Arrangements [2018] OJ L320/28–34.

[14] Consolidated version of the Treaty on the European Union (TEU) and the Treaty on the Functioning of the European Union (TFEU) [2012] OJ C 326/1–390.

necessitates the flexible use of ordinary legal frameworks to guarantee a pragmatic approach to crisis management.

The narrative of emergency has become a distinct feature of EU migration and asylum policies, as epitomised by the crowded migrant hotspot[15] of Moria on Lesbos and the stream of case law by the European Court of Human Rights (ECtHR) on the living conditions therein.[16] This narrative has left its imprint on the reform of the Common European Asylum System (CEAS).[17] This reform, reignited by the New Pact on Migration and Asylum of 2020[18] and endorsed by the European Parliament in April 2024[19] and by the Council in May 2024,[20] coupled with other legislative initiatives, such as the reform of the Schengen Borders Code,[21] confirms that the EU institutions have used the crisis narrative 'as an instrument of political mobilisation and legal reform,'[22] in an attempt to prevent the centrifugal thrusts of Member States' unilateral responses.[23]

Lively debates have arisen about the rhetoric of emergency and the narrative of migration as an emergency for Europe.[24] Equal attention has been paid to emergency law-making concerning migration,[25] but more awareness is necessary about the implications of this emergency-driven law-making from a constitutional and institutional perspective. This would contribute to identifying the potential benefits and pitfalls of adopting emergency-response mechanisms and their impact on the constitutional fabric of EU law.

To this end, after designing a typology of the main emergency response mechanisms adopted at the EU level for the governance of migration and asylum (Section II), this chapter explores three core implications that are relevant at

[15] Regulation (EU) 2019/1896 of the European Parliament and of the Council of 13 November 2019 on the European Border and Coast Guard and repealing Regulations (EU) No 1052/2013 and (EU) 2016/1624 [2019] OJ L295/1–131, Art 2 (23), defines 'hotspot area' as 'an area created at the request of the host Member State in which the host Member State, the Commission, relevant Union agencies and participating Member States cooperate, with the aim of managing an existing or potential disproportionate migratory challenge characterised by a significant increase in the number of migrants arriving at the external borders'.

[16] See, eg, *H.A. and others v Greece*, Appls Nos 4892/18 and 4920/18, 13 June 2023.

[17] See more specifically Nicolosi, 'Addressing a Crisis through Law: EU Emergency Legislation and its Limits in the Field of Asylum' (2021) 17 *Utrecht Law Review* 19.

[18] European Commission, Communication to the European Parliament, the Council, the European Economic and Social Committee and the Committee of the Regions on a New Pact on Migration and Asylum, COM(2020) 609 final, 23 September 2020.

[19] European Parliament, Plenary Session of 10 April 2024, Press Release at www.europarl.europa.eu/news/en/press-room/20240408IPR20290/meps-approve-the-new-migration-and-asylum-pact.

[20] Council of the EU, Press Release (14 May 2024) at www.consilium.europa.eu/en/press/press-releases/2024/05/14/the-council-adopts-the-eu-s-pact-on-migration-and-asylum/.

[21] Regulation (EU) 2024/1717 of the European Parliament and of the Council of 13 June 2024 amending Regulation (EU) 2016/399 on a Union Code on the rules governing the movement of persons across borders [2024] OJ L/2024/1717, entered into force in July 2024.

[22] G Campesi, 'Defining "Crisis" in Migration Governance: A Critical Legal Mapping of EU Crisis Response Mechanisms' (2024) 26 *European Journal of Migration and Law* 32.

[23] See in this regard Nicolosi (n 5).

[24] See, eg, D Siegel, 'The "Crises' of Lesbos" (2021) 4 *Utrecht Law Review* 10.

[25] See Campesi (n 22) and Nicolosi (n 17).

the constitutional level. These concern, respectively, the balance of powers (Section III), the legislative dynamics (Section IV) and fundamental rights (Section V). The chapter will then devise some possible corrections and safeguards that could contain or prevent any risks of constitutional drift determined by emergency response mechanisms (Section VI) and finally offer some conclusions (Section VII).

II. A TYPOLOGY OF EMERGENCY RESPONSE MECHANISMS IN EUROPEAN MIGRATION LAW

A definition of what may count as an emergency is important for determining what types of measures can be adopted. However, insofar as they involve unforeseen circumstances, emergencies by their nature escape strict definitions and are often seen as 'inherently indefinable'.[26] Scholars have stressed that in the areas of migration and asylum management, 'what counts as a crisis […] is defined in a range of radically different ways in existing EU legal instruments'.[27] Nonetheless, in these specific areas of EU law, two complex 'situations of necessity' have been associated with a crisis. In general, these can be considered either as situations for which the legal framework has detailed specific legislative exceptions, such as derogations from the ordinary legislation, or situations which allow for a particular procedure aiming at the adoption or implementation of an ad hoc instrument that can set aside the ordinary legislation.

The first category of situations includes events or circumstances that constitute or risk bringing about a serious threat to public policy or internal security in a Member State, as in the case of the Schengen Borders Code,[28] but also many provisions of the Common European Asylum System (CEAS).[29] The second category refers to the sudden inflow of third country nationals, as established in Article 78(3) TFEU or the Temporary Protection Directive (TPD).[30] These broad categories of circumstances have been regulated through various measures adopted over the past years as responses to migration crises, namely 'a set

[26] K Lovey, *Emergencies in Public Law. The Legal Politics of Containment* (Cambridge University Press, 2016) 60.

[27] Campesi (n 22) 39.

[28] See, eg, Regulation (EU) 2016/399 of the European Parliament and of the Council of 9 March 2016 on a Union Code on the rules governing the movement of persons across borders (Schengen Borders Code) [2016] OJ L 77/1–52, Arts 25 (1) and 28 (1).

[29] For a synoptical overview of these provisions, see European Council on Refugees and Exiles (ECRE), 'Derogating from EU Asylum Law in the Name of "Emergencies": The Legal Limits Under EU Law', *Legal Note* (June 2020) www.ecre.org/wp-content/uploads/2020/06/LN_6-final.pdf.

[30] Council Directive 2001/55/EC of 20 July 2001 on minimum standards for giving temporary protection in the event of a mass influx of displaced persons and on measures promoting a balance of efforts between Member States in receiving such persons and bearing the consequences thereof (hereinafter 'TPD') [2001] OJ L 212/12–23, Art 5.

of tools, including specific measures for deviating from ordinary migration and asylum governance procedures'.[31]

Emergency-response mechanisms in the form of derogations or specific legislative tools have been embedded in the governance of migration and asylum policies since at least the Treaty of Amsterdam.[32] Nonetheless, an emergency-driven approach was prompted by the 2015 Agenda on Migration,[33] which initiated a series of emergency response mechanisms resulting in a variety of instruments that are different in nature, scope and stage of advancement in the legislative process. Giuseppe Campesi advanced a classification of emergency mechanisms in the areas of migration and asylum into two generations, starting with the establishment of the Schengen Area, with a new generation adopted in the aftermath of the migratory pressure of 2015.[34]

However, a different typology of these emergency response mechanisms can be carved out from their nature and scope. As illustrated in the recapitulative Table 1 below, a broad distinction can be made between ad hoc instruments, on the one hand, and emergency clauses that have been included in many legislative instruments, on the other. Despite their heterogeneity, these mechanisms pursue a common goal, as they all allow temporary adaptations in the legal framework that make possible 'a swift and effective response capable of guaranteeing the continuance of the political system and a return to its regular functioning'.[35]

Table 1 A typology of emergency-response mechanisms

Category	Scope	Instrument
Emergency ad hoc instruments	Binding	▪ Temporary Protection Directive ▪ Relocation decisions ▪ Crisis regulation
	Non-binding	▪ Recommendation on an EU mechanism for preparedness and management of crises
Emergency clauses	Binding	▪ Schengen Borders Code ▪ Asylum Procedures Directive and Regulation ▪ Return Directive and recast Proposal
Externalisation measures	Non-binding	▪ EU-Turkey Statement ▪ Memorandum of Understanding EU–Tunisia ▪ Joint Declaration EU–Egypt ▪ Joint Declaration on the Strategic and Comprehensive Partnership with Jordan

[31] Campesi (n 22) 28.
[32] Treaty establishing the European Community (Consolidated version 1997) [1997] OJ C 340/173–306, Art 64.
[33] European Commission, 'A European Agenda on Migration' (Communication) COM(2015) 240, 13 May 2015.
[34] Campesi (n 22) 33 ff.
[35] Martín Rodríguez (n 6) 270.

Ad hoc instruments include legislative and non-legislative measures. The first category encompasses three different legislative instruments that address a situation of emergency determined by the large influx of third country nationals. The oldest EU law act dealing with large-scale displacement, namely the 2001 TPD, is one of these instruments. This directive defines temporary protection as a 'procedure of exceptional character to provide, in the event of a mass influx or imminent mass influx of displaced persons from third countries … immediate and temporary protection'[36] and was for the first time activated upon Russia's 2022 invasion of Ukraine.[37] A second set of instruments includes the two 2015 Council's Decisions on the relocation of asylum seekers from Greece and Italy. The Decisions were adopted as provisional measures under Article 78(3) TFEU and constitute an emergency-response mechanism setting out mandatory quotas to alleviate the disproportionate burden put on frontline States by the high number of asylum applications.[38]

Eventually, the emergency-driven approach was formalised in a specific Regulation addressing situations of crisis and force majeure in the field of migration and asylum, known as 'Crisis Regulation', adopted in the context of the new Pact on Migration and Asylum.[39] Significantly, one of the novelties of this Regulation is the introduction of a new type of situation that could qualify as a 'situation of crisis', proposed in response to the Belarus–EU border crisis, which began in 2021. This refers to the instrumentalisation of migrants by a third country or non-state actor that 'encourages or facilitates the movement of third-country nationals or stateless persons to the external borders or to a Member State, with the aim of destabilising the Union or a Member State, and where such actions are liable to put at risk essential functions of a Member State, including the maintenance of law and order or the safeguard of its national security'.[40] Essentially, this Regulation, which will enter into force in 2026, creates a threefold legal regime to manage asylum and migration in

[36] TPD, Art 2 (a).

[37] Council Implementing Decision (EU) 2022/382 of 4 March 2022 establishing the existence of a mass influx of displaced persons from Ukraine within the meaning of Article 5 of Directive 2001/55/EC, and having the effect of introducing temporary protection [2022] OJ L 71/1–6. For more references see M Ineli-Ciger, 'Reasons for the activation of the temporary protection directive in 2022: A tale of double standards' in S Carrera and M Ineli-Ciger (eds), *EU Responses to the Large-Scale Refugee Displacement. An Analysis on the Temporary Protection Directive and Its Implications for the Future EU Asylum Policy* (European University Institute, 2023) 59.

[38] Council Decision 2015/1523 of 14 September 2015 establishing provisional measures in the area of international protection for the benefit of Italy and of Greece [2015] OJ L239/146; Council Decision 2015/1601 of 22 September establishing provisional measures in the area of international protection for the benefit of Italy and of Greece [2015] OJ L248/80. For a broader analysis see SF Nicolosi, 'Emerging Challenges of the Temporary Relocation Measures under EU Asylum Law' (2016) 41 *European Law Review* 338.

[39] Regulation (EU) 2024/1359 of the European Parliament and of the Council of 14 May 2024 addressing situations of crisis and force majeure in the field of migration and asylum and amending Regulation (EU) 2021/1147 [2024] OJ L 22 May 2024 [hereinafter 'Crisis Regulation'].

[40] Crisis Regulation (EU) 2024/1359, Art 1(4)(b).

three exceptional situations: a crisis determined by a mass influx, a crisis triggered by the instrumentalisation of migrants, and force majeure. These special regimes allow the Member States to sidestep the ordinary legal framework with a range of derogations including delaying the registration of applications, and adjusting procedures, including border procedures, and deadlines also in the context of transfers of asylum applicants to the responsible State under the new Asylum and Migration Management Regulation.[41] Despite referring to different situations, the Regulation generalises the nature of the emergency response, while the broad definitions, especially the reference to 'instrumentalisation', can lower the threshold for Member States to apply these emergency measures.[42]

The rise of the instrumentalisation of migrants as another situation of crisis illustrates the osmotic connection between the national and European dimensions of the governance of migration. Tracking many national developments at the borders of the EU, especially in Greece and the Baltic countries, the President of the European Commission, Ursula von der Leyen, referred in her 2021 State of the Union address to the instrumentalisation of migrants by Belarus as 'a hybrid attack to destabilise Europe',[43] and by the end of the year, the European Commission announced a package of legislative proposals and other measures addressing the issue of instrumentalisation,[44] including the Proposal for an ad hoc Regulation addressing situations of instrumentalisation in the field of migration and asylum.[45] This instrument aimed to set up an emergency procedure for migration and asylum management in cases of instrumentalisation of migrants by a third country.[46] However, in light of the negotiations for the overall reform of the CEAS and the failed attempt to agree on a Council's general approach on the Instrumentalisation Regulation, this instrument was later merged with the Crisis Regulation 2021/1147.

[41] Regulation (EU) 2024/1351 of the European Parliament and of the Council of 14 May 2024 on asylum and migration management, amending Regulations (EU) 2021/1147 and (EU) 2021/1060 and repealing Regulation (EU) No 604/2013 [2024] OJ L/1351. For an analysis of all the derogations established by the Crisis Regulation, see M Ineli-Ciger, 'Navigating the Labyrinth of Derogations: A Critical Look at the Crisis Regulation' (*EU Immigration and Asylum Law and Policy Blog*, 10 June 2024).

[42] In this sense see also V Apatzidou, 'Derogations in Exchange of Increased Responsibility: How Can This Fix the Broken Promise for More Solidarity in the EU?' (2024) 3 *European Journal of Migration and Law* 317, 330 ff.

[43] European Commission, 'State of the Union 2021, President von der Leyen's speech' of 15 September 2021, state-of-the-union.ec.europa.eu/state-union-2021_en.

[44] For more references see M Gkliati, 'Let's Call It What It Is: Hybrid Threats and Instrumentalisation as the Evolution of Securitisation in Migration Management' (2023) 8 *European Papers, Insight* 561.

[45] European Commission, Proposal of 14 December 2021 for a Regulation of the European Parliament and of the Council addressing situations of instrumentalization in the field of migration and asylum COM(2021) 890 final.

[46] See the critical comments by ECRE on the Crisis Regulation, May 2024, at ecre.org/comments-paper-regulation-on-addressing-situations-of-crisis-and-force-majeure-in-the-field-of-migration-and-asylum/.

The second category of ad hoc instruments includes a plethora of soft law measures of which the Recommendation on an EU mechanism for preparedness and management of crises related to migration is the most recent and noteworthy example.[47] This is complementary to the mechanism established under the new Crisis Regulation, as it aims to provide the European Commission with timely and updated information to determine the existence of a situation of crisis and offer a framework for a coordinated and preventive European approach.

Apart from these ad hoc instruments, the emergency toolbox includes several clauses integrated into various legislative acts in the broad areas of migration and asylum, including the Schengen Borders Code (Articles 25, 28 and 29); the Asylum Procedure Directive (Article 31 (3)) and the Return Directive (Article 18).[48] A notable characteristic of these clauses is the delineation of emergencies under conditions defined by significant threats to the essential values of public order and national security. These are values that are not defined in the Treaties and that the Court of Justice has framed in broad terms, leaving to the Member States' wide discretion in contextualising the possible threats.[49] Interestingly, as will be discussed in greater detail in Section 4, Member States have even invoked, though unsuccessfully, the national security clause *ex* Article 72 TFEU to derogate from the emergency legislation, namely the mentioned Relocations Decisions.[50]

The emergency narrative had the effect of broadening the application of these clauses. For instance, the recent amendment to the Schengen Borders Code has expanded the array of situations in which a serious threat to public policy or internal security in a Member State may be considered to arise. These situations range from terrorist attacks or threats thereof, and threats posed by serious organised crime, to large-scale public health emergencies, exceptional situations characterised by sudden large-scale unauthorised movements of third-country nationals between the Member States, putting a substantial strain on the overall resources and capacities of well-prepared competent authorities and which is likely to put at risk the overall functioning of the area without internal border control, and large-scale or high-profile international events.[51]

[47] Commission Recommendation (EU) 2020/1366 of 23 September 2020 on an EU mechanism for preparedness and management of crises related to migration C/2020/6469 [2020] OJ L 317/26–38.

[48] See respectively Schengen Borders Code; Directive 2013/32/EU of the European Parliament and of the Council of 26 June 2013 on common procedures for granting and withdrawing international protection (recast) [2013] OJ L 180,/60–95, Art 31 (3); Directive 2008/115/EC of the European Parliament and of the Council of 16 December 2008 on common standards and procedures in Member States for returning illegally staying third-country nationals [2008] OJ L 348/98–107. For a more complete overview of these clauses, see ECRE (n 29) 10–11.

[49] See, eg, Court of Justice, Case C-373/13 *HT v Land Baden-Württemberg*, ECLI:EU:C:2015:413, paras 78–79.

[50] Case C-715/17 *Commission v Poland, Hungary and the Czech Republic*, ECLI:EU:C:2020:257, para 70.

[51] Regulation (EU) 2024/1717, Art 25.

The new Asylum Procedure Regulation confirms the possible derogations in case 'a disproportionate number of third-country nationals or stateless persons make an application for international protection within the same period of time, making it unfeasible to conclude the admissibility procedure within the set time limits'. In such cases, the determining authority may extend the time limits.[52] The proposal to recast the Return Directive also keeps the emergency clause. This clause allows for extended periods for judicial review 'in situations where an exceptionally large number of third-country nationals to be returned places an unforeseen heavy burden on the capacity of the detention facilities of a Member State or on its administrative or judicial staff'.[53] The Member State has, however, a duty to inform the European Commission when resorting to the exceptional measures under this clause as well as when these measures have ceased. This duty of information is to be seen as a manifestation of the principle of loyal cooperation. In this regard, the last paragraph of the emergency clause prevents the Member States from derogating from their general obligation to take all appropriate measures to ensure the fulfilment of their obligations under the Directive (or future Regulation), thereby upholding the obligation under Article 4(3) TEU.[54]

This complex emergency response toolbox essentially provides procedures and conditions for the national authorities to derogate from ordinary procedures and legislation, thereby creating, as will be discussed in greater detail in Section 4, a sort of *lex specialis*. The proliferation of ad hoc instruments and clauses for addressing situations of emergency has constitutional implications, raising questions about institutional balance, legislative dynamics and impact on fundamental rights. These three aspects will be analysed in the following Sections.

It is nonetheless worth stressing that the growing trend towards the externalisation of migration controls exemplified by the recent deals concluded with third countries, such as Tunisia and Egypt,[55] can also be understood as part

[52] Regulation (EU) 2024/1348 of the European Parliament and of the Council of 14 May 2024 establishing a common procedure for international protection in the Union and repealing Directive 2013/32/EU [2024] OJ L 2024/1348, Art 35(2)(a).

[53] Proposal for a Regulation of the European Parliament and of the Council establishing a common system for the return of third-country nationals staying illegally in the Union, and repealing Directive 2008/115/EC of the European Parliament and the Council, Council Directive 2001/40/EC and Council Decision 2004/191/EC, COM(2025) 101 final, Art 47.

[54] On the principle of sincere cooperation, see extensively M Klamert, *The Principle of Loyalty in EU Law* (Oxford University Press, 2014).

[55] See respectively Memorandum of Understanding (MoU) on a strategic and comprehensive partnership between the EU and Tunisia, 16 July 2023, ec.europa.eu/commission/presscorner/detail/en/IP_23_3887; Joint Declaration on the Strategic and Comprehensive Partnership between the Arab Republic of Egypt and the European Union, 17 March 2024, at neighbourhood-enlargement.ec.europa.eu/news/joint-declaration-strategic-and-comprehensive-partnership-between-arab-republic-egypt-and-european-2024-03-17_en. For a critical analysis see E Xanthopoulou, 'Mapping EU Externalisation Devices through a Critical Eye' (2024) 26 *European Journal of Migration and Law* 108.

of the narrative of emergency. These deals continue and expand the rationale behind the 2016 EU–Turkey Deal,[56] namely reducing the pressure on the EU's external borders and dissuading asylum seekers and economic migrants from embarking on life-threatening journeys. The legal nature and scope of these 'deals' have been controversial and are still the subject of academic debates. But far from being considered formal agreements, these instruments constitute an example of the informalisation of the management of the EU's external borders to prevent the rise of situations of emergencies.[57]

III. THE BALANCE OF POWERS IN SITUATIONS OF MIGRATORY PRESSURE

A situation of emergency generally tilts the balance of powers by allowing authorities at various levels of governance to take urgent measures.[58] Within the EU legal order, adopting and implementing the emergency toolbox to govern migration and asylum shows twofold implications from the perspective of the balance of powers. On the one hand, it affects vertically the balance between the Union as a whole and its Member States; on the other hand, it influences horizontally the inter-institutional balance of powers.

Despite the criticism raised about its opaque normative contours,[59] the principle of institutional balance, introduced by the Court of Justice in its landmark decision in *Meroni*[60] as a principle requiring that each institution exercises its powers with due regard for the powers of the other institutions,[61] has been playing an overriding function of safeguarding against any abuse within the EU legal order.[62] The principle of institutional balance is enshrined in Article 13(2) TEU which states that each institution 'shall act within the limits of the powers conferred on it in the Treaties, and in conformity with the procedures, conditions and objectives set out in them'. The same Article confirms that mutual

[56] EU–Turkey Statement, Press Release (18 March 2016) available at www.consilium.europa.eu/en/press/press-releases/2016/03/18/eu-turkey-statement/.

[57] It is worth noting in this regard that the General Court, Case T-192/16 *NF v European Council*, ECLI:EU:T:2017:128, para 71, stated that the Statement 'cannot be regarded as a measure adopted by the European Council, or, moreover, by any other institution, body, office or agency of the European Union'. For a broader analysis see N Idriz and E Kassoti (eds), *The Informalisation of the EU's External Action in the Field of Migration and Asylum* (Springer, 2022).

[58] F Britos Bastos and A De Ruijter, 'Break or Bend in Case of Emergency?: Rule of Law and State of Emergency in European Public Health Administration' (2019) 10 *European Journal of Risk Regulation* 610. *Amplius*, see C Eckes, P Leino-Sandberg and AW Ghavanini (eds), *The Dynamics of Powers in the European Union* (Hart Publishing, 2024).

[59] See especially M Chamon, 'The Institutional Balance, an Ill-Fated Principle of EU Law?' (2015) 21 *European Public Law* 371.

[60] Case C-9/56 *Meroni*, ECLI:EU:C:1958:7, 152.

[61] See also Case C-70/88 *Parliament v Council*, ECLI:EU:C:1990:217, para 22.

[62] K Lenaerts and A Verhoeven, 'Institutional Balance as a Guarantee for Democracy in EU Governance' in C Joerges and R Dehousse (eds), *Good Governance in Europe's Integrated Market, Collected Courses of the Academy of European Law* (Oxford University Press, 2002) 34.

sincere cooperation helps maintain institutional balance, as the institutions share responsibility for the legal act, which is adopted through a spirit of loyal cooperation.

Apart from its inter-institutional dimension, the migratory pressure has contributed to reopening the debate about a wider notion of institutional balance as encompassing the vertical relation between the Union and the Member States.[63] In *Région Wallone*, the European Court of Justice expressly mentioned that the institutional balance provided for by the Treaties also governs the conditions under which the Member States participate in the functioning of the supranational institutions.[64] Nonetheless, in a significant series of cases, the Court has lately denied the vertical direction of institutional balance,[65] maintaining that this is to be seen as separate from the principle of conferral or attribution of powers which is better suited to explain the dynamics between the Member States and the Union.

However, as mentioned in Section I, the scant references to emergency competences in EU primary law have prompted the EU institutions to be flexible in the exercise of their powers, resulting in an array of secondary legislation dealing with situations of emergency. While, as has been pointed out, 'every allocation of crisis response competence affects the institutional environment',[66] the flexible use of institutional powers and competences in the areas of migration and asylum management has also contributed to a 'process of power redistribution'.[67] As will be illustrated in the following sub-section, this has significant implications for the vertical institutional balance, since it essentially calibrates the role of the supranational entity in favour of the Member States' stances.

A. The Vertical Balance of Powers

The intergovernmental imprint has been a distinct feature of the migration and asylum policies.[68] While the Treaty of Lisbon has significantly reduced the intergovernmental nature of these policies, the migratory pressure of the past years has determined an intergovernmental shift in the governance of migratory emergencies. In general, the stronger institutional oversight placed by the most recent reforms at the EU level has not prevented the Member States from playing a major role when confronted by situations of emergency

[63] This view was originally proposed by E Vos, 'The Rise of Committees' (1997) 3 *European Law Journal* 210–29, 223; *contra*, see Chamon (n 59) 378.

[64] Case C-95/97 *Région wallonne v Commission*, ECLI:EU:C:1997:184, para 6.

[65] See, eg, Case C-38/06 *Commission v Portugal*, ECLI:EU:C:2010:108, para 49. For more references see Chamon (n 59) 379–380.

[66] Campesi (n 22) 44.

[67] ibid, 45.

[68] See more extensively T Givens and A Luedtke, 'EU Immigration Policy: From Intergovernmentalism to Reluctant Harmonization' in TA Börzel and RA Cichowski (eds), *The State of the European Union, 6: Law, Politics, and Society* (Oxford University Press, 2003) 291.

that have effects on the whole Union. An illustration of this power redistribution is offered by the role of the European Council.

Since at least the Presidency's Conclusions of June 2015,[69] the European Council has been playing a major role in the governance of migration,[70] boosting the rise of an emergency-driven approach which steered the process of reform of the CEAS and the Schengen Area. This approach led to the Council's adoption of the Relocation Decisions under Article 78(3) TFEU, based on the points decided at the European Council of June 2015.

Furthermore, the European Council's expansive interpretation of its mandate under Article 15 TEU – to define the political agenda and priorities for the Union as a whole – has frequently led it to act beyond the formal framework established by the Treaties. A distinct feature of this approach is the reliance on 'informality', both as a departure from conventional institutional structures and through the use of international legal instruments not governed by EU law. A notable example is the 2016 EU–Turkey Deal, which exemplifies this informal approach. Additionally, since 2015, the vast majority of the more than 25 European Council's Conclusions addressing migration emphasise the importance of enhancing cooperation with third countries and strengthening border management. This emphasis was reiterated at the European Council summit on 17 October 2024, where leaders called for 'intensifying cooperation with third countries of origin'.[71]

The European Council has been acting as the control room of EU emergency policy-making, explaining, on the one hand, that in times of emergency, European leaders aim to demonstrate to citizens that the crisis is being managed at the highest political level.[72] On the other hand, this dominant role entails a shift to inter-governmentalism as the preferred mode of governance during emergencies. In other words, in times of emergencies, especially if these affect core political affairs such as asylum or migration, the Member States tend to retain control of the integration process by adopting ad hoc instruments or triggering emergency clauses that allow the Member States to deviate from the ordinary EU legislation.

[69] European Council, Conclusions, EUCO 22/15, 26 June 2015.

[70] For more references see S Smeets and N Zaun, 'What is intergovernmental about the EU's "(new) intergovernmentalist" turn? Evidence from the Eurozone and asylum crises' (2020) 44 *West European Politics* 852.

[71] European Council, Conclusions, EUCO 25/24, 17 October 2024. For references see also Lucas Rasche, 'The EU needs a new migration diplomacy' (Policy Brief, Hertie School Delors Centre, 7 February 2023) at www.delorscentre.eu/en/publications/migration-diplomacy. It is worth stressing that this trend towards informality is common to other policy areas, see B De Witte, 'Euro crisis Responses and the EU Legal Order: Increased Institutional Variation or Constitutional Mutation?' (2015) 11 *European Constitutional Law Review* 448.

[72] See in this regard the Statement by the former European Council's President Donald Tusk, Press Release 593/17, 17 October 2017, www.consilium.europa.eu/en/press/press-releases/2017/10/17/tusk-invitation-letter-euco/pdf.

This is visible both in the proliferation of emergency clauses for reasons of public security or public order in Member States, and their frequent invocation. As has been stressed by Pablo Martín Rodríguez, instead of endowing EU institutions with more powers, these measures 'enable a Member State to escape from its EU commitments'.[73] This was not, as claimed by Giuseppe Campesi,[74] exclusively a distinct feature of the first-generation mechanisms, such as the 2006 Schengen Borders Code, but is still visible in the recent governance of migration and asylum policies.[75] The governments of the Member States, acting collectively within the European Council, become the institutional actors vested with the political authority to declare a state of emergency and thus shape the agenda.[76]

This intergovernmental drift is not counter-acted by the fact that the migratory pressure pushed the European Council to expand the role of technical actors, such as supranational migration agencies like the European Border and Coast Guard Agency (Frontex) or the EU Agency for Asylum (EUAA).[77] On the contrary, apart from their organisational structure, which includes Member States' representatives on their Management Boards, the operational performance of these agencies is largely contingent on cooperation with national authorities and dependent on the national policies' priorities. This is well illustrated by the launch by Frontex of a Rapid Border Intervention in the Aegean Sea Region, following the Greek National Security Council's decision to suspend the right to asylum for one month as of 1 March 2020 at the culmination of a series of national emergency measures to curb the arrival of migrants.[78] Accordingly, while contributing to understanding the EU as technocratic or 'executive-led by design',[79] it is worth stressing that the changing role of the European Council as well as the rise of EU migration agencies has brought about a redistribution of the vertical powers in which the executive branches of the Member States play a significant role in the governance of migration and asylum policies.

[73] Martín Rodríguez (n 6) 271.

[74] Campesi (n 22) 45.

[75] See the recent controversial temporary reintroduction of border controls by Germany, based on Article 25 of the Schengen Borders Code, German Federal Ministry of the Interior and Community, Press release (9 September 2024) www.bmi.bund.de/SharedDocs/pressemitteilungen/EN/2024/09/binnengrenzkontrollen_en.html.

[76] In this regard see also J White, 'Emergency Europe' (2015) 63 *Political Studies* 300.

[77] For references see D Fernández-Rojo, *EU Migration Agencies: The Operation and Cooperation of FRONTEX, EASO and EUROPOL* (Edward Elgar, 2021).

[78] For a critical treatment see Human Rights Watch (HRW), 'Greece Restarts Suspended Asylum Procedure', 5 June 2020, available at tinyurl.com/36sb34m8.

[79] P Leino-Sandberg and P Minkkinen, 'From Separated Powers to Consensual Executive Government in the EU' in Eckes, Leino-Sandberg and Ghavanini (n 58) 24. See also D Curtin, *Executive Power of the European Union. Law, Practices, and the Living Constitution* (Oxford University Press, 2009).

B. The Horizontal Balance of Powers

The new overriding role of the European Council is not only a sign of an intergovernmental reshuffle of the vertical balance of powers since it also influences the inter-institutional dynamics horizontally. As has been argued, 'on immigration-related issues, the European Council has shown willingness to keep control over future EU developments'.[80] This was particularly visible at the onset of the migratory emergency, in June 2014, when the European Council essentially set the EU political agenda while the new European Parliament had just been elected and the new European Commission had yet to be nominated.

The European Council continued that path by leaving limited room for manoeuvring in the emergency decision-making process.[81] One example is the adoption of the Relocation Decisions following the European Council's Conclusions of June 2015. These Conclusions left very little space for the institutions mentioned in Article 78(3) TFEU, namely the European Commission and the Council, let alone the European Parliament, which has a consultative role, about the substantive aspects of the measures to be adopted. Accordingly, the power of legislative initiative by the European Commission was significantly compressed, the involvement of the European Parliament was minimal, and the Council mostly ratified the points made by the European Council.

While the Court of Justice clarified that the legislative institutions are not bound by political decisions taken by the European Council as representatives of heads of state or governments,[82] it remains questionable whether, in a situation of necessity such as the migratory pressure experienced in 2015, the legislative institutions could justifiably refrain from acting in accordance with the European Council's decisions. As a result, in situations of necessity, the principle of sincere cooperation as a primary safeguard of the institutional balance can be undermined by the circumstance that each institution does not monitor its powers against the powers of the other institutions.

Drawing on experience from the financial and public debt crisis, scholars argued that the European Council as a political institution should exercise its constitutional powers, especially by making major efforts to deal with urgent matters.[83] However, while as an intergovernmental institution, the European Council is better placed to take action in times of emergency, its broad mandate

[80] Y Pascouau, 'The European Council's strategic guidelines and immigration: Can the EU be bold and innovative?' (*European Policy Centre Commentary*, 25 June 2014) available at https://epc.eu/publication/The-European-Councils-strateg-1cb59c/. See also M Carammia, S Princen and A Timmermans, 'From Summitry to EU Government: An Agenda Formation Perspective on the European Council' (2016) 54 *Journal of Common Market Studies* 809.

[81] In this regard, D Moloney and S Princen, 'Assessing the role of the European Council and the European Commission during the migration and COVID-19 crises' (2023) 47 *West European Politics* 1556, 1577, stressed that 'as the crisis deteriorated, initiatives were based on EUCO's [European Council's] priorities of increased security'.

[82] Case C-106/19 *Italy v Council and Parliament*, ECLI:EU:C:2022:568, para 144.

[83] De Witte (n 71).

under Article 15(1) TEU needs an effective system of checks and balances to ensure that the exercise of its mandate does not compromise the competences of other institutions. It is worth reiterating that Article 13(2) TEU provides, in a horizontal relationship, that the institutions shall act only within the limits accorded to them by the Treaties. As stressed by the Court of Justice, 'the Treaties set up a system for distributing powers among the different [...] institutions, assigning to each institution its own role in the institutional structure of the Community and the accomplishment of the tasks entrusted to the Community'.[84] This means that the institutions must respect the powers and competences of the other institutions.

However, the role played by the European Council during emergencies compresses the role of the other institutions, due to the broad formulation of its general mandate that often extends beyond treaty provisions, compared to the role of the other institutions. The European Parliament's role as well as the role of other institutions is, in fact, much more specific in the letter of the Treaties. For instance, the European Parliament becomes active when treaty provisions unambiguously stipulate its involvement in the respective procedure, or its position cannot be circumvented. Accordingly, in a protracted state of emergency, the exercise of the European Council's mandate can limit the transparency of the decision-making and this can amount to democratic deterioration.[85] In this regard, the Court of Justice stated that the legislative process is guided, by virtue of Article 1(2) in conjunction with Article 10(3) TEU, by the principle of transparency vis-à-vis the citizens, thus is capable of strengthening the 'democratic foundation' of a decision.[86]

Sceptical towards the incorporation of the constitutional principle of separation of powers into the EU, scholars have argued that the EU Treaties 'define an institutional "division of labour" providing optimal efficiency to the common objective of European integration rather than to enable cross-institutional democratic oversight'.[87] Nonetheless, such democratic oversight is existential for an organisation which is established as a community of values (Article 2 TEU). As will be argued in Section VI, even in emergency situations, the role of institutions like the European Parliament should safeguard checks and balances against arbitrariness or the pre-emption of formal decision-making.

[84] Case C-316/91 *Parliament v Council*, ECLI:EU:C:1994:76, para 11.

[85] See also K Schilde and S Wallace Goodman 'The EU's Response to the Migration Crisis: Institutional Turbulence and Policy Disjuncture' in M Riddervold, J Trondal and A Newsome (eds), *The Palgrave Handbook of EU Crises* (Palgrave-Macmillan, 2021) 449; and J Müller Gómez, W Wessels and J Wolters, 'The European Parliament and the European Council: A Shift in the Balance of Power?' in O Costa (ed), *The European Parliament in Times of EU Crisis. European Administrative Governance* (Palgrave-Macmillan, 2019) 53.

[86] Case C-59/18 *Italy v Council*, ECLI:EU:C:2022:567, para 95.

[87] Leino-Sandberg and Minkkinen (n 79) 23. Similar scepticism was also expressed by K Lenaerts, 'Some Reflections on the Separation of Powers in the European Community' (1991) 28 *Common Market Law Review* 11, 12.

IV. THE IMPACT OF THE MIGRATORY PRESSURE ON THE LEGISLATIVE DYNAMICS

The adoption of a complex toolbox to deal with migratory emergencies also raises questions about the relationship between these emergency measures and ordinary legislation. As has already been argued, 'situations of emergency offered an opportunity to get more flexibility from the existing EU legislative framework, in an attempt to provide for a unitary, decisive, and rapid action, rather than what would otherwise have been a slower, and differentiated, Member State response'.[88] The possibility to develop some emergency competences for the EU is thus to be seen as an attempt to contain unilateral legislative responses by the Member States. This is why it has also been maintained that 'finding a legal basis for the emergency measures and respecting the procedure and limits of the existing clauses become the crucial points'.[89]

In modern liberal constitutionalism, of which the EU is an example,[90] a situation of emergency is dealt with by assigning emergency powers to the executive that could thereby adopt special emergency legislation.[91] However, as discussed in Section III, a situation of emergency within the EU legal order produces a shift in the balance of powers to inter-governmentalism. Such a shift also affects the quality of the legislation, generally for the purpose of providing a framework for the Member States to derogate from the ordinary legislation. This is the logic informing the emergency toolbox adopted over the years to address situations of crisis or emergency in the areas of migration and asylum.

Both the ad hoc instruments and the emergency clauses, discussed in Section II, could be technically regarded as *lex specialis* involving limited and temporary derogations from the ordinary legislation, like in the case of the Dublin Regulation on the State responsible for an application for international protection.[92] This approach was ultimately formalised by the new Crisis Regulation 2021/1147 which, as has been emphasised, 'includes various ways to derogate from different EU instruments'.[93] The same logic applies to the emergency clauses included in the most relevant legislation, such as the Schengen Borders Code or the Asylum Procedures Directive. As regards the latter, the

[88] Nicolosi (n 5) 74.

[89] Martín Rodríguez (n 6) 271.

[90] See more extensively and critically M Fichera, *The EU and Constitutional Time. The Significance of Time in Constitutional Change* (Edward Elgar, 2023).

[91] J Ferejohn and P Pasquino, 'The law of the exception: A typology of emergency powers' (2004) 2 *International Journal of Constitutional Law* 210.

[92] Regulation (EU) No 604/2013 of the European Parliament and of the Council of 26 June 2013 establishing the criteria and mechanisms for determining the Member State responsible for examining an application for international protection lodged in one of the Member States by a third-country national or a stateless person (recast) [2013] OJ L 180/31–59. This Regulation will be replaced by Regulation (EU) 2024/1351 of the European Parliament and of the Council of 14 May 2024 on asylum and migration management, amending Regulations (EU) 2021/1147 and (EU) 2021/1060 and repealing Regulation (EU) No 604/2013 [2024] OJ L 2024/1351.

[93] Ineli-Ciger (n 41).

Covid-19 health emergency constituted a recent scenario in which the emergency clause under Article 31(3) was used to provide possible extensions of the time-frame for registration and examination of asylum applications.[94]

The normative paradigm of *lex specialis* provides for at least three general limits within which the emergency legislation will apply. These limits are especially common to the ad hoc instruments, namely the Temporary Protection Directive, the Relocation Decisions and the new Crisis Regulation. These instruments are, in fact, limited *ratione materiae*, as they only apply in a situation of crisis as defined by the instruments themselves; *ratione temporis*, as the period of time during which these measures will be applicable must be indicated; and *ratione personae*, as the measures address a specific group of third-country nationals.

The *lex specialis* paradigm acts as a safeguard of legal certainty in a situation of emergency that could lead the Member States to adopt unilateral measures with the risk of compromising the uniformity of EU law.[95] Accordingly, the *lex specialis* paradigm offers two possible advantages: it injects the necessary flexibility into the legal order and attempts to regulate the relationship with ordinary legislation through a clear system of derogations. The Court of Justice has not extensively outlined the role and scope of the *lex specialis* in EU law.[96] Nevertheless, in the case law concerning the Relocation Decisions, the Court was given a chance to provide helpful clarifications, confirming the possibility for the Council to derogate, on the basis of Article 78(3) TFEU, from ordinary secondary law.[97] However, as has been stressed by Steve Peers, these exceptional measures must still comply with primary law.[98]

Additionally, while highlighting the need to respond rapidly to a particular emergency that the Member States were facing, the Court concluded that the measures adopted based on Article 78(3) TFEU must be circumscribed, limited to responding swiftly and effectively to a specific crisis.[99] This distinguishes the emergency measures from the legislation that is to be adopted under Article 78(2) TFEU, whose normative goal, as I have argued, 'would be to normalise the asylum policy in a way to prevent sudden situations of emergency that will adversely impact the policy area'.[100]

[94] For more references see SF Nicolosi, 'Health Emergency and Asylum Law in the European Union' (2022) 34 *International Journal of Refugee Law* 398.

[95] For a critical analysis see S Weatherill, *Law and Values in the European Union* (Oxford University Press, 2016) 28 ff.

[96] In this regard, see E Hancox, 'Judicial approaches to norm overlaps in EU law: A case study on the free movement of workers' (2021) 58 *Common Market Law Review* 1057. For more references see G Conway, *The Limits of Legal Reasoning and the European Court of Justice* (Cambridge University Press, 2012) 201.

[97] Case C-643/15 *Slovakia and Hungary v Council*, ECLI:EU:C:2017:631, para 78.

[98] S Peers, 'A Pyrrhic victory? The ECJ upholds the EU law on relocation of asylum-seekers' (*EU Law Analysis Blog*, 8 September 2017).

[99] *Slovakia and Hungary v Council* (n 97) para 77.

[100] Nicolosi (n 5) 76.

The Court also offered another crucial clarification about the scope of the *lex specialis* established through ad hoc instruments such as the Relocation Decisions. By addressing the use of the public order and security clause under Article 72 TFEU, in the joined cases of *Commission v Poland, Hungary and the Czech Republic*, the Court established that this clause cannot be invoked unilaterally without any control by the European institutions.[101] On the contrary, since the emergency measures regulated the possibility of denying relocation if applicants with a risk profile were identified, thereby establishing a derogation, the Member States cannot merely refer to the existence of public order and security concerns in order not to apply the emergency measures.[102] In essence, the Court clarified that Article 72 TFEU is not a clause that allows for general derogations, but is to be seen as a clause to contain or guide the EU legislature in regulating in more specific contexts how the possible derogations from the relevant EU legislation can be taken into consideration.[103] Despite the flexibility afforded by a *lex specialis* regime, a system of derogations does not compromise the constitutional structure of the legal order as long as it remains temporally limited. Otherwise, there is a risk of undermining the effectiveness of ordinary legislation. An illustration is offered by the debate on the further extension of the TPD for those who fled the armed conflict in Ukraine.[104] The TPD was implemented on 4 March 2022 for one year, as established in Article 4(1) TPD,[105] automatically extended by one additional year, and then, pursuant to Article 4(2) TPD, extended up to one more year, until 4 March 2025,[106] followed by a further extension until 4 March 2026.

The extensive interpretation of Article 4(2) TPD allowing for an extension of an extra year beyond 2025 is against the letter and spirit of the Directive, which allows for up to three year maximum extension. The possible re-activation of the TPD, based on a new Council's decision by the qualified majority on a Commission's proposal will be also problematic.[107] Such a continuation of an exceptional legislative framework would create a situation of uncertainty that contradicts the rationale behind temporary protection, whose objective is to

[101] *Commission v Poland, Hungary and the Czech Republic* (n 50) para 146.

[102] ibid.

[103] See also Case C-808/18 *Commission v Hungary*, ECLI:EU:C:2020:1029, para 75.

[104] See Council of the EU, Justice and Home Affairs Council (Home Affairs), meeting of 13 June 2024, available at www.consilium.europa.eu/en/meetings/jha/2024/06/13/.

[105] Council Implementing Decision (EU) 2022/382 of 4 March 2022 establishing the existence of a mass influx of displaced persons from Ukraine within the meaning of Article 5 of Directive 2001/55/EC, and having the effect of introducing temporary protection ST/6846/2022/INIT [2022] OJ L 71/1–6.

[106] Council Implementing Decision (EU) 2023/2409 of 19 October 2023 extending temporary protection as introduced by Implementing Decision (EU) 2022/382 [2023] OJ L 240.

[107] For an overview of the possible options, see ECRE, 'Transitioning out of the Temporary Protection Directive. Analysis of the Main Options Available to Ensure a Smooth Transition out of the TPD Regime for People Displaced From Ukraine' Policy Paper No 13, February 20024, at ecre.org/wp-content/uploads/2024/02/ECRE-Policy-Paper-13_Transitioning-Out-of-the-Temporary-Protection-Directive.pdf.

grant immediate protection. At the same time, State authorities continue the ordinary procedures for international protection. In other words, a continual extension of the TPD would unnecessarily set aside ordinary legislation (namely the CEAS) and undermine access to international protection (refugee status or subsidiary protection). It would thus have implications for fundamental rights, which will be more broadly discussed in the next Section.

V. THE FUNDAMENTAL RIGHTS IMPLICATIONS OF EMERGENCY MEASURES IN THE AREAS OF MIGRATION AND ASYLUM

The sense of urgency determined by the migratory pressure on the EU has especially prioritised security objectives with limited attention to the position of migrants and their rights. Security concerns have been a distinct feature in EU migration law and policies, at least since the establishment of the Schengen Area and the Dublin rules on the State responsible for an asylum application, that contributed to the 'social construction of migration into a security question'.[108]

However, the migratory pressure of 2015 and the *mise-en-oeuvre* of an emergency-proof legal toolbox, especially pursuing the twofold goal of curbing the migratory flows and enhancing border controls, has exacerbated the crisis narrative. This narrative has framed security as an issue of general interest for the EU[109] and has impacted the reform of the CEAS and the Schengen system. In emergency situations, as explained in Section IV, the law permits deviations from the ordinary legislative process and, to a certain extent, can allow the suspension of individual rights when they conflict with the public interest, provided that this is strictly necessary. However, as has been emphasised, 'by frequently recalling migration as crises in their discourses, the EU and its Members States normalize and perpetuate the uses of volatile and arbitrary borders against [...] refugees [...] procreating a migration management crisis'.[110]

The hotspots at the borders of the EU, especially in the Greek islands, have become the example *par excellence* of a perpetuated situation of emergency that has created dire living conditions, as confirmed by the European Court of Human Rights (ECtHR). On 4 April 2023, in *A.D. v Greece*, the Strasbourg's judges found for the first time that the living conditions of the applicant at the Samos Reception and Identification Centre had fallen short of the requirements

[108] J Huysmans, 'The European Union and the Securitization of Migration' (2000) 38 *Journal of Common Market Studies* 751, 753. For an explanation of how the concept of border security found its way into the supranational EU legislation on border control, see Å Gustafsson, 'The "Border Security" Concept in EU Law' (2024) 3 *European Journal of Migration and Law* 341.

[109] See, eg, European Commission, Communication on the EU Security Union Strategy, COM(2020) 605 final, 24 July 2020.

[110] B Nur Osso, 'The Border, the Law, the Social: The Spatiotemporality of EU's Creeping Crisis of Migration Management and the Struggles of "Access"' (2023) Helsinki Legal Studies Research Paper Series No 79, at doi.org/10.2139/ssrn.4641005.

of Articles 3 and 8 of the European Convention on Human Rights (ECHR), which offer protection against inhuman or degrading treatment and respect for private and family life, respectively.[111] The case was followed by other rulings by the ECtHR reiterating that the conditions in the Samos 'hotspot' amounted to inhumane and degrading treatment.[112] More recently, in the cases of *A.R. v Greece* and *M.A. and other v Greece*, after recalling its previous case law related to the general principles concerning the living conditions of asylum seekers, the Court found that the applicants' living conditions (in Chios and once again in the Samos hotspot) were incompatible with Article 3 ECHR.[113]

The preponderance of security concerns in crisis management especially in situations of emergency raises the question about the compatibility of emergency measures with fundamental rights. In *Carpenter*, the Court addressed this question in relation to situations in which the Member States rely on reasons of internal security or public order to derogate from EU law, confirming that these national measures must comply with fundamental rights.[114] Admittedly, similar considerations extend to emergency measures adopted by the Union. As general principles of EU law, fundamental rights are binding on the EU institutions and are applied by the Court of Justice to determine the lawfulness of any adopted measure.[115] The EU institutions are equally bound by the Charter of Fundamental Rights of the EU (EU Charter) which, pursuant to Article 52(3), is to be applied with due regard to the ECHR.[116] In particular, as the Charter rights that correspond to rights under the ECHR have the same meaning and scope as the latter, this means that non-derogable ECHR rights, such as the right to life and the prohibition of torture or inhuman or degrading treatment which are also codified in the Charter (Articles 3, 4 and 19, have to be taken into account by any EU measures adopted to address emergencies.

Moreover, the 2016 Interinstitutional Agreement on Better Law-Making requires new legislative initiatives with significant societal and fundamental

[111] European Court of Human Rights (ECtHR), *Case of A.D. v Greece*, Appl No 55363/19, judgment of 4 April 2023. For an analysis see K Schayani and M Maydell, 'Inhuman and Degrading "Hotspots" at the EU Borders: An Analysis of How the ECtHR Rejects the Attempt to Push Asylum Seekers Into De Facto Legal Vacuums at the Borders of the EU' (*Völkerrechtsblog*, 27 April 2023).

[112] See, eg, ECtHR, *M.L. v. Greece*, Appl Nos. 8386/20 and *M.B. v Greece*, Appl No 8389/20, judgment of 23 November 2023. These cases were about pregnant women, thus stressing how the consequences for vulnerable migrants could be even harsher.

[113] ECtHR, *A.R. v Greece*, Appl No 59841/19, judgment of 18 April 2024; *M.A. v. Greece*, Appl. No. 15192/20, judgment of 3 October 2024. For references see M Baumgärtel, 'Whatever happened to Greek hotspots? The routine handling of routine violations in M.A. and others v. Greece' (*Strasbourg Observers*, 11 October 2024) at strasbourgobservers.com/2024/10/11/whatever-happened-to-greek-hotspots-the-routine-handling-of-routine-violations-in-m-a-and-others-v-greece/.

[114] Case C-60/00 *Carpenter v Secretary of State for the Home Department*, ECLI:EU:C:2002:434, para 41.

[115] See T Tridimas, *The General Principles of EU Law*, 2nd edn (Oxford University Press, 2007).

[116] Charter of Fundamental Rights of the European Union (EU Charter) [2012] OJ C 326/391–407.

rights impact to be supported by ex ante impact assessment.[117] However, the legislative proposals underpinning the Pact on Migration and Asylum, including the Crisis Regulation, lacked such an assessment, justified by an emergency narrative.

This omission has been criticised by the European Parliament[118] which raised fundamental rights concerns. For instance, delayed registrations of asylum requests[119] inevitably result in delays for applicants to have access to their rights for a protracted period.[120] Still, a systematic analysis of this Regulation and its system of derogations in light of the other legislative instruments that have been adopted provides for further scenarios in which fundamental rights guarantees can be downgraded in emergency situations. This is the case of the Asylum Procedures Regulation which imposes restrictions on the liberty of applicants undergoing border procedures. In cases where these procedures are extended, particularly under the provisions of the Crisis Regulation, the duration of these limitations can become excessively prolonged. The situation is even more worrisome because no specific mandatory and independent monitoring is foreseen for situations of crisis and force majeure by the Crisis Regulation.

VI. CONTAINING THE DISTORTIVE EFFECTS OF EMERGENCY MEASURES IN MIGRATION AND ASYLUM MANAGEMENT

While confirming the attempt to consolidate the preparedness and resilience approach of the EU facing situations of necessity, emergencies pose challenges to the Union's constitutional set-up. Drawing from the specific areas of migration and asylum, as has been argued in the previous Sections, emergency response mechanisms can generate distortive effects on the legal order. These include an alteration of the institutional balance with a shift to inter-governmentalism, a set of legislative derogations from the ordinary legislation and fundamental rights implications. Some normative considerations are, therefore, relevant to explain that even emergency-response mechanisms have to offer constitutional safeguards to correct the mentioned distortive effects and preserve the integrity of the EU legal order.

[117] Interinstitutional Agreement between the European Parliament, the Council of the European Union and the European Commission on better law-making [2016] OJ L 123/1, point 12.

[118] European Parliament, 'The European Commission's Legislative Proposals in the New Pact on Migration and Asylum'. Study requested by the LIBE Committee, July 2021, at www.europarl.europa.eu/RegData/etudes/STUD/2021/697130/IPOL_STU(2021)697130_EN.pdf, 11.

[119] Crisis Regulation (EU) 2024/1359, Art 6.

[120] A-H Neidhardt, 'The Crisis and Force Majeure Regulation: Towards Future-Proof Crisis Management and Responses?' European Policy Centre (EPC) Policy Study (June 2024) 19, www.epc.eu/en/publications/The-Crisis-and-Force-Majeure-Regulation-Towards-future-proof-crisis-m~5bb29c.

A first constitutional safeguard concerns the respect of sincere cooperation as a principle regulating both the relations between the Union and its Member States and the EU inter-institutional dynamics. As stressed by Robert Schütze, Article 13(2) TEU constitutes the 'horizontal extension of the principle of sincere cooperation in Article 4(3) TEU'.[121] Institutional balance and sincere cooperation thus constitute 'an indissoluble whole'.[122] The Court also had the chance to clarify that 'inter-institutional dialogue … is subject to the same mutual duties of sincere cooperation as those which govern relations between Member States and the Community institutions'.[123] This means that just like the Member States, the EU institutions must refrain from undermining the attainment of treaty objectives. Additionally, the Court connected sincere cooperation with fundamental values, such as the rule of law.[124] No matter how much flexibility is needed for EU institutions to adapt their powers in urgent situations, the duty of sincere cooperation must serve as a check against concentrating power and decision-making in any single institution, such as the European Council. This duty must also limit the reliance on informal procedures or meta-institutional arrangements, an example of which is the reference to 'European leaders' with reference to the EU-Turkey Statement.[125]

Second, while a certain shift to intergovernmental decision-making can be necessary to ensure that a situation of emergency is addressed through the support of consensual action by the Member States, it is crucial for enhancing democratic legitimacy that, for example, the European Parliament proactively exercises its oversight as established by the Treaties. These include the possibility that the President of the European Parliament be invited to open the meeting of the European Council (Article 235(2) TFEU). Moreover, the Treaty establishes an obligation for the President of the European Council to submit a report to the Parliament at the end of the meetings (Article 15(6)(d) TEU).

Still, relevant emergency measures can be regularly reviewed. Emergency clauses that allow the Member States to set aside ordinary legislation, such as those included in the Schengen Borders Code, usually require a duty of notification vis-à-vis the EU institutions. Similarly, in the case of the Union's ad hoc instruments, such as the Temporary Protection Directive or the Crisis Regulation, the European Parliament can provide democratic and political oversight as it is well-positioned to incorporate fundamental rights considerations into the emergency decision-making process. In this connection, it is worth stressing that Article 6(4) of the Crisis Regulation establishes a duty for the Commission to report to the European Parliament and the Council on the application of the

[121] R Schütze, *European Union Law*, 3rd edn (Oxford University Press, 2021) 79.

[122] P Koutrakos, 'Institutional Balance and Sincere Cooperation in Treaty-Making Under EU Law' (2019) 1 *International and Comparative Law Quarterly* 1, 6.

[123] Case C-204/86 *Greece v Council*, ECLI:EU:C:1988:450, para 16.

[124] Case C-2/88 *Zwartveld and Others*, ECLI:EU:C:1990:440, paras 16–17.

[125] *NF v European Council* (n 57) para 69.

Council's implementing decision authorising derogations *ex* Article 4 of the Regulation. The European Parliament is hence tasked with assessing the effectiveness of the measures undertaken in resolving the situation of crisis, thereby contributing to determining whether these measures continue to be necessary and proportionate.

Third, the respect for sincere cooperation is inherently linked with another more general constitutional safeguard, namely the need to comply with the general principles of EU law, including fundamental rights, as provided for by Article 6 TEU.[126] This is of vital importance, because, as argued in Section V, emergency mechanisms in the areas of migration and asylum, including the new Crisis Regulation which adds instrumentalisation as a situation of crisis, are extremely politicised measures that tend to prioritise security concerns over the protection of fundamental rights for migrants. It is therefore essential that core principles and values, such as the respect for fundamental rights, set out in EU primary law are not compromised by security objectives nor by a system of derogations established through emergency legislation. All derogations must be applied based on necessity and for no longer than allowed by the legal framework. Scholars have also noted that an approach focused on the general principles of legal certainty and legitimate expectations can be helpful when emergency measures adopted by the EU can downgrade individual safeguards.[127] As stated by the Court of Justice, the principle of legal certainty requires 'that rules of law be clear and precise and predictable in their effect, so that interested parties can ascertain their position in situations and legal relationships governed by EU law'.[128]

Furthermore, as has been mentioned, fundamental right impact assessments should accompany any ad hoc legislative instrument designed to address situations of emergency. One of the prerequisites for complying with the commitments under the 2016 Interinstitutional Agreement on Better Law-Making is the ex ante impact assessment, according to which any new legislative initiatives expected to have significant societal and fundamental rights impacts should be accompanied by robust evidence demonstrating their coherency, necessity, proportionality and compliance with the EU Charter.[129] Apart from strengthening the link between competence and evidence beyond just the Commission's explanation of the use of a legal basis,[130] an ex ante impact assessment could contribute to our understanding of how fundamental rights can be safeguarded when an emergency mechanism is triggered.

[126] For references see eg O de Schutter, 'Fundamental Rights and the Transformation of Governance in the European Union' (2007) 9 *Cambridge Yearbook of European Legal Studies* 133.

[127] Martín Rodríguez (n 6) 266.

[128] Case C-48/14 *Parliament v Council*, ECLI:EU:C:2015:91, para 45.

[129] Interinstitutional Agreement between the European Parliament, the Council of the European Union and the European Commission on better law-making [2016] OJ L 123/1, point 12.

[130] For a broader discussion see SF Nicolosi, 'Evidence-Based Policymaking in European Union Asylum Law: Potential and Pitfalls' (2022) 24 *European Journal of Law Reform* 68.

Fundamental rights considerations must be also integrated into the soft law arrangements concluded by the Union with external partners, such as neighbouring third countries, to curb irregular migration and securitise the EU borders. Regrettably, most of these initiatives take place informally and outside the procedures established by the Treaties, making it difficult to secure appropriate judicial control from the Court of Justice.[131]

Finally, it must be stressed that the heterogeneity of emergency-response mechanisms creates an excessive and often protracted system of exceptions and derogations set out in special emergency legislation that sets aside ordinary rules. The unnecessary prolongation of special regimes, as in the case of temporary protection for those fleeing the armed conflict in Ukraine, is undesirable for at least two reasons. First, it contributes to fragmenting the conditions of migrants in need of protection within the EU. Migrants covered by special regimes, like temporary protection, risk not having access to refugee status or subsidiary protection within a reasonable time.[132] Second, it undermines legal certainty and facilitates the abuse of derogating measures by the Member States. It is thus pivotal that the time limits established in the legislation for the application of exceptional regimes are strictly respected and that these special regimes are considered provisional and only justified by a situation of necessity, such as the temporary impossibility of a national asylum system to smoothly process all applications for international protection.

These normative corrections arguably fall short of the pragmatism required by a situation of emergency. Yet, they are necessary not only for preserving the EU rule of law in emergency situations but also for ensuring adequate resilience and emergency-proof sustainability of the legal order.

VII. CONCLUSION

Emergency situations are nothing new in the European integration process;[133] however, recent crises have prompted an unprecedented number of emergency-response mechanisms in various policy fields. The EU's approach to migration and asylum policies, heavily influenced by the narrative of emergency, reflects a broader trend towards the 'crisification' of EU law and governance. This approach has resulted in a complex legal framework that relies on a mix of ad hoc instruments and emergency clauses embedded in various legislative

[131] For a more specific analysis see, eg, T Strik and R Robbesom, 'Compliance or complicity? An analysis of the EU-Tunisia deal in the context of the externalisation of migration control' (2024) 71 *Netherlands International Law Review* 199.

[132] See also the criticism by ECRE, 'The EU is stretching the limits of the Temporary Protection Directive beyond 2025, but is it enough?' Op-Ed (14 June 2024) at ecre.org/op-ed-the-eu-is-stretching-the-limits-of-the-temporary-protection-directive-beyond-2025-but-is-it-enough/.

[133] See in this regard O Blin, 'Les crises de la construction européenne' in J Larrieu (ed), *Crise(s) et Droit* (Toulouse, LGDJ, 2012) 241.

acts, allowing for temporary adaptations to the legal framework in response to unforeseen circumstances. While devised to equip the EU with the necessary legal toolbox to cope with an emergency, this chapter explained that the proliferation of such measures has significant constitutional implications.

As illustrated throughout this chapter, the proliferation of emergency measures results in a change in the institutional balance. This change leads to a shift towards inter-governmentalism. Additionally, these measures introduce legislative exceptions to standard procedures or rules, which, if extended, can create legal uncertainty. Furthermore, there are implications for fundamental rights that may undermine core values and obligations.

To address these challenges, I argued that constitutional safeguards are necessary. Such safeguards are inherent in the fabric of the EU legal order and include duties of sincere cooperation for the Member States and the Union's institutions. Still, respect for general principles of EU law requires ensuring compliance with fundamental rights at different levels of the law-making process, from preliminary impact assessments of emergency measures to careful monitoring at the implementation stage. Finally, emergency mechanisms must be temporary, clearly defined, and subject to regular review to prevent the erosion of legal certainty and the abuse of derogations. Despite their normative nature, these safeguards are essential to maintaining the integrity of the EU's legal order during crises.

8

Economic Crises and EU Migration Law: A Blast from the Past

ALEZINI LOXA

I. INTRODUCTION

In EU migration law, accounts of crisis and its relation to law abounded in the wake of events which occurred in the period of 2015–2016.[1] The increased arrival of migrants and refugees, and the way Member States responded to this, revealed a series of problems inherent to EU migration and asylum law and created a need for change.[2] By turning the focus away from the 2015–2016 migration crisis which has been exhaustively examined in the relevant literature, this chapter will analyse a different crisis at a different historical moment. Specifically, it will revisit the history of EU labour migration policy, and demonstrate the role that the 1970s oil crisis played in its development. In so doing, the analysis will show that there is a thread connecting economic crises and EU migration governance which has been overlooked in the scholarship and which has had implications both for migrants' rights and for EU integration in general.

To develop the argument, Section II revisits the history of EU migration law and traces its emergence in the early years of Community law. The reader should note that the focus of the investigation is on labour migration to the exclusion of instruments related to asylum and border management. With these delimitations in mind, the historical analysis suggests that the approach of Community

[1] See contributions in S Carrera, J Santos Vara and T Strik (eds), *Constitutionalising the External Dimensions of EU Migration Policies in Times of Crisis: Legality, Rule of Law and Fundamental Rights Reconsidered* (Edward Elgar, 2019); R Dickson, *Migration Law, Policy and Human Rights: The Impact of Crisis in Europe* (Routledge, 2022); M Scipioni, 'Failing Forward in EU Migration Policy? EU Integration after the 2015 Asylum and Migration Crisis' (2018) 25 *Journal of European Public Policy* 1357.

[2] Initially by the collapse of the Dublin System, A Loxa and V Stoyanova, 'Migration as a Constitutional Crisis for the European Union' in S Stijn and V Stoyanova, *Migrants' Rights, Populism and Legal Resilience in Europe* (Cambridge University Press, 2022), section 5.3.1 and then by the collapse of Schengen, J Rijpma, 'Let's not forget about Schengen' (*EU Migration Law Blog*, 12 March 2021).

institutions to the regulation of EU labour migration was fundamentally altered by the 1970s oil crisis. After that economic crisis, short-termism became the defining feature of EU migration law. Section III situates the relevant empirical material within Runciman's theoretical framework on short-termism and democratic governance in times of crisis.[3] In this regard a conceptual clarification is due. The concept of crisis is so broadly used today that offering a clear-cut and all-encompassing definition is challenging.[4] For purposes of the present analysis, 'crisis' should be understood to mean 'a situation characterised both by fundamental threat and fundamental choice'.[5] Such a definition manages to capture core elements of the intellectual history of the concept and allows us to relate the economic threat experienced in the 1970s and the way in which the fundamental choice made by the Community institutions has left its imprint on EU migration law to this day.[6] Finally, Section IV concludes the analysis.

II. REVISITING THE HISTORY OF EU LABOUR MIGRATION LAW

The literature positions the development of EU migration law in the late 1980s and early 90s in the context of transnational security cooperation between the Member States.[7] There is a prevalent view that before the Maastricht Treaty, the EU had no competence to regulate migration, which was instead regulated through bilateral agreements. Yet this view has been challenged.[8] Specifically, the early determining stages of EU migration law can be traced back to the 1950s and 60s. A close examination of soft-law material, archival documents and Community law highlights that Community institutions were concerned with the regulation of labour migration a lot earlier, with migrants gaining extensive EU law rights by Association Agreements.[9] Drawing a

[3] D Runciman, 'What Time Frame Makes Sense for Thinking about Crises?' in PF Kjaer and N Olsen (eds), *Critical Theories of Crises in Europe: From Weimar to the Euro* (Rowman & Littlefield International, 2016).

[4] See R Koselleck and MW Richter, 'Crisis' (2006) 67 *Journal of the History of Ideas* 357, 399 who mention imprecision and vagueness in the use of the term crisis as a symptom of a historical crisis.

[5] Runciman (n 3) 4.

[6] Runciman (n 3) 5–6 discussing the problems of the definition but also Koselleck and Richter (n 4) 361 who mention that across the legal, theological and medical uses of the concept, it has historically been applied 'to life-deciding alternatives meant to answer questions about what is just or unjust, what contributes to salvation or damnation, what furthers health or brings death'.

[7] Indicatively see the ad hoc group on immigration set up at the initiative of the UK presidency in 1986, the Coordinator's group on the free movement of persons set up following the Rhodes European Council 1998, and the Trevi ministers' group and the immigration ministers' group under the Belgian presidency in 1987. See also Statewatch European Monitoring and Documentation Centre on justice and home affairs in the European Union, 'Key texts on justice and home affairs in the European Union, Volume 1 (1976–1993)'.

[8] A Loxa, *Sustainability and EU Migration Law: What Place for Migrants' Rights* (Doctoral Thesis (monograph), MediaTryck Lund, 2023).

[9] A Loxa, *Sustainability and EU Migration Law, Tracing the History of a Contemporary Concept* (Cambridge University Press, 2025).

picture of that history in broad strokes in this section, it will be argued that the Community labour migration policy has been fundamentally affected by the 1970s crisis which shaped the short-term approach to EU labour migration that is still at play today. To put it simply, there is an era before and after the 1970s oil crisis as regards the common regulation of labour migration. These two periods will be examined in turn to showcase how the end of post-war growth following the 1970s oil crisis affected the response to migration. Specifically, it will be shown that after this crisis, short-term approaches became prevalent. By 'short-term approach', I refer to the regulation of migration with no regard to the fluctuation of the economy, but rather with emphasis on sovereign control demanding abrupt border closure in case of recession and no consideration of the migrants' position within host societies. This is contrasted with long-term approaches, by which I mean the regulation of migration with due regard to the fluctuating economic demands of the internal market and safeguards for both migrants and the economy. The way in which short-termism has gained prevalence in migration has had implications not only for the specific policy area, but also for EU integration in general, as will be discussed in Section III.

A. The Common Approach to Labour Migration before the 1970s Oil Crisis

The 1950s and 60s were characterised by rapid economic development and an increased need for labour migration.[10] During that time, migration movements comprised mainly guest workers, and they were regarded as a short-term phenomenon, regulated by the demands of the market.[11] The need for workers in the industries of the Member States framed the Community migration policy in a very progressive way. First, free movement of workers was included in EU primary law to alleviate Italian unemployment and provide manpower to the industries of other European states.[12] Due to the open formulation of the Treaties, various authors have argued that the relevant provisions could cover non-Community workers as well.[13] At the same time, it appears that the Member

[10] Programme de politique économique à moyen terme (1966–1970) [1967] OJ 79/1513; Commission of the European Communities, Bulletin of the European Communities (1969) 6 23.

[11] Commission Communication to the Council and the European Parliament on Immigration, SEC (91) 1855 final para 9; JF Hollifield, *Immigrants, Markets, and States: The Political Economy of Postwar Europe* (Harvard University Press, 1992) 72.

[12] First under Art 69 ECSC with limitation for skilled workers, and then under Art 48 EEC Treaty. F Fauri (ed), *The History of Migration in Europe: Perspectives from Economics, Politics and Sociology* (Routledge, 2015).

[13] DF Edens and Sc Patijn, 'The Scope of the EEC System of Free Movement of Workers' (1972) 9 *Common Market Law Review* 322 with a focus on overseas territories; A Campbell, *Common Market Law* (Supplement 2/71, Longmans, 1971). See D Thym, 'Institutional and Constitutional Framework' in E Tsourdi and P De Bruycker (eds), *Research Handbook on EU Migration and Asylum Law* (Edward Elgar, 2022) 57 with reference to SAW Goedings, *Labor Migration in an Integrating Europe: National Migration Policies and the Free Movement of Workers; 1950–1968* (Sdu Uitgevers,

States did not perceive the Treaty of Rome as creating an obligation for them to employ Community migrants to begin with.[14] Instead, Member States saw free movement as a labour migration framework that created obligations of preferential treatment to Community migrant workers only as long as the national workforce was not sufficient to fulfil labour needs. This national perception of the Treaty framework at the time was not very different from what is in place today regarding the principle of Union preferences in the labour market.[15]

This initial framework regulating free movement for Community migrants was put into motion through secondary law adopted in successive steps in 1961, 1964 and 1968.[16] In the secondary law of the period, free movement was structured as a labour mobility scheme aimed at addressing the uneven distribution of manpower between the Member States. The economic expansion of the Community was pursued through the 'optimum valorization of the technical abilities of human beings' residing in the Member States.[17] At the same time, in a context of continuous growth, Member States also employed manpower from outside the Community to fulfil their needs.

In relation to this, the Community concluded Association Agreements with all the main countries that supplied labour to the Community industries.[18] These Agreements did not regulate residence rights for migrant workers,

2005) suggesting that this was not the intention of the drafters. The same point is also raised in D Thym, 'Ambiguities of Personhood, Citizenship, Migration and Fundamental Rights in EU Law' in L Azoulai, S Barbou des Places and E Pataut (eds), *Constructing the Person in EU Law : Rights, Roles, Identities* (Hart Publishing, 2016) 122.

[14] European Community Information Service, Press Notice, Common Market takes initial step toward free mobility for workers, 15 June 1961.

[15] Council Resolution of 20 June 1994 on Limitations on Admission of Third-Country Nationals to the Member states for employment [1996] OJ C 274/3, General criteria. The overall approach of the Council was that Member States should in principle refuse entry to all TCN workers. Entry should only be considered in case of vacancies that could not be filled by Community workers or TCN workers already permanently residing in a Member State.

[16] Règlement n° 15 relatif aux premières mesures pour la réalisation de la libre circulation des travailleurs à l'intérieur de la Communauté [1961] OJ 57/1073; Directive du Conseil en matière de procédures et pratiques administratives relatives à l'introduction, l'emploi et le séjour des travailleurs d'un État membre, ainsi que de leur famille, dans les autres États membres de la Communauté [1961] OJ 80/1513; Règlement n° 38/64/CEE du Conseil du 25 mars 1964 relatif à la libre circulation des travailleurs à l'intérieur de la Communauté [1964] OJ 62/965; Council Directive 64/240/EEC of 25 March 1964 on the abolition of restrictions on the movement and residence of Member states' workers and their families within the Community [1964] OJ 62/981; Council Directive 64/221/EEC of 25 February 1964 on the co-ordination of special measures concerning the movement and residence of foreign nationals which are justified on grounds of public policy, public security or public health [1964] OJ 56/850; Regulation (EEC) No 1612/68 of the Council of 15 October 1968 on freedom of movement for workers within the Community [1968] OJ L 257/2; Council Directive 68/360/EEC of 15 October 1968 on the abolition of restrictions on movement and residence within the Community for workers of Member states and their families [1968] OJ L 257/13.

[17] Professor Giuseppe Petrilli, Member of the Commission, Chairman of the Social Affairs Group, The Social Policy of the Commission European Economic Community, Bulletin de La Communauté Économique Européenne (1959) 2 6.

[18] Association Agreement with Greece 1961, with Turkey 1963; with Morocco, Algeria and Tunisia 1978, Yugoslavia 1983.

but they did guarantee equal treatment for them and their families in terms of working conditions and social rights in the host state. The provisions of the relevant agreements were not only later found to have direct effect but were also interpreted by the Court as specific expressions of the general non-discrimination provisions found in the text of the Treaties.[19] Next to the Association Agreements, soft law documents produced by the Community institutions emphasised the need for an aligned approach to labour migration. Specifically, the first Commission reports on free movement of workers generally discussed the number of labour migrants employed in Community Member States, regardless of their origin.[20]

The overview of the labour market situation by reference to all migrant workers in general and not exclusively Community migrants continued even after a framework was put in place which prioritised Community workers.[21] Especially during the late 1960s the production capacities of national industries were so closely dependent on labour mobility that there were discussions on including third-country nationals in the Community scheme of mobility in order to meet Community labour needs.[22] Any opening-up of the Community labour market in this way would always take place with oversight, so as to prevent unlimited access of foreign workers to national markets, which was seen as possibly limiting the quality of life for nationals.[23] Similar considerations continued as long as post-war growth continued. For example, the First Medium-term Economic Policy Programme issued by the Commission in 1967 showed that recourse to manpower from non-Member countries would become necessary as the years passed. Less than two decades after the establishment of the Communities, the Commission started pushing for comparative studies of

[19] The Court first found that such agreements can have direct effect in Case 12/86, *Demirel / Stadt Schwäbisch Gmünd*, ECLI:EU:C:1987:400, [1987] ECR 3719. For a detailed analysis of the clauses of the relevant agreements and the case law see Loxa (n 9) chs 4 and 7.

[20] See MA Bertrand (1957), Rapport fait au nom de la Commission des affaires sociales sur la migration et la libre circulation des travailleurs dans la Communauté, Exercice 1957–1958, Première session extraordinaire, Document 5.

[21] See Commission (1965), Libre circulation et migrations des travailleurs dans la Communauté. Bilan annuel des activités de compensation et de placement au sein de la Communauté (art 25 § 4 du règlement no 15/61, art 36 § 4 du règlement no 38/64, 48ff); Commission (1966), La libre circulation de la main-d'œuvre et les marches du travail dans la CEE, Rapport établi en application des dispositions des articles 29 et 36 du règlement n° 38/64 relatif à la libre circulation des travailleurs, 36 ff; Commission (1967), La libre circulation de la main-d'œuvre et les marches du travail dans la CEE, Rapport établi en application des dispositions des articles 29 et 36 du règlement n° 38/64 relatif à la libre circulation des travailleurs à l 'intérieur de la CEE, 16-19; Commission (1968), La libre circulation de la main-d'œuvre et les marches du travail dans la CEE, Rapport établi en application des dispositions des articles 29 et 36 du règlement n° 38/64 relatif à la libre circulation des travailleurs à l 'intérieur de la CEE, 34 ff.

[22] MA Bertrand (1957) Rapport complémentaire fait au nom de la Commission des Affaires sociales sur la migration et la libre circulation des travailleurs dans la Communauté, Exercice 1957–1958 Première session extraordinaire, Document 11; Commission (1960), Synthèse des rapports établis en 1960 sur la situation actuelle du service social des travailleurs migrants dans les six pays membres de la C.E.E.

[23] Bertrand, Document 11, para 55.

national recruitment policies to establish whether there existed common interests that could form the basis for closer cooperation in this field.[24] Next to this, in the 1974 Action Programme in Favour of Migrant Workers and their Families we find the first explicit articulation of the need for a Community migration policy and for the implementation of non-discrimination between Community and non-Community migrant workers.[25] The idea underlying the approach of the Community institutions was that all migrant workers regardless of origin contribute to the economic development of the Member States, and relatedly to the prosperity of the resident population, and for this they should enjoy a common set of rights.

Overall, before the 1970s oil crisis there existed no clear-cut differentiation between Community and non-Community migrants, as both groups of migrant workers were thought to make the same contribution to the Community project, and the different action plans put forward were meant to cover both. In the 'golden age' of sustained economic growth from the 1950s to the 70s the Commission was trying to set up a system that would ensure the best use of human capital available in the Member States. As a result, the paths of regulating migration were aligned for both Community and non-Community migrants, as the main objective served by the regulation of migration was to ensure the functioning of a common labour market. Member States were required to safeguard free movement for Community workers and respect their obligations towards the Community manpower before hiring non-Community workers, while non-Community migrants from associated countries enjoyed protection from discrimination, and in some cases also security of residence rights from Association Agreements.[26] One could add that as long as the Member States' economies needed migrant labour, there was no issue with attributing rights in a coherent way to all migrants regardless of origin.

[24] This led to the adoption of Commission Decision 85/381/EEC of 8 July 1985 setting up a prior communication and consultation procedure on migration policies in relation to non-member countries [1985] OJ L 217/25 which was challenged in Joined Cases 281, 283, 284, 285 and 287/85, *Federal Republic of Germany and others v Commission of the European Communities*, ECLI:EU:C:1987:351, [1987] ECR 2303 for lack of competence. The Court confirmed that migration policy fell under the social field and could be regulated by action adopted under Article 118 EC but declared two provisions void for falling outside the community powers. Commission Decision 88/384/EEC of 8 June 1988 setting up a prior communication and consultation procedure on migration policies in relation to non-member countries [1988] OJ L 183/35 was adopted subsequently.

[25] Action Programme in Favour of Migrant Workers and their Families COM(74)2250 final; Council Resolution of 9 February 1976 on an Action Programme for Migrant Workers and Members of Their Families [1976] OJ C 34/2. While these measures were strictly speaking adopted in the wake of 1973, it took some time for the effects of the oil crisis to be reflected in law.

[26] See eg the case law on Decision 1/80 implementing the EEC–Turkey Agreement analysed in view of migrants' rights in Loxa (n 9) ch 7. See also Case C-416/96, *Eddline El-Yassini*, ECLI:EU:C:1999:107, [1999] ECR I-1209 on a limited right to remain as long as someone is in employment in view of the non-discrimination clause of the EEC-Morocco Association Agreement.

B. The Common Approach to Labour Migration after the 1970s

The impetus driving a uniform approach to the Community regulation of migration only lasted as long as growth lasted. Specifically, by the early 1980s and with the effects of the oil crisis experienced by the Member States, the category of 'workers' slowly became differentiated based on nationality. Member States hesitated to extend rights to all migrants, for fear that they would not be able to guarantee social progress for their own citizens. Instead of equal rights for all migrants engaged to the project of growth, the Council shifted its approach and instead referred to equal opportunities to make a contribution.[27] And while the rights of Community workers were already developed by that stage and were informed by a kind of solidarity between the different Member States that were all implicated in the same development project, this type of solidarity could not extend to migrants whose state of origin was not implicated in the project at all. In this context, we see a shift in the approach to labour migration with short-termism guiding the Council and restricting any long-term approach to regulating labour migration by the Commission.

Specifically, the period following the 1970s crisis began with national bans on migration as a means to address national unemployment.[28] Next to these national bans, or perhaps due to their appearance, the approach in the Council shifted and the emphasis was now placed on the present economic needs (or lack thereof) in the Member States. The approach of the Council is brought to the fore when juxtaposed with the Commission and its various proposals to regulate migration. Especially after the adoption of the Single European Act and with awareness of the constantly changing socio-economic circumstances, the Commission emphasised the need to create a system that could accommodate and regulate the fluctuation of population movements and, relatedly, labour demand and supply in Member States.[29] At the same time the Commission also demanded maximum protection for legally resident migrants so as to promote their social advancement and social cohesion within Member States.[30] Contrary to that, the Council continuously rejected any attempt at regulation as long as there was no labour demand to be filled. Instead, through series of resolutions adopted in 1994 on migrant workers, self-employed migrants and migrant students, the Council emphasised national competence over migrant admission

[27] Council Resolution of 16 July 1985 on Guidelines for a Community Policy on Migration [1985] OJ C 186/3.

[28] See the 1994 Council resolutions but also retrospective analysis in Communication from the Commission, On Immigration, SEC (91) 1855 final, para 17; Commission, DG Employment, Industrial Relations and Social Affairs, Unit: Freedom of movement, Migration policy, Immigration Policies in the Member States: Between the need for Control and the Desire for Integration, Working Document, Summary Report of the information network in migration from non-EC Countries (RIMET) year of reference 1991, V/1020/92, 23. See also D O'Keeffe, 'The Free Movement of Persons and the Single Market' (1992) 17 *European Law Review* 3.

[29] On Immigration, SEC(91)1855 final para 69.

[30] ibid paras 3, 69.

and the need to maintain and, if necessary, reinforce restrictive measures on admission.[31] By following such an approach, the Council was not concerned with the constantly changing economic circumstances and their interaction with labour migration but rather with the lack of unlimited demand for labour at times when geopolitical events pointed to the potential creation of more migration. Specifically, increased unemployment and political instability pointed to potential movements from the Mediterranean.[32] In addition to this, the fall of the Soviet Union and the process of accession of the Central and Eastern European Countries pointed to the potential of increase in labour migration.[33] Towards the mid-1990s, growth began to slowly resume, and this created extra demand for labour in specific sectors.[34] In parallel, a new challenge appeared: that of an ageing EU population which would no longer be able to support the development needs of the Member States.[35] All these were taking place in a period of continued national unemployment next to settled migrant communities, which were increasingly facing racism and xenophobia.[36] What was missing was not the understanding of the relation of labour migration to the economic needs of Member States. Rather what was missing was a long-term perception behind the function of migration in contemporary societies.[37]

[31] Council Resolution of 30 November 1994 relating to the limitations on the admission of third country nationals to the territory of the Member states for the purpose of pursuing activities as self-employed persons [1996] OJ C 274/7. 1994, Council Resolution of 20 June 1994 on Limitations on Admission of Third-Country Nationals to the Member states for employment [1996] OJ C 274/3; Council Resolution of 30 November 1994 on the admission of third-country nationals to the territory of the Member states for study purposes [1996] OJ C 274/10.

[32] Commission of the European Communities, Directorate General for Information, Europe Information Development, The countries of the Greater Arab and Maghreb and the European Community. DE 68, January 1991; Commission Communication, The future of relations between the Community and the Maghreb, SEC(92)401 final. See also Commission Communication, Strengthening the Mediterranean Policy of the European Union: Establishing a Euro-Mediterranean Partnership, COM(94)427.

[33] HAEU, GJLA-246, Commission of the European Communities, Directorate General External Relations, Task force Enlargissement, Enlargement and the Community's Relations with its Mediterranean Neighbours, Brussels 2 March 1992, RDM/m 4; Commission Communication, On Immigration, SEC(91)1855 final paras 8–9.

[34] See the retrospective description of the 1990s trends in migrant employment in Commission Communication, On a Community immigration policy COM(2000)757 final, Annex 1, The Demographic and Economic context.

[35] Commission Communication, On immigration and asylum policies, COM(94)23 final para 9.

[36] The Parliament was pushing for different measures to address this issue. See initially European Parliament, Committee of Inquiry into the Rise of Fascism and Racism in Europe, Report on the findings of the inquiry, Evrigenis Report and indicatively, Parliament resolution on racism and xenophobia, adopted on 10 October [1991] OJ C 280. The Council also issued declarations on the matter. See Maastricht European Council, Presidency Conclusions, 16.12.1991, Annex 3 Declaration on racism and xenophobia; Corfu European Council 24–25 June 1994, Presidency conclusions, Annex III: Implementation of the Franco/German initiative against racism and xenophobia and Resolution of the Council and the representatives of the Governments of the Member states, meeting within the Council of 5 October 1995 on the fight against racism and xenophobia in the fields of employment and social affairs [1995] OJ C 296/10.

[37] cf H de Haas, *How Migration Really Works: The Facts about the Most Divisive Issue in Politics* (Basic Books, 2023).

The prevalent short-termism led to the rejection of two Commission Proposals that were put forward with the aim of creating a system that has inbuilt guarantees to ensure the development of the Member States in changing economic and demographic circumstances.[38] Acknowledging that the economic growth of the 1950s and 1960s would not return, and that the current labour market situation would not allow for a liberal migration policy, the Commission remained realistic as to the fact that the zero immigration target envisioned by Member States could not be realised. In the explanatory memorandum of the first Proposal of 1997, the Commission suggested the creation of a system that could ensure the continued benefits of migration for the EU development project. The idea behind this system was to allow the market to function, while avoiding a labour force expansion at a time when unemployment was already a problem in the Member States. The proposal envisioned a framework for the conclusive regulation of migration at the EU level and addressed the admission of migrants for employment, independent economic activity, training, study, non-gainful activity, family reunification, and the attribution of progressive rights to long-term residents. This proposal was eventually withdrawn in 2001 and replaced by a second proposal for a Directive which sought to harmonise the admission of migrants for the purpose of paid employment and self-employed activities.[39] The aim was to provide rights to migrants, while allowing Member States to limit admission for economic migration in case of limited labour demand. Specifically, the framework would permit a quick reaction to changing economic and demographic circumstances, and admission would be allowed only if there was an economic need on behalf of the Member States, or if such migrants had a beneficial effect on the national economies. This proposal was eventually withdrawn in 2006, after failing to gather support from the Council, which did not want to address the matter of horizontal admission for all categories of migrants.

It is not clear as to why these proposals were rejected by the Council, ie, whether the issue was the need of Member States to maintain competence on regulating migration, the assumed risks for their economies, or the fact that the proposals, especially the 1997 one, would lead to a system of residence and movement equally extensive to that applicable to EU migrants. In any case, at least until the early 2000s the only measure that was adopted on migration was the regulation on admission of students, which came with no economic cost, and which still incorporated specific limits to avoid the possibility of students entering the EU to find employment. These different approaches on the function of migrants for EU economies blocked every attempt to harmonise admission until the 2000s, but they did allow the adoption of instruments guaranteeing a

[38] Proposal for a Council Act establishing the Convention on rules for the admission of third-country nationals to the Member States COM(97)387 final.

[39] Proposal for a Council Directive on the conditions of entry and residence of third-country nationals for the purpose of paid employment and self-employed economic activities COM(2001)0386 final.

minimum set of rights to migrant workers.[40] Following these, the Commission only put forward proposals that could gather support by the Council. This is how we have ended up with the sectoral legislation which is in place today and which has been criticised not only for failing to secure the rights of migrant workers but more fundamentally for not promoting any market efficiency due to the way in which migrants receive residence but not effective free movement rights under EU law.[41]

Behind the current incoherent system of regulation that neither supports migrants' rights nor effectively serves the needs of the EU economy is the persistence of short-termism behind decision-making in EU politics. The above brief historical reconstruction of the EU labour migration policy hints at the opposing approaches of the Commission and the Council in relation to EU law-making. Specifically, in the regulation of entry and rights for non-EU migrants the Commission has emphasised the need to guarantee a more efficient allocation of resources and the proper functioning of the EU economy. Each proposal that has been put forward by the Commission included safeguards that could guarantee the functioning of such a system, also in times of recession.[42] In contrast to the Commission's approach, the Council has been taking into account considerations related to the specific economic circumstances at the national level. Tying migrant rights to the achievements of economic objectives was emphasised only during the years prior to the oil crisis.[43] Since then, the Member States have repeatedly acknowledged the need to commit to the common project of growth

[40] See Council Directive 2003/86/EC of 22 September 2003 on the right to family reunification [2003] OJ L 251/12; Council Directive 2003/109/EC of 25 November 2003 concerning the status of third-country nationals who are long-term residents [2003] OJ L 16/ 44.

[41] On the relevant legislation see Directive (EU) 2016/801 of the European Parliament and of the Council of 11 May 2016 on the conditions of entry and residence of third-country nationals for the purposes of research, studies, training, voluntary service, pupil exchange schemes or educational projects, and au pairing (recast) [2016] OJ L 132/21; Directive 2014/66/EU of the European Parliament and of the Council of 15 May 2014 on the conditions of entry and residence of third-country nationals in the framework of an intra-corporate transfer [2014] OJ L 157/1; Council Directive 2009/50/EC of 25 May 2009 on the conditions of entry and residence of third-country nationals for the purposes of highly qualified employment [2009] OJ L 155/ 17 (Blue Card Directive 2009) and Directive (EU) 2021/1883 of the European Parliament and of the Council of 20 October 2021 on the conditions of entry and residence of third-country nationals for the purpose of highly qualified employment, and repealing Council Directive 2009/50/EC [2021] OJ L 382/1 (Blue Card Directive 2021); Directive 2014/36/EU of the European Parliament and of the Council of 26 February 2014 on the conditions of entry and stay of third-country nationals for the purpose of employment as seasonal workers [2014] OJ L 94/375. On the fragmented and inefficient nature of the legislative instruments see Commission Staff Working Document, Executive Summary of the Fitness Check on EU Legislation on legal migration SWD(2019)1055 PART 2/2, Annex 5; Resolution of 20 May 2021 on new avenues for legal labour migration (2020/2010(INI)) [2022] OJ C 15/196; Resolution of 25 November 2021 with recommendations to the Commission on legal migration policy and law (2020/2255(INL)) [2022] OJ C 224/69. See also European Parliament Research Service, Recast of Directive 2003/109/EC: Status of third-country nationals who are long term residents in the EU, EPRS BRI(2024)757361.

[42] For a detailed analysis of the relevant proposals see Loxa (n 9) ch 6.

[43] Loxa (n 9) ch 3.

in political declarations, but when it comes to the negotiation of specific legal instruments, the focus turns to ensuring economic growth in the short term and within each national setting.[44]

In a sense, the above dissonance between the Council and the Commission also points to the limits of solidarity between Member States when the EU project does not deliver unhindered growth for all the members of the club.[45] The problem is aggravated by the fact that economic considerations in the Council are shaped by the immediate economic circumstances on the ground, with no thought as to how to align migration with the future needs of national economies. Furthermore, even though the Council is supposed to reflect the collective political interests of Member States in the common EU project, national considerations predominate.[46] Especially regarding non-EU migrants, when Member States are up against national unemployment or recession, it is impossible for them to agree on any migration-related measure that could lead to the attribution of rights. This is, of course, also connected to the shared competence on migration and the fact that even if Member States can foresee the demand for workers, they know that they can fulfil this demand through national migration law measures.[47] What this short-termism means for the quality of EU law-making, but also for EU integration, will be explored in the next section.

III. TIMEFRAMES OF CRISIS, DISADVANTAGES OF SHORT-TERMISM AND EU MIGRATION LAW

Following the historical reconstruction of EU labour migration policy in the previous section, the following should have become clear. The first is the intimate connection of EU labour migration policy and economic crises experienced by the Member States. The second is the defining effect of the 1970s oil crisis for the Council's short-termism in law-making on migration. With these in mind, the historical development of EU labour migration law will be situated in a broader theoretical discussion on crisis, governance and short-termism which can gain insight from critical theories on crisis and specifically, from the work of Runciman.[48]

[44] ibid ch 6.

[45] See also X Groussot and E Karageorgiou (eds), 'Special Issue on the Principle of Solidarity' (2023) 6(2) *Nordic Journal of European Law*.

[46] See on this N Jürgen Neyer, 'Saving Liberal Europe: Lessons from History' in A Bakardjieva Engelbrekt and X Groussot (eds), *The Future of Europe: Political and Legal Integration Beyond Brexit* (Hart Publishing, 2019) 24.

[47] See, eg, parallel schemes allowed for highly skilled workers which some Member States make extensive use of. Commission Staff Working Document, Executive Summary of the Fitness Check on EU Legislation on legal migration SWD(2019)1055.

[48] Runciman (n 3).

Runciman has demonstrated the conceptual ambiguities inherent in the idea of crisis, connected them to temporal ambiguities and described the effects of crisis for democratic governance in ways that could find analogous application in the area of EU migration, but also of EU integration more broadly.[49] To do that, Runciman begins by drawing on Koselleck's work on the concept of crisis and its ambiguities. According to Koselleck, crisis 'can be conceptualised as both structurally recurring and utterly unique'.[50] Runciman builds on this tension inherent in the idea of crisis and, unlike Koselleck, whose work drew on twentieth century revolutionary settings, Runciman instead focuses on the concept's evolution in the twenty-first century and democratic settings.[51] A central concern for him is the difficulty of pinning down a specific time frame of crisis and the interaction between different temporal conceptions of crisis. He argues that 'a distinctive feature of the contemporary understanding of crisis is the interplay and mismatch between different time frames, which creates problems for thinking about our long-term future'.[52] To demonstrate this feature, he identifies specific difficulties or background problems behind the inability to pin down the time frame of crisis.[53] Next, he goes on to identify another series of problems which he considers relevant to crisis as experienced in the contemporary democratic context: the mutually reinforcing problems of ubiquity, unpredictability and durability.[54]

Drawing on Alexis Tocqueville and his work on American democracy, Runciman reminds us that 'the short termism of democratic politics creates long-term advantages because it means that no crisis is ever allowed to reach its moment of truth (and, therefore its moment of ultimate danger)'.[55] By following a short-term approach and focusing on the problems at hand, crises are downplayed into a series of more manageable problems.[56] As Runciman suggests, the worst-case scenario is 'forestalled by never being encountered in full'.[57] While acknowledging the importance of this aspect of short-termism for democracy, Runciman also identifies a series of disadvantages. First, he points to the consequences short-term responses can have given that they are fragile and susceptible to failure.[58] Second, he suggests that once the durability of democracy is revealed (which is the long-term advantage of short-termism), it

[49] ibid.

[50] Koselleck and Richter (n 4) 374.

[51] Runciman (n 3) 4.

[52] ibid.

[53] ibid 4–7. He calls the difficulties definitional, experiential and perspectival. The first relates to the difficulties of definition, the second on the dependence of the time frame upon the various groups who experience the crisis, and the third relates to the perspective of those who did not experience the crisis at all.

[54] Runciman (n 3) 7–11.

[55] ibid 14; A de Tocqueville in HC Mansfield and D Winthrop (eds), *Democracy in America* (University of Chicago Press, 2002).

[56] Runciman (n 3) 12.

[57] ibid.

[58] ibid.

can become self-defeating.[59] By applying Tocqueville's insights on the inherent problems of democracy to the 2008 crisis and beyond, Runciman argues that the adaptability and flexibility which was key in addressing the worst of the crisis is also the reason behind the absence of longer-term solutions.[60]

I suggest that Runciman's analysis of the short-termism of democratic governance in situations of crisis finds perfect application in the area of EU migration law. Over 50 years after the oil crisis we are still suffering from overreliance on short-termism to avoid the worst which is predicted but never arrives in the area of migration. The implications which Tocqueville and Runciman identified in relation to short-termism and democracy can be extended by analogy to this specific policy area of EU law and provide new input on the problems of EU integration. While the advantages of short-termism are clear – EU integration moving forward – the disadvantages are also embedded in this area and fundamentally set it up for failure. In a more abstract sense, this proposition also relates to Streek's suggestion that the 1970s oil crisis was the prelude to an ongoing crisis.[61]

As to the first implication of short-termism for the fragility of the solutions adopted to handle crises, the following should be noted. The resolution of the 1970s oil crisis through border closures and migration bans took place within a fundamentally short-term horizon where the broader relation of labour migration and economic development could not be seen. The fragility of such a solution took attention away from structural issues of the economy and gave room to populist responses blaming migration for every economic downturn.[62] At the same time the sectoral regulation which is the result of such short-termism fails to achieve the objectives of aligning EU migration law to the needs of the market and is constantly revised.[63] Effective mobility of migrant labour in the internal market is constantly demanded and constantly failing.[64]

[59] ibid.

[60] ibid.

[61] W Streeck in P Camiller and D Fernbach trs, *Buying Time: The Delayed Crisis of Democratic Capitalism*, 2nd edn (Verso, 2017).

[62] cf Haas (n 37).

[63] Indicatively the first Directives on Students and Researchers (Directives 2005/71 and 2004/114) were revisited less than a decade after their first adoption. (The Commission proposal was issued in 2013 and led to the adoption of Directive 2016/81.) The Blue Card Directive also lasted less than a decade before receiving a revision that did not bring much change (Directive 2009/50 was recast by Directive 2021/1883 while the proposal to recast was issued in 2016). The Single Permit Directive adopted in 2011 has had a better fate with its revision proposed in 2022 and the recast just agreed in April 2024. See most recently the Commission's attempt to shape a regular migration policy that can address the economic needs in Commission Communication, Attracting skills and talent to the EU COM(2022)657 final.

[64] As attested also by the most recent attempt to revise the Long-term residents directive with uncertain outcome, Proposal for revision of Long-term residents Directive COM(2022)650 final 4, Explanatory memorandum Art 16–18. See also Council Document, Proposal for a Directive of the European Parliament and of the Council concerning the status of third-country nationals who are long-term residents (recast) – Presidency compromise text, ST 10528/1/23 REV 1, Brussels, 21 June 2023, already limiting some elements of the Commission proposal. See also European Parliament Research Service, Recast of Directive 2003/109/EC: Status of third-country nationals who are long term residents in the EU, EPRS BRI(2024)757361.

On the second implication of the self-defeating nature of short-termism, we would have to connect EU labour migration, crisis governance and competence. The self-defeating nature of short-termism for democracy identified by Runciman would in our case be extended by analogy to the self-defeating nature of short-termism for EU integration. This is for two reasons. First, the way in which EU migration law has developed points to the institutional failure to perceive labour migration as an issue of common and shared concern among the Member States.[65] The shared competence of the EU on migration means that Member States can eventually admit the labour they need in order to keep their economies running via national migration schemes. This allows them to individually cover labour demands and to achieve the needed growth without regard to growth on the collective level. The existence of and insistence on national frameworks, which do not guarantee sufficient rights to migrants, create barriers to the development of regulation at EU level. Where a position could be filled internally by the movement of a person from one Member State to another, this is now subject to barriers and delays that make it no different from entering the EU for the first time, adversely affecting integration in a common labour market. Second, Runciman reminds us that the short-termism of western democracies in the ways they address crises is characterised by smugness and panic at the same time. Specifically, he has suggested that 'The knowledge that Western democracies have come to possess that they can survive whatever the world throws at them could yet prove their fatal flaw.'[66] We could argue the same about the EU, with various scholarly works praising the EU for its success in addressing the crises that have been experienced through short-termism and decisions that are potentially controversial from a democratic perspective.[67] However, especially in the area of migration, populists have started to draw on this durability to portray the EU as both the cause of the crisis and the one unable to provide any substantive solutions to it.[68] It is uncertain for how long this situation can be sustained.

Finally, a third effect of short-termism which Runciman does not identify, but which is cause for concern as regards the short-termism of EU law, is the incoherence and injustice it produces. Specifically, the short-termism which has guided the EU response to labour migration has resulted in instruments plagued by internal and external incoherence. Apart from incoherence in the terms used in the various instruments, resulting most notably in the lack of an intelligible concept of

[65] See P Craig, 'Institutions, Power, and Institutional Balance' in P Craig and G de Búrca (eds), *The Evolution of EU Law* (Oxford University Press, 2021) raising the same point also for the migration crisis.

[66] Runciman (n 3) 14; D Runciman, *The Confidence Trap: A History of Democracy in Crisis from World War I to the Present* (Revised edition, Princeton University Press, 2018).

[67] D Hodson, *Circle of Stars: A History of the EU and the People Who Made It* (Yale University Press, 2023); For a more nuanced longue-durée account see L van Middelaar, *The Passage to Europe: How a Continent Became a Union* (Liz Waters tr, Yale University Press, 2013).

[68] See N Zaun and A Ripoll Servent, 'Perpetuating Crisis as a Supply Strategy: The Role of (Nativist) Populist Governments in EU Policymaking on Refugee Distribution' (2023) 61 *JCMS: Journal of Common Market Studies* 653; see also G Noll, 'Viciously Circular: Will Ageing Lock the European Union into Immigrant Exclusion?' in S Smet and V Stoyanova (eds), *Migrants' Rights, Populism and Legal Resilience in Europe* (Cambridge University Press, 2022).

integration, there are also vast differences among the rights migrants are granted by different instruments.[69] The rights migrants enjoy under EU migration law are defined horizontally in the Single Permit Directive and differentiated based on the function of different categories of migrants for the EU economy, with more rights attributed to those who are needed more.[70] Essentially the legal system put in place attributes more rights to those who are seen as crucial for the development of the EU project.[71] It can hardly be imagined that fair treatment of migrants, as demanded by Article 79(1) TFEU, implies differentiated attribution of rights based on how crucial a migrant is for the EU economy. In parallel, while there is an understanding of the need to promote mobility for certain individuals crucial to the project of growth, the economic fears of Member States, their short-term approach to migration and their ability to attract such individuals by parallel national schemes has led to the introduction of so many conditions for the exercise of mobility rights that in practice it is almost impossible to meet them all.[72] Such unfair attribution of rights makes no sense in view of long-term considerations. To put it simply, we might know what type of migrants the EU economy needs today, but we cannot predict what type of migrants will be most needed in the future.

Overall, we see that the short-termism of the Council in the area of migration jeopardises both the durability of the solutions offered and the durability of the EU as such due to institutional failure and lack of legitimacy. At the same time this short-termism also produces unfair results which cannot and should not be accommodated by a system based on the rule of law, the protection of human rights and respect for human dignity under Article 2 TEU.

IV. CONCLUSION

While EU scholarship has examined in great depth the so-called migration crisis of 2015–2016, this chapter revisited the history of EU labour migration law in order to bring to light the effects of the 1970s oil crisis for the development of

[69] See Loxa (n 8) 322–31 for a detailed overview of the matter; also S Iglesias Sánchez, 'Free Movement as a Precondition for Integration of Third-Country Nationals in the EU' in E Guild, K Groenendijk and S Carrera (eds), *Illiberal liberal states: immigration, citizenship, and integration in the EU* (Ashgate, 2009). See earlier K Groenendijk, 'Legal Concepts of Integration in EU Migration Law' (2004) 6 *European Journal of Migration and Law* 111 with reference to free movement as well.

[70] Directive 2011/98/EU of the European Parliament and of the Council of 13 December 2011 on a single application procedure for a single permit for third-country nationals to reside and work in the territory of a Member State and on a common set of rights for third-country workers legally residing in a Member State [2011] OJ L 343/1. See also the recast version voted by the Parliament in April 2024 on first reading and pending for adoption in the Council.

[71] These are high-skill workers. See Loxa (n 8) 293.

[72] The problems persist even after the adoption of the recast Blue Card Directive, cf T de Lange and Z Vankova, 'The Recast EU Blue Card Directive: Towards a Level Playing Field to Attract Highly Qualified Migrant Talent to Work in the EU?' (2022) 24 *European Journal of Migration and Law* 489.

the relevant legal area. The purpose was to demonstrate a connection between economic crises and their effects for migration governance in the EU which has been understudied from a legal perspective.

To do so the chapter began by a historical reconstruction of EU labour migration, and suggested that the Community institutions followed a fundamentally different approach to migration before and after the 1970s oil crisis. The economic threat experienced by the Community industries at the time lead to a short-termist response that has been guiding the Council's position, but also law-making, in the era from the 1980s onwards. By identifying the oil crisis as the crucial event propelling the establishment of short-termism in EU migration governance, the chapter connected this area to a broader understanding of the 1970s as the beginning of an ongoing crisis.[73]

Relating the relevant empirical material to the theoretical framework of Runciman on crisis, short-termism and its effects for democratic governance, it appears that short-termism has had significant implications not only for EU migration law but for EU integration at large which are structured around three major fault lines.

The first is the fragility of the solutions offered as a response to a crisis. From the 1970s onwards migration has been made a scapegoat for every economic downturn. This has made it impossible to adopt common legislation that can offer a reasonable and long-term solution to the migration demand in the Member States. The second is the self-defeating nature of the solutions offered. While the durability of the EU seems to be achieved through these short-term approaches to migration, the failure by institutions to perceive migration as an issue of common concern prevents integration and feeds populist representations of the EU.[74] The third and final fault line relates to the incoherence and injustice that are entrenched in the relevant framework. The instruments of EU migration law are characterised by great internal and external incoherence, and they create different rights based on how much a migrant is needed for the EU economy. Such an unfair model of attribution of rights not only sits uneasily with the foundational values of EU primary law, but it also becomes self-defeating as there is no concern for how migrant labour might have a role to play in an anticipated green and just transition.[75]

In a broader political reality that does not seem promising, one can only hope that insights gained by looking at the past and bringing to the fore the problems which arise from short-termism can inform political debate, or even lead to legal change with due consideration for the long-term future.[76]

[73] Streeck (n 56).

[74] cf R McCrea, 'Forward or Back: The Future of European Integration and the Impossibility of the Status Quo' (2017) 23 *European Law Journal* 66; See also Loxa and Stoyanova (n 2) for a different account with a focus on constitutional deficits in EU asylum law.

[75] See A Vandeplas et al, 'The Possible Implications of the Green Transition for the EU Labour Market', European Economy Discussion Papers, Publication Office of the European Union 2022.

[76] See A van Rij et al, 'How will gains by the far right affect the European Parliament and EU?' Chatham House Explainer, 11 June 2024. cf B Davies, 'Why EU Legal History Matters – A Historian's Response' (2013) 28 *American University International Law Review* 1337.

9

Legal Sources in Times of 'Crisis' – How Sweden's Migration Courts Responded to the 2016 Temporary Migration Law

LOVISA HÄCKNER POSSE

I. INTRODUCTION

THE LEGAL LITERATURE on emergencies tends to take, as its starting point, a division between the normal and the exceptional (special law will displace normal law; normal times will be taken over by a continuous state of exception, etc).[1] Today, however, there is an increasing need to go beyond this dichotomy. As highlighted by the legal scholar Karin Loevy, far from being a space of political exception and legal vacuum, emergencies should be viewed 'as processes, rather than momentary events; as involving a plurality of response agents rather than one centralised executive; as opportunities for norm production and legal and institutional mobilisation, rather than occasions for the suspension of law and legality'.[2] Since crisis management takes place in complex institutional settings, studies of these settings, including their norms and practices, are essential to fully comprehend the response capacities that are being mobilised in perceived emergencies.[3]

This chapter, which builds on my doctoral thesis,[4] draws on these insights and analyses the Swedish migration courts' responses to the Temporary Act (2016:752) – a law that was enacted 2016 as a response to the 'refugee crisis' with the aim of adapting Sweden's migration policy to minimum levels under EU law.[5] The

[1] For an overview of theoretical endeavours that are tied to such a distinction, see K Loevy, *Emergencies in Public Law – Legal Politics of Containment* (Cambridge University Press, 2016) 2–5.

[2] ibid 5.

[3] ibid 124.

[4] L Häckner Posse, *Integrationskrav i domstol – En studie av hur svenska migrationsdomstolar förhåller sig till nationella politiska ambitioner och övernationella källor* (Lund University, 2024).

[5] SFS 2016:752.

chapter focuses on how theories of the 'rules of the game' in these courts – that is, theories of the courts' decision-making practices in times of 'normalcy' – affect our understanding of emergency management, especially as regards the relationship between domestic legislators and domestic courts, and whether these theories are empirically supported. It makes three key points: first, it argues that theories of how Swedish courts have adapted to the Europeanisation of public law inform our understanding of what room the domestic legislator has for manoeuvring in responding to perceived threats. Second, it identifies discrepancies between the theories just mentioned and the Swedish migration courts' application of the Temporary Act. Third, it argues that we need more evidence-based studies of the role of domestic courts in declared emergencies. This is primarily for two reasons: first, such studies can help rework theories of how the indeterminacy of law can be used to influence legal outcomes, including the outcomes of 'crisis' legislation. Second, such studies can help us move beyond theoretical endeavours that are tied to a division between the normal and the exceptional. The Swedish migration courts' responses to the Temporary Act is a clear example of how 'crisis' legislation raises questions not only about emergency practices, but equally about the general norms and practices that govern public law decision-making.

The chapter is organised as follows. First, in Section II, it provides an overview of how public law scholarship tends to conceptualise the decision-making practices of Swedish courts, especially considering the Europeanisation of the Swedish legal order. In Section III, a brief overview of the Temporary Act and the history of the migration courts is outlined. In Section IV, the legislative process of the Temporary Act is studied to show the conflicting views underpinning the decisions-making practices of the migration courts. In Section V, the migration courts, and the way they apply the Temporary Act, is examined by focusing on the role of EU and ECHR law arguments in the courts' application of the income requirement for family reunification. Lastly, the chapter discusses the identified gap between theory and practice and the way in which it can help rework theories of the decision-making practices of Swedish courts, including their role(s) in declared crises.

II. A POLYCENTRIC OR MONOCENTRIC METHOD? THEORIES IN THE LEGAL LITERATURE OF HOW SWEDISH COURTS HAVE ADAPTED TO THE EUROPEANISATION OF THE LEGAL ORDER

The public law literature often highlights that Swedish courts are in the wake of a major change: while the legal order of the past was primarily a means of realising national political ambitions, the Europeanisation has created a legal order with other focus areas.[6] EU law and the ECHR have resulted in a

[6] Häckner Posse (n 4) 38, 214. The focus on realising political ambitions should be understood in the light of the emergence of the Swedish welfare state.

domestic legal order that focuses on the protection of rights, not least since national policy is being monitored and constrained by supranational courts. Thus, many agree that today Swedish courts are less focused on pursuing national political ambitions (such as objectives of limited immigration) and more focused on ensuring compliance with supranational sources of law, which in the context of family reunification primarily means the EU Family Reunification Directive[7] and the right to family life in Article 8 of the ECHR (for a more detailed description of how the Temporary Act relates to these latter sources, see Section V). Yet the literature contains several, partly contradictory, theories of *how* Swedish courts ensure compliance with EU law and the ECHR. As I have argued elsewhere, the different views can be categorised by using two schematised positions: the *polycentric position* and the *monocentric position*.[8] As will be discussed later in this chapter, the positions are likely to influence our perceptions of how legal reasoning should be conducted to influence legal outcomes, as well as our understanding of the role of domestic courts in public law 'emergencies'.

According to the *polycentric* position, Swedish courts are accustomed to taking EU law and ECHR obligations into consideration (including case law from the Luxembourg and Strasbourg courts), even in the absence of explicit consideration of such obligations in traditional domestic legal sources (such as statutes and preparatory works). The Europeanisation of the Swedish legal order has dissolved older legal hierarchies: today, the will of the domestic legislator is one of several interests that the domestic courts consider, which means that preparatory works (such as government bills) have become a less important means of statutory interpretation. The polycentric position further distances itself from the legal method of Scandinavian legal realism, ie, to a goal-oriented approach to legal sources and to the view that general legal principles and human rights are of secondary importance. Moreover, the parties to the case increasingly steer contemporary court proceedings, which means that the polycentric character of law can be used for strategic purposes (eg, by arguing that national legislation breaches the EU Family Reunification Directive or Article 8 of the ECHR).[9]

According to the *monocentric* position, Swedish courts still depend on detailed interpretations of EU law and ECHR law obligations. The Europeanisation takes place in a context of established ways of thinking, which means that Swedish courts still consider the national legislator to be the 'engine' of legislative development. The monocentric position emphasises, inter alia, the doctrine of dualism – ie, the idea that international law regulations require national legislative measures to be domestically applicable. Rather than

[7] Council Directive 2003/86/EC of 22 September 2003 on the right to family reunification [2003] OJ L 251/12.
[8] Häckner Posse (n 4) 38.
[9] ibid 38–46; n 7.

dissolving older legal hierarchies, the Europeanisation of the legal order makes Swedish courts study traditional domestic sources (such as statutes and preparatory works) with an increased focus on the domestic legislator's interpretations of Sweden's international obligations. The monocentric position also highlights that Swedish courts largely study case law from domestic higher courts.[10]

Both the polycentric and the monocentric position highlight that Swedish courts thoroughly explain how they interpret sources of law, including conflicts and ambiguities in these sources.[11] For instance, the polycentric position stresses that the Europeanisation requires transparency and that domestic courts need to 'explain more thoroughly why they do not intervene to protect the rights that individuals claim to have'.[12] Although a high workload sometimes makes this difficult, the courts see it as a central task to explain how they interpret and navigate the polycentric landscape. As regards the monocentric position, the courts' focus on traditional legal sources does not mean that they engage in a 'mechanical' law application. For instance, the courts examine how different preparatory works should be ranked and explain how they interpret contradictory or ambiguous statements in these latter sources.[13]

It may be noted that neither the polycentric nor the monocentric position discusses whether the law application in 'normal times' differs from the law application in times of 'crisis'. Studies that address public law issues of Swedish crisis legislation have devoted more attention to the design of such legislation than to the domestic courts' implementation and application.[14] Yet, as mentioned above, it is likely that the positions inform our understanding of the courts' role in emergency management, including the courts' position in the system of checks against abuse of authority. Although the positions represent different views on the relationship between the domestic courts and the domestic legislator, where the monocentric position emphasises a closer connection,

[10] Häckner Posse (n 4) 47–51; L Häckner Posse and H Lärka, 'Hiding In Plain Sight? Conceptualizations of Databases in Migration Law and International Tax Law' (2023) 117 *AJIL Unbound* 151 doi.org/10.1017/aju.2023.22.

[11] Häckner Posse (n 4) 60–61.

[12] I Cameron, 'Den svenske domaren och internationella normer – några reflektioner' in F Wersäll et al (eds), *Svea hovrätt 400 år* (Norstedts Juridik, 2014) 510.

[13] Häckner Posse (n 4) 51.

[14] cf T Johansen, *Krisjuridik: Rättsliga befogenheter från olycka till höjd beredskap* (Norstedts Juridik, 2024); H Wenander, 'Sweden: Non-binding Rules against the Pandemic – Formalism, Pragmatism and Some Legal Realism' (2021) 12 *European Journal of Risk Regulation* 127; M Zamboni, 'Swedish legislation and the migration crisis' (2019) 7 *The theory and practice* 101. It can further be noted that the migration courts are rarely the focus of discussions in legal scholarship on how Swedish courts have adapted to Europeanisation. The existing research on the migration courts has mainly discussed their evaluation of evidence in asylum cases. cf L Johannesson, *In Courts We Trust – Administrative justice in Swedish migration courts* (Stockholm University, 2017); A Meyerson, *To believe or not to believe – is that the question?: a critical study of how the Swedish migration courts handle their responsibility to judge in asylum cases* (University of Gothenburg, 2023); R Thorburn Stern, 'Foreign Law in Swedish judicial decision-making: playing a limited role in refugee law cases' in GS Goodwin-Gill and H Lambert (eds), The *Limits of Transnational Law Refugee Law, Policy Harmonization and Judicial Dialogue in the European Union* (Cambridge University Press, 2010) 186.

both positions suggest that Swedish courts, when applying legislation (including 'crisis' legislation), focus on issues of compliance with supranational norms.

III. THE MIGRATION COURTS AND THE TEMPORARY ACT – A BRIEF BACKGROUND

Since 2006, the decisions of the Swedish Migration Agency – the authority that decides on residence permit applications – can be appealed to a migration court. The migration courts are part of Sweden's administrative courts, which means that judges who rule on migration law cases also decide on other public law issues. There are four migration courts in Sweden, each being responsible for different geographical regions. The decisions of the courts can be appealed to the Migration Court of Appeal, which is part of the Administrative Court of Appeal in Stockholm. Before 2006, applications for residence permits were handled by the state administration. The main purposes of the 2006 court reform were to strengthen the rule of law and to increase transparency, based on the idea that increased judicial review would create greater legitimacy for the Swedish migration control system (both among the public and among residence permit applicants).[15]

Moreover, and as stated in the beginning of this chapter, in 2016, the Swedish government enacted a Temporary Act (2016:752) that restricted the possibility of being granted a residence permit in Sweden. The law, which intended to create a 'respite' for Swedish refugee reception in the wake of the so-called refugee crisis, provided, inter alia, for temporary residence permits for refugees (instead of permanent ones) and significantly limited the possibility of family reunification in Sweden. The law was initially intended to apply for three years, but in 2019 it was extended for another two years. In 2021, many of the provisions of the Temporary Act were incorporated into the ordinary Aliens Act (2005:716). It is thus not surprising that the legislative changes that followed the 'crisis' have been described as a paradigm shift in Swedish migration policy.

One consequence of the Temporary Act was that the income requirement for family reunification was significantly extended. Over the past two decades, many European countries have introduced such requirements – rules that are often referred to as *civic integration*.[16] In Sweden, the requirement was first introduced in 2010 but, due to its many exceptions, it was very rarely applied. In 2016, the number of exceptions to the requirement was reduced, meaning that the requirement became applicable in a large proportion of family reunification

[15] Johannesson (n 14) 69–72.

[16] C Joppke, 'Beyond national models: Civic integration policies for immigrants in Western Europe' (2007) 30 *West European Politics* 1; S Wallace Goodman, 'Integration requirements for integration's sake? Identifying, categorising and comparing civic integration policies' (2010) 36 *Journal of Ethnic and Migration Studies* 753.

cases.[17] The Temporary Act thus meant that Swedish migration authorities were given new tasks, which highlights that emergencies are not equivalent to the suspension of legal norms.[18] The Act further required that individuals who wanted to reunite with family members in Sweden (the sponsors) were able to support not only themselves, but also the migrating family members. (As will be clarified below, the Swedish legislation was thus adapted to the minimum levels of the EU Family Reunification Directive.)[19] According to the legislator, the objective of limiting the numbers of asylum seekers could be achieved by restricting the possibility of family reunification in Sweden, meaning that asylum and family reunification were seen as intertwined policy areas.[20] The Temporary Act also shifted the purpose of the income requirement: while the 2010 requirement was primarily linked to an objective of promoting 'integration' and 'self-sufficiency', the Temporary Act primarily presented the requirement as a tool to create a 'respite' for Swedish refugee reception (this is not to say, however, that these objectives are fundamentally different).[21]

As will be described in the following, the Temporary Act further resulted in a discussion on the role and the decision-making practices of Swedish courts. The discussion largely reflected the positions outlined above – the polycentric position and the monocentric position.

IV. THE LEGISLATIVE PROCESS OF THE TEMPORARY ACT – A DISPUTE OVER THE ROLE(S) OF SWEDISH COURTS

Sweden has a tradition of sending legislative drafts to different bodies for non-binding consultation, such as authorities within the judicial system.[22] In early 2016, the government's proposal for a temporary migration law was sent out for such consultation. In their consultation responses, the migration courts (among others) questioned whether the proposal was compatible with Sweden's international obligations. In particular, the compatibility of the limited possibilities for family reunification with Article 8 of the ECHR was questioned. Yet the migration courts seem to have been at least as concerned about having to decide on the issue of compatibility themselves.[23] The government's proposal included so-called *safety valves*, ie, provisions stating that several of the Temporary Act's

[17] Häckner Posse (n 4) 89–93.

[18] cf O Gross and F Ní Aoláin, *Law in times of crisis: emergency powers in theory and practice* (Cambridge University Press, 2006) 66.

[19] See n 7. In addition to being self-supporting, the sponsor must have a home of sufficient size and standard to accommodate the applicants.

[20] Häckner Posse (n 4) 90.

[21] ibid 92.

[22] T Bull, 'Judges without a Court – Judicial Preview in Sweden' in T Campbell, KD Ewing and A Tomkins (eds), *The Legal Protection of Human Rights: Sceptical Essays* (online edn, Oxford Academic, 2011) doi.org/10.1093/acprof:oso/9780199606078.003.0019.

[23] Häckner Posse (n 4) 93–97.

restrictions would not be applicable in cases where the rejection of an application for residence permit would constitute a violation of 'Sweden's international obligations'.[24] According to the courts, the tradition of dualism made it inappropriate for them to consider international obligations in each individual case. They thus asked for clarification on which obligations the domestic legislator had in mind.[25]

Despite the criticism aired during the consultation process, the Swedish legislator chose to include the safety valves in the Temporary Act. According to the legislator, the migration courts already interpreted national legislation in light of EU law and the ECHR, ie, when applying the ordinary Aliens Act, which meant that the safety valves did 'not entail a completely new task' for the courts.[26] However, the final government bill contained some statements from the legislator regarding the relationship between the Temporary Act and supranational norms. In particular, the legislator emphasised the importance of ensuring that the courts' law application was in accordance with the ECHR and with the principle of the best interests of the child.[27] Yet the government bill also stressed that the purpose of the safety valves was to 'eliminate any risk of the Swedish rules being contrary to the ECHR or to *any other* Swedish convention commitment', which seems to indicate that the courts were also expected to consider conventions that were not explicitly mentioned in the preparatory works.[28] Moreover, the legislator emphasised the importance of considering how the ECHR had been interpreted by the ECtHR (although without making any direct references to case law from the Strasbourg court).[29] The government bill further contained a general evaluation of the compatibility of the Temporary Act with EU law and ECHR obligations, in which the government emphasised that the act would only apply for three years and that 'due to the burden placed on the Swedish asylum system [...] it is compatible with the [ECHR] to postpone family reunification for this period'. At the same time, however, the government highlighted the need for individual assessments.[30]

The consultation process of the Temporary Act thus revived a fundamental discussion of how Swedish courts have adapted to the Europeanisation of the legal order. By insisting on the safety valves, the domestic legislator seems to have been concerned that the migration courts, in the absence of such provisions, would not apply the Temporary Act, ie, on the grounds that it was contrary to superior norms. Yet the courts' responses indicate that they did not want to engage in such a policy intervention, or at least that they considered themselves

[24] SFS 2016:752 (ss 11 and 13).

[25] Häckner Posse (n 4) 95; Government Bill, Prop. 2015/16:174, *Tillfälliga begränsningar av möjligheten att få uppehållstillstånd i Sverige* (Temporary restrictions on the possibility to obtain residence permits in Sweden) 159.

[26] Government bill (n 25) 53.

[27] ibid 79.

[28] ibid 54.

[29] ibid 79.

[30] ibid 41–43.

to be in need of the legislator's interpretations of EU law and the ECHR to take a position on the issue. While the legislator's view coincided with the polycentric position, the courts' responses corresponded with the monocentric position. In other words, the consultation process expressed conflicting views on the decision-making practices of Swedish courts. The consultation process further highlights that it can be difficult to identify whether statements about such practices are empirical or normative. For instance, whether the courts considered themselves incapable of assessing issues of EU law and ECHR compatibility (that is, in the absence of thorough consideration in the preparatory works), *or* that they felt that the responsibility should not be imposed on them but that they were able to take on the task as a last resort (eg, in the absence of detailed preparatory works).[31] This underlines the need for combining studies of 'law on the books' with studies of the actual decision-making practices of domestic courts.

V. THE MIGRATION COURTS' APPLICATION OF THE TEMPORARY ACT – A PRACTICE NOT FULLY CAPTURED BY THE LEGAL LITERATURE

This section, which is based on a qualitative study conducted in my previous work, looks at how Sweden's migration courts de facto applied the Temporary Act, by focusing on their application of the income requirement for family reunification. The empirical data consists of 418 court cases decided in 2017 from three of Sweden's four migration courts.[32] As clarified below, the courts' applications deviate from both the polycentric and the monocentric position.

A. The Absence of the Polycentric Position in the Migration Courts' Application

As noted earlier in this chapter, the polycentric position argues that Swedish courts are accustomed to (ex officio) considering EU law and ECHR obligations, including case law from the CJEU and the ECtHR. Further, the parties to the case increasingly steer contemporary court proceedings, eg, by arguing that national legislation breaches EU law or the ECHR. To determine whether the migration courts' application of the income requirement correlates with the polycentric position, we first need to examine how the requirement is regulated

[31] cf Häckner Posse (n 4) 96–97. Furthermore, since the aim of the courts' criticism was for the legislator to fully abandon the safety valve design, their consultation responses contained few clarifications on how they intended to apply the provisions.

[32] For a more detailed account of the data collection and methodology, see Häckner Posse (n 4) 32–36. Since the study's approach is qualitative, I do not claim to achieve statistically significant results. In the following, when I comment on the courts' applications, I refer to how the courts deal with the income requirement in the decisions I have studied.

in EU and ECHR law; that is, how the requirement relates to the EU Family Reunification Directive (FRD) and Article 8 of the ECHR.[33]

As regards EU law, the FRD contains several provisions on the ability of Member States to impose income and housing requirements on third-country nationals who reside in Europe.[34] However, the Directive does not oblige Member States to apply such requirements, meaning that states have the possibility of applying more 'generous' rules on family reunification than those provided for in the Directive.[35] This was also emphasised by the Swedish legislator in 2016: by adapting the Swedish legislation to the minimum levels of the FRD, the expectation was that asylum seekers would 'choose' other Member States over Sweden (a strategy that has been referred to as 'negative nation branding').[36] Moreover, the CJEU has ruled, on several occasions, on the compatibility of Member States' legislation with the Directive's income requirement.[37] On the one hand, the Court has repeatedly stated that the objective of the FRD is to promote family reunification, and that the leeway that states are recognised as having when applying the Directive must not be used in a manner which would undermine this objective. On the other hand, the Court has frequently accepted that Member States impose various forms of socio-economic requirements on sponsors, including in the name of 'integration'. The CJEU case law on the FRD is thus characterised by ambivalence, emphasising both the rights and obligations of third-country nationals.[38]

As mentioned above, the income requirement further relates to the right to family life in Article 8 of the ECHR. The case law of the ECtHR on the right to family life is extensive.[39] To summarise this jurisprudence, it can be

[33] See n 7.

[34] Article 7 (n 7).

[35] cf Häckner Posse (n 4) 77.

[36] T Gammeltoft-Hansen, 'Refugee policy as "negative nation branding": The case of Denmark and the Nordics' (2017) 2017 *Danish Foreign Policy Review* 99. As Gammeltoft-Hansen highlights: 'Rather than preventing access to asylum per se, policies of indirect deterrence are designed to make the asylum system and protection conditions appear as unattractive as possible, thereby achieving a "beggar-thy-neighbour" effect in pushing asylum seekers towards other countries' (ibid 100).

[37] Case C-540/03 *European Parliament v Council of the European Union* ECLI:EU:C:2006:429, [2006] ECR I-5769; Case C-578/08 *Rhimou Chakroun v Minister van Buitenlandse Zaken* ECLI:EU:C:2010:117, [2010] 3 CMLR 5; Case C-558/14 *Mimoun Khachab v Subdelegación del Gobierno en Álava* ECLI:EU:C:2016:285, [2016] 3 CMLR 29; Joined Cases C-356/11 and C-357/11 *O & S v Maahanmuuttovirasto and Maahanmuuttovirasto v L.* ECLI:EU:C:2012:776, [2013] 2 WLR 1093; Case C-153/14 *Minister van Buitenlandse Zaken v K & A* ECLI:EU:C:2015:453, [2016] 1 CMLR 9; Case C-550 *A & S v Staatssecretaris van Veiligheid en Justitie* ECLI:EU:C:2018:248, [2018] 3 CMLR 20.

[38] Häckner Posse (n 4) 78–82; D Kostakopoulou, 'The Anatomy of Civic Integration' in F Anthias and M Pajnik (eds), *Contesting Integration, Engendering Migration – Theory and Practice. Migration, diasporas and citizenship* (Palgrave-MacMillan, 2014) 37.

[39] For an overview, see S Carrera and Z Vankova, *Human rights aspects of immigrant and refugee integration policies – A comparative assessment in selected Council of Europe member states* (Council of Europe, 2019) rm.coe.int/168093de2c.

said that Article 8 does not include a general right to family reunification.[40] As has been extensively analysed elsewhere, the Court claimed early on that it was 'well established in international law' that states have a right to control the entry and residence of aliens. Further, when considering whether there is a legitimate interference with the right to family life in the context of migration, the ECtHR tends to attribute a wide margin of appreciation to the states parties.[41] Yet the Court has found on several occasions that it is contrary to Article 8 to deny family reunification, especially in relation to children and refugees.[42] Moreover, the ECtHR case law is casuistic, meaning that Article 8 requires a case-by-case examination.[43] In recent years, the Court has also ruled on the relationship between Article 8 and civic integration. (However, part of the ECtHR case law on civic integration came after 2017; that is, after the domestic court cases studied in this chapter.)[44] As described in the previous section, the link between the income requirement and the ECHR was also made clear by the Temporary Act and its preparatory works. The Act contained safety valves stating, inter alia, that if the requirement was not met, family reunification should still be granted if a rejection of an application for residence permit would constitute a violation of Sweden's international obligations. Although the instructions in the preparatory works on how to apply the safety valves were brief, the legislator

[40] That the right to family life can be restricted is also clear from the second paragraph of Article 8, which states that a state may restrict the right to family life if it is 'necessary in a democratic society in the interests of national security, public safety or the economic well-being of the country, for the prevention of disorder or crime, for the protection of health or morals, or for the protection of the rights and freedoms of others'.

[41] *Abdulaziz, Cabales & Balkandali v United Kingdom* App no 9214/80, 9473/81, 9474/81 (ECtHR, 28 May 1985); M-B Dembour, *When humans become migrants: study of the European Court of Human Rights with an Inter-American counterpoint* (Oxford University Press, 2015) 96–119. The Court's approach in the migration context can be compared to how it has interpreted the margin of appreciation in the context of climate crisis. In this latter context, the Court has emphasised that states have a reduced margin of appreciation regarding the reduction targets that they must set and implement to ensure compliance with Article 8. See *Varein Klimaseniorinnen Schweiz and others v Switzerland* App no 53600/20 (ECtHR, 9 April 2024).

[42] For an overview, see Carrera and Vankova (n 39) 11.

[43] T Spijkerboer, 'Structural Instability: Strasbourg Case Law on Children's Family Reunion' (2009) 11 *European Journal of Migration and Law* 271.

[44] *Okubamichael Debru v Sweden* App no 49755/18 (ECtHR, 25 July 2024); *D.H. and others v Sweden* App no 34210/19 (ECtHR, 25 July 2024); B.F. *and others v Switzerland* App no 13258/18, 15500/18, 57303/18, 9078/20 (ECtHR, 4 July 2023); *Dabo v Sweden* App no 12510/18 (ECtHR, 18 January 2024); *Haydarie v The Netherlands* App no 8876/04 (ECtHR, 20 October 2005); *Konstantinov v The Netherlands* App no 16351/03 (ECtHR, 26 April 2007). Furthermore, Article 7 of the EU Charter establishes a right to respect for family life. The starting point of the Charter is that the rights expressed therein should be at least equivalent to those of the ECHR. It may also be noted that the UN Convention on the Rights of the Child (CRC) contains a specific provision on family reunification (Article 10), stating, inter alia, that 'applications by a child or his or her parents to enter or leave a State Party for the purpose of family reunification shall be dealt with by State Parties in a positive, humane and expeditious manner'. Moreover, Article 3 of the CRC establishes the principle of the best interests of the child. Sweden ratified the CRC in 1990, but it was not incorporated into and given the status of Swedish law until 2020. However, the principle of the best interests of the child has been enshrined in the Swedish Aliens Act since 1989.

emphasised the importance of considering how the ECHR had been interpreted by the ECtHR.[45]

How then do the migration courts' practices relate to the polycentric position? That is, how (if at all) do the courts refer to EU law and the ECHR? In general, the polycentric position is not supported by the migration courts' cases on the income requirement. With a few exceptions, the migration courts do not refer directly to sources in EU or ECHR law.[46] Below are two examples of how the courts' application deviates from the polycentric position.

The first example concerns how the courts assess sponsors' ability to support themselves. According to the Temporary Act, the sponsor's income must be at least equivalent to the reserve amount, ie, the part of the salary that may not be seized when the Swedish Enforcement Authority carries out seizures (an amount which is intended to cover the person's housing cost and general cost of living).[47] In the courts' application of the income requirement, the reserve amount is generally treated in a schematic manner, meaning that if the income does not reach the amount, the sponsor is not considered to meet the requirement.[48] In their assessments, the migration courts make no references to the case law of the CJEU, including the *Chakroun* case.[49]

In the *Chakroun* case, the CJEU stated that Member States, when applying the income requirement of the FRD, 'may indicate a certain sum as a reference amount', but not 'impose a minimum income level below which all family reunifications will be refused, irrespective of an actual examination of the situation of each applicant'.[50] The migration courts, however, tend to assess each source of income separately and without elaborating on the situation of the applicant. For example, suppose a sponsor refers to her salary, her savings, and the income of her spouse – sources which, when added together, exceed the reserve amount. In these situations, the courts disqualify the sponsor's salary on the grounds that it is not sustainable, disqualify the savings on the grounds that they do not generate returns, and disqualify the spouse's income on the grounds that the income must come from the sponsor – that is, without discussing whether the sources taken together would nevertheless meet the requirement. The courts' reasoning often puts individual variations in the background, meaning also that they seem reluctant to engage in explicit overall assessments. This does not mean that their rulings are contrary to EU law, or that reasoning based on CJEU case law would have led to a different outcome. Given the assumption that all sources of law involve contradiction, references to a certain legal source can be made to protect different interests and claims (the CJEU's case law is also brief when it comes

[45] Government bill (n 25) 79.
[46] Häckner Posse (n 4) 111, 161–67.
[47] SFS 2016:850 (section 1).
[48] Häckner Posse (n 4) 115–17.
[49] n 37.
[50] See para 48 (n 37).

to clarifying how an individual assessment of the income requirement should be made).[51] Yet the migration courts' reasoning, not least the absence of references to the CJEU's case law, makes it difficult to argue that their application corresponds with the polycentric position.[52]

The second example concerns how the migration courts apply one of the safety valves, ie, the provision of the Temporary Act stating that if the income requirement is not met, family reunification should still be granted if the rejection of an application for residence permit would constitute a violation of Sweden's international obligations. In general, the courts' application of the safety valve is characterised by cursory reasoning; that is, it consists of a statement that 'a rejection of a residence permit does not violate Sweden's international obligations'. This is also the case when the appellant invokes circumstances clearly related to the ECtHR's case law (for instance, that the sponsor is a refugee, meaning that family reunification is not possible in the country of origin, or that the sponsor's children are living under difficult conditions in the home country).[53] If the courts discuss international obligations in addition to the standard wording just mentioned, they refer to how the Migration Court of Appeal has interpreted Article 8 of the ECHR. Thus, the migration courts do not refer directly to ECtHR case law.[54] Again, this does not mean that the courts' application breaches the ECHR.[55] On the one hand, the Strasbourg court has emphasised that an assessment under Article 8 must contain a statement of reasons.[56] On the other hand, in 2022, the Court accepted that Swedish migration authorities 'mainly referred in abstract terms to the relevant provisions of the Temporary Act and to international conventions'.[57] Yet the migration courts' application of the safety valve clearly deviates from the polycentric position.[58]

B. The Absence of the Monocentric Position in the Migration Courts' Application

When applying the income requirement, the migration courts mainly refer to domestic statutes, preparatory works, and case law from the Migration Court

[51] cf D Kennedy, 'The Hermeneutic of Suspicion in Contemporary American Legal Thought' (2014) 25 *Law and Critique* 91.

[52] Häckner Posse (n 4) 124–27, 136–37.

[53] ibid 161–167; *Ahmut v the Netherlands* App No 21702/93 (ECtHR, 28 November 1996); *Sen v the Netherlands* App No 31465/96 (ECtHR, 21 December 2001); *I.M. v Netherlands* App No 41226/98 (ECtHR, 25 March 2003); *Tuquabo-Tekle and Others v the Netherlands* App No 60665/00 (ECtHR 1 December 2005); *Osman v Denmark* App No 38058/09 (ECtHR, 14 June 2011); *Gül v Switzerland* App No 38058/09 (ECtHR, 19 February 1996).

[54] Häckner Posse (n 4) 171.

[55] ibid 173.

[56] *El Ghatet v Switzerland* App No 56971/10 (ECtHR, 8 November 2016).

[57] *M.T. and others v Sweden* App No 22105/18 (ECtHR, 20 October 2022).

[58] Häckner Posse (n 4) 187–88.

of Appeal.[59] These are sources highlighted by the monocentric position. Yet the courts' reasoning does not correlate with this position either. This can be illustrated by once again examining their application of one of the safety valves and their assessments of sponsors' ability to support themselves.

According to the monocentric position, the Europeanisation of the legal order makes Swedish courts study traditional domestic sources with an increased focus on the domestic legislator's interpretations of Sweden's international obligations. The position further highlights that Swedish courts engage in explicit interpretation of vague and conflicting statements in such sources, eg, preparatory works. As regards the compatibility of the Temporary Act with supranational norms, the preparatory works are indeed brief (which was also criticised by the migration courts during the consultation process). Yet, the preparatory works contain *some* statements on how the courts should proceed when applying the safety valves. As mentioned earlier, the preparatory works consist partly of general evaluations of the compatibility of the law with the ECHR and partly of statements emphasising the need for an individual assessment that considers the case law of the Strasbourg court. When applying the safety valve, the migration courts reiterate the general statement that 'due to the burden placed on the Swedish asylum system [...] it is compatible with the [ECHR] to postpone family reunification for this period'. The courts seem to view this statement as a complete proportionality assessment under Article 8 of the ECHR that can be applied to all cases that concern the income requirement. The fact that the preparatory works also contain other statements cannot be deduced from the migration courts' reasoning (eg, that 'an individual assessment of the right to family reunification should be made in each individual case' and/or that the courts should consider how the ECHR has been interpreted by the Strasbourg court). The courts thus seem reluctant to discuss vague or contradictory statements in the preparatory works.[60]

The preparatory works further contain several statements on how sponsors' ability to support themselves should be assessed – statements that are often ambiguous. Also in this context, the courts use some statements in the preparatory works in a schematic manner and without discussing other statements in the same sources that seem to jeopardise the former ones. For instance, the preparatory works states that 'normally, student loans should not be considered an acceptable source of income, but an absolute prohibition of student loans as a source of income could lead to an unreasonable result and to an impediment to the utilisation of high competence'.[61] The migration courts consistently disqualify student loans with reference to the first part of the statement (ie, that normally, student loans should not be considered an acceptable source of

[59] ibid 192.
[60] ibid 194, 172–73.
[61] Swedish Government Official Reports, SOU 2008:114, *Försörjningskrav vid anhöriginvandring* (Maintenance Requirement for Family Reunification) 90.

income) and without discussing whether a disqualification of student loans in the individual case would lead to an unreasonable result. Thus here again, the courts seem unwilling to discuss vague and conflicting statements in the preparatory works.[62] This is not to say, however, that an application that had emphasised the contradictions in the preparatory works would have led to a different outcome: like EU and ECHR law, preparatory works can be used to justify different legal outcomes.[63]

C. Fidelity to the National Legislator or to the Objective of 'Respite'?

As shown in the previous sections, the migration courts seem to have been unwilling (or unable) to intervene in the 2016 migration policy by using EU and ECHR law arguments – that is, either by independently drawing on sources of EU law or the ECHR (cf the polycentric position) or by examining how such obligations have been discussed by the national legislator (cf the monocentric position). What then are the migration courts doing? How do they argue, if not in the ways suggested by Swedish legal scholarship?

As indicated above – and as I have described in more detail elsewhere – the migration courts use a variety of modes of argumentation when applying the income requirement.[64] For instance, the courts divide questions of law into several isolated sub-questions, meaning, inter alia, that when they identify deficiencies in relation to one source of income (ie, one of these sub-questions), the sponsor's sources of income are disqualified as a whole. The courts further use some statements in the sources of law in a schematic manner and without discussing other statements in the same sources that jeopardise the former ones. Of course, such modes of argumentation can be used in different ways, that is, to justify different outcomes. The courts' application of these modes, however, appears to be in line with the national policy objective that followed the 2015 'refugee crisis', eg, with the intention to create a 'respite' for Sweden.[65] This suggests that the Swedish legislator had considerable room for manoeuvring in realising the objective of limiting migration. This does not necessarily mean that the migration courts consider themselves loyal to the national legislator. Although the courts are implementing a political will for 'respite', they seem reluctant to discuss this and

[62] Häckner Posse (n 4) 124–26.

[63] ibid 200.

[64] ibid 193–97.

[65] ibid 196–97. This relates to the results of previous research on Sweden's migration courts, which indicates that judges at the courts use a sceptical approach to asylum applicants to distance themselves from a perceived political discourse of generosity. See further Johannesson (n 14). On the one hand, and since the Temporary Act reflected a restrictive shift in Sweden's migration policy, it seems unlikely that the courts' preservation of a respite post-2015 was an attempt to distance themselves from a political goal of a generous migration policy. On the other hand, it is conceivable that the migration courts perceive a restrictive application of migration laws as a less political (and more legal) activity than a less restrictive application, that is, regardless of the current political landscape.

other political objectives. For instance, the courts do not discuss how their application relates to the different purposes of the income requirement that have been put forward by the domestic legislator in the last decade (eg, the purpose of promoting 'integration' and the purpose of reducing migration). Moreover, the courts do not follow some of the instructions put forward by the legislator in the preparatory works, eg, the instruction to study case law from the Strasbourg court when applying the Temporary Act, which can be interpreted as the courts showing some disloyalty to the national legislator. It is thus plausible that the courts, in the wake of the 2015 'crisis', primarily linked the protection of a 'respite' to a perceived community spirit, ie, that they considered their mission to be the protection of an 'important public interest' rather than to demonstrate loyalty to the domestic legislator. It is also conceivable, however, that the courts assumed that a 'respite' was the main object of the legislator's will, meaning that discussions of the ambiguities and conflicts in the sources of law were deemed superfluous. But whatever the reason, the practices of the migration courts diverge from theories in the legal literature of how Swedish courts have adapted to the Europeanisation of the legal order.[66] Moreover, the migration courts' practice clearly raises questions about their application of law in times of 'normalcy', ie, general questions about what Europeanisation means for the decision-making practices of Swedish courts.

VI. REWORKING THE THEORIES OF THE DECISION-MAKING PRACTICES OF SWEDISH COURTS

We noted above that the migration courts' application of the Temporary Act diverges from theories in the public law literature. Thus, a follow-up question arises: Does this matter? Is the discrepancy a problem? As emphasised above, nearly all sources of law can be used to justify different legal outcomes. This means that neither the polycentric nor the monocentric position represents a particular attitude towards migration or family reunification. Yet the positions claim to describe the 'rules of the game' in Swedish courts, meaning that they influence our perceptions of how legal reasoning should be conducted to influence legal outcomes. The positions thus inform individuals who want to use the indeterminacy of law to critique domestic legislation, including emergency laws.[67] According to the polycentric position, these individuals should focus on demonstrating EU law and ECHR incompatibility in court, eg, by making attorneys and public counsels argue more intensively that domestic legislation breaches the FRD or Article 8 of the ECHR. According to the monocentric position, these individuals should instead ascertain that such obligations are given prescriptive weight by the domestic legislator in the preparatory works, eg, by ensuring that consultative bodies discuss such

[66] ibid 197–98.
[67] ibid 200–201.

obligations in the legislative processes by which emergency legislation is enacted and/or extended.[68] Considering the migration courts' application of the income requirement, however, both strategies seem misleading. This suggests that we need more evidence-based studies of the role of domestic courts in declared emergencies. As will be clarified below, such studies can also help rework theories of the decision-making practices of Swedish courts.

As regards the polycentric position, it takes as its starting point the idea that the Europeanisation of the Swedish legal order has narrowed the national legislator's leeway. The rulings of the migration courts on the income requirement challenge this assumption (albeit without completely rejecting it). On the one hand, the Temporary Act is an example of national policy being subjected to a European law discourse, not least through the above-mentioned safety valves. In addition, the ECJ and the ECtHR have, on several occasions, provided interpretations of the FRD and Article 8, which can be interpreted as European law formalising national laws on family reunification and limiting national discretion.[69] On the other hand, the migration courts do not seem to automatically adapt their reasoning to this case law. This raises questions about the conditions for polycentric reasoning. What is required for EU law and ECHR law arguments to gain a foothold in domestic courts? Although these questions seem crucial for fully comprehending emergency management in public law settings, as well as public law decision-making in general, the literature on Swedish courts currently provides few answers. One potential way forward could be for this literature to draw inspiration from socio-legal research that examines how administrators on the ground deal with European migration rules (this would probably also benefit the latter research, which rarely focuses on lower courts).[70] Another way forward could be to examine the extent to which legal mobilisation is a prerequisite for courts to argue in a polycentric manner.[71] A further dimension that seems to deserve more attention in contemporary theories on Swedish courts is the issue of workload. The Temporary Act led to an increased flow of cases to the migration courts. It seems plausible that the increased workload encouraged quick assessments of the income requirement and that such assessments required legal reasoning that put individual behaviour and variations into the background.[72] Yet, the absence of references to sources of European law does not appear to be specific to the migration courts: empirical studies of other

[68] cf Häckner Posse and Lärka (n 10) 152.

[69] N Dörrenbächer and T Strik, 'Implementing migration policies' in A Weinar, S Bonjour and L Zhyznomirska (eds), *The Routledge Handbook of the Politics of Migration in Europe* (Routledge, 2018) 64; Häckner Posse (n 4) 204.

[70] For an overview, see Dörrenbächer and Strik (n 69). For an example from legal sociology examining asylum appeals boards in Norway and Denmark, see S Scott Ford, *Entangled asylum in the Nordic region: legal sociology and human rights* (Bristol University Press, 2025).

[71] DR Kelemen, *Eurolegalism: the transformation of law and regulation in the European Union* (Harvard University Press, 2011); J Karlsson Schaffer, M Langford and M Rask Madsen, 'An Unlikely Rights Revolution: Legal Mobilization in Scandinavia Since the 1970s' (2024) 42 *Nordic Journal of Human Rights* 11.

[72] Häckner Posse (n 4) 196.

Swedish courts of first instance point in a similar direction.[73] Previous research also indicates that Swedish courts are generally reluctant to request preliminary rulings from the CJEU, which can make it difficult for principles of EU law to enter Swedish law.[74]

As regards the monocentric position, it assumes that the Europeanisation of the Swedish legal order is compatible with Swedish legal traditions, ie, that Swedish courts can ensure the impact of the ECHR, as long as domestic preparatory works provide clear guidance on how these commitments are to be applied. Yet the migration courts' application of the safety valve raises questions about how statements in preparatory works regarding rights can be used without compromising the governance required by the Convention. As described earlier in this chapter, the ECtHR's case law on Article 8 is casuistic, meaning that the Court's reasoning relates primarily to the circumstances of the individual case. What is the role of preparatory statements in a Europeanised legal landscape (statements that are, by definition, general)? How can such statements be formulated and used without jeopardising the effectiveness of the Convention? Here again, the literature offers surprisingly few answers.[75]

VII. CONCLUSION

This chapter has highlighted that theories of domestic courts do not always coincide with the courts' actual decision-making practices. Yet by comparing such theories with the actual practices of courts, legal scholarship is more likely to be able to adequately account for public law's effects, including the implications of 'crisis' legislation. Moreover, the chapter has illustrated that 'crisis' legislation raises questions not only about emergency practices, but also about the general norms that govern the institutional settings in which such legislation is to be applied. One example is the consultation process of the Temporary Act, which revived a general discussion of how Swedish courts have adapted to the Europeanisation of the legal order. Another example is the cursory EU and ECHR law reasoning that characterised the migration courts' application of the act – a circumstance that raises as many questions about the courts' law application in times of 'normalcy' as it does about their law application in times of 'crisis'. This echoes Loevy's call to transcend the division between normal and exceptional and to thoroughly examine the space within which the practices of emergency management take place.[76]

[73] M Derlén and J Lindholm, 'Från Champagne till Ramlösa: EU-domstolens rättspraxis i svenska underinstanser' (2017) 4 *Europarättslig tidskrift*, 695.

[74] M Wind, 'The Nordics, the EU and the Reluctance Towards Supranational Judicial Review' (2010) 4 *J.Com.Mar.St.* 1039.

[75] Häckner Posse (n 4) 206.

[76] Loevy (n 1) 5.

Part IV

Climate Change

10

Who Decides, and How, When Things Fall Apart? Climate Emergency, Public Participation and the Role of EU Law

CHIARA ARMENI

I. INTRODUCTION

As sudden catalysts of change, crises are an intrinsic element of the EU integration and transformation.[1] Over time and through multiple economic and political shocks, the EU legal order has embraced change as part of its constitutional core.[2] Today, climate change embodies a global 'polycrisis' showing 'unprecedented convergence of risk'.[3] It acts as a threat multiplier by exacerbating other crises:[4] from a humanitarian to a health crisis,[5] from a socio-ecological to a 'democratic' crisis.[6] This makes it hard to define what 'climate crisis' really means, and to predict its effects and decision-makers' response to it. Beyond these multiple risks, climate change reshapes the time perspective of the legal and policy agenda. When science tells us there is no time to lose, urgency redesigns the conceptual understanding and practical assumptions of decision-making. As Andrew Wilson and Ben Orlove point out, 'time constrains – perceived or actual – can adversely affect the ability to

[1] D Dinan, N Nugent and WE Paterson (eds), *The European Union in Crisis* (Palgrave Macmillan, 2017); M Dawson, H Enderlein, and C Joerges (eds), *Beyond the Crisis: The Governance of Europe's Economic, Political and Legal Transformation* (Oxford University Press, 2015).

[2] T Beukers, B de Witte, C Kilpatrick (eds), *Constitutional Change through Euro-Crisis Law* (Cambridge University Press, 2017).

[3] R Heinberg, 'From Climate Crisis to Polycrisis' (2024) 98 *World Literature Today* 32, 32.

[4] S Goodman et al, 'National Security and the Threat of Climate Change' (The CNA Corporation, 2007).

[5] L Baxter et al, 'The Relationship between Climate Change, Health, and the Humanitarian response' *Lancet Public Health* (5 November 2022) 161–63.

[6] Parliamentary Assembly of the Council of Europe, Recommendation 2214 (2021) adopted on 29 September 2021.

make good decisions'.[7] Climate change has limited visibility in the Treaties,[8] but the rich and constantly evolving EU legal and policy framework on climate change shows the connection between climate change and legal transformation in the EU. However, recent pressure to reframe climate change as an emergency is problematic and fits uneasily with the EU legal order and decision-making process.

This chapter explores the jagged contours of an emergency framing of the climate crisis, and its implications for public participation in decision-making in the EU. First, it points to the difference between emergency as a reaction to specific events, and emergency as a strategy for urgent action on climate change. It explores the difference between the EU's competence to react to the specific climate-induced emergencies (eg, floods, wild-fires) under a reactive emergency framing, and the lack of a constitutional arsenal granting broader emergency powers to the EU to decide when climate change is a strategic emergency. Second, it focuses on what emergency-induced urgency means for democratic participation in both its constitutional[9] and environmental law articulation in the EU, drawing on the examples of climate targets, and public participation in climate governance and decisions on renewable energy projects.[10] The chapter argues that although urgency can help support climate action, it comes with risks for public participation. While one should be cautious about claiming causality here, the chapter places this framing within the multiple pressures on democracy in a time of climate crisis.[11]

Ultimately, the chapter calls for intensifying the legal right to participate in environmental decision-making by paying attention to time. Time critically connects emergencies and participation. It is central to today's proliferation of emergency framings that reshape the 'temporality of exceptionality', representing emergencies as a 'taken-for-granted way of apprehending and governing events and situations'.[12] Time also defines the orthodoxy of public participation in decision-making as a requisite for access to information, debate and deliberation. Yet in a crisis, lack of time is a barrier to meaningful participation and a justification for emergency measures, highlighting the tensions between emergency and participation as decision-making modes.

The chapter is structured as follows. In Section II, it examines the twin notions of 'crisis' and 'emergency' and how the EU legal order can (and cannot) respond

[7] AJ Wilson and B Orlove, 'What do we mean when we say climate change is urgent?' (Centre for Research on Environmental Decisions Working paper, 2019) 283.

[8] See Article 191.1 TFEU.

[9] Article 2 Treaty on the European Union (TEU).

[10] UNECE Convention on Access to Information, Public Participation in Decision-Making and Access to Justice in Environmental Matters (Aarhus, 25 June 1998) UNTS 2161, 446 (hereinafter 'Aarhus Convention'). The EU signed the Aarhus Convention in June 1998 and submitted its instrument of approval on 17 February 2005.

[11] C Armeni and M Lee, 'Participation in a time of climate crisis' (2021) 48 *JoLS* 549.

[12] B Anderson, 'Emergency Futures: Exception, Urgency, Interval, Hope' (2017) 65 *The Sociological Review* 463.

to climate change framed as an emergency. Section III discusses the legal foundations of public participation within EU constitutional and environmental law. The chapter then explores the ways in which urgency constrains and reshapes the space for public participation in EU climate law, offering three examples in Section IV. Section V returns to public participation in climate decision-making and discusses the importance of intensifying participatory rights in the EU by increasing the salience of time.

II. CLIMATE EMERGENCY, CRISES AND THE EU LEGAL ORDER

The relationship between crisis and emergency is complex and nuanced. Borrowing from medical science, Frank Fischer describes a crisis as 'a situation in which a complex, highly uncertain, and often unexpected system starts to function or operate poorly and the causes of the malfunctioning are not well known'.[13] When this situation becomes an existential threat to institutional arrangements and societal order, a crisis triggers emergency responses.[14] 'Emergency' is therefore just one, among many, socio-political framing used to understand and respond to a crisis.[15] The reference to 'emergency' as a framing for contemporary societal shocks has expanded in recent years across different domains.[16] But the term evokes different things for different people. For some, it can include a space for optimism.[17] Ben Anderson conceptualises an emergency as 'a "mode of eventfulness" characterised by the hope that action will make a difference as harms, damages or losses emerge'.[18] It emphasises the space still available for 'anticipatory action'.[19] For others, emergencies are circumstances where things fall apart. This is where law and reason fail, opening the realm of exception.[20] From this perspective, climate change is feared as 'a catastrophe in slow motion'.[21]

[13] F Fischer, *Climate Crisis and the Democratic Prospect – Participatory Governance in Sustainable Communities* (Oxford University Press, 2017) 22.

[14] ibid 23.

[15] P Hodder and B Martin, 'Climate Crisis? The Politics of Emergency Framing' (2009) 44 *Economic and Political Weekly* 55, 53.

[16] P Adey, B Anderson and S Graham, 'Introduction: Governing Emergencies: Beyond Exceptionality' (2015) *Theory, Culture and Society* 3.

[17] R Solnit and T Young Lutunatabua (eds), *Not Too Late: Changing the Climate Story from Despair to Possibility* (Haymarket Books, 2023).

[18] B Anderson, 'Governing Emergencies: the Politics of Delay and the Logic of Response' (2015) 41 *Transactions of the Institute of British Geographers* 14, referring to L Berlant, *Cruel Optimism* (Duke University Press, 2011).

[19] B Anderson, 'Preemption, Precaution, Preparedness: Anticipatory Action and Future Geographies' (2010) 34 *Progress in Human Geography* 777.

[20] N Rogers, *Law, Fiction and Activism in a Time of Climate Change* (Routledge, 2020) 168–69.

[21] RT Pierrehumbert, 'Climate Change: A Catastrophe in Slow Motion' (2006) 2 *CJIL* 573.

Understanding the nuances between crisis and emergency gets more complicated when it comes to climate change.[22] The emergency framing is frequently being used but also contested in policy and governance discourse.[23] Yet it is not a homogeneous concept. It varies in operationalisation and aims, partially because of the different ways actors make sense of the climate crisis and its impact. In exploring emergency framings in sustainability studies, James Patterson and colleagues point to two main ways in which framings act in environmental science and politics. First, an emergency framing can be used as a reaction to specific environmental issues and unprecedented events. It can be, for instance, a response to climate-induced disasters, such as droughts, floods, hurricanes and wild-fires. This framing focuses on relief from impact, going back to normal and occasionally 'build[ing] back better'.[24] As a response, this type of emergency also speaks to Anderson's 'anticipatory action', supporting risk preparedness.[25] It draws upon the idea of anticipatory climate governance where action is focused on 'containing reducible risks, which can be acted upon in the present through improved knowledge infrastructures and strategic planning processes'.[26] Reactive deployment of an emergency framing mobilises emergency action across different scales and by different actors such as governments (eg, national and local), disaster management services and agencies, sometimes including the military, as well as local communities and non-governmental organisations (NGOs).

Second, looking beyond – but often in combination with – specific impacts in defined locations, an emergency framing can be deployed as a strategy 'to mobilise attention, resources and effort to address the issue where action is lagging'.[27] This recourse to emergency framings challenges the status quo that led to the crisis and points to the inadequacy of law and politics. As Patterson and colleagues argue, 'emergency-as-strategy is about creating an exception to the norm as a political intervention to make an existing situation visible in a new way'.[28] Rather than focusing on specific events, this framing is mostly used to describe the 'elevated salience'[29] of the climate crisis and foster change.[30] This is in line with visions of the climate crisis as situations where law and reason

[22] J Mazon, D Pino and M Vinyoles, 'Is Declaring a Climate Emergency Enough to Stop Global Warming? Learning From the COVID-19 Pandemic' (2022) 4(848587) *Frontiers in Climate* 1–5.

[23] See, eg, L Holmes McHugh, M Carmen Lemos and T Hope Morrison, 'Risk? Crisis? Emergency? Implications of the new climate emergency framing for governance and policy' (2021) 12 *Wiley Interdisciplinary Reviews: Climate Change* 1.

[24] See United Nations, Sendai Framework for Disaster Risk Reduction 2015–2030 (2015).

[25] Anderson (n 19).

[26] K Muiderman et al, 'Four approaches to anticipatory climate governance: Different conceptions of the future and implications for the present' (2020) 11(e673) *WIREs Climate Change* 7 (discussing four approaches to anticipatory climate governance).

[27] J Patterson et al, 'The Political Effects of Emergency Frames in Sustainability (2021) 4 *Nature Sustainability* 841, 842.

[28] ibid.

[29] Wilson and Orlove (n 7) 5.

[30] Patterson (n 27) 842.

fail, leading to a state of exception.[31] Jocelyn Stacey engages with this framing, arguing that since we cannot anticipate extreme events and predict our response, 'the emergency undermines any conception of the rule of law that equates law with pre-existing rules [and] reveals the inevitability and necessity of executive discretion'.[32] This connects with the legal scholarship on the difficult relation between political and legal grounds of a state of exception.[33]

This second type of emergency framing is gaining traction as a strategic imaginary in policy and political discourse worldwide and is mobilised by different actors than those acting under a reactive framing. Scientists use it to 'tell it like it is'.[34] Activists mobilise it to demand urgent climate action as a last resort before ecological collapse.[35] Litigants use it to hold states accountable for alleged violations of their national and international legal obligations due to climate inaction or insufficient ambition.[36] Increasingly, this framing has also been employed by institutions, governments, and regional and local authorities as a conceptual foundation of climate emergency declarations.[37] In November 2019, for instance, the European Parliament declared a climate emergency stating 'its own commitment, to urgently take the concrete action needed in order to fight and contain this threat before it is too late'.[38]

These two framings are conceptually different: whereas climate emergency as a reaction focuses on well-defined emergency action on disaster relief and loss and damages, climate emergency as a *strategy* calls on special powers to cope with the unprecedented and exceptional nature of the climate crisis as a whole. However, these two conceptualisations of emergency – i.e. as a reaction and as a strategy – associate both the optimistic and catastrophist visions of emergencies with ideas of climate risk and transformation, blurring their boundaries.[39] In practice, the implications of these types of emergency framings vary with

[31] N Rogers, *Law, Fiction and Activism in a Time of Climate Change* (Routledge, 2020) 168–69.

[32] J Stacey, *The Constitution of the Environmental Emergency* (Hart Publishing, 2018) 16 (though her conceptualisation of emergency is more concerned with defending environmental regulation than with demanding urgent action).

[33] The legal and philosophical complexities of this scholarship are beyond the scope of this chapter. See G Agamben, *State of Exception* (Chicago University Press, 2005).

[34] WJ Ripple et al, 'World Scientists' Warning of a Climate Emergency' (2020) 70 *BioScience* 8, 8.

[35] LD Bevan, T Colley and M Workman, 'Climate change strategic narratives in the United Kingdom: Emergency, Extinction, Effectiveness' (2020) 69 *Energy Research and Social Science* 101580, 1.

[36] See ECHR, Grand Chamber, *Verein Klimaseniorinnen Schweiz and others v Switzerland* (Application no. 53600/20) Judgment 9 April 2024 (especially para 419–420 on climate change as a 'polycentric issue'). See also: Request for an advisory opinion on the climate emergency and human rights submitted to the Inter-American Court of Human Rights by the Republic of Colombia and the Republic of Chile, 9 January 2023.

[37] For a review, see J Stacey, 'The Public Law Paradoxes of Climate Emergency Declarations' (2022) 11 *TEL* 291.

[38] European Parliament resolution of 28 November 2019 on the climate and environment emergency (2019/2930(RSP)).

[39] U Beck, *The Metamorphosis of the World: How Climate Change is Transforming Our Concept of the World* (Polity, 2016).

context and time.[40] This suggests that although distinct, the two framings are interconnected. For example, an emergency framing for a specific event can call for strategic change in climate action at a broader scale to increase resilience. Similarly, calls for a state of exception (often implied in the climate emergencies declarations) can also characterise reactive uses of emergencies through expanded executive powers to address a specific climate-induced disaster. However, while interconnected, these two ways of conceptualising the climate emergency imply two different types of mobilisation of EU law.

A. Emergency as Reaction

When a climate emergency framing is used to prevent and respond to distinct climate catastrophes, EU law has a constitutionally defined role. Under Article 196 of the Treaty on the Functioning of the European Union (TFEU), the EU has a supportive competence towards Member States in decisions on civil protection and prevention of disasters. In this policy area,[41] the Union 'shall encourage cooperation between Member States in order to improve the effectiveness of systems for preventing and protecting against natural or man-made disasters'.[42] Its action aims to 'support and complement Member States' action […] in risk prevention, in preparing their civil-protection personnel and in responding to natural or man-made disasters within the Union'. This helps 'promote swift, effective operational cooperation within the Union between national civil-protection services'[43] and ensure 'consistency in international civil-protection work'.[44] The Union's supportive competence leaves discretion to the Member States as legal harmonisation is excluded.[45]

Building on this constitutional framework, the EU Civil Protection Mechanism was established in 2013 and revised in 2021.[46] The mechanism extends to climate disasters defined as 'any situation which has or may have a severe impact on people, the environment, or property, including cultural heritage'.[47] Its objective is to 'strengthen the cooperation between the Union and the Member States and to facilitate coordination in the field of civil protection

[40] Patterson et al (n 27).
[41] Article 196.1(a) TFEU.
[42] Article 196.1 TFEU.
[43] Article 196.1(b) TFEU.
[44] Article 196.1(c) TFEU.
[45] Article 196.2 TFEU. This is complemented by Article 214.1 TFEU on the Union's humanitarian aid operations.
[46] Decision No 1313/2013/EU on a Union Civil Protection Mechanism (OJ L 347). The EU Civil Protection Mechanism follows the Community Civil Protection Mechanism set up in 2001 under Euratom, whose financial instrument expired in 2013. See Council Decision 2001/792/EC establishing a Community mechanism to facilitate reinforced cooperation in civil protection assistance interventions (OJ L 297). See also Council Decision 2007/779/EC establishing a Community Civil Protection Mechanism (OJ L 314).
[47] Article 1, Regulation (EU) 2021/836 amending Decision No 1313/2013/EU on a Union Civil Protection Mechanism (OJ L 185).

in order to improve the effectiveness of systems for preventing, preparing for and responding to natural and man-made disasters'.[48] It also aims to foster solidarity between Member States.[49]

B. Emergency as Strategy

In combination with emergency responses to climate impact, the notion of climate emergency evokes a vision of a radical change of exceptional scale to avoid societal and ecosystems' collapse. In this case, the emergency framing demands a rupture with the past, rather than urgent action to go back to normal. This meaning of climate emergency aligns with Patterson and colleagues' definition of emergency as a strategy to reject the status quo and justify the need for exceptional climate measures.

But when an emergency framing is used as strategy for exceptional climate action, the role of law is tricky. This is primarily due to a mismatch between the political understanding to an emergency and what an emergency means in legal terms. From a political perspective, declaring a climate emergency could help justify more drastic measures. Yet the extent to which an emergency government and institutions will be able to achieve better results on climate change than would an ordinary one is unclear. Emergency framing can be useful for attracting attention and raise an issue's profile in the political and policy agenda. But the suggested positive effects of emergency framings on the quality of climate action are questionable. Over-reliance on emergency framing can even induce a boomerang effect, increasing political polarisation.[50] In legal terms, the declarations of climate emergency announced thus far have no effect in many jurisdictions, including the EU. These statements and declarations are made primarily by legislative bodies rather than by the executive branch under pre-existing emergency legislation. This is because a climate emergency framing does not fit squarely with the legal and institutional standards of the state of emergency exception and its implications.[51] In law, a state of emergency triggers a provisional suspension of constitutional rights and guarantees, such as the separation of powers and checks and balances.[52] Precisely because of their disruptive consequences on the constitutional order, emergency laws are – by their very nature – extraordinary and temporary frames. It is this extraordinary and temporary essence that makes us accept a limitation of the most fundamental

[48] Article 1.1. Decision No 1313/2013/EU on a Union Civil Protection Mechanism (OJ L 347).

[49] Article 1 Regulation (EU) 2021/836 on a Union Civil Protection Mechanism. On Member States' solidarity in the Treaty, see Article 42(7) TEU (solidarity on foreign policy) and Article 222 TFEU (general solidarity clause).

[50] P Sol Hart and EC Nisbet, 'Boomerang effects in science communication: How motivated reasoning and identity cues amplify opinion polarization about climate mitigation policies' (2012) 39 *Communication Research* 701.

[51] Stacey (n 37).

[52] ibid.

set of constitutional rights and procedural guarantees. But here lies the paradox: while climate disruption threatens ecological, institutional and social stability, a state of exception is ill-suited to the nature and challenges of climate change. Unprecedented measures, supported by a good dose of 'creative legal engineering' are of course required.[53] However, climate change lacks the temporary condition of states of exception, since climate mitigation and adaptation measures are not thought to be provisional. For the climate crisis to develop its 'elevated salience',[54] it must be normalised rather than made exceptional.[55] This assumption aligns with Bruno de Witte's observation that 'there is undoubtedly a crisis situation there, but climate change policies do not require the adoption of "special laws"'.[56]

From an EU law perspective, EU constitutional law does not provide the Union with exceptional decision-making powers in the event of a climate emergency. This is due to the absence of a comprehensive emergency regime within EU constitutional law, comparable to most of its Member States' constitutions. Emergency-relevant provisions are scattered across primary and secondary law, but there is no general framework for triggering a legal state of emergency under EU constitutional law.[57] While this has not been a barrier to action on an emergency footing in the past, it restricts the possibility of a legal construction of a climate emergency as a justification for ambitious measures. This means that EU constitutional law restricts the EU's capacity to deal with climate change (as a whole) as an emergency. In the absence of an EU constitutional framework for declaring a state of climate emergency under EU law, the legitimacy of taking emergency measures to tackle the climate crisis becomes a crucial issue. This concern arguably highlights the central role of public participation in addressing climate change as an emergency within the EU, as explored in the following section.

III. PUBLIC PARTICIPATION IN EU CONSTITUTIONAL AND ENVIRONMENTAL LAW

The link between the climate crisis and democratic decision-making is being increasingly highlighted by human-rights institutions and courts.[58] Democratic

[53] B De Witte, 'The European Union's COVID-19 recovery plan: The legal engineering of an economic policy shift' (2021) 58 *CMLR* 635.

[54] Wilson and Orlove (n 7) 5.

[55] On the normalisation of crises, see RJ Holton, 'The idea of crisis in modern society' (1987) *British Journal of Sociology* 502.

[56] B De Witte, 'Guest Editorial: EU emergency law and its impact on the EU legal order' (2022) 59 *CMLR* 3, 4.

[57] ibid.

[58] See Parliamentary Assembly of the Council of Europe, Recommendation 2214 (2021) adopted on 29 September 2021 and Resolution 2399 (2021) entitled 'Climate Change and Rule of Law' adopted on 29 September 2021. See also eg ECHR, Grand Chamber, *Verein Klimaseniorinnen Schweiz and others v Switzerland* (Application no. 53600/20) Judgment 9 April 2024, especially para 420 on the democratic decision-making process as a space for weighing conflicts triggered by the climate crisis.

values, principles and rights constitute the fabric of the EU. Under the Treaty of the European Union, democracy is one of the values on which the Union is founded.[59] A commitment to democracy shapes the constitutional configuration of the Union, as well as of its Member States, whose compliance with its founding values constitutes a condition for joining the Union.[60] This democratic value is given 'concrete expression'[61] through several principles, including the promotion of good governance and the participation of civil society.[62]

A democratic ideal defines how the EU works. Representative democracy is the mode of internal functioning of the EU, ultimately shaping its institutional setting. Citizens are 'directly represented at Union level in the European Parliament elected by direct universal suffrage every five years.[63] They are also indirectly represented by their Heads of State or government within the European Council and by their governments in the Council, who are 'themselves democratically accountable either to their national Parliaments, or to their citizens'.[64]

Representation is combined with opportunities for participatory democracy. The Treaty provides that 'every citizen shall have the right to participate in the democratic life of the Union' and that '[d]ecisions shall be taken as openly and as closely as possible to the citizen'.[65] In order to make participation meaningful, the EU commits to giving its citizens and representative associations 'the opportunity to make known and publicly exchange their views' and to 'maintain an open, transparent and regular dialogue with representative organizations and civil society'.[66] The Treaty imposes an obligation on the Commission to 'carry out broad consultations with parties concerned in order to ensure that the Union's actions are coherent and transparent' and take note of any initiative put forward by a significant number of citizens.[67] These are broad principles guiding the Union's actions and its relationship with its citizens and civil society. But they do not imply a particularly ambitious commitment to democracy other

[59] Article 2 TEU.

[60] Based on the reading of Article 49 TEU in Case C-621/18 *Wightman and Others v Secretary of State for Exiting the European Union* ECLI:EU:C:2018:999, [2018] ECR 999, para 63 and Case C-619/18 *Commission v of Poland* (Independence of the Supreme Court) ECLI:EU:C:2019:531, [2019] ECR 531 para 42.

[61] Case C-418/18 P *Puppinck and others v Commission* ECLI:EU:C:2019:1113, [2020] 4 WLR 20, para 64 – concrete expression.

[62] On the rich case law, see K Lenaerts, 'The Principle of Democracy in the Case law of the European Court of Justice' (2013) 62 *ICLQ* 271. See also K Lenaerts, 'New Horizons for the Rule of Law Within the EU' (2020) 21 *GLJ* 29.

[63] See Article 14(1) and (2) TFEU. However, a principle of degressive proportionality (ie, the principle of per head representation combined with the principle that the larger the population of a Member State, the lower the weighting per head) applies and Member States have discretion on the system of proportional representation they use and its elements. See Decision 2018/937 establishing the composition of the European Parliament, OJ 2018, L 165l/1. BVerfG, case 2 BvE 2/08, 30 June 2009.

[64] Article 10.3 TFEU.

[65] Articles 10 and 3 TEU.

[66] Article 11(2) TEU.

[67] Articles 11(3) and (4) TEU.

than ensuring public consultation on those actions.[68] In an effort to strengthen participation, the European Citizens' Initiative (ECI) enables citizens to 'take the initiative of inviting the European Commission, within the framework of its powers, to submit any appropriate proposal on matters where citizens consider that a legal act of the Union is required for the purpose of implementing the Treaties'.[69] Nevertheless, the ECI imposes strict conditions and does not oblige the Commission to act on the initiative.[70] Despite recent reforms, its capacity to 'democratise' EU decision-making remains contested.[71]

The EU constitutional commitment to democracy also shapes decision-making on environmental protection. This is remarkably expressed by the institutionalisation of individual rights to information, public participation in decision-making and access to justice under the UNECE Aarhus Convention, to which both the EU and its Member States are contracting Parties.[72] The Convention recognises a right for individuals and NGOs to participate in decision-making on specific activities (eg, activities listed in its annex I and any other activity that 'may have a significant effect on the environment', such as the development of energy infrastructure projects);[73] on the preparation of plans, programmes, and policies;[74] and on the preparation of 'executive regulations and other generally applicable legally binding rules that may have a significant effect on the environment'.[75] As Maria Lee and Carolyn Abbot show, the Aarhus participation pillar has until recently been relatively neglected (compared to the access-to-information or access-to-justice pillars) by environmental NGOs who have paid less attention to its legal mobilisation through courts or political advocacy.[76] However, the right to participate is in many respects the Convention's most democratically-spirited pillar (and the focus here), building its legal edifice on access to information and access to justice as 'facilitative rights'.[77]

The Aarhus Convention reflects environmental decision-making as a multistage, complex process covering a wide and diverse range of decisions. Procedural safeguards for participation are stronger with respect to

[68] M Dawson, 'Better regulation and the future of EU regulatory law and politics' (2016) 53 *Common Market Law Review* 1209.

[69] Article 11(4) TEU. On this, see J Mendes, 'Participation and the role of law after Lisbon: a legal view on Article 11 TEU' (2011) 48 *CMLR* 1849.

[70] A Karatzia, 'The European Citizens' Initiative and the EU Institutional balance: On realism and the possibilities of affecting lawmaking' (2017) 54 *CMLR* 177.

[71] M Dawson and Fs de Witte, *EU Law and Governance* (Cambridge University Press, 2022) 67–68. See also M Dougan, 'What are we to make of the citizens' initiative?' (2011) 48 *CMLR* 1807.

[72] UNECE (n 10). See M Lee, 'The legal institutionalization of public participation in the EU governance of technology' in R Brownsword, E Scotford and K Yeung (eds), *Oxford Handbook on the Law and Regulation of Technology* (Oxford University Press, 2017) 620.

[73] Article 6 Aarhus Convention.

[74] Article 7 Aarhus Convention.

[75] Article 8 Aarhus Convention.

[76] C Abbot and M Lee, 'NGOs Shaping Public Participation Through Law: The Aarhus Convention and Legal Mobilisation' (2024) 36 *JEL* 85.

[77] E Barritt, *The Foundations of the Aarhus Convention* (Hart Publishing, 2020) 28.

participation of 'the public concerned' – ie the 'public affected or likely to be affected by, or having an interest in, the environmental decision-making[78] – on decisions related to specific activities.[79] It then becomes gradually more flexible in relation to participation by the public (in general) with respect to decisions on plans, programmes and policies, as well as decisions on executive regulations and other binding rules.[80] The Aarhus model is viewed as an illustration of 'a moment of democratic optimism' for environmental decision-making.[81] Although it does not explicitly refer to the idea of environmental democracy, it enshrines a series of rights that 'facilitate and protect democratic expression in the context of environmental decision-making'.[82] The details of the rights guaranteed by Aarhus will be discussed in Section V. For the time being, it suffices to observe that the legally protected rights of the Aarhus Convention reflect and connect with the Treaties' commitment to democratic accountability (eg, through an obligation for public authorities to give reasons for a decision and for Member States to provide access to justice on environmental matters),[83] transparency (eg, through the right to access to environmental information and the obligation to publish the final decision and its reasons),[84] and inclusion (eg, through its broad scope for participation of individuals as well as of environmental NGOs).[85]

Over the years, the Convention has had a substantial impact on the legal construction and implementation of procedural environmental rights in the EU environmental acquis[86] and their interpretation by the Court of Justice of the European Union.[87] It represents an example of how environmental law helps translate often distant values into everyday processes for environmental protection. Its legal implementation through secondary law has been a key driver of

[78] Article 2 of the Aarhus Convention states that, for purposes of this definition, 'non-governmental organizations promoting environmental protection and meeting any requirements under national law shall be deemed to have an interest'.

[79] However, Parties are allowed to adopt or maintain more stringent provisions.

[80] Articles 7 and 8 Aarhus Convention.

[81] M Lee, 'The Aarhus Convention 1998 and the Environment Act 2021: Eroding Public Participation' (2023) 86 *MLR* 1.

[82] Barritt (n 77) 27. More extensively on this point, see ch 3.

[83] Articles 6(9) and 9 Aarhus Convention.

[84] Articles 4, 5 and 6(9) Aarhus Convention.

[85] Article 6(4) Aarhus Convention.

[86] Directive 2003/4 on public access to environmental *information* OJ 2003, L 41/26; Directive 2003/35 providing for public participation in respect of the drawing up of certain plans and programmes relating to the environment OJ 2003 L 156/17; Regulation 1367/2006 on the application of the provisions of the Aarhus Convention on access to information, public participation in decision-making and access to justice in environmental matters to Community institutions and bodies [2006] OJ L 264/13.

[87] See, eg, Case C-427/07 *Commission v Ireland* ECLI:EU:C:2009:457, [2009] ECR I-6277; Case C-263/08 *DLV v Stockholms kommun* ECLI:EU:C:2009:631, [2009] ECR I-9967; Case C-115/09 *Trianel* ECLI:EU:C:2011:289, [2011] 3 CMLR 15; Case C-240/09 *LZ VLK v Ministry of Environment of Slovakia* ECLI:EU:C:2011:125, [2012] QB 606; Case C–826/18 *LB and others v College van burgemeester en wethouders van de gemeente Echt-Susteren* ECLI:EU:C:2021:7, [2021] 2 CMLR 18.

the entrenchment of procedural environmental rights in the EU.[88] It is therefore relevant to this chapter to investigate the ways in which climate emergency framings influence the exercise of participatory rights in a time of climate crisis. The next section explores this question by unwrapping the (somehow familiar)[89] tensions between the urgency of action and the participatory commitments at play, and the ways in which EU climate law and governance addresses them.

IV. URGENCY AND PARTICIPATION

Although a state of climate emergency cannot be formally triggered in EU law, time pressure inhabits the political discourse on climate change, inevitably shaping legal and institutional responses. Since its origins, EU climate law and governance has been built upon a growing sense of urgency. An explicit reference to a climate 'emergency' is absent in the 2019 European Green Deal, but the urgency of increased climate action shapes it. Of course, the EU is used to acting under time pressure, and an emergency governance approach has unquestionably been adopted to respond to other – often interconnected – crises.[90] In most of these cases, the democratic legitimacy of these measures has been questioned.[91] However, it can be argued that what we see with respect to climate change has the potential to reshape the familiar legal guarantees for public participation in environmental decision-making. This argument will be illustrated through the examples of climate targets (subsection A) participation in climate governance (subsection B) and decision-making on renewable energy projects (subsection C) in the EU.

A. Climate Targets and Expertise

The Commission constructs its narrative of climate urgency upon scientific expertise, in particular upon the Intergovernmental Panel on Climate Change findings that 'emissions need to be reduced with far more urgency than previously anticipated'.[92] This scientific grounding informs the resolve to '[a]ct now or it will be too late'.[93] The message is clear: 'We have a responsibility to act

[88] C Hilson, 'The Visibility of Environmental Rights in the EU Legal Order: Eurolegalism in Action?' (2018) 25 *JEPP* 1589.

[89] M Lee et al, 'Public Participation and Climate Change Infrastructure' (2013) 25 *JEL* 33, 35.

[90] See (n 1) and (n 2) and, more recently, E Massetti and T Exadaktylos, 'From Crisis to Crisis: The EU in between the Covid, Energy and Inflation Crises (and War)' (2022) 60 *JCMS* 5.

[91] See, eg, C Kreuder-Sonnen and J White, 'Europe and the transnational politics of emergency' (2022) 29 *JEPP* 953.

[92] Commission, 'A Clean Planet for all – A European strategic long-term vision for a prosperous, modern, competitive and climate neutral economy' COM(2018) 773 final, 5.

[93] Commission 'Stepping up Europe's 2030 climate ambition Investing in a climate-neutral future for the benefit of our people' COM(2020) 562 final, 3.

decisively in the interest of future generations'.[94] This sense of urgency constitutes the context of legal choices. The European Climate Law (ECL) builds on the realisation that climate change is an 'existential threat'[95] and that science evidences 'the need to rapidly step up climate action' and 'urgently' reduce greenhouse gas emissions (GHG).[96] The ECL explicitly acknowledges the European Parliament's 2019 climate emergency resolution, therefore placing its own normative framework firmly within this narrative.[97]

Urgency coupled with the long-term policy perspective is the empire of targets and deadlines. The ECL enshrines a legally binding EU-wide target to reduce the EU net GHG emissions by at least 55 per cent by 2030 (compared to 1990 levels) and achieve carbon neutrality by 2050.[98] The target aims to support 'economic and societal transformation, high-quality jobs, sustainable growth, and the achievement of the United Nations Sustainable Development Goals', as well as the achievement of the Paris Agreement's temperature target 'in a just, socially balanced, fair and cost-effective manner'.[99] An intermediate target of 55 per cent GHG emission reduction by 2030 is also set to achieve the final objective.[100] In 2024, building on the advice of the European Scientific Advisory Board on Climate Change,[101] the Commission recommended a 90 per cent net GHG emissions reduction by 2040 compared to 1990 levels, launching a discussion with all stakeholders to shape a legislative proposal as required under the ECL.[102] Deadlines are setting the pace of Member States and Commission obligations.[103] The 'Fit for 55' legislative package implements the European Green Deal through new and existing legislation in virtually all EU policy areas.

As regulatory tools, climate targets have multiple merits: they help coordinate stakeholders' action on a common objective, plan and manage resources for the future. They provide a clear tool for civil society to hold governments accountable for their actions as contributing to achieving the targets.[104] Yet climate targets are contested.[105] An over-reliance on climate targets and deadlines tend to suggest a

[94] ibid referring to IPCC, *Global Warming 1.5°* (2019).

[95] Preamble, para 1., Regulation 2021/1119 establishing the framework for achieving climate neutrality, OJ 2021, L 243/1 (hereinafter 'ECL').

[96] ibid para 3.

[97] ibid para 19.

[98] Article 2(1) European Climate Law.

[99] ibid para 4.

[100] Article 4 European Climate Law.

[101] European Scientific Advisory Board on Climate Change (ESABCC) 'Scientific advice for the determination of an EU-wide 2040 climate target and a greenhouse gas budget for 2030–2050' (15 June 2023).

[102] Commission, 'Securing our future: Europe's 2040 climate target and path to climate neutrality by 2050 building a sustainable, just and prosperous society' COM/2024/63 final, 6.2.2024.

[103] Regulation 2018/1999 on the Governance of the Energy Union and Climate Action OJ 2018, L 328/1.

[104] S Theil, 'Cautious scrutiny: The Federal Climate Change Act case in the German Constitutional Court' (2023) 86 *MLR* 263.

[105] C Hilson, 'Hitting the Target? Analysing the Use of Targets in Climate Law' (2020) 32 *JEL* 195.

shift from 'governing by law to governance by numbers', where 'rules give way to objectives'.[106] This leads to an institutional setting in which quantification and statistical objectives shape the social order and the institutional response to crises. But this approach is insufficient to address the polycentric nature of climate change. An economy-wide binding climate target tells us little about its underlying values and choices, the differential contribution of various socio-economic groups to climate change, or vulnerability to climate risk or decarbonisation. Broader issues, such as the impact of and on inequality, are difficult to integrate.[107] Of course, the ECL is a framework law and the implementing legislation will set the details, including on distributive choices to be made. Existing environmental and social legislation still apply and will adapt to align with the targets. A lot is left to Member States and to the Fit-for-55 implementing legislation. However, one could agree with Chris Hilson that 'climate targets need to move beyond the recent headline shouting phase to a position where the pros and cons of various choices around targets are better understood'.[108]

Targets are also contested as they often reflect technocratic decisions, shaping assumptions around 'carbon numbers'[109] to be hit by a certain deadline.[110] Expertise – economic, environmental, legal, scientific – is certainly crucial here.[111] Recourse to expert knowledge is conveniently relied upon as the main strategy to prove the substantive quality of decision through irrefutable facts, validated by methodology and quantitative assessment, and subject to peer review. Law is part of this technical expertise story, as it is mobilised in various ways by multiple actors, including the EU institutions, environmental NGOs and scholars.[112]

Despite its merits, an unmitigated confidence in experts is problematic. First, technocratic approaches to environmental decision-making might close the space for and influence of public participation in decision-making. They often squeeze out socio-cultural values from the realm of what counts as 'good reason' for a decision.[113] Any form of overreliance on technical expertise is likely to

[106] A Supiot, *Governance by Numbers: The Making of a Legal Model of Allegiance* (Bloomsbury, 2017) 29 (drawing particularly from labour and employment law).

[107] P Gazzotti et al, 'Persistent inequality in economically optimal climate policies' (2021) 12 *Nature Communication* 3421.

[108] Hilson (n 105) 197.

[109] Hulme (n 23).

[110] On 'climate deadline-ism', S Asayama et al, 'Why setting a climate deadline is dangerous' (2019) 9 *Nature Climate Change* 570.

[111] For a review, M Ambrus et al, *The Role of Experts in International and European Decision-Making Processes: Advisors, Decision-Makers or Irrelevant Actors?* (Cambridge University Press, 2014).

[112] E Korkea-aho and P Leino-Sandberg (eds), *Law, Legal Expertise and EU Policy-Making* (Cambridge University Press, 2022); C Abbot and M Lee, *Environmental Groups and Legal Expertise – Shaping the Brexit process* (UCL Press, 2021). On EU law expertise specifically, A Vauchez and B de Witte (eds), *Lawyering Europe – European Law as a Transnational Social Field* (Oxford University Press, 2013).

[113] S Jasanoff, *Design on Nature – Science and Democracy in Europe and the United States* (Princeton University Press, 2007).

refute values with facts.[114] Although important for the quality of the outcome, technical framings will always tend to limit the lay public's ability to influence.[115] Second, but connected to the first argument, a bold reliance on techno-scientific expertise as justification for a decision has been widely challenged as naïve.[116] Knowledge is rarely complete, as some elements remain unknown, while others are the subject of scientific controversies, or evolve too rapidly to be pinned down with conclusive certainty.[117] Climate targets are strictly dependent to their underlying models. The Commission notes for instance that assessment of 'the portfolio of options' to reach the climate neutrality targets 'builds upon scientific literature and inputs from a wide range of stakeholders – business, nongovernmental organisations, think tanks and the research community – as well as integrated modelling allowing to better understand the transformation of and complex interactions between the energy, industry, buildings, transport, agriculture, forestry and waste sectors'.[118] Science, privileged participants, and technical modelling shape the available options. This inevitably reduces the contribution of 'non-expert' participants and their values and lived experience. This perceived pressure for rapid action and targets can hardly evade its 'real tension' with a legal commitment to participation discussed above.[119]

B. Repositioning Participation

The centrality of climate targets in the European Climate Law influences the role of the legal right to participate. More specifically, while public participation remains an important element, the ECL seems to reposition its normative purpose: from participation in decision-making to participation in achieving the collective 'carbon numbers'.[120] This trend started to become visible through a series of Commission Communications. In 2018, the Commission pointed out that '[c]limate change can only be tackled if people actively engage, as consumers and as citizens'.[121] The achievement of a net-zero EU 'should be based on the empowerment of all citizens and consumers in making change possible and proper information to the public'.[122] The Commission further states that

[114] M Lee, 'Beyond Safety? The Broadening Scope of Risk Regulation' in C O'Cinneide (ed), *Current Legal Problems 2009* (Oxford University Press, 2010).
[115] M-F Cuéllar, 'Rethinking Regulatory Democracy' (2005) 57 *Administrative Law Review* 411.
[116] F Sandbach, *Environment, Ideology and Policy* (Blackwell, 1980).
[117] B Wynne, 'Uncertainty and Environmental Learning: Reconceiving Science and Policy in the Preventing Paradigm' (1992) 2 *Global Environmental Change* 111. See also U Beck, *The World at Risk* (Polity, 2009) 115 describing contemporary society as a 'non-knowledge society' which is the contradictory 'product of more and better knowledge'.
[118] Commission (n 92) 6.
[119] Lee et al (n 89) 35.
[120] Hulme (n 23).
[121] Commission (n 92).
[122] ibid.

'[a]longside government policies and regulation, citizens, communities and organisations have their part to play'.[123] In 2020, the Commission launched the European Climate Pact 'to engage with different stakeholders and civil society with the aim to commit them to climate action and more sustainable behaviour'.[124] The Pact primarily encourages information sharing and awareness, and provides a space for sharing ideas and work on 'ambitious actions, both at individual and collective level'. There is an emphasis in the Pact on participation as a collaborative space for enabling information exchange and dialogue between actors with an abundance of resources (including income, time and education) and access (including market, institutional, procedural, knowledge and legal access) to change their behaviour and act. The Commission highlights that 'citizens are crucial partners in the fight against climate change, and can support it through political mobilisation and consumer choices. They can greatly contribute to decarbonisation by making more sustainable purchase decisions and lifestyle choices, but need to be assisted by actionable and reliable information'.[125] 'Ambition and urgency' are among the Pact's core values.[126]

Individual and social behavioural change in climate policy is a source of controversy.[127] Drawing on a narrative of responsibilities of the public, the ECL's provision on public participation shifts from the Aarhus-type of participation in decision-making to public engagement in achieving the targets. This is visible at three stages. First, participation is presented as an opportunity to enable and empower 'all parties of society [...] to take action towards a just and socially fair transition to a climate-neutral and climate-resilient society'.[128] In this process, the Commission's task will be to 'facilitate an inclusive and accessible process at all levels [...] for the exchange of best practice and to identify actions to contribute to the achievement of the objectives' of the ECL.[129] Participation here is not about the decision-making process. It is primarily about the Commission nudging stakeholders to take their share in implementing the target. Participation is encouraged from a more fluid and less legally determined group representing 'all parts of society'. While drafted in an inclusive manner, this generic reference, omitting clear indications of who, as a minimum, should be included, comes with the risk that powerful

[123] Commission (n 93).

[124] Commission, 'European Climate Pact' COM(2020) 788 final 3. The Pact stresses the co-benefit of climate action for citizens.

[125] Commission (n 93).

[126] Commission (n 124) 9.

[127] See, eg, K Ehrhardt-Martinez et al, 'Consumption and Climate Change' in RE Dunlap and RJ Brulle (eds), *Climate Change and Society – Social Perspectives* (Oxford University Press, 2015). See also E Shove, 'On the difference between chalk and cheese – a response to Whitmarsh et al's comments on "Beyond the ABC: climate change policy and theories of social change"' (2011) 43 *Environment and Planning A* 262; L Whitmarsh, S O'Neill, I Lorenzoni, 'Commentary. Climate change or social change? Debate within, amongst, and beyond disciplines' (2010) 43 *Environment and Planning A* 258; E Shove 'Beyond the ABC: climate change policy and theories of social change' (2010) 42 *Environment and Planning A* 1273.

[128] Article 9.1 European Climate Law.

[129] ibid.

voices and interests will be prioritised.[130] Second, the Commission 'may' rely on ongoing processes of consultation and the 'multilevel climate and energy dialogues' at national level provided by the Governance of the Energy Union and Climate Action Regulation ('Governance Regulation').[131] This is an important cross-reference to other institutionalised spaces where participation can happen in the Member States. Under the Governance Regulation, Member States must establish integrated National Energy and Climate Plans, but its provision on participation is relatively soft.[132] Finally, informal engagement with 'citizens, social partners and stakeholders' is an important element of the right to participate under the ECL.[133]

Certainly, the ECL's approach to participation could be seen as another example of stakeholder consultation, traditionally favoured by the Commission.[134] However, Kati Kuvolesi and colleagues find that the EC merely 'pays lip service to public participation [as] these provisions are vague and lack concrete means to strengthen the inclusiveness and openness of climate policymaking'.[135] The Commission's view of the purpose of participation as helping achieve the climate targets – rather than defining them – is problematic. It highlights the responsibility of individual everyday actions to contribute to the top-down climate objective, rather than the value of an inclusive participatory process. This presents another example of what has been called 'the silent erosion of rights to participate' in a time of climate crisis, where choices are made and voices are selected.[136]

C. Participation and Renewables Acceleration

The urgency of reaching the EU climate targets also affects participation in ways that are perhaps less visible, yet more concrete. In recent years, for instance, the authorisation process of renewable energy projects under the Renewable Energy Directive has become a symbolic battlefield between streamlining the permitting process for new infrastructure and ensuring public participation, in particular within national planning law and the Environmental Impact Assessment (EIA) procedure.[137] In the EU, this tension has recently arisen in the establishment of

[130] M Lee and C Abbot, 'The Usual Suspects? Public Participation under the Aarhus Convention' (2003) 66 *MLR* 80.

[131] Article 9.2 European Climate Law.

[132] Article 10 Regulation 2018/1999 on the Governance of the Energy Union and Climate Action (OJ 2018, L 328/1).

[133] ibid.

[134] Communication, 'European governance – A white paper', COM(2001) 428 final – OJ C 287.

[135] K Kulovesi, S Oberthür, H van Asselt and A Savaresi, 'The European Climate Law: Strengthening EU Procedural Climate Governance?' (2024) 36 *JEL* 23, 40.

[136] Armeni and Lee (n 11).

[137] C Armeni, 'Participation in Environmental Decision-making: Reflecting on Planning and Community Benefits for Major Wind Farms' (2016) 28 *JEL* 415. See also R Cowell and P Devine-Wright, 'A "Delivery-Democracy Dilemma"? Mapping and Explaining Policy Change for Public Engagement with Energy Infrastructure' (2018) 20 *JEPP* 499.

'renewables acceleration areas', which are 'specific location[s] or area[s], whether on land, sea or inland waters, which a Member State designated as particularly suitable for the installation of renewable energy plants'.[138] By 21 February 2026, Member States must ensure that one or more plans are adopted by the competent authorities to identify these areas following an EIA as well as another impact assessment under the Natura 2000 directive 'if they are likely to have a significant impact on Natura 2000 sites'.[139] Opportunities for public participation in the decision-making on the plans designating such areas must be provided.[140] In those areas, the permitting process is fast-tracked.[141] What is important here is that new projects in a designated acceleration area will be 'exempt from the requirement to carry out a dedicated environmental impact assessment'.[142] A simpler screening procedure is required to establish if any proposed project is 'highly likely to give rise to significant unforeseen adverse effects [...] which were not identified during the environmental assessment of the plans designating' the area.[143] While participation is still in principle a core requirement of this procedure, this streamlining and the scaling-up of consultation at the level of plans, with only a screening requirement included in the process, raises questions regarding the scope for participation in this context. The acceleration of renewable energy projects is part of the EU energy agenda's twin decarbonisation and securitisation objectives. Here the emergency framing focuses on the need to speed up deployment and accelerate authorisation. Cutting procedure and time for public consultation reinforces the assumption that public participation causes delays in implementation of the target, which in turns means that the time for participation often gets reduced when speed and efficiency are prioritised.

The tensions between urgency and participation are not exclusive to specific projects. They should be seen within a wider – contested – trend of reducing administrative burdens for infrastructure development and a simplification of stakeholder consultation under the Better Regulation Agenda.[144] This tension is visible within the public consultation provision of the Governance Regulation. Article 10 of the Regulation requires that 'each Member State ensure that the public is given early and effective opportunities

[138] New Article 2(2) point 9(a) Directive (EU) 2018/2001 on the promotion of the use of energy from renewable sources (recast) (inserted by Article 1 Directive (EU) 2023/2413 as regards the promotion of energy from renewable sources (OJ L, 2023/2413).

[139] New Article 15c(2), ibid. cf Directive 2001/42/EC on the assessment of the effects of certain plans and programmes on the environment (OJ L 197) and Article 6(3) of Directive 92/43/EEC on the conservation of natural habitats and of wild fauna and flora (OJ L 206).

[140] ibid new Article 15(d)(1).

[141] ibid new Article 16(a)(3).

[142] ibid new Article 16(a)(4).

[143] ibid.

[144] Communication, 'Better regulation: Joining forces to make better laws', COM/2021/219 final. See also Art 10 of the Governance Regulation on public consultation requiring that each Member State 'limit administrative complexity when implementing its obligation to ensure public participation'. In so doing, the Regulation implicitly translates urgency into a need to reduce red tape and accelerate implementation at the Member State level.

to participate in the preparation of the draft integrated national energy and climate plan'.[145] The public must be informed, without specific indication of the content and context of the information. 'Reasonable time frames' must be established to allow 'sufficient time for the public to be informed, to participate and express its views'.[146] While rather minimal and unspecific, these provisions broadly align with the Aarhus-model's (equally minimal) standards. However, the Regulation requires that each Member State 'shall limit administrative complexity when implementing its obligation to ensure public participation'.[147] In so doing, the Regulation implicitly translates urgency into the need to reduce red tape and accelerate implementation at the Member State level. Although participation is in principle a good thing, in practice it tends to represent an inconvenience and an administrative burden for the implementation of ECL and the governance framework and its associated targets. At least when it is so perceived, administrative streamlining and simplification is likely to be prioritised.

While climate emergency framings are not explicitly mobilised through law here, the urgency visible in these legal arrangements implicitly reminds us how time can serve as both a constrain upon and an enabler of participation. Building on this argument, in the following section, the chapter calls for the intensification of the legal rights to participate in the EU precisely because of – rather than despite – the time pressure of climate action by strengthening the salience of time in the decision-making process.

V. TIME FOR PARTICIPATION

Time has been a quiet, somehow uncomfortable guest throughout this chapter. This section emphasises its role in supporting – rather than constraining – participation at different levels. Time is central to participation and to emergencies. Time pressure can be used to justify technocratic decision-making, bypassing other participants. But time is also an enabler when participation is allowed to unfold and have an impact. The Aarhus Convention is hugely preoccupied with time. When it comes to decisions on authorisation of specific activities (eg, a renewable energy infrastructure), the Convention requires Parties to identify and then notify the public concerned (ie, the public affected or likely to be affected by the decisions, including NGOs) of an authorisation procedure, 'early in the process' and 'in an adequate, *timely* and effective manner'.[148] It requires clear timeframes to be established. Enough time must be provided to inform the public about a decision-making process on a proposed activity so the

[145] ibid Article 10.
[146] ibid.
[147] ibid.
[148] Article 6 Aarhus Convention (emphasis added).

public might prepare. This includes time to bring in their own experts who can help give weight to their argument.[149]

Having time is a condition for participation to make the difference. Participation must take place at a moment when all options are still open and people have a real opportunity to influence decisions. Time is not only important with regard to the actual formal decision-making process. Even before a decision is made, the Convention 'encourages exchanges of information between the applicant and the public 'where appropriate', and all relevant information to the decision-making process should be provided to the public 'as early as possible'.[150] This centrality of time works as an enabler of richer public inclusion and cannot be negotiated, if we are serious about our democratic commitments, including in the EU. To strengthen the value of participation as a contribution to the quality of decisions in a time of crisis, we should recognise and intensify the legal function of time for participation.

The EU should reinforce the construction and protection of time for participation. It should address the administrative streamlining trends from the lens of justice and participation. Alternatives need time to be evaluated, contested and chosen through a collective process. Courts are also confronted with alternatives, as choices on the emission reductions models for instance are increasingly contested.[151] Consequences need to be assessed by the largest possible groups of people. Justification is an essential element of what justice means and a key aspect of democracy and the rule of law.[152] Explaining how the outcome of the consultation will be considered is crucial and takes time. Law always provides for the right to be given reasons, which takes time.

The intensification and protection of time is a condition for inclusion. Participation does not only require protection of institutional time, ie periods for participation set aside in the process. It also needs to ensure time for participants to engage in practice, while everyday life goes on. Time is a scarce resource especially for those whose level of education, socio-economic status and cultural background makes it harder to take time off from work and family care. Extended social protection – eg childcare, employment, education – could help free up time for those whose voices tend to be less heard. The role of Member States is central here, but the EU could strengthen

[149] J Hawkins, '"We Want Experts": Fracking and the Case of Expert Excess' (2020) 32 *JEL* 1.

[150] Article 6 Aarhus Convention.

[151] See, eg, the Belgian 'Klimaatzaak' Civ. [Tribunal of First Instance] Brussels (ch 4), 17 June 2021, case 2015/4585/A [188–190].

[152] This is also a central point of the Better Regulation Agenda in the EU (n 144 above). For a discussion, see J Nowag and X Groussot, 'From Better Regulation to Better Adjudication? Impact Assessment and the Court of Justice's Review' in S Garben and I Govaere (eds), *The EU Better Regulation Agenda: A Critical Assessment* (Hart Publishing, 2020). On reason-giving see also Better Regulation Case C-114/19 *European Commission v Danilo di Bernardo* ECLI:EU:C:2020:457; Case C-12/03 *Tetra Laval v Commission* ECLI:EU:C:2005:87, [2005] ECR I-987; Case C-310/04 *Spain v Council*, ECLI:EU:C:2006:521, [2006] ECR I-7285.

the connection between social rights and participation by increasing the salience of time in this context.[153]

Framing the climate crisis as an emergency is a way to depoliticise decision-making, 'to take things off the table to get things done'.[154] Recognising that participation takes time, and extending and protecting the time offered for participation would counter this trend and resist technocracy. Re-politicising EU climate law and policy away from 'governance by number' is an important step toward strengthening legal rights to participation. This does not mean rejecting expertise. It means demanding that decisions be made based on a richer set of positions and interests,[155] which requires that the most marginalised groups have sufficient time to form and express their views.

At a broader level, the legal framework should move from a focus on delivery to a focus on the process. The climate transition is not only about how to achieve the targets quickly. The EU pays attention to the distributive effects of the climate neutrality targets and has made a commitment to a just transition.[156] But more profoundly, we need to make collective choices that consider a wider set of values, potential impacts and economic and non-economic costs and benefits. This requires a wider inclusion of diverse groups among the public, who may come up with a very different assessment. By extending and protecting time for participation, we can construct law as an enabler of democratic processes and of the constitutional values guaranteed by Article 2 of the TEU, showcasing the co-benefits of the climate transition.[157] Deliberative experiments, especially citizens assemblies, are being conducted in many Member States as an alternative and innovative model of participation to shape more ambitious climate laws and policies.[158] These experiments are not a panacea for the ailments of existing democratic systems.[159] Nor will they necessarily be able to quench scepticism towards participation and solve technocratic barriers. However, they can complement the landscape of environmental democracy and help set aside time for participation across the EU.

[153] On this connection, K Arabadjieva and S Bogojević, 'The European Green Deal: Climate Action, Social Impacts and Just Transition Safeguards' (2024) *YEL* 1 (advance access).

[154] J White, *In the Long Run* (Penguin, 2024).

[155] Armeni and Lee (n 11)12–17.

[156] C Armeni, 'What justice? The scope for public participation in the European Union Just Transition' (2023) 60 *CMLR* 1027, 1030.

[157] É Laurent, 'The European Green Deal: from growth-strategy to social-ecological transition?' in European Trade Union Institute, *Social Policy in the European Union: State of Play* (2020) 97–111, available at www.etui.org/sites/default/files/2021-01/07-Chapter5-The%20European%20Green%20Deal.pdf.

[158] L-A Duvic-Paoli, 'Re-imagining the Making of Climate Law and Policy in Citizens' Assemblies' (2022) 11 *TEL* 235.

[159] A Machin, 'Democracy, Agony, and Rupture: A Critique of Climate Citizens' Assemblies' (2023) 64 *German Political Science Quarterly* 845.

VI. CONCLUSION

The climate crisis is not just an existential threat to the EU. It is also a test for the EU legal order, and an opportunity to strengthen its democratic foundation and ensure the protection of the legal right to participate in environmental decision-making. Decision-makers at EU and Member State levels are under time pressure to deliver on climate targets, while at the same time reaffirming the importance of public engagement in how these are reached. In this chapter, it was argued that when time pressure is at play, public participation is likely to be eroded and its values and purpose recede into the background, ceding pride of place to quantifiable objectives and technocratic decisions. EU constitutional law is ill-equipped to deal with the climate crisis through the strategy implied by calling it an emergency, which calls for swift and radical action or a state of exception to which participation is a barrier. Instead of stressing the urgency of the crisis, the EU should stress the role time plays in a participatory democracy: truly democratic decision-making takes time. At a moment when environmental democracy is under threat in many ways in the EU, this could offer a (perhaps modest but) much-needed starting point for going back to politics in climate decision-making.

11

Climate Emergency, Vulnerability and Justice: The Ambivalent Dynamic of the European Green Deal

NATHALIE HERVÉ-FOURNEREAU

I. INTRODUCTION

ONE THING IS sure: the climate emergency is real. Six of the nine biogeophysical boundaries of the Earth system are exceeded, putting the 'safe operating space for humanity'[1] at risk. According to the Doughnut Economics Action Lab, none of the 140 countries studied currently live within a space of ecological security and social justice.[2] According to the European Environment Agency (EEA), Europe is warming at twice the rate of other continents. Among the 36 major climate risks for Europe identified in the EEA's assessment, 21 need action now, with eight of them being particularly urgent.[3] In its communication on climate risks in 2024, the Commission exclaims that 'the climate crisis is one of the most existential of all the threats we face'.[4]

What is the role of the EU in this regard? It has called for a radical transformation aimed at establishing a just and prosperous society as part of the European Green Deal (EGD).[5] But how can the EU effectively achieve its ambitious goal of becoming the world's first carbon-neutral continent by 2050, while ensuring that no one is left behind and mitigating further ecosystem degradation? The EGD is not as unequivocal as it may appear. A Promethean vision of technology, combined with a persistent 'business as usual' economic growth paradigm remains embedded within its framework. The final tumultuous year of the mandates of the President of the European

[1] J Rockström et al, 'A safe operating space for humanity' (2009) 461 *Nature* 742.

[2] AL Fanning et al, 'The social shortfall and ecological overshoot of nations' (2022) 5 *Nature Sustainability* 26.

[3] European Environment Agency, *European Climate Risk Assessment* (EEA Report 01/2024), available at www.eea.europa.eu/en/analysis/publications/european-climate-risk-assessment.

[4] COM (2024) 91 final.

[5] COM (2019) 640 final.

Commission (Commission) and the European Parliament (EP) highlights threats to the transformative ambitions of the EGD. In November 2024, the President of the Commission, Ursula Von der Leyen, affirmed that 'we must and will stay the course on the goals of the European Green Deal', but importantly added that 'the first major initiative of the new Commission will be a Competitiveness Compass'.[6] The second pillar of this compass will be a joint plan for decarbonisation and competitiveness. In her first speech for her second mandate in July 2024, she further emphasised that 'we have to reconcile climate protection with a prosperous economy', arguing that 'this is not a matter of competitiveness but also a matter of intergenerational fairness'.[7] In many ways, the nexus of climate emergency, vulnerability, and justice represents a highly complex issue.

The EU's understanding and approach to this nexus reveal the ambivalent dynamics underpinning the EGD. Among the numerous Herculean tasks associated with the EGD, this intricate nexus emerges as a critical legal challenge, as will be discussed in Section II. Yet it remains insufficiently addressed in both the EGD and its implementation. The spatiotemporal dimensions of this nexus constitute a uniquely complex legal issue, analysed in Section III. Moreover, integrating this nexus into EU decision-making processes raises significant concerns regarding the socio-ecological coherence of EU policies, particularly given the imperative to strengthen democratic foundations for realising the ambitions of the EGD, as debated in Section IV. The final part of this chapter, Section V, concludes.

II. THE GREEN DEAL AT THE NEXUS OF CLIMATE EMERGENCY, VULNERABILITY AND JUSTICE

The nexus between the climate emergency, vulnerability, and justice is obvious and an ever-pressing issue. As voiced in 2020 by Rosemary A DiCarlo, UN Under-Secretary-General for Political Affairs and Peacebuilding: 'the risk of a vicious cycle of climate disaster and insecurity […] undermines our core objectives of conflict prevention and sustaining peace'.[8] More recently, in his address to the Security Council, António Guterres, the UN Secretary-General recalled that 'climate and conflict were the main causes of acute food insecurity

[6] Speech by President of the Commission, Von der Leyen to the European Parliament Plenary (27/11/2024), available at neighbourhood-enlargement.ec.europa.eu/news/speech-president-von-der-leyen-european-parliament-plenary-new-college-commissioners-and-its-2024-11-27_en.

[7] Statement at the European Parliament by President of the Commission, Ursula von der Leyen (18/7/2024), available at neighbourhood-enlargement.ec.europa.eu/news/statement-european-parliament-plenary-president-ursula-von-der-leyen-candidate-second-mandate-2024-2024-07-18_en.

[8] The Fifth Arria-formula Meeting on 'Climate and security risks: the latest data' (April 2022), available at dppa.un.org/en/climate-change-multiplying-factors-lead-to-insecurity-millions-rosemary-dicarlo-tells-arria-formula.

for almost 174 million people in 2022'.[9] He also urged the Security Council 'to consider how it can best address the interlinked threats to climate, food security and international peace and security'.[10]

The European Council drew attention to the impact of climate change on international security as early in 2007.[11] More recently, the Commission and the High Representative of the Union for Foreign Affairs and Security Policy have promoted a 'new outlook on the climate and security nexus',[12] and in their joint communication in 2023, they reaffirm that climate change and environmental degradation contribute to increased risks of insecurity, including 'greater migratory movements and displacement, pandemics, social unrest, instability, and insecurity'.[13]

The cost of inaction in the face of climate change is already significant, particularly for those who are most vulnerable. At the opening of the Climate Action Summit in November 2024, the UN Secretary-General urged that 'the COP 29 must tear down the walls of climate finance'.[14] In its recent opinion on the economic impact of climate change, the EESC mentions that 'the preliminary data indicate annual costs of EUR 600 billion for the period 2024–2030'.[15] The EEA similarly emphasises the major costs of climate change in Europe, estimating the economic damage caused by, for instance, floods in the EU over the past 30 years at more than €170 billion, affecting 5.5 million people.[16] The EEA also indicates that projections of the economic costs of climate change are set to increase significantly.[17] In its communications on climate risks, the Commission further confirms that 'the costs and benefits of avoided damage to society as a whole cannot be accurately calculated.' It also concludes that, without radical mitigation and adaptation measures, the EU's GDP could be reduced by around 7 per cent by the end of the century. Moreover, due to limitations in the availability of data and inherent uncertainties, these estimates do not encompass all the social and environmental consequences of the adverse

[9] Open Debate on the impact of climate change and food security on the maintenance of peace and security (13 February 2024) available at www.un.org/sg/en/content/sg/statement/2024-02-13/secretary-generals-remarks-the-security-council-high-level-open-debate-the-impact-of-climate-change-and-food-insecurity-the-maintenance-of-intl-peace-and-security.

[10] ibid.

[11] At the request of the European Council, the Commission and the High Representative of the Union for Foreign Affairs and Security Policy had presented a paper on climate change and international security in 2008 (S113/08), see www.consilium.europa.eu/uedocs/cms_data/docs/pressdata/en/reports/99387.pdf.

[12] Joint Communication, A new outlook on the climate and security nexus: Addressing the impact of climate change and environmental degradation on peace, security and defense (2023) 19 final.

[13] ibid.

[14] Secretary-General's remarks to World Leaders Climate Action Summit at COP 29 (12 November 2024) available at www.un.org/sg/en/content/sg/statement/2024-11-12/secretary-generals-remarks-world-leaders-climate-action-summit-cop29-delivered.

[15] Climate change and its impacts on the economy, ECO/45, October 2024.

[16] EEA Report (n 3).

[17] ibid.

effects of climate change, which are challenging to quantify only in monetary terms. As the UN Secretary-General poignantly stated at COP 29: 'this is a story of avoidable injustice [underscoring that] the rich cause the problem, and the poor pay the highest price'.[18]

Inaction on climate and environmental issues adversely affect both current and future generations, threatening the planet's habitability. The exacerbation and proliferation of environmental, social, and economic vulnerabilities are undeniable. Similarly, the imperative to transform our development models toward a sustainable trajectory may also increase socio-environmental vulnerabilities or even create new ones, potentially leading to significant political and socio-economic tensions and opposition and creating injustices. In 2019, the European Parliament declared a 'climate and environment climate emergency',[19] calling for a just and equitable ecological transition. The EGD confirms that such a transition 'can only succeed if it is conducted in a fair and inclusive'[20] manner. The EGD aims to accelerate the EU's decarbonisation process, with the central objective of making the EU the first carbon-neutral continent by 2050.[21] The EGD is thus presented as a novel European growth strategy that emphasises that 'the most vulnerable are most exposed to the adverse effects of climate change and environmental degradation',[22] and therefore concludes that it is essential to ensure a just and inclusive transition to avoid exacerbating existing vulnerabilities or creating new ones.

A. European Green Deal: The Ambition for a Fair Ecological Transformation of the EU's Socio-Economic System

There are two main aspects of what I call the 'socio-ecological oath' in the EGD: 'do no harm' and 'leave no one behind' in ensuring the socio-economic internal market mechanisms. The central objective of this oath is to ensure that all EU policies are mobilised in a systematic and coherent manner to guarantee the success of this just transition to a sustainable future. This oath is designed not only to integrate the social and environmental costs of inaction and/or inadequate environmental protection, but also the significant risks arising from the disproportionate distribution of the costs and benefits of an ecological transition process. The 8th Environment Action Programme also recognises that limited attention has been paid to the extent of vulnerability and social inequality in the face of environmental risks.[23]

[18] Secretary-General's remarks to World Leaders Climate Action Summit at COP 29 (n 14).
[19] Resolution of 28/11/2019 on the climate and environment emergency (2019/2930 (RSP).
[20] COM (2019) 640 final.
[21] Regulation (EU) 2021/1119 of the EP and of the Council of 30/6/2021 establishing the framework for achieving climate neutrality [2021] OJ L 243/1.
[22] COM (2019) 640 final.
[23] Decision (EU) 2022/591 [2022] OJ L 144/22.

In this regard, the EGD underscores the guiding role that the European pillar of Social Rights will play in ensuring that no one is left behind, particularly in addressing the twin challenge of energy efficiency and affordability. Consequently, the EGD emphasises that the need for a socially just transition must be reflected in European and national policies, not only in terms of working conditions but also in employability. Such an imperative requires not only a comprehensive assessment of the current socio-environmental vulnerabilities and inequalities, but also a thorough examination of the complex socio-environmental consequences of the transition process promoted by the EGD. However, the EGD does not provide sufficient clarity regarding the model of social and environmental justice that underpins its ambitious objective of 'designing a set of profoundly transformative policies'.[24]

The Just Transition Fund and the Social Climate Fund[25] are two key examples of the EGD's commitment to ensuring that no one is left behind. These financial instruments are designed to support regions particularly vulnerable to the energy transition due to their reliance on fossil fuels, as well as households and small businesses impacted by rising energy costs. Not to be overlooked, the current action plan of the European Pillar of Social Rights calls for 'a new social rule that guarantees solidarity between generations'[26] and contributes to the 'success'[27] of the EGD for all Europeans.

The implementation of the social pillar of the EGD has been one of the priorities of the Belgian Presidency of the Council of the EU in 2024. At the request of the Presidency, the European Economic and Social Committee (EESC) has identified, in an exploratory opinion, a series of measures to design a more comprehensive just transition policy framework. Under the aegis of the Belgian Presidency, the Just Transition conference in March 2024 further confirmed the urgent need to strengthen the interactions between the social and environmental foundations of the EGD, at the risk of undermining the edifice as a whole.

A Eurobarometer survey conducted at the end of 2022 revealed that these concerns were already acute, with only 50 per cent of respondents agreeing that the EU was doing enough to ensure a fair transition.[28] Similarly, a 2023 Eurobarometer survey indicated that 67 per cent of respondents considered that their government was not doing enough to tackle climate change.[29] At the same time, a Eurobarometer survey published in the spring of 2024 confirmed widespread concern among citizens regarding the direct impact of environmental issues on their daily lives and health.[30] Similarly, another Eurobarometer survey

[24] COM (2019) 640 final.

[25] Regulation (EU) 2021/1056 establishing the Just Transition Fund [2021] OJ L 231/1. Regulation (EU) 2023/955 establishing a Social Climate Fund [2023] OJ L 130/1.

[26] COM (2021) 102 final.

[27] ibid.

[28] Available at europa.eu/eurobarometer/surveys/detail/2672.

[29] See europa.eu/eurobarometer/surveys/detail/2954.

[30] See europa.eu/eurobarometer/surveys/detail/3173.

revealed that the fight against poverty and social exclusion, alongside public health, ranked among the top priorities for citizens leading up to the European elections in June 2024.[31]

In light of such data, it is crucial to assess the relevance of the actions taken by the EU and its Member States in meeting the ambitious targets of the EGD while respecting the socio-ecological Oath. However, it is important to acknowledge that the EGD represents a significant normative dynamic, despite prevailing uncertainties regarding the capacity and political will to achieve an ecological transformation of the European economic system in line with the socio-ecological oath.

B. A Real Normative Dynamic

Although not legally binding, the EGD has led to the adoption of a plethora of strategies,[32] action plans,[33] and legislative texts under various EU policies. As a result, some EU policies that were previously underdeveloped or relatively indifferent to climate issues are now receiving renewed attention considering the objectives of climate neutrality and the circular economy. Furthermore, the Commission has emphasised the importance of sustainable financing,[34] placing public and private finance and investment at the centre for the EGD's success. Similarly, the objective of strengthening corporate social responsibility has resulted in the adoption of a binding framework for large companies on due diligence,[35] sustainable investments and non-financial reporting.[36] Moreover, the combined impact of Covid-19 and the war in Ukraine has reinforced the prominence of the energy transition on the European agenda.

In November 2024, the EP's 'legislative train schedule' identified 168 'carriage' acts for the implementation of the EGD:[37] in addition to the 98 legislative acts already adopted, the list also includes several texts that are still pending or have yet to be submitted by the Commission. While it is true that the EGD emphasises the need for a just and inclusive transition and the importance of strengthening the social dimension of sustainable development, this is not new. The EU's first sustainable development strategy already advocated for a long-term vision combining economic growth,

[31] See europa.eu/eurobarometer/surveys/detail/3272.

[32] COM (2020) 380 final; COM (2020) 381 final; COM (2022) 675 final.

[33] COM (2020) 98 final.

[34] Finance durable COM (2021) 390 final; Strategy for Financing the transition to a sustainable Economy.

[35] Directive (EU) 2024/1760 on corporate sustainability due diligence [2024] OJ L 2024/1760.

[36] Regulation (EU) 2020/852 on the establishment of a framework to facilitate sustainable investment [2020] OJ L 198/13; Directive (EU) 2022/2464 on regards corporate sustainability reporting [2022] OJ L 322/15.

[37] See www.europarl.europa.eu/legislative-train/theme-a-european-green-deal.

social cohesion and environmental protection.[38] While the EGD's normative dynamic is undoubtedly significant, and differs in terms of concrete actions from previous sustainable development strategies, the implementation of its social dimension remains incomplete and fragmented. This raises the question of whether the intersection of the EGD and social justice could be considered a missed opportunity.

i. An Ambivalent Sustainability Trajectory

The EGD also has a 'dark side' that can breed future disenchantment. Despite the EGD's rhetoric of transformation and radical innovation, several major uncertainties persist. A key issue is the nature of the interactions between the economic, social, environmental and cultural pillars, as well as the relative weight of each in balancing the rights, interests and needs of all people and stakeholders – an issue at the core of the ongoing debate between strong and weak sustainability. Is the greening of the European social market economy model, grounded in planetary boundaries and framed within the social doughnut, truly underway? While answering this question lies beyond the scope of this Chapter, it remains crucial to understanding the challenges of effectively addressing socio-ecological vulnerabilities and emergencies.

The EGD stresses the need for substantial investments required to move towards a long-term sustainability trajectory. However, both the EU and its Member States face a series of constraints and pitfalls. Beyond quantitative considerations, the allocation of these funds, as well as the fair distribution of the benefits and risks inherent in any profound transformation of production and consumption patterns, remains a contentious issue. Since June 2023, a highly turbulent political climate has swept across Europe, marked by a wave of protests against the EGD, including demonstrations within the EP's hemicycle ahead of the 2024 elections. In response to calls from France[39] and Belgium[40] – later echoed by other Member States – for a 'regulatory pause' on climate and environmental matters,[41] Commission Vice-President Frans Timmermans firmly rejected such a break, arguing that 'we don't have the luxury of a pause'.[42] The chaotic process surrounding the adoption of the regulation on nature restoration,[43] the renewal of the glyphosate registration,[44] the rejection of the

[38] COM (2001) 264 final.

[39] See www.elysee.fr/emmanuel-macron/2023/05/11/accelerer-notre-reindustrialisation-le-president-presente-sa-strategie.

[40] Ce Gijs, 'Belgian PM wants to hit "pause" on nature restoration rules' *Politico* (24 May 2023).

[41] See www.epp.eu/news/epp-summit-statement-2.

[42] Eurativ-France (4 May/2023).

[43] Regulation (EU) 2024/1991 of the EP and of the Council on nature restoration, OJEU L 2024/1991.

[44] Commission implementing Regulation (EU) 2023/2660 renewing the approval of the active substance glyphosate (for a period of 10 years), OJEU L 2023/2660.

pesticide regulation proposal by the EP,[45] and the absence of a proposal to revise the REACH regulation[46] all illustrate the impact of these significant turbulences.

Notably, and as mentioned, Ursula von der Leyen's speeches at the start of her second term differ significantly[47] from the inaugural address of her first term.[48] The industrial dimension of the EGD is now presented as *the* primacy focus, aiming to achieve strategic autonomy for the EU and ensure the competitiveness of European companies. This shift in priorities raises questions about the legal interpretation of the EGD's commitment to 'do no harm' and to ensure that no one is left behind.

III. LEGAL CONSIDERATIONS OF THE SPATIOTEMPORAL DIMENSIONS OF THE CLIMATE EMERGENCY

The concept of emergency has become the prevailing temporal framework in contemporary legal production.[49] In his speeches, UN Secretary-General António Guterres underscores the unprecedented nature of these complex temporalities, stating that 'every second counts [and that] delay means death'.[50] At the 2020 Climate Summit, he called on world leaders to 'declare a state of climate emergency in their countries until carbon neutrality is achieved'.[51] The urgency of the situation, as outlined in scientific assessments of environmental and socio-ecological vulnerabilities, underscores the shortcomings of current policies. It is evident that inaction, coupled with the lack of ambitious measures, has generated existing vulnerabilities and will create new ones. The EGD is presented as a response to the climate and environmental emergency, advocating for urgent action without invoking a state of emergency. The distinction between the common legal framework and the exceptional nature of a state of emergency is legally significant. However, the implementation of the EGD is confronted with spatiotemporal discordances that risk exacerbating social and ecological vulnerabilities, potentially creating conflict between them. The need to address current socio-ecological vulnerabilities in tandem thus requires a trans-generational perspective, while also recognising the rights of future generations – all as discussed next.

[45] COM (2022) 305 final.

[46] The Commission specified in its 2023 work programme that the proposal to revise the REACH regulation would be presented (COM 2022 (548 final).

[47] See neighbourhood-enlargement.ec.europa.eu/news/statement-european-parliament-plenary-president-ursula-von-der-leyen-candidate-second-mandate-2024-2024-07-18_en.

[48] See ec.europa.eu/commission/presscorner/api/files/document/print/en/speech_19_4230/SPEECH_19_4230_EN.pdf.

[49] Such observation was made in François Ost, *Le temps du droit* (Odile Jacob, 1999).

[50] See news.un.org/en/story/2022/02/1112852.

[51] See www.un.org/sg/en/content/sg/statement/2020-12-12/secretary-generals-remarks-the-climate-ambition-summit-bilingual-delivered-scroll-down-for-all-english-version.

A. Between Urgent Legal Action and the State of Climate Emergency

The Treaty on European Union (TEU) does not confer a general competence to declare a state of emergency on the EU. However, specific provisions address emergency situations,[52] as well as severe threats or 'difficulties caused by natural disasters or exceptional occurrences beyond'[53] the control of a Member State, thereby justifying EU assistance, including the adoption of provisional measures.

While the symbolic political significance of declarations of climate and environmental emergency cannot be disregarded, exceptional emergency regimes are not without significant risks and challenges to democracy and the rule of law.[54] Experiences from the implementation of states of emergency in Member States during the Covid-19 pandemic further underscore this inadequacy.[55] It is essential to highlight that the democratic foundation for structural changes towards sustainable modes of consumption and production – ensuring that no one is left behind – requires the comprehensive and long-term integration of these processes within the framework of ordinary law and the rule of law. In its November 2019 resolution, the EP underscores that 'no emergency should ever be used to erode democratic institutions or to undermine fundamental rights; whereas all measures will always be adopted through a democratic process'.[56] It also calls on decision-makers to 'urgently take the concrete action needed in order to fight and contain this threat before it is too late'.[57]

Most strategies and legislation adopted to implement the EGD stress the need for urgent action. Climate and environmental emergencies have been compounded by other crises, such as the Covid-19 pandemic and soaring energy prices resulting from Russia's aggression in Ukraine. In response, the EU adopted temporary emergency measures[58] based on Article 122(1) TFEU,[59] allowing Member States to provide financial support to individuals and companies most vulnerable to the rising energy prices.[60] The adoption of Council

[52] Article 28 TEU (Common Foreign and Security Policy), Article 78 TFEU (Asylum and Immigration).

[53] Article 122-2 TFEU.

[54] A Van Lang, 'L'urgence climatique: faut-il un droit d'exception' in S Robert (ed), *Droit et sécurité climatique, un nouveau registre de la lutte contre le réchauffement planétaire* (Mare Martin, 2024). See also «*Urgence (s) écologique(s) : quelle(s) urgence(s) pour le droit ?* » coord. N Hervé-Fournereau and A Langlais, 'Revue juridique de l'environnement 2022, numéro spécial'.

[55] EP resolution of 12/7/2023 on the COVID-19 pandemic: lessons learned and recommendation for the future, OJEU 2024 C/2024/4003. See also 2023 Rule of Law Report COM (2023) 800 final.

[56] EP resolution of 28 November 2019 on the climate and environment emergency, ibid.

[57] ibid.

[58] Council Regulation (EU) 2022/2578 establishing a market correction mechanism to protect Union citizens and the economy against excessively high prices [2022] OJ L 335/45.

[59] The provision states: 'Without prejudice to any other procedures provided for in the Treaties, the Council, on a proposal from the Commission, may decide, in a spirit of solidarity between Member States, upon the measures appropriate to the economic situation, in particular if severe difficulties arise in the supply of certain products, notably in the area of energy'.

[60] Council Regulation (EU) 2022/1854 on an emergency intervention to address high energy prices [2022] L 261I (note – no longer in force).

Regulation (EU) 2022/2577,[61] extended for a further one-year period in 2023,[62] illustrates the use of targeted temporary measures to address 'short-term energy emergencies [and] exceptional circumstances.'[63] One of the temporary measures introduced in this regulation establishes a presumption that renewable energy projects constitute an overriding public interest, including health and safety, which may justify temporary derogations from several EU environmental laws.[64] The objective of accelerating the implementation of renewable energy sources is further demonstrated by the reduction in the time required to grant permits. It must be emphasised that there exists a certain degree of porosity between emergency regimes and ordinary law, which may be open to scrutiny. Several temporary emergency provisions adopted to address exceptional and abnormal situations have subsequently evolved into permanent legal norms within the framework of ordinary law. Directive (EU) 2023/2413[65] exemplifies this point by 'normalising' one of the emergency measures in Council Regulation (EU) 2022/2577. Specifically, it considers that until climate neutrality is achieved, renewable energy plants are presumed as being in the overriding public interest and serving public health and safety. This encompasses the permit-granting authorisation procedure, grid connection, and storage assets, unless Member States envisage territorial restrictions, of which the Commission must be notified. In a similar vein, in order to ensure the security of supply of net-zero technologies within Europe and to contribute to the European Union's open strategic autonomy, Regulation (EU) 2024/1735[66] grants priority status to net-zero technology production projects located in net-zero acceleration valleys, recognising them as being of public interest and potentially qualifying them as projects of overriding public interest. This prioritisation of emergencies is not neutral and may result in problematic spatiotemporal discordances, impacting the integrated consideration of social and environmental vulnerabilities within the EGD transition process.

B. The Imperative to Address Ecological and Social Vulnerabilities in Tandem

In the context of its ecological transition, the EU faces a dual spatiotemporal challenge: addressing urgent social and environmental crises alongside

[61] Council Regulation (EU) 2022/2577 laying down a framework to accelerate the deployment of renewable energy [2022] OJ L 335/36.

[62] Council Regulation (EU) 2024/223 amending Regulation (EU) 2022/2577, OJEU 2024/2023, no longer in force.

[63] Council Regulation (EU) 2022/2577 (n 61).

[64] Directive 2011/92/EU of the EP and of the Council on the assessment of the effects of certain public and private projects on the environment [2012] OJ L 26/1.

[65] [2023] OJ L 2023/2413.

[66] Regulation (EU) 2024/1735 establishing a framework of measures to strengthen the Europe's net-zero technology manufacturing ecosystem [2021] OJ L 2024/1735.

long-term social and environmental vulnerabilities, both within and beyond its borders, arising from its patterns of production and consumption. Concurrently, it must reconcile its actions with often conflicting timeframes that may impede the achievement of long-term objectives. These challenges are further exacerbated by socio-economic and legal barriers, increasing the risk of spatial and temporal discordances.

It is imperative to recognise the spatial dimensions of these challenges, emphasising the need for targeted action in regions and cities most vulnerable to the impacts of climate change and environmental degradation, as well as those that will bear the greatest burden in the pursuit of climate neutrality. The protection of the EU's outermost and overseas regions is particularly urgent, given their socio-economic and environmental vulnerabilities.[67] Additionally, regions heavily dependent on fossil fuels have been prioritised for transitional financial support mechanisms to facilitate their energy and climate transitions.[68] While the EU's dependence on external sources of critical raw materials, technologies, and other essential products poses a significant risk to its strategic open autonomy, it is equally important to acknowledge that the EU's external environmental and social footprint must not be overlooked. Measures taken to address this dependency must not obscure the EU's international climate commitments, nor its responsibility to contribute meaningfully to global efforts to combat climate change, including through fair and sustainable practices beyond its borders. However, the challenges of extra-territorialising the ambitions of the EGD – without causing harm or leaving anyone behind – are exemplified by issues such as deforestation, carbon leakage, and the legal recognition of corporate sustainability due diligence.

Achieving articulation and coherence across different time scales is undoubtedly a complex legal task, situated at the intersection of economic, social, political, and ecological temporalities.[69] This underscores the need for a multi-annual action programme and territorial just transition plans[70] with binding interim targets. The 2050 horizon for achieving carbon neutrality and living within planetary boundaries represents an ambitious and essential trajectory for planning the necessary socio-economic transformations. The Commission intends to propose a binding interim greenhouse gas emission reduction target for 2040;[71] thereby illustrating the need to move beyond the traditional short-term policy approach. Similarly, the systematic use of monitoring mechanisms, scenarios, and strategic foresight tools[72] addresses the need to anticipate and adapt policies based on the results obtained. Projecting into the long term

[67] COM (2024) 435 final.
[68] Regulation (EU) 2021/1056 establishing the Just Transition Fund, [2021] OJ L 231/1.
[69] T Soleilhac, *Le temps et le droit de l'environnement* (PhD thesis, University of Lyon, 2006).
[70] Regulation (EU) 2023/955 establishing a Social Climate Fund [2023] OJ L 130.
[71] COM (2024) 63 final.
[72] COM (2023) 376 final.

presents a challenge for decision-makers due to increasing uncertainty, yet it is crucial for anticipating and addressing the risks of ecological irreversibility and tipping points. Therefore, if 'policy is the direction and the course, can law not be seen as the construction of the ship, its rigging, and its buoyancy'[73] – guiding present and future generations back into a safe operating space for humanity, particularly for the most vulnerable populations, territories, and ecosystems?

C. Current Socio-ecological Vulnerabilities and the Rights of Future Generations

European integration is part of a long-term process aimed at 'creating an ever-closer union among the peoples of Europe'.[74] The EU explicitly promotes 'solidarity between generations and protection of the rights of the child'.[75] Furthermore, the Charter of Fundamental Rights of the EU underscores that the 'enjoyment of these rights entails responsibilities and duties with regard to other people, to the human community, and to future generations'.[76] Since 1973, the EU's environmental policy has been guided by a long-term perspective, while remaining grounded in the present. The 7th Environment Action Programme, with its priority objectives for 2020, advances a 'clear long-term vision for 2050'.[77] In this current Environment Action programme, the legislator underscores the imperative of setting the 'pace for ensuring the prosperity of present and future generations globally, guided by the intergenerational responsibility'.[78] In her speech to the EP in November 2019, Von der Leyen defended a 'generational transition towards climate neutrality'.[79] The EGD thus embraces this vision by pursuing a fair ecological transition committed to 'improving the quality of life of current and future generations'.[80] The EGD's twofold injunction to 'do no harm' and 'leave no one behind' extends into the long term and resonates with the objective of sustainable development defined as a 'development that meets the need of the present without compromising the ability of future generation to meet their own needs'.[81]

[73] My own translation of Jean Carbonnier: 'la politique est la direction, le cap, le droit étant la construction du navire, son gréement, sa flottaison' as cited in J Commaille, *L'esprit sociologique des lois*, (PUF Publishing, 1994) 250.

[74] Preamble of the Treaty on European Union (TEU).

[75] Article 3 TEU.

[76] Preamble of the Charter of Fundamental Rights of the EU.

[77] Decision 1386/2013/EU on a General Union Environment Action Programme to 2020, [2013] OJ L354/171.

[78] Article 2, Decision (EU) 2022/591 on a General Union Environment Action Programme to 2030 [2021] OJ L 114.

[79] See ec.europa.eu/commission/presscorner/api/files/attachment/858838/Speech%20by%20President-elect%20von%20der%20Leyen%20at%20the%20EP%20-%20as%20delivered%20in%20EN-FR-DE.pdf.

[80] COM (2019) 640 final.

[81] Article 3 TEU.

The legal challenge lies in ensuring that decisions made today do not render future generations vulnerable by imposing an unsustainable ecological and social debt.[82] The urgency of taking immediate action to safeguard what remains for future generations is particularly evident in light of the irreversible environmental risks and potential future severe damage as exemplified by nuclear energy and long-lived radioactive waste. These issues starkly illustrate the significant risk of transferring an enormous burden to future generations, along with a disproportionate distribution of risks, efforts, and resources between generations, particularly affecting vulnerable individuals, communities, territories, and ecosystems.

The overarching objective of Council Directive 2011/70/Euratom is to ensure a 'responsible and safe management of spent fuel and radioactive waste to avoid imposing undue burdens on future generations'.[83] However, the Commission's 2024 report on the implementation of this legislation highlights that 'the targets set in some national programmes are not sufficiently ambitious and envisage long implementation periods that risk burdening future generations'.[84] Furthermore, the report acknowledges that, due to incomplete national data, it was not 'possible to provide an overall EU inventory long-term forecast'.[85] The Commission also stressed that due to the fact that 'the current lack of operational deep geological disposal facilities leads to continuously increasing amounts of stored intermediate and high-level waste and spent fuel', it appears difficult to ensure 'sufficient long-term storage capacity and developing sustainable disposal solutions'.[86] Such an observation cannot fail to raise concern. The Commission has already highlighted that several consequences of climate change are either irreversible or cause severe damage. As early as 2007, it emphasised that adaptation measures are 'not an alternative to reducing greenhouse gas emissions',[87] particularly considering the risks of exceeding critical temperature thresholds and their severe and irreversible consequences, including large-scale population displacement.

The determination of the long-term scale (eg, 20, 30, 100 years, or even longer) is therefore fundamentally challenging. Would it not be prudent to refrain from adopting measures whose consequences extend beyond a specific temporal horizon, given the inherent uncertainties? Would the precautionary principle be overlooked? Moreover, how can the reversibility of the storage of long-lived radioactive waste be effectively ensured? The capacity and freedom of present and future generations to live well within the limits of the planet will largely depend on the reversibility of technological choices made today, as well

[82] COM (2019) 22 final.
[83] Article 1, Council Directive 2011/70/Euratom establishing a Community framework for the responsible and safe management of spent fuel and radioactive waste (2011) OJ L 199/48.
[84] COM (2024) 197 final.
[85] ibid.
[86] ibid.
[87] COM (2007) 354 final.

as on the reduction of greenhouse gas emissions, as enshrined in the EU Climate Neutrality Regulation 2021/1119.

In response to the escalating climate and environmental risks and emergencies, the consideration of future generations in EU decision-making has gained increasing attention. Some EU legislative instruments underscore the need to adopt or strengthen obligations, for the protection of future generations.[88] Similarly, the various strategies and action plans developed within the EGD also highlight the importance of reinforcing such imperative, framed from a perspective of intergenerational equity and transgenerational solidarity. However, the legal status of future generations remains unsettled within EU Law.

Directive 2011/70/Euratom on radioactive waste qualifies as an 'ethical obligation' for each Member State to 'avoid undue hardship on future generations'[89] in one of its recitals, urging them to take 'reasonable steps to ensure' the achievement of this objective. Notably, the concept of 'rights of future generations' was invoked in the 2022 conclusions of the Council and the representatives of the governments of the Member States meeting within the Council, concerning environmental engagement among young people. In these conclusions, it was asserted that 'inter-generational solidarity and justice should be addressed in decision-making processes on protecting the environment so that the benefits for present generations do not stand in conflict with the rights of future generations.'[90] In the CJEU's case law, there are only a few instances invoking the duty to protect future generations, with the singular exception of three preliminary references submitted by a German court.[91] These cases concerned the consequences of the Dieselgate scandal. However, the German court advanced arguments akin to a plea for the recognition of the rights of nature through an expansive interpretation of the EU Charter of Fundamental Rights, thereby contributing to the fulfilment of the duty to protect future generations as well as the intergenerational and intertemporal protection of freedom.[92] Here the applicants did not explicitly refer to future generations or the consideration of the long term when arguing the lack of ambition in the 2018 Climate and Energy Legislative Package.[93] The CJEU has yet to assess the nature and legal scope of a duty of protection towards future generations. Moreover, the restrictive interpretation of the already stringent

[88] Regulation (EU) 2023/1115 (deforestation), Regulation (EU) 2021/1139 of the EU and of the Council establishing the European Maritime, Fisheries and aquaculture Fund [2021] OJ L 247/1.

[89] Article 24, Council Directive 2011/70/Euratom [2011] OJ L 199.

[90] Conclusions of Council and the representatives of the government of the Member States meeting within the Council-Fostering engagement among young people as actors of change in order to protect the environment, see [2022] OJ C 159/9.

[91] Landgericht Erfurt – note that in 2024, two of these cases have been removed from the register: Case C-506/21 *UM v Mercedes-Benz-Daimler AG* ECLI:EU:C:2024:248; Case C-388/21 *A v B* ECLI:EU:C:2024:276. Case C-276/20 *A.G.E./B AG*, supplement to the request for preliminary ruling 24 April 2024.

[92] See Case C-388/21 *A v B* [2021] OJ C 382/15.

[93] Case C-565/19 P *A. Carvalho & others* ECLI:EU:C:2021:252, [2022] 2 CMLR 8.

conditions for public access to its courtroom partly explains this situation. Furthermore, in cases against the Commission's delegated regulations,[94] on the inclusion of nuclear energy and gas as transitional activities in the taxonomy of sustainable investments (Regulation (EU) 2020/852) the applicants do not invoke the protection of future generations under the Charter of Fundamental Rights in seeking the annulment of these regulations[95] or the Commission's refusal to conduct an internal review.[96] The parties argue a breach of environmental principles, such as the precautionary and integration principles, as well as the EGD's 'do no harm' oath, now renamed the 'do no significant harm' principle in Regulation (EU) 2020/852.[97] This Regulation stipulates that the technical assessment criteria must account for the long-term effects of a given economic activity. In this context, enabling activity 'shall qualify as contributing substantially to one or more environmental objectives'[98] if it 'does not lead to lock-in of assets that undermine long-term environmental goals, considering the economic life of those assets', and 'has a substantial positive environmental impact on the basis of life-cycle considerations'.[99] Furthermore, the Regulation outlines general assumptions under which an economic activity is deemed to cause significant harm, including, for instance, 'the long-term disposal of waste [that] may cause significant and long-term harm to the environment'.[100] The CJEU's decision on Austria's action for annulment of these delegated regulations is eagerly awaited,[101] particularly given the Court's questionable interpretation of these texts in cases of other actions that were dismissed as inadmissible.[102]

Several European courts, particularly domestic courts, are contributing to the legal process of the fundamentalisation of future generations by adopting an intertemporal analysis of human rights and recognising States'

[94] See eg Commission Delegated Regulation (EU) 2022/1214 amending Delegated Regulation (EU) 2021/2139 as regards economic activities in certain energy sectors and Delegated Regulation (EU) 2021/2178 as regards specific public disclosures for those economic activities [2022] OJ L 188/1.

[95] Action for annulment against Commission Delegated Regulations see eg Case T-567/22 *ATPN v Commission* ECLI:EU:T:2023:189.

[96] Appeals under the internal review procedure (Aarhus Regulation), see eg Case T-575/22 *Robin Wood v Commission*: Case T-579/22 *ClientEarth v Commission* ECLI:EU:T:2025:862; Case T-583/22 *Fédération environnement durable v Commission* ECLI:EU:T:2025:863; Case T-214/23 *Greenpeace v Commission*; Case T-449/24 *Dryade v Commission*.

[97] Regulation (EU) 2020/852 on the establishment of a framework to facilitate sustainable investment [2020] OJ L 198/13.

[98] ibid Article 3.

[99] ibid.

[100] ibid Article 17.

[101] Case T-625/22 *Austria v Commission* ECLI:EU:C:2023:227.

[102] See Case T-567/22 (C-340/23 P, *ATPN v Commission* ECLI:EU:C:2024:806): Although the application was declared inadmissible, both the General Court and the Court of Justice nevertheless engaged with the substantive merits of the case. Specifically, they dismissed the applicants' contention that the regulation would have a direct impact on the development of the nuclear industry within the EU. This interpretation is open to question, particularly as it appears to underestimate the strategic financial significance of the information provided to investors in this sector.

legally binding obligation to protect them.[103] Judges are also progressively integrating long-term considerations into their reasoning. This approach is exemplified by the German Constitutional Court, which recognised 'an advance interference-like effect on the freedom of the complainants'.[104] The Court held that the allocation of CO_2 emissions poses an 'irreversible legal risk to future freedom' and concluded that the 2019 Climate Law's failure to specify minimum greenhouse gas reduction requirements after 2030 violated Article 20a of the Basic Law. According to the Court, this provision imposes 'an obligation to safeguard fundamental freedom over time and to spread the opportunities associated with freedom proportionately across generations.'[105] The Court further emphasised that 'one generation must not be allowed to consume large portions of the CO_2 budget while bearing a relatively minor share of the reduction effort, if this would involve leaving subsequent generations with a drastic reduction burden and expose their lives to serious losses of freedom',[106] and must not leave future generations with no choice other than 'to engage in radical abstinence' to preserve the 'natural foundations of life'.[107] In 2023, in its interpretation of Article 1 of the Constitutional Charter for the Environment,[108] the French Constitutional Council ruled that 'when adopting measures likely to cause serious and lasting harm to a balanced environment that respects health, the legislator must ensure that the choices made to meet present needs do not compromise the ability of future generations and other peoples to meet their own needs, while preserving their freedom of choice in this regard'.[109] Although widely praised by legal scholars, this decision has been subject to critique,[110] particularly with regard to the principle of reversibility enshrined in Law 2016-1015 on nuclear waste storage. Concerns have also been raised regarding risks extending beyond the operational lifespan of the site (100 years). Will future generations truly have the freedom and capacity to reconsider such technological storage decisions made by the current legislator without bearing an immeasurable burden? Similar concerns arise with other technologies, such as geological carbon storage and industrial carbon

[103] Among the numerous academic legal publications on future generations see eg E Brown Weiss, *In Fairness to Future Generations: International Law, Common Patrimony and Intergenerational Equity* (Transnational Publication, 1989) 416.

[104] Order 24/03/2021, BvR 2656/18, BvR 78/20, BvR 96/20, BvR 288/20, recital 183.

[105] ibid recital 183.

[106] ibid recital 192.

[107] ibid recital 193.

[108] Article 1 of the Charter for the Environment: 'Everyone has the right to live in a balanced environment which shows due respect for health'; Interpretation of this article in light of the 7th paragraph of the preamble of the Charter: 'In order to ensure sustainable development, choices designed to meet the needs of the present generation should not jeopardise the ability of future generations and other peoples to meet their own needs'.

[109] Décision 2023/1066 QPC.

[110] M Moliner-Dubost, 'Droit des générations futures à un environnement équilibré et respectueux de la santé et stockage des déchets radioactifs: La prudente audace du Conseil constitutionnel (observations sur deux oxymores)' (janvier 2024) 1 *Actualité juridique collectivités territoriales* 35.

capture solutions or geoengineering technologies,[111] even if these are intended to be temporary or transitional. As stressed by the ECHR in the case of *Verein Klimaseniorinnen*, 'in the specific context of climate change, intergenerational burden-sharing assumes particular importance both in regard to the different generations of those currently living and in regard to future generations'.[112]

While the consideration of the spatiotemporal dimensions offers promising legal advances, several potential challenges persist. In light of these considerations, the EESC emphasised that the 'principle of intergenerational justice should be central to policy-making'[113] and to the implementation of the EGD, while ensuring better representation and inclusion of all individuals within our democracies. Ensuring an ecosystemic approach to the Nexus within a reinforced democratic framework is, therefore, indispensable.

IV. THE NEED FOR A STRATEGIC LEGAL FRAMEWORK FOR A JUST ECOLOGICAL TRANSITION

The EGD advocates for a systemic approach to achieving its objectives. While this imperative is not new, it assumes greater significance considering the ambitions of the EGD. The Commission acknowledges that the success of the EGD depends significantly on the implementation of such an approach and the socio-environmental coherence of its actions. However, despite the adoption of financial mechanisms aimed at mitigating some of the social impacts of the ecological and energy transition, the EESC has highlighted that 'the EU lacks a dedicated and comprehensive strategy for integrating the social dimension into the green and just transition'.[114] As such, designing an integrated strategy for a just transition, grounded in a genuine model of socio-environmental justice, appears imperative. Such a systemic and ambitious strategic framework would therefore require a new design for the balance of interests and rights to ensure a just and inclusive ecological transition. Paradoxically, although the EGD emphasises that the involvement and commitment of the public and all stakeholders is crucial, it does not make any explicit reference to democracy. While the Commission's proposal to diversify forms of dialogue and consultation may contribute to fostering engagement with the EGD's objectives, one must question: to what extent is the voice of vulnerable groups truly incorporated, and how are their rights defended? These points are further discussed next.

[111] A Langlais and M Lemoine-Schonne, *Construire le droit des ingénieries climatiques au croisement des enjeux climatiques et écosystémiques* (UGA Ed, 2024).

[112] Application n°53600/20, recital 420.

[113] A Blueprint for a European Green and Social Deal: Based on well-being economy, Own-initiative opinion, [2024] OJ C/6879.

[114] Exploratory opinion, 'What EU policies are needed for enterprises/business to become competitive in a fair, sustainable, stronger and more resilient way to realise the European Green Deal' [2024] OJ C/6873.

A. The Ecological Transition Anchored in a Model of Social and Environmental Justice

Notwithstanding the imperative to leave no one behind, the implementation of the EGD does not necessarily guarantee a genuine transformation of the European economic model. The current prioritisation of the industrial dimension of the EGD warrants caution, given the risks of perverse effects arising from a 2.0 instrumentalisation of demands for flexibility and social resilience under the guise of a liberal ecological transition. Likewise, the coordination of economic and employment policies within the framework of the European Semester and the Stability and Growth Pact rigorously shapes the fiscal trajectory of Member States. Indeed, this economic governance of the EU seeks to achieve the objective of sound and sustainable public finances, fostering robust, sustainable, and inclusive growth aligned with the EU's priorities, such as the ecological transition, social and economic resilience, and the EPSR. According to Regulation (EU) 2024/1263 on the effective coordination of economic policies and multilateral budgetary surveillance, each Member State must submit to the Commission its medium-term fiscal structural plans addressing common EU priorities, including a 'fair green and digital transition, including climate objectives […] social and economic resilience, including the European Pillar of Social Rights; energy security […]'.[115] Nevertheless, the obligation for Member States to maintain public debt at a maximum of 60 per cent of GDP and the public deficit at 3 per cent, while simultaneously increasing investments in ecological, energy, and digital transitions, ensuring social equity, combating poverty, and promoting social inclusion, seems to represent a demand to square the circle.

The EESC has, on several occasions, advocated for reforming the Stability and Growth Pact and introducing a 'golden rule' for social and environmental public investments. Both the EESC and the European Committee of the Regions argue that excluding 'high-quality and well-targeted net public investment'[116] from the calculation of Member States' net public deficits under the EU's budgetary rules, along with spreading their costs over the entire duration of their life cycle, would help preserve the social and ecological foundations essential for the well-being of future generations. Such measures would also contribute to the implementation of the EGD and the SDGs while ensuring budgetary sustainability. The EESC further suggests attaching social and environmental conditionalities to other investments to support a just ecological transition, focusing on those most in need.[117] Although the 2024 economic governance framework reflects a degree

[115] [2024] OJ L 1263.

[116] Opinion of the European Committee of the Regions, 'Economic governance review' [2021] OJ C 37/28.

[117] Exploratory opinion at the request of the Belgium Presidency, Advancing the EU's just transition policy framework: what measures are necessary? (14 December 2023).

of flexibility, the inclusion of such a golden rule has sparked resistance, particularly among EU institutions and Member States, due to concerns over potential fiscal slippage and the short-term exacerbation of public deficits.

These debates highlight the pressing need for a stronger and systematic integration of social and environmental requirements into the framework of EU economic governance. Ensuring the socio-environmental coherence of EU policies must be a priority, particularly given the risks of orchestrated conflicts, as evidenced by recent demonstrations against the EGD, which have set the social pillar against the environmental pillar of the ecological transition. This tension is further illustrated by two actions for annulment brought by Poland in Case C-445/23: here, Poland sought the annulment of Decision (EU) 2023/852 regarding the number of allowances to be placed in the market stability reserve for the EU GHG emission allowance trading system until 2030.[118] In parallel, Poland sought interim relief, requesting that the Court stay the execution of the decision – a request that was ultimately rejected.[119] The Polish government argued that the decision 'may lead to a decrease in mining employment and a rise in unemployment and, as a result, to greater social inequalities between Member States and increased social exclusion'.[120] Furthermore, in its application for interim measures, Poland emphasised the risk of a worsening social situation, which could potentially trigger social unrest and undermine public order. Similarly, in case C-444/23, Poland challenges Regulation (EU) 2023/851, which strengthens CO_2 emission performance standards for new passenger cars and mandates the phase-out of combustion engine car sales by 2035.[121] More specifically, it contended that the EU legislator failed to uphold several constitutional obligations, including the duty to promote the well-being of EU peoples, ensure social justice, combat social exclusion, and comply with the prohibition of discrimination based on property. Moreover, it argued that this regulation risks exacerbating disparities in living standards and creating 'transport exclusion for poorer people'.[122] Pending the Court's interpretation, these two cases underscore the critical need to support a just ecological transition process underpinned by substantial financing, with an urgent priority on reducing inequalities and addressing vulnerabilities.[123] In this context, the EP explicitly stressed the necessity for all EU funding to integrate social justice 'as a guiding principle to make the Union more resilient in the face of growing threats to health and well-being', as well as environmental justice 'to ensure a fair redistribution of projects to disadvantaged communities disproportionately affected by underinvestment

[118] Action brought on 17/7/2023, Case C-445/23 *Republic of Poland v EP and Council of the EU.*
[119] Order of the Vice-President of the Court, 18 September 2023, Case C-445/23 R *Poland v Parliament.*
[120] Action brought on 17/7/2023, Case C-445/23, *Republic of Poland v EP and Council of the EU.*
[121] ibid.
[122] ibid.
[123] SWD (2024) 621 final.

in essential infrastructure and the fight against pollution and climate change'.[124] Nevertheless, it would be inaccurate to suggest that the EGD's recognition of socio-economic and territorial vulnerabilities has not led to measures aimed at mitigating and compensating for the adverse effects of the climate and energy transition. Indeed, instruments such as the Just Transition Fund,[125] the InvestEU 'Just transition' programme[126] and the Social Climate Fund[127] exemplify this approach, providing essential social safety nets for individuals, groups, and economic or regional entities particularly vulnerable to the transition toward a low-carbon economy.

Similarly, the regulations on carbon neutrality and renewable energy require Member States to pay particular attention to vulnerable and marginalised individuals and groups, specifically within the scope of their obligation to plan and implement relevant actions.[128] This approach further strengthens the application of Principle 20 of the European Pillar of Social Rights, which guarantees access to essential services, based on the constitutional principles of equality and non-discrimination. The introduction of definitions of 'energy poverty'[129] and 'transport poverty',[130] alongside emerging concepts such as 'water poverty',[131] underscores the increasing imperative to consider social vulnerability arising from the impacts of climate change and the energy transition. While these developments represent significant progress, they remain, nevertheless, limited in scope. Moreover, the effective protection of ecosystems that are currently vulnerable or at risk of becoming so, including those under strict protection, continues to be overshadowed and remains at risk of being instrumentalised for conflicting purposes, including climate-related objectives. With respect to the projections of the EGD investment plan,[132] the allocation of funds, including those deployed by Member States, remains insufficient to meet the scale of investments required, particularly in critical areas such as housing renovation and sustainable mobility.[133] Consequently, improving the coordination of

[124] Resolution of 15 March 2023 on the European semester for economic policy coordination: employment and social priorities for 2023, OJEU V/2023/402.

[125] Regulation (EU) 2021/1056 establishing the Just Transition Fund [2021] OJ L 231.

[126] Regulation (EU) 2021/523 [2021] OJ L 107/30. See also the third pillar of this Just transition Mechanism: Regulation (EU) 2021/1229 [2021] OJ L 274/1.

[127] Regulation (EU) 2023/955 establishing a Social Climate Fund [2023] OJ L 130.

[128] See Articles 3; Article 24 in Regulation (EU) 2018/1999 on the Governance of the Energy Union and Climate Action [2018] OJ L 328/1. See also Article 11 in Regulation (EU) 2021/1056 establishing the Just Transition Fund [2021] OJ L 231; and Article 3 in Directive (EU) 2024/1275 on the energy performance of buildings [2024] OJ L1275.

[129] See Article 2 in Regulation (EU) 2023/955 establishing a Social Climate Fund [2023] OJ L 130; Article 2 of Directive (EU) 2023/1791 on energy efficiency [2023] OJL 231/1.

[130] See Article 2 in Regulation (EU) 2023/955 establishing a Social Climate Fund [2023] OJ L 130.

[131] Opinion of the EESC on Access to Water: tackling water poverty and its implications for social policy [2023] OJ C-349/60.

[132] COM (2020) 21 final.

[133] The ETS-funded Social Climate Fund, which includes contributions from Member States, will mobilise €87 billion from 2026 to 2032.

these various funding mechanisms, alongside conducting comprehensive impact assessments, will enhance both their socio-ecological efficiency and overall effectiveness.[134]

Formulated a few months before the adoption of the EGD, the EESC's observation regarding the injunction 'Leave no one behind' in the implementation of the SDGs remains highly relevant. It entails re-powering as many people as possible to play a positive role as active citizens, maximising the accessibility of 'investments, new lifestyles, consumption patterns and sustainable technology to all people, groups and regions in the transition process'.[135] At the intersection of 'Leave no one behind' and 'Do no harm', the EU must firmly anchor its ecological transition process in a multidimensional spatiotemporal conception of socio-environmental justice. It is essential to move beyond a narrow conception of social and environmental justice and address the root causes of vulnerabilities, rather than focusing solely on the necessary financial compensation and temporary support measures aimed at mitigating the disproportionate burdens on the most vulnerable in the face of urgency. An integrated strategy must prioritise risk anticipation, prevention, and the enhancement of capabilities throughout life through strong social investments, alongside the resilience of ecosystems. Such structurally transformative transition strategy must place solidarity and both environmental and social justice at the forefront, with the aim of preventing any regression in the level of protection. Accelerating the greening of the EU social model – based on systems of collective social protection, public services, and social dialogue that uphold social rights – is therefore essential in light of the stimulating actions of the International Labour Organisation for a just transition and an ecological society for all,[136] as recognised by the Commission.[137] Equally important is strengthening the social dimension of EU environmental policy and the effective implementation of environmental legislation to ensure that no one is left behind. As the Council points out, 'equity and solidarity are fundamental principles of the Union's policies for a fair and inclusive ecological transition';[138] it therefore crucial to substantially strengthen these actions. Such a holistic and ambitious strategic framework would call into

[134] Regulation (EU) 2021/1060 laying down common provisions on the European Regional Development Fund, the European Social Fund Plus, the Cohesion Fund, the Just Transition Fund and the European Maritime, Fisheries and Aquaculture Fund, and financial rules for those and for the Asylum, Migration and Integration Fund, the Internal Security Fund and the Instrument for Financial Support for Border Management and Visa Policy [2021] OJL 231/159.

[135] Own-Opinion of the EESC, 'Leaving no one behind when implementing the 2030 sustainable Development Agenda' (30 October 2019), available at www.eesc.europa.eu/en/our-work/opinions-information-reports/opinions/leaving-no-one-behind-when-implementing-2030-sustainable-development-agenda-own-initiative-opinion.

[136] ILO, 'Guidelines for a just transition towards environmentally sustainable economies and societies for all' (2016) available at www.ilo.org/publications/guidelines-just-transition-towards-environmentally-sustainable-economies.

[137] COM (2020) 14 final.

[138] Council Recommendation on ensuring a fair transition towards climate neutrality [2022] OJ C 243/35.

question the adequacy of the current balance of interests and rights within the EU decision-making process, ensuring an effective consideration of social and ecological vulnerabilities.

B. Towards a New Balance of Interests and Rights

In the context of the climate emergency, it is imperative to reassess the legal balances between interests and rights, designing frameworks that aim to prevent harm and ensure that no one is left behind. At the intersection of present and future challenges, a reasoned and renewed reconciliation of public interest objectives must be achieved. Moreover, it is critical to delineate the conditions under which the overarching concept of public interest can guide the reconfiguration of legal hierarchies, thereby accelerating a just and inclusive ecological transition. The effective implementation of the EGD must be integrated into the entire decision-making process, from data collection to the obligation to report to citizens on the adopted measures, with the goal of 'contributing to public awareness and support for the decision taken'.[139] Under the Green Oath 'do no harm', the Commission has committed to revising its Better Regulation guidelines to more effectively incorporate the SDGs and the objectives of the EGD. However, with respect to the imperative of leaving no one behind – although not formally designated as an oath – the Commission refers to the mechanisms to be established under the Investment Plan for a Sustainable Europe. What, then, will be the legal significance of integrating this imperative into the regulatory cycle, from the collection of evidence to its enforceability before the courts, particularly in light of the social rights guaranteed by the Charter of Fundamental Rights?

Since the launch of the EU's so-called *Better lawmaking* programme in 2002,[140] the Commission has established a series of mechanisms, including socio-economic and environmental impact assessments, evaluation procedures, and quality reviews reflecting a broader shift towards the proceduralisation of EU Law.[141] Impact assessments, for example, are designed to assist the institutional triangle in making 'well-informed decisions'[142] without replacing political choices made within the democratic decision-making process.[143] In

[139] Recital 2 of the Regulation (EC) 1367/2006 on the application of the provisions of the Aarhus Convention on Access to Information, Public participation in decision-making and Access to Justice in Environmental matters to Community institutions and bodies [2006] OJ L 264/13.

[140] COM (2002) 275 final.

[141] N Hervé-Fournereau, 'Démocratie et procéduralisation du droit de l'environnement de l'Union européenne' in S Adalid and F Michéa (eds), *Procéduralisation du droit de l'Union européenne* (Presses universitaires de Rennes, 2022) 335.

[142] Interinstitutional Agreement between the EP, the Council and the Commission [2016] OJ L 123/1.

[143] ibid.

accordance with its commitment to the EGD, the Commission revised its Better Regulation guidelines in 2021[144] to further strengthen territorial impact assessments and introduce a rural test.[145] It also specified that each impact assessment of legislative proposals will consider the necessary synergies and trade-offs between the SDGs.[146] Similarly, it underscores the importance of grounding legislation in data and evidence, defined as 'multiple sources of data, information, and knowledge',[147] and enhancing data sharing through the new 'Fit for Future platform', established in 2020.[148] Furthermore, the Commission plans to substantially improve data collection concerning vulnerable population groups (children, people with disabilities, immigrants, Roma) at risk of poverty.[149] In its annual 2023 report on the principles of subsidiarity and proportionality, the Commission also commits to refining its analysis of the social impacts of the ecological transition, placing particular emphasis on 'greater attention to gender equality and equality in general'.[150]

What is more, while the explanatory memorandum accompanying legislative proposals outlines how each initiative complies with the principle of 'do no significant harm', it does not explicitly address the imperative to leave no one behind. However, as this injunction strongly resonates with the fundamental human rights enshrined in the EU Charter, compliance with these rights should be systematically incorporated into the impact assessments conducted by the EU institutions.[151] Furthermore, it would be appropriate to consider adopting guidelines to ensure compliance with the imperative to leave no one behind, addressed to both European and national institutions. These guidelines could draw inspiration, in particular, from the approach taken by the Commission regarding the application of the 'do no significant harm' principle under the Regulation establishing the Recovery and Resilience Facility.[152] Moreover, on several occasions, the EESC has urged the inclusion of a dedicated impact assessment for future generations and young people[153] within the Better Regulation guidelines, stressing the need to uphold the best interests of the child 'as a primary consideration'.[154] Under the current EU strategy for

[144] COM (2021) 219 final.
[145] COM (2023) 640 final.
[146] COM (2023) 700 final.
[147] COM (2021) 219 final.
[148] Commission Decision establishing the Fit for Future Platform [2020] OJ C 163/3.
[149] COM/2023/700 final.
[150] COM (2024) 493 final.
[151] COM (2020) 711 final.
[152] Commission Notice, 'Technical Guidance' [2023] OJ C/2023/111.
[153] Own-initiative opinion, 'A blueprint for a European Green and Social Deal, based on well-being economy' (19 September 2024), available at www.eesc.europa.eu/en/our-work/opinions-information-reports/opinions/blueprint-european-green-and-social-deal-based-wellbeing-economy.
[154] Article 3 of the Convention on the Rights of the Child (1989, into force 1990) which all Member States have ratified. According to Article 24 of the Charter of Fundamental Rights, 'in all actions relating children, whether taken by public authorities or private institutions, the Child's best interests must be a primary consideration.'

children's rights, the Commission has pledged to integrate a children's rights perspective into all relevant policies, legislation and funding programs.[155] Despite the Commission's efforts, in 2023, the EP called for a 'more integrated approach to sustainability that would better take into account the interplay of the economic, social and environmental impacts of EU policies and legislation'.[156] Similarly, the EESC proposed developing an 'intelligent evaluation matrix' by 'modelling the impact of substantial amendments by the co-legislator by objectifying the impact of certain parameters but also qualitative data'.[157] The EESC thus draws attention to a particularly sensitive issue: the significant weakening of environmental legislative proposals by the EP and the Council, undertaken without any prior impact assessment of these substantial modifications.[158] The Interinstitutional Agreement on Better Law-Making grants each institution the authority to determine 'the definition of a substantial amendment', thereby allowing for broad discretion without genuine interinstitutional coordination. The Commission acknowledges that impact assessments 'should be applied to the legislation as it is adopted at the end of the negotiation process'.[159]

It is essential to highlight the existing tensions between the urgency to act immediately despite incomplete data and the necessity of robust factual evidence to properly inform the legislator of the benefits, costs, and the added value of the action taken. The EESC explicitly called on the Commission to set 'realistic deadlines […] to conduct fully developed Impact assessments'.[160] The Commission recognises the importance of better anticipating and coordinating the need for evidence, particularly concerning the social and ecological impacts of the transition. In this regard, it specifically advocates for 'better mobilising and engaging the research community in the regulatory process from the start'[161] of the law-making process, as well for the establishment of a common data register.[162] More recently, however, a critical EESC opinion underscored the lack of a previous impact assessment as 'one of the major pitfalls' of the EGD, arguing that several initiatives were not subject to a solid economic, environmental, and social analysis aimed at preventing or mitigating negative impacts.[163] Several disputes have been

[155] COM (2021) 142 final.

[156] EP Resolution on EU regulatory fitness and subsidiarity and proportionality – Report on Better Law-Making covering 2020, 2021, 2022 [2024] OJ C4228.

[157] Opinion EESC on Communication Better Regulation: joining forces to make better law (22 October 2021).

[158] See eg the Regulation (EU) 2024/1991 on nature restoration [2024] OJ L.

[159] COM (2021) 219 final.

[160] Opinion EESC on Communication Better Regulation: joining forces to make better law (22 September 2021).

[161] COM (2021) 219 final.

[162] ibid.

[163] Exploratory opinion of the EESC Competitiveness of EU Businesses and the EU Economy/ European Green Deal, at the request of the Hungarian Presidency of the Council, adopted in section (5 September 2024).

brought before the CJEU due to the absence[164] or incompleteness of an impact assessment, as well as challenges related to public access to such assessments.[165] While the Court has emphasised that these impact assessments are not binding on the EU institutions,[166] it has also clarified that the institutions must be able to 'produce and set out clearly and unequivocally the basic facts which had to be taken into account'[167] to justify the legislative or regulatory act, thereby enabling citizens to 'understand the choices made by the EU institutions within the framework of the legislative process'.[168]

In challenges concerning the quality of impact assessments, applicants almost systematically invoke a violation of the principle of proportionality. In Case C-128/17, for example, Poland argued that Directive (EU) 2016/2284 on the reduction of national emissions of certain atmospheric pollutants failed to balance interests in accordance with both the principle of proportionality and the principle of equality. According to this Member State, the cost of implementing this legislation would lead to a decline in the standard of living, exacerbate poverty in Poland, and be higher than in other Member States. The two actions brought before the Court in 2023 by the same Member State follow a similar line of reasoning. According to settled case law, the principle of proportionality, which is a general principle of EU law, 'requires that acts of the EU institutions be appropriate for attaining the legitimate objectives pursued by the legislation at issue and do not go beyond what is necessary in order to achieve those objectives; when there is a choice between several appropriate measures, recourse must be had to the least onerous, and disadvantages caused must not be disproportionate to the aims pursued'.[169] Furthermore, given these complex issues, which justify a broad margin of appreciation for the legislature, review by the EU courts 'has to be limited to verifying whether the exercise of such powers has been vitiated by a manifest error of appraisal or a misuse of powers, or whether the legislature has manifestly exceeded the limits of its discretion'.[170] Similarly, the CJEU has consistently held that it 'cannot substitute its assessment of scientific and technical facts for that of the EU legislature, on which the Treaty has conferred that task'.[171] Furthermore, as the Court has repeatedly affirmed, when fundamental rights are in conflict, 'the assessment of observance of the principle of proportionality must be carried out in accordance with the need to reconcile the requirements of the protection of those various rights,

[164] Case T-584/13, *BASF Agro e.a c/ Commission* ECLI:EU:T:2018:279.
[165] Case C-57/16 P *ClientEarth/Commission* ECLI:EU:C:2018:660, [2019] 1 CMLR 37.
[166] Case C-5/16 *Poland v EP and Council* ECLI:EU:C:2018:483.
[167] ibid para 153.
[168] *ClientEarth/Commission* (n 165) para 84.
[169] Case C-128/17 *Republic Poland v EP and Council* ECLI:EU:C:2019:194, para 94.
[170] Case C-5/16 *Republic of Poland v EP and Council* ECLI:EU:C:2018:483, para 150.
[171] ibid para 95.

striking a fair balance between them'.[172] However, the Court specifies that it is essential to 'take account of the importance of that fundamental right as it results from the system implemented by the Charter as a whole'.[173] In accordance with Article 52 of the Charter of Fundamental Rights, 'any limitation on the exercise of the rights and freedoms [...] must be provided for by law and respect the essence of those rights and freedoms'. In compliance with the principle of proportionality, the same Article explains that such limitations 'may be made only if they are necessary and genuinely meet objectives of general interest recognised by the Union or the need to protect the rights and freedoms of others'.

Given the complexity of balancing interests and rights to achieve a just transition, the necessity of robust impact assessments becomes even more evident, as they enable the judge to 'verify the material accuracy of the evidence relied upon, its reliability, and its consistency in assessing a complex situation'.[174] Thus, beyond the judge's review of whether the reasoning is substantiated and whether any manifest errors affect its validity, the legislator's compliance with the legal obligation to state reasons for the legal act ensures that its scope and justifications can be understood, thereby allowing the parties to effectively defend their rights.[175]

The EGD's 'Do no harm' principle reflects a certain logic of conciliation, ostensibly ensuring a high level of protection. But can such conciliation be justified when the most vulnerable not only face multiple risks but also suffer the compounded effects of climate change and an unjust transition? More critically, how can conciliation be justified when it concerns individuals and groups whose essential fundamental rights – such as the right to dignity or the right to life – are not merely threatened but substantially affected? In such cases, hierarchy cannot be optional. Determining the criteria for assessing the substantial threshold of impact is crucial, and their application must be carried out on a case-by-case basis. Moreover, a just balance of human rights, interests, and needs cannot be confined to the establishment of temporary corrective and financial compensation mechanisms or restoration schemes, particularly for the most vulnerable ecosystems. It is crucial to strengthen the anticipatory and preventive pillar of social and environmental justice as well as the empowerment pillar of this model, throughout the entire socio-ecological transition process. The voices of vulnerable must also be also heard to ensure a democratic and just ecological transition.

[172] Case C-752/18 *Deutsche Umwelthlife eV/Freistaat Bayern* ECLI:EU:C:2019:1114, para 50; Case C-13/23 *cdVet Naturprodukte/Niedersachsisches Landsamt* ECLI:EU:C:2024:175, para 40.

[173] Case C-476/23 *Star Post EOOD/Komisia za regulirane na saobshteniata* ECLI:EU:C:2024:921, para 39.

[174] Case C-405/07 P, *Netherlands v Commission of the European Communities* ECLI:EU:C:2008:613, [2008] ECR I-8301, para 55.

[175] Case T-368/11 *Polyelectrolyte Producers Group and Others v Commission* ECLI:EU:T:2013:53, para 101.

C. Strengthening EU Democratic Decision-making and Enhancing Access to Justice

An authentic model of social and environmental justice must combine a redistributive logic with elements of procedural and recognition justice. In accordance with the subsidiarity principle found in the EU Treaties, the EU must ensure that decisions are taken as openly as possible and as closely to the citizen as possible. While the EU is founded on representative democracy, citizens have 'the right to participate in the democratic life', as listed in Article 10 of the Treaty of the EU. Nevertheless, disenchantment and mistrust persist, fuelling criticism of the democratic deficit in European integration. Indifference, lack of awareness and accessibility, the technical complexity of issues, and linguistic and digital divides – these are all factors that contribute to the exclusion of the most vulnerable citizens and those who 'have the least opportunity to present their concerns to decision-makers'.[176] As a result, the voices of vulnerable entities or those in vulnerable situations too often remain unheard, diluted by those of other stakeholders, and sometimes even instrumentalised, leading to their marginalisation both in the EU decision-making process and at the Member State level. This raises significant concerns about their true participation in democratic life and their access to justice to defend their rights. However, the EGD and the 8th Environment Action Programme remain largely silent regarding the necessary transformations of the current model of democracy and multi-level governance. Under the current EU legal framework, environmental democracy follows a procedural model driven by the Aarhus Convention and is primarily decentralized at the Member State level. While the EGD mentions the revision of the 1367/2006/EC Aarhus Regulation, the Commission has chosen to prioritise consultation mechanisms, a series of dialogues on the green transition,[177] and other exchange platforms. However, questions remain as to whether vulnerable individuals and groups can effectively participate in these mechanisms and forums, except if one assumes that the organisations representing them engage with a strong activism within such informal consultative arenas.

Moreover, in a recent opinion on the role of young people in the ecological transition,[178] the EESC calls for their voices, as well as those of their organisations, to be heard so that they can contribute to decision-making process at all levels. As part of the EU Strategy on the Rights of the Child (2021),[179] will the establishment of the European Participation Platform, dedicated consultations for children, and support for the *Education for Climate* coalition – aimed at making children ambassadors of the EGD – be sufficient to ensure that their

[176] EP resolution of 30/5/2018 on the interpretation and implementation of the Interinstitutional Agreement on Better Law-Making, P8_TA(2018)0225.
[177] COM/2024/163 final.
[178] SOC/753-EESC-2023.
[179] COM (2021) 142 final.

voices are truly heard, particularly those of young people experiencing intersecting social and environmental vulnerabilities? How can we better integrate migrants, persons with disabilities, marginalised groups, ethnic minorities, indigenous populations, and those in precarious conditions into the decision-making process – groups that are not only highly exposed to climate and environmental risks but also disproportionately affected by poorly thought-out and designed transition policies? The Roma constitutes the largest minority group in the EU but the Council Recommendation on Roma inclusion[180] and the EU's Roma strategy[181] do not address the EGD or the impact of the ecological transition process on these communities. Furthermore, the EESC reiterated its call for the 'formal recognition of climate refugees'[182] and advocated for the reform of European asylum and migration policies to include specific protections.[183] However, the Migration and Asylum legislative package adopted in 2024 fails to explicitly distinguish climate refugees from others categories of refugees, either in the definition of a refugee or in the rights and reception conditions for beneficiaries of international protection.[184] Finally, several scholars[185] have critically examined the EU's compliance with the rights of indigenous peoples, particularly in terms of obtaining their 'free and informed consent prior to the approval of any project affecting their lands or territories and other resources'.[186] As part of the implementation of the EGD, a process is underway to integrate the rights of indigenous people into EU legislation. For instance, Article 10 of the Regulation (EU) 2023/1115 on deforestation includes among the criteria of the risk assessment carried out by operators, the 'consultation and cooperation in good faith with indigenous peoples in the country of production or parts thereof [as well as] the existence of duly reasoned claims by indigenous peoples […] regarding the use or ownership of the area used for the purpose of producing the relevant commodity'. Nevertheless, it remains to be seen whether these commitments, whose implementation has been postponed until December 2025, will be effectively fulfilled. Similarly, among the criteria for the Commission's recognition of strategic projects in the raw materials sector under Regulation 2024/1252 is the requirement of respect for the rights of indigenous peoples. To benefit from such recognition, in cases where a project has the potential to affect indigenous peoples, the project promoter must submit a

[180] Council Recommendation on Roma equality, inclusion and participation [2021] OJ C 93/1.
[181] COM (2020) 620 final.
[182] Resolution on jointly tackling an existential threat: social partners and civil society for implementation of ambitious climate action [2023] OJ C 75/1.
[183] C Cournil, 'Les déplacés climatiques, les oubliés de la solidarité internationale et européenne. De la gouvernance au contentieux' (2022) 22 *Revue des Droits de l'Homme*.
[184] Regulation (EU) 2024/1348 establishing a common procedure for international protection in the Union [2024] OJ L 1348; Directive (EU) 2024/1346 laying down standards for the reception of applicants for international protection (recast) [2024] OJ L /1346.
[185] I Bellier, 'Europe and the rights of indigenous people' (2020) 50 *Ethnologie Française* 513.
[186] United Nation Declaration on the Rights of Indigenous Peoples, 2007, Article 32.

plan to the Commission that includes measures for 'meaningful consultation',[187] the consultation outcomes, and 'where appropriate, fair compensation for those people'.[188] This last element raises concerns about the potential misuse of consultation processes, especially in the contentious mining sector. In light of the Arctic climate emergency, the EESC rightly stresses the need to involve indigenous representatives in EU–Arctic dialogues, given the heightened risk of rights violations from expanding resource extraction projects.[189]

The success of the EGD's transformative vision undoubtedly depends on democratic and inclusive governance capable of fostering understanding, innovation, and broad stakeholder support. Ad hoc public consultations and other platforms certainly provide a pragmatic means of facilitating discussions and the exchange of data and best practices between stakeholders and EU and national authorities. However, these mechanisms risk excluding the most vulnerable and marginalised groups. Despite efforts to promote constructive dialogue, these forums may also be used to build socio-economic and political alliances of resistance, ultimately undermining the socio-environmental transition and hindering legislative progress. It is therefore essential to strengthen existing institutional mechanisms for social and civil dialogue, ensuring the effective exercise of rights to information, participation, and access to justice in environmental matters. European institutions remain committed to strengthening social dialogue, 'a cornerstone of the European social model',[190] to actively contribute to the socio-environmental transition while making 'sure that no one is left behind'.[191] The EESC and the EP specifically highlight the key role of social partners[192] and the necessity of their mandatory consultation, thus amplifying the voices of workers undergoing occupational retraining and contributing, through collective bargaining, 'to the design of sustainable workplaces and the promotion of green, competitive, and decent jobs'.[193] As the representative body of organised civil society, the EESC also advocates for a comprehensive strategy to enhance civil dialogue and participatory democracy, particularly for vulnerable or marginalised for whom increased efforts are required to mitigate growing inequalities.[194] Among registered European Citizens' Initiatives (ECI), only a limited number

[187] Article 7 Regulation 2024/1252.

[188] ibid.

[189] Opinion EESC, 'Developing Europe's strategy for the Artic dialogue with civil society', EESC-2024-3182-AC.

[190] COM (2023) 40 final; Council Recommendation of 12/6/2023 of on strengthening social dialogue in the European Union [2023] OJ L1389.

[191] Opening speech by Van Der Leyen at the Val Duchesse Social Partners Summit (31 January 2024), available at ec.europa.eu/commission/presscorner/detail/en/speech_24_574.

[192] EP Resolution on strengthening social dialogue [2023] OJ C 1225.

[193] Exploratory Opinion, requested by the Czech Presidency, on Social dialogue within the green transition, [2022] OJ C 486/95.

[194] Exploratory Opinion, requested by the Belgian Presidency, on Strengthening civil dialogue and participatory democracy in the EU: a path forward, SOC/782-2023.

integrate both social and environmental dimensions such as the recent ECI *HouseEurope! Power to Renovation*, which supports the creation of affordable housing while adhering to the EGD's climate objectives.[195]

As outlined below, the EGD has so far been limited to referring to the revision of the Aarhus Regulation[196] and the Commission's adoption of measures aimed at improving access to justice for citizens and NGOs before national courts. The studies commissioned by the EESC and the EP on the rights of nature within the EU context or legal framework[197] have not yet led to concrete proposals. Despite criticisms of these legal constructs, the legal recognition of the personality and rights of the highly vulnerable Mar Menor lagoon in Spain[198] raises fundamental questions regarding democratic governance, the ecological incoherence of public policies, and the evident ineffectiveness of the EU's environmental legislation. It also underscores the key role of environmental NGOs and their active use of existing EU legal mechanisms, despite the challenges they face – such as the internal review procedure for EU administrative acts that may contravene environmental law. The European Ombudsman's public consultation on transparency and participation in the EU's environmental decision-making process specifically sought to assess whether citizens and their representatives could 'exercise their right to democratic scrutiny in an area of high importance and public interest'.[199]

Strengthening the role of environmental organisations in EU decision-making would likely have implications for defending their interests before the ECJ. However, it appears that the strict constitutional conditions governing public access to ECJ against EU legislative and regulatory acts, coupled with the ongoing application of the *Plaumann* jurisprudence,[200] may limit the extent to which these NGOs can participate more effectively in the EU decision-making process. What is more, in *Carvalho*, the EJC concluded that the mere fact that the applicants were affected differently by climate change was 'not in itself sufficient to establish [their] standing to bring an action for annulment of a measure of general application'[201] such as the 2018 climate and energy legislative package. The Court held that the applicants had failed to demonstrate that these contested acts 'distinguished them individually from all other natural or legal persons concerned by those provisions just as in the case of the addressee'.[202] This case law of the ECJ contrasts with the more

[195] [2025] OJL 123.

[196] Regulation (EU) 2021/1767 of the EP and the Council revised the regulation (CE) 1367/2006.

[197] M Carducci et al, 'Towards an EU Charter of the Fundamental Rights of Nature' (EESC Study 1/2020).

[198] Law 19/2022 of 30/9/2022 Boletin official del Estado, n°237, 3/10/2022, p 135131.

[199] Overview of responses to the European Ombudsman's public consultation on transparency and participation in EU decision making related to environment, see www.ombudsman.europa.eu/fr/document/en/168767.

[200] Case 25/62, *Plaumann v Commission* ECLI:EU:C:1963:17, [1964] CMLR 29.

[201] ibid para 40.

[202] ibid para 50.

progressive interpretations made by other national courts or even the ECHR.[203] In several judicial disputes, plaintiffs have invoked their vulnerability – due to factors such as age (young, elderly, etc), disabilities, or geographical location – to argue for a relaxation of the conditions for access to justice and the qualification of victim in order to seek compensation for violations of their fundamental rights caused by the adverse impacts of climate change. However, given the current sensitive political climate of European integration, it seems unlikely that the CJEU will adopt a bold stance, even though more than 23 years have passed since Advocate General Jacob called for a renewed and adapted interpretation of case law to account for the peculiarities of environmental disputes.[204]

V. FINAL NOTE

The final note will be kept short. There is much in the EGD to be applauded. Ultimately, it shows commitment to climate action by European leaders and the EU institutions. But the deal is, as discussed here, highly ambivalent, especially in how the climate emergency, vulnerable parties of society, and justice will be taken into consideration jointly. What is needed to make the EGD's ambitions real is action on three fronts: ecological transition anchored in a model of social and environmental justice; better balancing of interests and rights; and strengthening EU democratic decision-making and enhancing access to justice. The three objectives must be joined in a nexus, or we may face the tragic opposite of the EGD, namely a 'Dark Deal' aimed at regressing the EU's sustainability trajectory and rolling back environmental legislation. Under the pretext of an urgent need to simplify EU legislation – a central pillar of the Commission's 2025 work programme – the forthcoming presentation of an 'omnibus package on sustainability'[205] risks opening a dangerous Pandora's box for democracy and the rule of law, standing in stark contrast to social and environmental justice. More specifically, it risks putting aside the promises made in the EGD to achieve a fair socio-ecological transition.

[203] G Winter, 'Climate protection before the European Court of Human Rights: KlimaSeniorinnen and Duarte Agostinho Cases in Perspective' (2024) 84 *Heidelberg Journal of International Law* 457.

[204] See Case C-50/00 P *Union de Pequenos Agricultores/Conseil* ECLI:EU:C:2002:197.

[205] Commission, 'A simpler and faster Europe: Communication on implementation and simplification (2024-2029)', available at commission.europa.eu/document/download/8556fc33-48a3-4a96-94e8-8ecacef1ea18_en?filename=250201_Simplification_Communication_en.pdf&prefLang=fr.

Part V

Covid-19 Pandemic

12

Discretion in the Context of the Covid-19 Pandemic and EU/EEA Law: A Study of the Precautionary and Proportionality Principles in Emergency Situations

XAVIER GROUSSOT AND KATHARINA GIRBINGER

I. INTRODUCTION

THE OUTBREAK OF the Covid-19 pandemic posed an unparalleled challenge not only to global health but also to the European Union's structures. Its rapid transmission and severe consequences for public health systems, economies, and social frameworks worldwide brought about an unmatched crisis that necessitated immediate and comprehensive action. Unsurprisingly, the initial response to the outbreak of the Covid-19 pandemic in the EU Member States was hectic and uncoordinated.[1] The divergent responses revealed a lack of unity between the Member States and posed a significant challenge to the foundational value of European solidarity.[2] The sacrosanct principle of free movement protected by the EU/EEA Treaties and the EU Charter of Fundamental Rights (EUCFR) was also jeopardised during the pandemic. Indeed, Member States implemented national regulations and constraints affecting the EU's internal market and the Schengen area, including the reintroduction of internal border controls and travel restrictions to curb the virus's spread.[3] The national measures that were enacted, from border controls

[1] D Thym and J Bornemann, 'Schengen and Free Movement Law During the First Phase of the Covid-19 Pandemic: Of Symbolism, Law and Politics' (2021) 5 *European Papers – A Journal on Law and Integration* 1146.

[2] AM Pacces and M Weimer, 'From Diversity to Coordination: A European Approach to COVID-19' (2020) 11 *EJRR* 283.

[3] K Farrant Shaw, *The Court of Justice of the European Union: Rule of Law Guardian for the Public Health Derogation* (Brill Nijhoff, 2022) 105, 129. The EU institutions provided a practical

to lockdowns, underlined the urgent need for rapid and decisive actions to contain the pandemic.

These national responses prompted a re-evaluation in EU law of the principles of precaution and of proportionality in the face of a public health emergency, as demonstrated by the *Nordic Info* case (but also the *LDL* case in the EFTA Court),[4] wherein the Court of Justice of the European Union (CJEU or Court) sought to balance the objectives of national measures with their impact on the free movement of individuals.[5] Particularly, this case was the first occasion for the CJEU to apply the precautionary principle in relation to the free movement of persons.[6] It also offered a unique opportunity to articulate the relationship between EU fundamental principles (especially the relationship between the precautionary and proportionality principles) in times of a health emergency – here, the Covid-19 pandemic. For this chapter, the *Nordic Info* case, which is marked by a very high degree of discretion granted to the Member States, is essential for testing whether the adjudicative and constitutional practice developed by the CJEU during this health crisis can be seen as respecting the EU rule of law, and whether this practice can be transposed to other types of emergencies outside the field of public health, eg environmental or economic emergencies.

From legal and adjudicative perspectives, emergencies are generally marked by elevated deference to public/executive authorities as courts allow these authorities to adopt precautionary measures and to take abrupt and intrusive decisions that would fall outside the ambit of the rule of law if adopted during 'normal circumstances', ie non-emergency circumstances. Interestingly, in EU law and during the pandemic, the general 'state of emergency' derogation clause (Article 347 TFEU/Article 123 EEA) was not activated to justify the heavy restrictions imposed by the Member States on the application of the individual rights

path for the Member States towards progressively lifting the restrictions on the free movement of persons like the introduction of the EU Digital Covid-19 certification system. See also S Coutts, 'Citizenship, Coronavirus and Questions of Competence' (2020) 5 *European Papers – A Journal on Law and Integration* 429, 432: 'The flexibility of the European legal system giving the Member States leeway to exercise core state functions is one of the strengths of the systems and shows that EU law in effect 'facilitates and manages its own limitation in the face of imperative needs'.

[4] Case C-128/22 *Nordic Info* ECLI:EU:C:2023:951, [2024] 2 CMLR 48. See also case E-5/23 *Criminal Proceedings against LDL* (henceforth *LDL*) in the EFTA Court (21 March 2024. This chapter focuses on the *Nordic Info* case, and draws a parallel with the EFTA Court's *LDL* case which follows the principles established by *Nordic Info* when it comes to proportionality and discretion. As we shall see, the influence of EEA law on EU law should be noted especially in relation to the application of the precautionary principle through the *Kellogg's* case (see Section III).

[5] See H Van Eijken, and J piconet Rijpma, 'Stopping a Virus from Moving Freely: Border Controls and Travel Restrictions in Times of Corona' (2021) 17 *Utrecht Law Review* 34; A Iliopoulou-Penot, 'La Citoyenneté de l'Union aux temps du coronavirus' in E Dubout and F Picod (eds), *Coronavirus et droit de l'Union européenne* (Bruylant, 2021) 178–80; and S De Vries, X Groussot and GT Petursson, *Balancing Fundamental Rights with the EU Treaty Freedoms: the European Court of Justice as Tightrope Walker* (Eleven International, 2012).

[6] I Goldner Lang, 'Laws of Fear in the EU: Precautionary Principle and Public Health Restrictions to Free Movement of Persons in the Time of COVID-19' (2021) 14 *EJRR*.

as enshrined in the free movement principles/fundamental rights protected by the EU/EEA Treaties and the EU Charter of Fundamental Rights (EUCFR).[7] To put it differently, the rule of law (*l'état de droit*) was still applicable in EU law, since the 'EU state of emergency' under Article 347 TFEU was not recognised during the Covid-19 pandemic. There was thus no suspension of EU law and its network of principles (to which the principles of precaution and of proportionality pertain).

Due to the absence of a 'state of emergency' in EU law, and in facing the unique challenges brought about by the Covid-19 pandemic, the European Union and its Member States found themselves treading a delicate line between protecting public health and respecting individuals' freedoms and fundamental rights.[8] The CJEU eventually had to deal with this difficult balancing of interests at the adjudicative level, which can also be understood as walking a line between the need to respect the rule of law and the need to grant a high degree of discretion to the EU Member States in times of emergency (what we call 'emergency discretion' in this chapter). How has the Court, in its adjudicative practice, dealt with the application of the rule of law against emergency discretion? This chapter shows that the CJEU has 'scaffolded'[9] the EU rule of law with several substantive and procedural requirements that are in fact derived from the application and interpretation of the precautionary principle and the principle of proportionality in tandem. In other words, a high level of discretion is granted to the Member States in times of emergency; but it is a 'controlled level of discretion' ensured by specific substantive and procedural safeguards established by the CJEU through the application of these two entangled principles. Is this a new type of judicial review relied on by the CJEU in 'emergency situations' or can it be traced back to other judicial review practices in fields related to high levels of discretion? This chapter intends to study the two above-mentioned questions, and is divided into five further sections.

Section II discusses the issues of discretion and emergency in the specific context of the *Nordic Info* case. Section III analyses the issue of discretion by considering the precautionary principle as a general principle of EU law and as forming an integral part of the test of proportionality. Section IV focuses on the application of the EU principle of proportionality (particularly looking at its increased structuration with the CJEU's use of a 'balancing test' and a 'procedural test' within proportionality) and its relation to discretion. In Section V,

[7] Article 347 TFEU reads as follows: 'Member States shall consult each other with a view to taking together the steps needed to prevent the functioning of the internal market being affected by measures which a Member State may be called upon to take in the event of serious internal disturbances affecting the maintenance of law and order, in the event of war, serious international tension constituting a threat of war, or in order to carry out obligations it has accepted for the purpose of maintaining peace and international security'.

[8] See de Vries et al (n 5).

[9] See ch 6 by J Stacey 'Scaffolding an Era of Emergency: Lessons from Canada's Emergencies Act' in this volume.

we evaluate whether it is possible to talk about a uniform concept of emergency discretion considering the findings of the previous Section and the simultaneous application of the precautionary and proportionality principles by the CJEU. Section VI draws conclusions about emergency discretion.

II. EMERGENCY SITUATIONS AND THE ISSUE OF DISCRETION IN THE *NORDIC INFO* CASE

Nordic Info is a preliminary ruling case that concerns, in essence, the interpretation of Directive 2004/38/EC (Citizens' Rights Directive, CRD)[10] and the Schengen Border Code (SBC). The reference was made by the Brussels Court of First Instance in proceedings between Nordic Info BV – a Belgian travel agency specialised in travel to and from Scandinavia – and the Belgian State, which pertained to compensation for the damage allegedly suffered by the company because of national measures restricting the free movement of persons adopted during the Covid-19 pandemic.

In March 2020, the WHO classified the coronavirus as a pandemic.[11] In consequence, the Belgian government amended the Ministerial Decree on emergency measures to limit the spread of the Covid-19 virus by introducing travel restrictions. The adopted legislation prohibited non-essential travel to and from Belgium. Travel between Belgium and countries of the European Union (EU), the Schengen area and the United Kingdom remained authorised with the exception of territories designated as 'red zones' based on epidemiological data. Furthermore, travellers coming from a red zone had to undergo testing and were subject to quarantine. As a result, Nordic Info BV had to cancel all trips scheduled for the summer season from Belgium to Sweden, a red zone.[12] Later, the list of countries designated as red zones was updated, with Sweden no longer classified as such. Nordic Info BV brought a civil liability action against the Belgian state claiming that the latter had acted wrongly in drawing up the amended national legislation and seeking compensation for the damage which it claimed to have suffered because of the introduction and subsequent amendment of the colour codes. The national court asked the CJEU two main questions, the first pertaining to the CRD and the second to the SBC. The essence of the referring court's concern was dealt with by its first question to the CJEU which focuses on the lawfulness of the restrictions (based on Article 27(1) and 29 of the CRD) in light of the free movement of persons which is enshrined both in the TFEU and the EU Charter of Fundamental Rights.[13] This question put forward by the

[10] Directive 2004/38/EC of the European Parliament and of the Council of 29 April 2004 on the right of citizens of the Union and their families to move and reside freely within the territory of the Member States amending Regulation (EEC) No 1612/68 and repealing Directives 64/221/EEC, 68/360/EEC, 72/194/EEC, 73/148/EEC, 75/34/EEC, 75/35/EEC, 90/364/EEC, 90/365/EEC and 93/96/EEC.

[11] WHO, Director General's opening remarks at the media briefing on Covid-19, 11 March 2020.

[12] This was outlined in their own statements of *Nordic Info* (n 4).

[13] See in particular paras 50–57 of the ruling in *Nordic Info* (n 4).

national court thus concerned the extent of the discretion that can be granted to a Member State in a situation of emergency.

The CJEU considered that all measures which prohibit, impede or render less attractive the exercise of the freedom of movement must be regarded as restrictions.[14] Therefore, not only total or partial travel bans, but also the obligation to undergo screening tests and observe quarantine constitute restrictions.[15] Contrary to what Nordic Info BV submitted, restrictions based on Articles 27(1) and 29 CRD could, according to the Court, be adopted even in the form of an act of general application.[16] And the Court ruled that to comply with the principle of proportionality, measures must be appropriate for attaining the objective of general interest pursued, be limited to what is strictly necessary, and not be disproportionate.[17] However, a Member State has some discretion when it comes to the degree of protection of public health and the way the latter is to be achieved. Therefore, the CJEU concluded that the fact that other Member States impose less strict rules than the Member State in question does not mean that the latter's measures are disproportionate. Moreover, it recalled the precautionary principle, affirming that if there is uncertainty as to the existence or extent of risks to human health, a Member State must be able to take protective measures without having to wait until the reality of those risks becomes fully apparent.[18] Following those fundamental remarks, the Court, although stating that it is for the referring court to ascertain whether the requirements of proportionality are satisfied, did provide some guidance to the national court.[19]

As a second question, the Court had to assess whether the introduced control of the restrictions amounted to border checks or the reintroduction of border controls in breach of the SBC.[20] The Court pointed to the wording of Article 25 SBC which – in contrast to Article 23(a) SBC – only refers to threats to public policy or internal security as grounds for reintroducing border controls. Therefore, the Court shared the AG's view that such a measure may be taken in the case of a health threat if and only if this is grave enough to also constitute 'a serious threat to public policy and/or internal security'.[21] (The Court had held already in previous cases that a health threat may constitute a serious threat to public policy.)[22] The Court also agreed with the AG that neither the provisions

[14] ibid paras 58–59. The Court refers eg to Case C-269/09 *Commission v Spain* EU:C:2012:439, para 54 and Case C-503/14 *Commission v Portugal* EU:C:2016:979, para 40, and confirms its previous case law.

[15] ibid.

[16] ibid para 62.

[17] ibid para 77. See also *LDL* (n 4), para 82.

[18] ibid paras 78–80. See also *LDL* (n 4), paras 83–85.

[19] ibid paras 83–90. See also *LDL* (n 4), paras 87–92.

[20] ibid 104–15.

[21] See AG Emiliou in Case C-128/22 *Nordic Info* ECLI:EU:C:2023:645, para 154.

[22] See *Nordic Info* (n 4) para 126 which refers to Case C-137/09 *Josemans* EU:C:2010:774, [2011] 2 CMLR 19, para 65. In this case public health was invoked as a derogation to the freedom to provide services.

of the CRD nor those of the SBC preclude, in principle, measures like those at issue in the main proceedings. According to the AG, this does not mean that public health and public policy coincide – the wording of Article 25(1) SBC is not qualified in such a way as to cover any type of threat. Ultimately, it is for the referring national court to ascertain whether the conditions and principles (the precautionary and proportionality principles) provided for by EU law are satisfied and thus whether the national legislation is lawful.

The *Nordic Info* Case constitutes a pivotal moment for the CJEU since it marks the first occasion ever for the Court to assess the compatibility of precautionary measures with the free movement of persons under EU law. This case encapsulates a complex dilemma: how to effectively address societal and public health threats while upholding the fundamental EU rights of individuals and citizens who are affected by such measures. This is clearly a thick political question which touches upon the heart of our democratic society and the values that should prevail in it.[23] From a more judicial perspective, this political dilemma can also be formulated in terms of balancing, as did the Advocate General in his Opinion. As AG Emiliou elegantly put it:[24]

> maintaining such a balance was no easy exercise. Keeping the pandemic under control while limiting the impact of the sanitary measures on civil liberties was, undoubtedly, a complex task. Public authorities had to make many political, economic and social choices, and rather quickly, given the rapidly evolving situation they were facing. In fact, it was probably one of the greatest challenges that public authorities have had to face in recent history.

As we shall see in greater detail in the next sections, the *Nordic Info* case provides a striking illustration of the CJEU's tendency to allow national authorities a certain degree of discretion in implementing public health measures, especially during emergency crises like the Covid-19 pandemic. By approving Belgium's travel restrictions, albeit with certain caveats and procedural safeguards, the Court implicitly acknowledges Member States' prerogative to adopt necessary measures to safeguard public health within their jurisdictions. This ruling aligns with a trend observed in recent years, where the CJEU has gradually taken a more lenient approach in reviewing Member States' measures concerning public health, public policy, public order and public security.[25] In doing so, the Court attempts to balance the imperative of protecting the principles of free movement and non-discrimination

[23] See AG Emiliou (n 21) paras 123 and 124, referring to AG Saugmandsgaard Øe who wrote in his Opinion in *Tele 2 Sverige* (Joined Cases C-203/15 and C-698/15, para 248) that this balancing exercise 'opens a debate about the values that must prevail in a democratic society and, ultimately, about what kind of society we wish to live in'.

[24] ibid AG Emiliou, para 125.

[25] See X Groussot and GT Petursson, 'Balancing as a Methodology of Constitutional Adjudication' in De Vries et al (n 5). See also S Heinikoski and T Hyttinen, 'The Impact of Covid-19 on the Free Movement Regime in the North' (2022) 91 *Nordic Journal of International Law* 84.

with the recognition of Member States' autonomy in responding to such urgent public health challenges. *Nordic Info* should be also analysed through a procedural lens and bearing in mind the overall rule of law rhetoric which has prevailed in the case law of the CJEU during the last few years. The importance of *Nordic Info*, in our view, lies particularly in the way it articulates strong safeguards (substantive and procedural) to protect the rule of law. This point is exemplified and developed in the next two Sections which concern the precautionary principle and the principle of proportionality.

III. THE PRECAUTIONARY PRINCIPLE AND 'EMERGENCY DISCRETION'

What is the role of the precautionary principle in the context of emergency action? This question was discussed by AG Emiliou in *Nordic Info* – a case concerning the lawfulness of national legislation that restricts the free movement of persons adopted in the context of the Covid-19 pandemic. It was the first time in which the dilemma – health protection in times of a pandemic versus free movement of persons – was deliberated:[26]

> The Court has never been called upon to rule on the compatibility with EU law of precautionary measures which shook, by their very nature and severity, one of the main foundations and [...] achievements, of the European Union [...] an area without internal frontiers, in which the free movement of persons is ensured.

The judgment in *Nordic Info* was delivered more than three and a half years after the WHO classified the Covid-19 outbreak as a pandemic and six months after it declared the pandemic had ended.[27] As a result of differing scientific evidence and no case law on the public health derogation to free movement of persons in a pandemic, public authorities were faced with one of the greatest challenges in recent history,[28] resulting in a variety of measures and controversies as regards the question on how to face Covid-19 and to what extent the public health derogation can be relied upon. Against this background the judgment has been long anticipated.

The logic followed in the judgment is largely based on the precautionary principle. This principle is enshrined in Article 191 TFEU with regards to Union policy on the environment. The CJEU has been employing this concept since the 1980s,[29] defining it as a 'general principle of Community law requiring the competent authorities to take appropriate measures to prevent specific potential risks to public health, safety and the environment, by giving precedence

[26] AG Emiliou in *Nordic Info* (n 21), para 4.

[27] See the WHO media briefings at www.who.int/news-room/speeches/item/who-director-general-s-opening-remarks-at-the-media-briefing---5-may-2023.

[28] AG Emiliou in *Nordic Info* (n 21), para 125.

[29] A seminal case in this regard is C-174/82 *Sandoz* ECLI:EU:C:1983:213, [1983] ECR 2445.

to the requirements related to the protection of those interests over economic interests'.[30] The principle was set out and thoroughly explained in a European Commission Communication from February 2000,[31] which has now become a milestone for the understanding of the precautionary principle – a principle often categorise as an autonomous principle of EU law stemming from Article 191 TFEU.[32]

In *Nordic Info*, the precautionary principle is featured in the context of the Covid-19 pandemic. However, the precautionary principle does not specifically (and only) apply to emergency health situations; it is constantly being related to 'scientific risk assessment' situations in the fields of public health and environmental laws. The CJEU stated in *Solvay* and *Pfizer Animal Health* that the application of the principle implies the existence of an unacceptable level of risk to human health.[33] Where there is uncertainty as to the existence or extent of such risks, it is settled CJEU case law that public institutions may take precautionary measures without having to wait until the reality and seriousness of those risks materialise.[34] In order to do so, a margin of discretion has to be granted to the Member States or the EU institutions in order to decide what, if any, type of precautionary measures to implement, and these are supposed to be evaluated on the basis of whether there was a clear misuse of power or a manifest error in the use of power.[35]

The precautionary principle, in contrast to that of proportionality,[36] is not explicitly mentioned in the EUCFR; but it is referred to in its legal explanations to clarify the concept of 'principles'[37] – specifically, that these do not give rise to 'direct claims for positive action by the Union's institutions or Member States' authorities'. This principle is thus qualified here as an interpretative tool and not a per se adjudicative principle. Yet it clearly derives from the CJEU case law on the bovine spongiform encephalopathy (BSE) during the 'mad cow disease' crisis in Europe (in the context of emergencies) and the free movement of goods case law regarding foodstuffs (outside the context of emergencies), and is often relied on by the EU institutions and Member States' authorities in health situations

[30] See Case T-74/00 *Artegodan v Commission* ECLI:EU:T:2002:283, [2002] ECR II-4945, para 184. See also Goldner Lang (n 6) 150.

[31] Communication of the Commission in 2000.

[32] WT Douma, 'The Precautionary Principle in the European Union' (2000) 9 *RECIEL* 141. See also A Donati, 'The Precautionary Principle under European Union Law' (2021) 49 *Hitosubashi Journal of Law and Politics* 43; and M Gignon et al, 'The Precautionary Principle: Is It Safe?' (2013) 20 *European Journal of Health Law* 261.

[33] See Case T-392/02 *Solvay Pharmaceuticals BV* ECLI:EU:T:2003:277, para 121; and Case T-13/99 *Pfizer Animal Health SA* ECLI:EU:T:2002:209, para 86.

[34] ibid, *Solvay*, paras 126 and 161; and *Pfizer*, para 387.

[35] The principle first emerged in the case law of the ECJ in *Sandoz* (n 29), para 16. See also, eg, Case C-192/01 *Commission v Denmark* ECLI:EU:C:2003:492, [2003] ECR I-9693 and Case C-24/00 *Commission v France* ECLI:EU:C:2004:70, [2004] ECR I-1277.

[36] See Article 52(2) EUCFR.

[37] See Article 52(5) EUCFR.

where a risk assessment reveals a certain degree of scientific uncertainty.[38] This is often done in order to justify the adoption of legislation or decisions that may infringe on the free movement rules of the TFEU.[39] As the CJEU put it (in regard to Member States' measures impairing free movement): 'in such circumstances, it must be accepted that a Member State may, in accordance with the precautionary principle, take protective measures without having to wait until the existence and gravity of those risks are fully demonstrated'.[40] In *Toolex*, the CJEU clarified that scientific uncertainty, which underlies the precautionary principle, can justify a prudent approach by Member States with regard to potential dangers.[41] Nevertheless, and importantly, the risk assessment cannot be based on purely hypothetical considerations.[42] Here it is striking that the EEA and CJEU case law in the early years of the third millennium made extensive use of the Commission guidelines from 2000 (a soft law instrument codifying and developing judicial practice on the precautionary principle). This instrument helped the CJEU and EFTA Courts clarify and structure the application of this principle of EU law.[43]

It appears clear from the Commission guidelines and the CJEU and EFTA's subsequent case law that the precautionary and proportionality principles influence each other. While the CJEU emphasised in judgments prior to *Nordic Info* that 'in exercising their discretion relating to the protection of public health, the Member States must comply with the principle of proportionality',[44] the proportionality test was affected by the precautionary nature of the mobility restrictions.[45] As the Advocate General pointed out in *Nordic Info*, both the scientific uncertainty of the situation and the discretion afforded to the

[38] See Case C-180/96 *United Kingdom v Commission* ECLI:EU:C:1998:92, [1998] ECR I-2265, Case C-157/96 *National Farmers' Union* ECLI:EU:C:1998:191, para 63 (though it does not explicitly mention the principle of precaution) and Case C-393/01 *France v Commission* ECLI:EU:C:2003:307.

[39] ibid, *United Kingdom v Commission* and *National Farmers' Union*, and Case C-236/01 *Monsanto Agricoltura Italia* ECLI:EU:C:2003:431. See also *Commission v Denmark* (n 35), para 39 on genetically modified food plants for use in agriculture. Reliance on Guidelines.

[40] ibid *United Kingdom v Commission*, para 99; *National Farmers' Union*, para 63, and *Commission v Denmark* (n 35), para 39.

[41] See Case C-473/98 *Toolex* ECLI:EU:C:2000:379 and Case E-3/00 *EFTASurveillance Authority v Norway*, '*Kellogg's*' (EFTA Court Report 2000/01, 73) [2001] 2 CMLR 47, paras 29–31. See also *LDL* (n 4) paras 84–86, where the EFTA Court elaborates on the precautionary principle.

[42] See eg ibid, '*Kellogg's*' para 29, and *Monsanto Agricoltura Italia* (n 39), para 106.

[43] See ibid *Kellogg's*, paras 25–30. See GT Petursson, 'Commentary on Articles 8-13 EEA' in F Arnesen et al (eds), *Agreement on the European Economic Area – A Commentary* (Nomos, 2018) 308. In *Kellogg's* the EFTA Court considered that States must run 'a comprehensive evaluation of the risk to health based on the most recent scientific information' (this logic was also used recently by CJEU in Case C-333/14 *Scotch Whiskey Association* ECLI:EU:C:2015:845, [2016] 1 WLR 2283). See also A Alemanno, 'The Precautionary Principle' in C Baudenbacher (ed), *The Fundamental Principles of EEA Law* (Springer, 2017) 839, 848. In a more recent line of cases where there is 'scientific uncertainty' concerning the actual effects of the restrictive measures, the CJEU has emphasised the need for a detailed proportionality analysis by the national courts, see *Scotch Whisky Association* (paras 64–65). See also Case E-16/10 *Philip Morris* [2012] 1 CMLR 24, paras 83–84.

[44] Case C-88/07 *Commission v Spain* ECLI:EU:C:2009:123, [2009] ECR I-1353, para 88. See also Case T-13/99 *Pfizer Animal Health* (n 33) paras 163, 410.

[45] Goldner Lang (n 6) 159.

Member States in public health issues affect the Court's standard of review.[46] Scientific uncertainty lowers the standard applied in assessing the legality of the legislature's choice of restrictive measures.[47] The legislator is expected to base his decision on the limited and unclear data available at the time and will be given a greater degree of discretion, provided that the choice of measure was reasonable, especially considering the question of necessity.[48]

However, the principle has never been applied to same extent and with the same severity as in the context of Covid-19.[49] Moreover, and in contrast to previous applications of the precautionary principle, the risks that had to be considered did not arise from actions, but rather from inaction.[50] The application of the precautionary principle presupposes that it is 'impossible to determine with certainty the existence or extent of the alleged risk because of the insufficiency, inconclusiveness or imprecision of the results of studies conducted, but the likelihood of real harm to public health persists should the risk materialize'.[51] Accordingly, despite the lack of any provision for the level of discretion enjoyed by decision-makers with regards to the public health derogation,[52] precautionary measures must be underpinned by scientific risk assessment – as a first limit. However, there remains a margin of appreciation for the final risk management.[53]

In *Nordic Info*, the Court refers to the precautionary principle to justify the discretion enjoyed by the Member States, acknowledging that it is for the latter to 'determine the degree of protection which they wish to afford […] and the way in which that degree of protection is to be achieved',[54] and that they can 'take protective measures without having to wait until the reality of those risks becomes fully apparent'.[55] In the context of Covid-19, there was not only scientific uncertainty as to the risks of the virus, there were also diverging views on the question what measures should be imposed to tackle the pandemic. At this point, proportionality comes into play, because where several measures are appropriate, only the least onerous one must be considered necessary. However, the precautionary principle lowers the threshold for the necessity test: Where there is uncertainty whether a less restrictive but equally effective measure exists, decision-makers enjoy discretion. This makes the assessment of proportionality more difficult and less intrusive. The Court

[46] AG Emiliou in *Nordic Info* (n 21), para 92. See also Donati (n 32) 57; and K de Smedt and E Vos, 'The Application of the Precautionary Principle in the EU' in HA Mieg (ed), *The Responsibility of Science* (Springer, 2022) 163, 177.

[47] Goldner Lang (n 6) 159.

[48] ibid.

[49] ibid.

[50] Case C-663/18 *BS v Ministère public* ECLI:EU:C:2020:938, [2021] 2 CMLR 5, para 92.

[51] Farrant Shaw (n 3) 109.

[52] Goldner Lang (n 6) 156.

[53] *Nordic Info* (n 4) para 78.

[54] ibid para 79.

[55] Case C-165/8 *Schräder* ECLI:EU:C:1989:303, para 21 regarding public health.

thus gave deference to the Member State in the decision to impinge on the right to free movement.

Two additional questions remain to be answered: What are the criteria for the risk assessment which must precede the application of precautionary measures, and how broad is the margin of discretion for managing this risk?

The first question was answered by the Court insofar as it found that commonly accepted scientific data, the trend in cases of infection and mortality, the fact of a national healthcare system being overwhelmed as well as the time of year had to be taken into consideration.[56] As for the margin of discretion, the CJEU held with regard to necessity that it must not be evident that a different measure would have sufficed.[57] Moreover, by stating that the referring court will have to take into account that similar measures were adopted by other Member States,[58] the Court seems to impose more limits: the measure must be reasonable, considering other legislative options.[59] This, however, leads to the question as to what is reasonable, the answer to which might differ among different social groups. Regarding border checks, the Court gives discretion regarding the intensity and frequency of controls, while holding that it may not extend to the point where the exercise of police powers are systematic; that is, it must be possible to clearly distinguish the controls from systematic checks on persons at the external borders.[60] The limit here derives from the law itself.[61] On the other hand, by ascertaining that a health threat can constitute a threat to public policy, the Court lowers the requirements objectively deriving from the law and broadens the decision-maker's range of possibilities for justifying measures on public health grounds.

This is a good example of the CJEU's reasoning throughout the judgment, which seems to be tolerant as to the restrictive measures that were taken. It is nevertheless surprising that the justification for this extensive interpretation is limited to the consideration that a threat to public policy 'entails the existence [...] of a genuine, present and sufficiently serious threat affecting one of the fundamental interests of society'[62] and that 'a pandemic of such a scale as that of COVID19' is liable to affect one of those interests, 'namely that of ensuring the lives of citizens'.[63] If we take a more methodical approach, a first observation is that the SBC does not expressly mention public health as a possible justification for the temporary reintroduction of border controls. In light of the rationale of Article 25 SBC which establishes an exception to the principle of movement across internal borders without border controls, this provision

[56] *Nordic Info* (n 4) para 82.
[57] ibid para 90.
[58] ibid para 83.
[59] Goldner Lang (n 6) 159.
[60] *Nordic Info* (n 4), para 122.
[61] Article 23(a)(iii) SBC.
[62] *Nordic Info* (n 4), para 126.
[63] ibid para 127.

must be interpreted strictly – as is also stated in recital 27 SBC – and not go beyond what the wording provides for. The AG, however, seems to deduce from recital 27 SBC that it is for the Court to define the concept of public policy[64] – which it did, subsuming public health under it. The Court's approach seems to find favour with the European Commission which envisages the possibility of equating public policy and public health in case of an extremely critical situation.[65] Even so, and with regards to other EU provisions like Article 27(1) CRD which explicitly allows for the justification of national restrictions on public health grounds, the Court's reasoning is little convincing.

Against this background, it is satisfying that the Commission in December 2021 made a proposal to amend the SBC[66] which was agreed upon by the European Parliament and the Council in February 2024.[67] The amended Article 25(1)(b) SBC provides that a serious threat to public policy or internal security may be considered to arise from large-scale public health emergencies.[68] This is a step towards more legal certainty. Returning to the restrictive measures adopted in the context of Covid-19, *Nordic Info* affirms that they can be considered a 'triumph of the much-disputed precautionary principle'.[69] Let's now have a look at the principle of proportionality in a more detailed manner and particularly at the use of procedural and substantive safeguards by the CJEU in its applications.

IV. THE STRUCTURATION OF PROPORTIONALITY IN 'EMERGENCY DISCRETION'

As seen in the previous Section, the precautionary principle has been integrated within the test of proportionality and particularly within the second limb of the test: the so-called necessity test or test of less restrictive means. This evolution is in fact part of a broader shift in the application of proportionality towards a more structured approach of this principle by substantive (the 'balancing test') and procedural (the 'procedural test') safeguards.[70] We will now focus this analysis by looking, first, at the structuration by substantive safeguards and, second, to structuration by procedural safeguards.

[64] AG Emiliou in *Nordic Info* (n 21), para 152.

[65] See European Commission, 'Covid-19 Guidelines for border management measures to protect health and ensure the availability of goods and essential services', C(2020) 1753 final, 16 march 2020, point V18.

[66] COM (2021) 891 final.

[67] Press release issued by the Commission on 6 February 2024, www.consilium.europa.eu/en/press/press-releases/2024/02/06/schengen-council-and-european-parliament-agree-to-update-eu-s-borders-code.

[68] L Schumacker, 'Proportionality of Internal Border Controls: From the Covid-19 Pandemic to the 2021 Proposal' (2022) 18 *CYELP* 151.

[69] Goldner Lang (n 6) 158.

[70] X Groussot, *General Principles of Community Law* (Europa Law Publishing, 2006).

Concerning substantive safeguards, the Court in *Nordic Info* provides a three-step proportionality test with the suitability of a legitimate objective as a first step, necessity as a second, and proportionality *stricto sensu* (balancing) as a last step.[71] This is noteworthy insofar as the Court usually assesses necessity and proportionality in the strict sense as alternatives rather than complements,[72] yet often leaves out proportionality *stricto sensu*. The seemingly more in-depth assessment of proportionality in *Nordic Info* can be linked to the function of the multiple steps of the principle.[73] While suitability and necessity guarantee the effectiveness of a measure, proportionality *stricto sensu* aims at weighing (balancing) the advantages against the disadvantages resulting from the contested measures.[74] It is only the balancing test that allows the Courts to consider the negative consequences of a measure for the interests of individuals and fundamental rights.[75] This attempt to reconcile the protection of human health with free movement within this last step 'opens a debate about the values that must prevail in a democratic society'[76] – a debate particularly lively when it comes to Covid-19 and the unprecedented impact of the measures that were taken in its context.

In fact, this was the first time the CJEU had to address the issue of balancing fundamental rights and the objective of combating a threat facing society in relation to a pandemic.[77] When fundamental freedoms are at stake, the proportionality test serves as the guardian of individual rights – in contrast to its function as an instrument for economic integration[78] – which could explain why the Court applied all of its steps in *Nordic Info*.[79] The nature of the restriction at issue thus has an impact on the intensity of the proportionality assessment.[80] Following *Schmidberger*, in case of a clash between free movement and EU fundamental rights, 'the interests involved must be weighed having regard to all the circumstances of the case in order to determine whether a fair balance was struck between those interests'.[81] Moreover, it is worth noting that the balancing test is constantly used by the CJEU when assessing restrictions on the EUCFR

[71] Goldner Lang (n 6) 152.

[72] W Sauter, 'Proportionality in EU law: A Balancing Act?' (2013) 15 *CYELS* 439, 448.

[73] See also *LDL* (n 4) paras 81–97, where the EFTA Court also uses a very structured proportionality test.

[74] AG Emiliou in *Nordic Info* (n 21) para 123. See also J Rivers, 'Proportionality and Variable Intensity of Review' (2006) 65 *CLJ* 174, 200. See also C Baudenbacher and T Haas, 'Proportionality as a Fundamental Principle of EEA Law' in Baudenbacher (n 43) 204, 209.

[75] P Craig, *EU Administrative Law* (Oxford University Press, 2006) 657. See Baudenbacher (n 43). According to him, under the balancing test, the burden of proof for 'unreasonableness' lies with the individual alleging that the authority acted unreasonably, and this is difficult to prove.

[76] AG Emilou *Nordic Info* (n 21) para 123.

[77] ibid para 4.

[78] T Tridimas, *General Principles of EU Law* (Oxford University Press, 2006) 191.

[79] This is a reading which is backed up using the balancing test in human rights cases based on Article 52(1) EUCFR.

[80] Sauter (n 72) 453.

[81] Case C-112/0 *Schmidberger* ECLI:EU:C:2003:333, para 81.

based on Article 52(1) EUCFR. Therefore, *Nordic Info* and *Schmidberger* can be viewed as falling into that category. In *Nordic Info*, the free movement of persons is also recognised by Article 45 of the EUCFR. It is for this reason that the third part of the proportionality test figures consistently in decisions pertaining to the legality of national measures that limit the exercise of fundamental rights guaranteed by the Charter of Human Rights of the European Union, and plays an important role in *Nordic Info*.[82] By providing a three-step analysis, the CJEU in *Nordic Info* seems to engage in a thorough and very structured proportionality assessment. However, it remains vague within the different steps, finding that a measure 'appears […] proportionate in the light of the precautionary principle, in so far as there was a significant probability' of the threat materialising.[83] The Court hereby gives a taste of the direction it suggests for the referring court to take, yet the attempted clarifications remain ambiguous. As elaborated in the previous section, a key element of *Nordic Info* is the precautionary principle which not only modifies the principle of proportionality but also finds a limit therein. The principle of proportionality, in turn, is characterised by the margin of appreciation enjoyed by the Member States.

Similarly to *Nordic Info*, the EFTA Court in *LDL* endeavoured to weigh interests in a *Schmidberger* style.[84] It is worth noting here that EFTA in *Holship* conducted a balancing of interest test to assess the legality of the prohibition of a blockade by union dock-workers in light of the free movement of establishments (Article 31 EEA).[85] The EFTA Court found that the refusal to authorise the boycott was in line with EEA law and noted that a boycott is likely to discourage or even prevent the establishment of companies from other EEA States and thereby constitutes a restriction on the freedom of establishment under Article 31 EEA. The European Court of Human Rights (ECtHR) eventually had to gauge whether the Supreme Court of Norway's refusal to authorise the boycott had remained within its wide margin of appreciation. Importantly, the ECtHR stated that, from the standpoint of Article 11 ECHR (on freedom of association), the EEA freedom of establishment enshrined in Article 31 EEA is not a counterbalancing fundamental right to freedom of association but rather just one element, albeit a significant one, to be taken into consideration in the valuation of proportionality.[86] This logic applied by the ECtHR may be of considerable importance to balancing in the context of emergencies such as in *Nordic Info* and *LDL*, and even if it confirms the broad margin of appreciation/discretion granted to the States, it displays the problematic of the test of balancing when economic rights are involved.

[82] *Nordic Info* (n 4) para 92.
[83] ibid para 97.
[84] See *LDL* (n 4) paras 94–95.
[85] See Case E-14/15 *Holship Norge AS v Norsk Transportarbeiderforbund* [2016] 4 CMLR 29.
[86] Application no. 45487/17 *Norwegian Confederation of Trade Unions (LO) and Norwegian Transport Workers' Union (NTF) v Norway* (2021).

Lastly, a condition for the enjoyment of that discretion is compliance with the rule of law – a Union value enshrined in Article 2 TEU.[87] This is exemplified in *Nordic Info* insofar as the Court examines whether several rule of law procedural standards are satisfied,[88] which now seems to be a trend in the Court's case law.[89] Notably, the Court expressly says that measures restricting freedom of movement on grounds of public policy, public security or public health must comply, first, with the principle of legal certainty; second, with the general principle of EU law pertaining to good administration; and third, to the right to an effective judicial remedy.[90] Legal certainty requires that 'legal rules be clear and precise and that their application be foreseeable by those subject to them'.[91] In *Laval*, for instance, the Court found that a measure cannot be justified where there is 'a lack of provisions [...] which are sufficiently precise and accessible'.[92]

The principle of good administration 'lays down [...] the obligation to state reasons for acts and decisions adopted by national authorities'.[93] The right to an effective judicial remedy comprises the right of access to a court or tribunal with the power to ensure respect for the rights guaranteed by EU law. Those requirements can be referred to as the public law element of proportionality intertwining fundamental freedoms with the rule of law. What remains unclear is the question whether those procedural requirements are a precondition for applying the proportionality test or if the former are part of the latter, leading to a proceduralisation of proportionality. In contrast to other cases, the procedural safeguards assessed in *Nordic Info* can be deduced from the CRD. The directive can therefore be considered *lex specialis* to the general proportionality test.

An argument for reviewing procedural aspects before delving into the three-step analysis of proportionality could be that if a measure does not comply with the principles of legal certainty, good administration and the right to an effective judicial remedy, there is no need for the remaining proportionality test – or that, even more drastically, it is then not possible to carry out the assessment of proportionality.[94] Even though the CJEU applied a similar structure in *Greenham Abel*[95] – procedural aspects before proportionality – it remains

[87] See eg Case C-896/19 *Repubblika and Il-Pim Ministru* ECLI:EU:C:2021:311, [2021] 3 CMLR 18.

[88] *Nordic Info* (n 4) paras 68–75.

[89] See, eg, Case C-95/01 *Greenham and Abel* ECLI:EU:C:2004:71, [2004] ECR I-1333, paras 35 and 50; Case C-244/06 *Dynamic Medien* ECLI:EU:C:2008:85, [2008] ECR I-505, paras 49–50; and Case C-341/05 *Laval* ECLI:EU:C:2007:809, [2007] ECR I-11767, para 110.

[90] *Nordic Info* (n 4) para 69.

[91] ibid.

[92] *Laval* (n 89) para 110.

[93] *Nordic Info* (n 4) para 69.

[94] M Hilling, 'Justifications and Proportionality: An analysis of the ECJ's assessment of national rules for the prevention of tax avoidance' (2013) 41 *Intertax* 294, 303.

[95] *Greenham and Abel* (n 89) para 35.

unclear if the Court will continue to apply this rationale where there is no secondary law at issue.

On the one hand, procedural safeguards could be considered an additional element of the Court's review in the sense that 'the CJEU should ensure that any exercise of the public health derogation by a Member State complies as a minimum with the EU rule of law procedural standards as well as being […] proportionate'.[96] Previous case law, however, seems to link the procedural aspects more closely with the actual proportionality test, denying proportionality because of a lack of legal certainty, for instance.[97] This approach seems to find favour among scholars who refer to it as a 'proceduralization of the requirements necessary to satisfy the proportionality test',[98] or who state, for example, that 'procedural guarantees of individual rights can play a role in the proportionality assessment'.[99]

Regardless of the theoretical question of where procedural requirements can find their place within the Court's analysis, the traditional substantive approach of proportionality – a review of the restrictions with regards to free movement – has been supplemented by a more procedural standard to assess the exercise of power and the lawfulness of national measures in light of human rights, so that the Court is engaging in a 'collateral view on grounds of proportionality'.[100] With this development, the Court 'has a potential for a much more powerful role as guardian of the EU's rule of law through stricter scrutiny of the exercise of the public health derogation'.[101] Also, the European Commission provided additional guidance during the Covid-19 pandemic in May 2020, emphasising the importance of considering not only the epidemiological situation and the necessity of measures but also the principle of proportionality. This entails a requirement to balance the benefits of maintaining broad restrictions against economic and social factors, accentuating the significance of economic and social considerations in assessing the continuation of free movement constraints.

V. IS THERE A CONCEPT OF 'EMERGENCY DISCRETION'?

It is now essential to understand the scope of the discretion granted to Member States and the EU institutions and how it relates to the issue of (the rule of) law. To try to define the contours of 'emergency discretion' vis-à-vis the (rule of) law

[96] Ferrant Shaw (n 3) 134.

[97] Case C-318/10 *SIAT* ECLI:EU:C:2012:415, [2012] 3 CMLR 35, para 59. In *Laval* (n 89) para 110, the Court reviewed procedural requirements at the end (or after) proportionality.

[98] C Barnard, *The Substantive Law of the EU: The Four Freedoms* (Oxford University Press, 2022) 191. Barnard contextualises procedural requirements as conditions necessary to satisfy the proportionality test.

[99] Sauter (n 72) 451.

[100] Tridimas (n 78) 194.

[101] Ferrant Shaw (n 3) 134.

will clearly help us in this task. As articulated lucidly by Joana Mendes reflecting on EU executive discretion:[102]

> The need to investigate the role of law in relation to discretion is more present than ever at a time of emergency in which, at the state level, legal constraints are relaxed, and in which the EU executive pledges to make full use of the flexibility that EU law allows for.

To put it differently, 'emergency discretion' softened the 'stringency of the law' by permitting Member States to rely on their executive powers in a more intrusive way towards individuals' rights, thus leading to a limitation of the theory of 'limited governance/power' which lies at the core of the rule of law and, arguably, constitutes its existential function. Therefore, it may be said that emergency discretion hampers the effectiveness of the substantive rule of law as protector of individual rights.

Going further, is it possible to posit that there is in EU law a common concept of 'emergency discretion'? Or is it merely a concept that should be included within a wider (and rather well-known) category of 'high level of discretion' granted to public or executive authorities in situations which do not need to be emergencies per se?[103] To draw on Ronald Dworkin, who liked to describe 'discretion' as a hole in a doughnut: Are we in fact talking about the same doughnut?[104] In this chapter, we have shown how discretion in health emergencies is often deeply entangled with the precautionary principle – a principle which brings a high level of discretion into the application of the principle of proportionality. We have also underlined that the CJEU's application of the proportionality test uses substantive and procedural safeguards that are aimed at controlling the level of discretion. As has been made evident in the analysis of the Court's case law, these safeguards are not specific to situations of emergency. They can also be found in environmental emergencies. However, it is uncommon to have this application in tandem in other emergency fields. For instance, in the context of economic emergency there is no principle of precaution that triggers a high level of discretion granted to the public/executive authorities.[105] As a result, it is difficult to say that there is a unified concept of 'emergency discretion' that incorporates the same parameters or criteria for determining discretion. Yet we can say, as seen previously, that the application of the precautionary principle brings an

[102] J Mendes, 'EU Executive Discretion: Again, in Times of Crisis (*EU Law Live*, Weekend Edition No. 15, 2 May 2020).

[103] See X Groussot, 'Constitutional Dialogues, Pluralism and Conflicting Identities' in M Avbelj and J Komárek (eds), *Constitutional Pluralism in the European Union and Beyond* (Hart Publishing, 2012) 319.

[104] R Dworkin, *Taking Rights Seriously* (Bloomsbury, 2013) 48.

[105] See, eg, A Zemskova, *The Rule of Law in Economic Emergency in the European Union* (DPhil thesis, Lund University, 2023) as well as the forthcoming manuscript; A Zemskova, *The Rule of Law in Economic Emergency in the European Union* (Routledge, forthcoming).

additional parameter or criterion and a higher level of discretion to the test of proportionality.

Moreover, we have considered in this chapter that in the assessment of proportionality in emergency situations, the balancing test and the procedural test are used to control the level of discretion. The parallel use of these two tests shows that substantive and procedural safeguards are not opposed to one another but instead complement each other in judicial review. There is therefore a clear *continuum* between substantive and procedural review and the use of the associated safeguards.[106] This insight is important for grasping with accuracy the scope and function of judicial review in EU law. In the end, it reveals how the rule of law is understood by the CJEU and demonstrates the prominence of the EU procedural rule of law in taming emergency discretion. It thus appears clear from the analysis of 'emergency discretion' that 'procedure may also serve as a source of political power. It is used to constrain national discretion and align national policies within the framework of set parameters thus shaping *communautaire* outcomes'.[107] In a similar vein, and as rightly noted by Angelica Ericsson in an analysis of the procedural discretion on national decisions falling within the scope of EU law:[108]

> the Court can show both deference and prescriptive assertiveness at the same time […] Rather than second guessing the merits of the national discretionary policy choices regarding the substantive risk assessment, the Court can focus its normative power towards streamlining national processes and structures, ultimately fostering effective judicial oversight.

In other words, the procedural conditions attached to the respect of the EU rule of law at the national level constitute flexible, adaptive and polymorphous tools of adjudication in the hands of (national and transnational) judges interpreting EU law.

Finally, it is worth remarking that the procedural dimension of the rule of law can take various procedural forms which are not directly related to the judicial review of a specific measure per se and that are sometimes not seen as expressions of discretion. This point is illustrated by the procedural use of the burden of proof by the CJEU and the role of the national courts in a preliminary ruling procedure under Article 267 TFEU. Concerning the burden of proof, and as Patricia Popelier lucidly puts it, with 'a high evidential standard, the Court

[106] This point is made in relation to ECHR, see J Gerards, 'Procedural Review by the European Court of Human Rights – a Typology of Functions for the Court's Reasoning' in X Groussot and D Harvey (eds), *Process-Oriented Federalism in EU Law* (EU Law Live Press, 2024) 107.

[107] T Tridimas, 'Process and Substance in EU Law: Imperfect Boundaries and Common Objectives' in Groussot and Harvey (ibid) 33. See generally, on the use of procedural safeguards as political power, X Groussot and D Harvey, 'Process-oriented Federalism in the European Union' in Groussot and Harvey (ibid) 7.

[108] A Ericsson, 'National Pre-Authorisation Schemes and the EU's Demands for Objectivity Safeguards – Allowing Policy Discretion while Streamlining Administrative Process' in Groussot and Harvey (ibid) 163.

of Justice adds procedural requirements that make it harder for the Member States to derogate from EU principles and limits the referring courts margin to assess the proportionality of a measure'.[109] The high evidential standard is not present, however, when a Member State has to prove the existence of less restrictive means in light of the precautionary principle (ie, when there is in fact uncertainty as to what measures should be imposed to face (in this case) the Covid-19 pandemic) just like the CJEU did in *Nordic Info*.[110] Concerning the role of national courts in the preliminary ruling procedure, the Court is deferring to them when it chooses to delegate the application of the test of proportionality to the referring national courts, as it did in *Nordic Info*.[111] In these situations, the referring national courts obviously enjoy 'a certain margin of discretion on the final outcome of the cases pending before them'.[112] In *Nordic Info*, both the low evidential burden and the deference to the national court point towards a wide margin of discretion for the Member State. Consequently, they can also be seen as key procedural elements expressing the concept of 'emergency discretion' in a major health crisis.

VI. CONCLUSION

The *Nordic Info* and *LDL* cases provide compelling examples of the CJEU's and EFTA Court's tendency to grant a certain degree of discretion to national authorities in implementing public health measures, particularly during emergencies like the Covid-19 pandemic. By upholding Belgium's travel restrictions in *Nordic Info*, albeit with certain procedural safeguards and caveats, the CJEU implicitly recognises the Member States' authority to adopt necessary measures to protect public health within their jurisdictions. This ruling reflects a broader trend in

[109] See P Popelier, 'Process Federalism Review in the European Union: Autonomy Concerns in the Spotlight, but What About Cohesion?' in Groussot and Harvey, ibid, 8. Popelier gives the example of *Scotch Whiskey Association* (n 43, paras 34–35) as a case where the CJEU adopted a high evidentiary standard. In this case, the precautionary principle was not applied. The ECJ has underlined the necessity for a detailed proportionality analysis by the national courts. This new standard of judicial review places scientific evidence and proportionality at the forefront of its rulings when the precautionary principle does not apply. EFTA jurisprudence has significantly influenced the understanding of judicial review and discretion in health-related matters in EU law, thus helping the CJEU establish a rigorous evidential standard for the national courts when applying the test of proportionality in the internal market context. The application of the precautionary principle, by contrast, serves to decrease the evidential standard.

[110] See Section III. Though scientific uncertainty reduces the standard required for the legality of the legislature's choice of restrictive measures, the burden of proof was still placed on the Member State to show that no breach was committed in the efficiency-means part of the proportionality test. By contrast, in the balancing test of proportionality (the third part), the burden is placed on the individual (see Baudenbacher (n 43)).

[111] See Sections II and IV. For an elaboration, see GT Pétursson, *The Proportionality Principle as a Tool for Disintegration in EU law – of Balancing and Coherence in the Light of the Fundamental Freedoms* (PhD Thesis, Lund University, 2014).

[112] G Gentile, 'EU Judicial Federalism: A Conceptual Analysis' in Groussot and Harvey (n 106) 96.

recent years, where the CJEU has adopted a more flexible stance when reviewing national measures concerning public health, public policy, public order, and public security. In doing so, the Courts in *Nordic Info* and *LDL* seek to balance the protection of the principles of free movement and non-discrimination with the acknowledgment of Member States' autonomy in responding to urgent public health challenges. Moreover, the *Nordic Info* and *LDL* cases should be analysed from a procedural perspective, considering the prevailing rule of law discourse that has influenced the CJEU's recent jurisprudence. In our view, the significance of *Nordic Info* and *LDL* lies particularly in the establishment of robust and structured safeguards – both substantive and procedural – to uphold the rule of law for the CJEU, the EFTA Courts and the national courts.

This chapter demonstrates that the CJEU and EFTA Courts have effectively 'scaffolded' the EU rule of law with substantive and procedural safeguards, derived from the intertwined application and interpretation of the precautionary principle and the principle of proportionality.[113] In other words, while Member States are granted significant discretion during times of emergency, this discretion is tightly regulated by the CJEU's imposition of specific safeguards. These safeguards ensure that emergency discretion remains controlled, guided by the substantive and procedural requirements rooted in the two principles. Put simply, there is discretion, but it is 'controlled discretion'. This controlled discretion is exercised through the application in tandem of the precautionary and proportionality principles. In addition, this chapter has shown the significance of the precautionary principle in emergency discretion. Nevertheless, we have underlined that the use of the precautionary principle in adjudication is not common to all the types of emergencies facing the EU, and that therefore, there is no unified concept of 'emergency discretion' that applies transversally, eg between health emergencies or economic ones.[114]

A key aspect in the application of the precautionary principle in Europe is the profound impact of EFTA case law, particularly the landmark *Kellogg's* case, on the recent jurisprudence of the CJEU, as explored in this contribution. EFTA jurisprudence has significantly influenced the understanding of judicial review and discretion in health-related matters, also helping the CJEU establish a rigorous evidential standard for the national courts when applying the test of proportionality in the internal market context when the principle of precaution is not relevant.[115] To conclude, this Chapter has examined the 'balancing of rights' approach – the principle of proportionality – used in EFTA case law, for example in the *Holship* and *LDL* decisions. In that respect, we have emphasised that the balancing of rights has also been scrutinised by the ECtHR, where economic rights were also to be weighed against non-economic fundamental rights, but

[113] See Sections III and IV.
[114] See Section V.
[115] See Sections III and V.

where balancing was interpreted in a different way by the ECtHR, and using a different method of balancing than the EFTA court.[116] In our view, this case shows the important role the ECtHR plays when issues of emergency discretion arise, especially in situations where economic and non-economic fundamental rights conflict. This dynamic is especially relevant as the EU continues to explore its potential accession to the ECHR, a development that would further integrate the ECtHR's influence into EU legal frameworks.[117]

[116] See Section IV.
[117] See V Stoyanova's ch 14 '*Review of Covid-19 Measures by the European Court of Human Rights: How to Avoid the 'Fair', the 'Balance' and 'the Fair Balance*' in this volume which discusses in detail the ECTHR case law during the Covid-19 pandemic.

13

The Covid-19 Pandemic and Parliamentary Oversight in Finland

TUUKKA BRUNILA, JANNE SALMINEN AND MEHRNOOSH FARZAMFAR*

I. INTRODUCTION

IN MANAGING THE Covid-19 pandemic, governments around the world resorted to the most extensive use of emergency measures since World War II.[1] This was also the case in Finland. In March 2020, the Finnish government, together with the president, declared a state of emergency in line with the Finnish constitution (731/1999) and the Emergency Powers Act (1552/2011).[2] As the pandemic continued, the government triggered a state of emergency once more, in March 2021. The first state of emergency lasted for three months (16 March–16 June) and the second for two months (1 March–27 April). The pandemic put a test to the new constitution, which was amended in 2000 to change Finland's political system from a semi-presidential to a parliamentary governance structure. This change brought about, among other things, a strengthening of the role of the parliament in overseeing and checking the executive branch. Similarly to other Nordic countries, the judiciary in Finland tends to be restrained in exercising review of executive powers as compared to other European countries.[3] It is the parliament that enjoys a strong role in *ex-ante* review of the constitutionality of legislative acts. Thus the pandemic saw the

* Salminen and Farzamfar have analysed and discussed this material also in Janne Salminen and others, 'Legislative Oversight in Finland during the States of Emergencies of the COVID-19 Pandemic', *COVID-19 and the Constitution: A Special Collection of Essays in Honour of the Thirtieth Anniversary of the Constitution of the Republic of Slovenia* (University of Ljubljana 2024). Brunila's research on this chapter has been funded by the Government of Finland as a part of the The Lessons of the Pandemic Crisis -project (PAKO).

[1] Venice Commission, *Interim Report on the Measures Taken in the EU Member States as a Result of the COVID-19 Crisis and Their Impact on Democracy*, The Rule of Law and Fundamental Rights (Strasbourg, 8 October 2020) 15.

[2] Valmiuslaki 1552/2011.

[3] See J Husa, 'Nordic Constitutionalism and European Human Rights – Mixing Oil and Water?' (2011) 55 *Scandinavian Studies in Law* 101; J Lavapuro, T Ojanen and M Scheinin, 'Rights-Based Constitutionalism in Finland and the Development of Pluralist Constitutional Review' (2011) 9 *International Journal of Constitutional Law* 505.

constitutional and parliamentary control of executive action in Finland being put to a test.[4] It raised the significant question whether this governance structure is effective in overseeing and controlling the use of emergency measures.[5]

In this chapter, we analyse how the Finnish Constitution facilitates parliamentary oversight and constitutional control of executive emergency measures. We first develop a theoretical perspective on parliamentary oversight (Section II). We then analyse the constitutional basis of emergency legislation in Finland and its limits in Section 23 of the constitution (Section III).[6] Thereafter, we analyse the special emergency legislation in Finland – that is, the Emergency Powers Act – from the perspective of legislative oversight (Section IV), as well as the relevance of the constitution in this regard. The decision-making mechanisms available under section 23 of the Finnish constitution and the Emergency Powers Act mean that the Finnish parliament has a legislative oversight mandate during states of emergency.

In addition, we highlight the role of the parliament in controlling the legality of emergency measures, a role that has been noted to serve to uphold the balance of power between the legislature and the executive.[7] While some have argued that the Finnish system in this context relies on political culture,[8] we argue that the Finnish Constitution and other relevant legislation offer an important example of parliamentary control during emergencies (Section V). What it shows is that although emergency exemptions are permitted in the Finnish legal system, parliamentary overview has shown that the grounds for such exceptions and their conditions must be provided explicitly in an independent parliamentary act. The necessity of such acts originates in the rule of law and respect for the principle of legality – a principle that has deep roots in both the Finnish constitution and legal tradition.[9] This chapter thus shows the close interconnection between emergency rules and the rule of law – both of which the parliament in Finland forcefully employed in the context of the Covid-19 pandemic.

[4] T Brunila and J Salminen, '"Regular Powers Are No Longer Enough" – Checks and Balances in Declaring a State of Emergency According to the Constitution of Finland' (2024) 70 *Scandinavian Studies in Law* 215; regarding the peculiarity of the Finnish system, see J Husa, 'Locking in Constitutionality Control in Finland' (2020) 16 *European Constitutional Law Review* 249.

[5] D Beetham, *Parliament and Democracy in the Twenty-First Century: A Guide to Good Practice* (Geneva, Inter-Parliamentary Union, 2007) 115; H Yamamoto, *Tools for Parliamentary Oversight: A Comparative Study of 88 National Parliaments* (Geneva, Inter-Parliamentary Union, 2007) 15.

[6] Suomen perustuslaki 731/1999.

[7] J Grogan and J Beqiraj, 'The Rule of Law as the Perimeter of Legitimacy for COVID-19 Responses' in J Grogan and A Donald (eds), *Routledge Handbook of Law and the COVID-19 Pandemic* (Routledge, 2022) 209; see also C Poyet, R Niemikari and T Raunio, 'What Makes Democratic Institutions Resilient to Crises? Applying a Novel Analytical Framework to the Case of Finland' (2024) 32 *Journal of Contemporary European Studies* 246.

[8] A Vedaschi and C Graziani, 'New Dynamics of the "Post-COVID-19 Era": A Legal Conundrum' (2023) 24 *German Law Journal* 1612, 1644.

[9] J Salminen, 'Finsk krishantering i fredstid – beredskapslagen tillämpas för första gången' [2020] *Svensk Juristtidning* 1116.

II. EMERGENCIES AND LEGISLATIVE OVERSIGHT

Emergencies often require a shift in the balance of power in favour of the executive.[10] In order to act swiftly and decisively, the executive must have the necessary authority to deal with the emergency.[11] A declaration of a state of emergency is often required by legal systems to confine the use of extraordinary measures to a limited period. In addition, the powers granted by the state of emergency are often legislated in advance, which strengthens the capacity of individuals to anticipate them.[12] Doing so is tied to questions of democratic legitimacy.[13] There are two reasons for this. First, preparing such legislation in advance ensures that emergency powers are democratically deliberated by the parliament and society at large. Second, it allows the legislature to uphold the normal legislative procedures also during emergencies.[14] This means that even if an emergency calls for some extraordinary measures, these measures are legitimate and legally authorised.

Most notably, the Venice Commission recommends this approach. The Commission distinguishes constitutional *de jure* and extra-constitutional *de facto* states of emergency.[15] An extra-constitutional state of emergency obtains when emergency measures are extra-legal (often due to a lack of constitutional provisions on emergency measures), so that 'authorities enact emergency measures without having officially declared a state of emergency'.[16] In contrast, a *de jure* state of emergency occurs when constitutional and legal regulations and constrains are established in advance. The Venice Commission recommends a *de jure* approach as it provides stronger guarantees of fundamental rights and protection of democracy. In this vein, the Commission recommends giving the parliament an active role.[17] The parliament must therefore have the capacity to exercise control over the declaration and termination of a state of emergency, as well as the actions taken

[10] Venice Commission (n 1) 16.

[11] C Bjørnskov and Sn Voigt, 'Emergencies: On the Misuse of Government Powers' (2022) 190 *Public Choice* 1. J Salminen and M Farzamfar, 'Legislative Oversight in Finland during the States of Emergencies of the COVID-19 Pandemic' in Saša Zagorc and Samo Bardutzky (eds), *COVID-19 and the Constitution: A Special Collection of Essays in Honour of the Thirtieth Anniversary of the Constitution of the Republic of Slovenia* (Ljubljana, Slovenia: University of Ljubljana, 2024) 457–476.

[12] T Brunila, 'Legislation, Emergencies and the Need for Swift Action: Tensions between the Executive Branch and Emergency Legislation during the COVID-19 Pandemic in Finland' [2025] *The Theory and Practice of Legislation* 31.

[13] G De Angelis and E De Oliveira, 'COVID-19 and the "State of Exception": Assessing Institutional Resilience in Consolidated Democracies – a Comparative Analysis of Italy and Portugal' (2021) 28 *Democratization* 1602, 1606.

[14] David Dyzenhaus argues that during emergencies only those emergency acts that have a legal basis are democratically legitimate. See D Dyzenhaus, 'States of Emergency' in M Rosenfeld and A Sajó (eds), *The Oxford Handbook of Comparative Constitutional Law* (Oxford University Press, 2012) 451.

[15] Venice Commission, *Respect for Democracy, Human Rights and the Rule of Law during States of Emergency – Reflections* (Council of Europe, 2020) 6.

[16] Venice Commission (n 1) 8.

[17] Venice Commission, *Rule of Law Checklist* (Council of Europe, 2016) 22.

over its course.[18] What is also important here is that power is not centralised with the executive: it does not both enjoy norm-issuing power and decide on exceptions to those norms.[19] It is these normative principles that are key to understanding parliamentary oversight during a state of emergency.

The main objectives of legislative oversight is the prevention of arbitrary power, making the government accountable and its actions transparent.[20] Various oversight tools exist to make governing more democratic and to foster trust and uphold democratic principles, including committees, commissions, and parliamentary inquiries.[21] Some scholars argue that parliamentary systems are less effective than presidential systems in that the latter separate the two branches – the executive and the legislatureä – more clearly.[22] Others argue that what is more relevant than the principle of separation of powers is the capacity of the legal framework to facilitate control.[23] This means that some constitutions have more oversight potential than others based on the mechanisms and tools established in them. This also applies to emergency governance.[24]

While a state of emergency requires delegating new powers and authorities to the executive, the checks and balances on the executive are crucial for protecting against the concentration of power and its arbitrary use. To limit these possibilities, which threaten the rule of law and the continuity of the democratic system, the role of the legislative branch is threefold. First, the parliament oversees the executive by assessing and demanding justifications for its actions. Second, the parliament limits executive authority by means of enforcing its constitutional limits (such as by means of sunset clauses that establish that the parliament is responsible for prolonging the state of emergency). Third, the parliament also acts as a legislator during emergencies, as sometimes the extraordinary situation requires new legislation for handling it. These are the three functions relevant in analysing parliamentary oversight in constitutions and in practice.

[18] Venice Commission (n 15) 9, 18.

[19] ibid 15.

[20] BA Rockman, 'Legislative-Executive Relations and Legislative Oversight' (1984) 9 *Legislative Studies Quarterly* 387, 415; Yamamoto (n 5) 9–10.

[21] Riccardo Pelizzo and Rick Stapenhurst, 'Tools for Legislative Oversight: An Empirical Investigation' in Rick Stapenhurst and others (eds), *Legislative Oversight and Budgeting – A world Perspective* (WBI Development Studies 2008) 21; Riccardo Pelizzo, 'Oversight and Democracy Reconsidered' in Rick Stapenhurst and others (eds), *Legislative Oversight and Budgeting – A world Perspective* (WBI Development Studies 2008) 31, 39; Kevin Deveaux, Natália Švecová and Tim Baker, *Parliaments Responding to a Pandemic: Lessons Learned for Emergency Planning* (Report from the House Democracy Partnership and The Swiss Agency for Development and Cooperation 2021) 11.

[22] David Beetham (n 5) 115, 128; Yamamoto (n 5) 11; however, Stapenhurst and Pelizzo suggest that parliamentary systems are better equipped to oversee executive powers. See Pelizzo and Stapenhurst (n 21) 20.

[23] Pelizzo (n 21) 44; E Houlihan and W Underwoord, *Emergency Law and the COVID-19 Pandemic: Global State of Democracy Thematic Paper 2021* (International Institute for Democracy and Electoral Assistance, 2021) viii; Deveaux, Švecová and Baker (n 21) 11.

[24] Houlihan and Underwoord (n 23) viii; De Angelis and De Oliveira (n 13) 5.

III. PARLIAMENTARY CONTROL IN FINLAND DURING A STATE OF EMERGENCY

Declaring a state of emergency under the Finnish Constitution and the Emergency Powers Act means delegating to the Finnish Government the authority to issue decrees for assigning various measures necessary for dealing with an emergency. During the Covid-19 pandemic, these delegations included a range of issues related to social welfare, healthcare services, employment, education, and restricting people's freedom of movement.[25] The main aims of these decrees were announced to be that of preventing the spread of the virus, protecting special groups of the population (such as the elderly and the immunocompromised), ensuring the adequacy of social welfare and healthcare personnel, and the capacity of intensive-care services during the crisis, as well as ensuring the supply of medications.[26] In this section, we examine how the Finnish Constitution regulates the act of declaring a state of emergency and authorises the parliament to exercise control over the government's actions.

The Finnish constitutional framework predicts and – to a certain extent regulates – states of emergency. When a state of emergency is declared, some additional powers may be added to normal regulatory frameworks in order to secure the livelihood of inhabitants, enforce the law, ensure respect for constitutional freedoms and human rights, and safeguard the territorial integrity and independence of the country. One part of the Finnish attitude towards possible future emergencies has been to prepare legislation for regulating procedures in advance.[27] The Finnish legislature has also tried to anticipate possible public powers needed in various types of emergencies. The main objective of the Finnish legislature has been to prepare for possible emergencies in order to regulate them before they occur. The prevailing mindset in responding to emergencies in Finland is that if there is an exceptional situation that requires special competences and measures, such measures should have been regulated in acts of parliament in advance.[28] It is especially the first two roles established above in Section 2, the parliament's role in overseeing and assessing the government's actions, and the parliament's role in limiting executive authority, that are relevant to our analysis.

[25] Salminen and Farzamfar (n 11); Mehrnoosh Farzamfar, Janne Salminen and Janna Tuominen, 'Governmental Policies to Fight Pandemics: Defining the Boundaries of Legitimate Limitations on Fundamental Freedoms: National Report on Finland' in Arianna Vedaschi (ed), *Governmental Policies to Fight Pandemic* (Brill Nijhoff 2024).

[26] Government Decrees (*valtioneuvoston asetukset*) M 1/2020 and M 2/2020 on the adoption of certain emergency powers within the Emergency Powers Act and Government Decrees M 3/2020, M 4/2020 and M 5/2020 on the application of the aforementioned powers were all given to Parliament on the same day and discussed by Parliament on 17.3.2020.

[27] See T Brunila, 'Legal Resilience and Legislative Emergency Preparation in Finland' (2025) 183 *Retfærd* 9. This is also the case more generally in Finnish political culture. See A-E Hyvönen and T Juntunen, 'From "Spiritual Defence" to Robust Resilience in the Finnish Comprehensive Security Model' in S Larsson and M Rhinard (eds), *Nordic Societal Security; Convergence and Divergence* (Routledge, 2021).

[28] Salminen and Mehrnoosh (n 11).

A. The Constitution

The Constitution of Finland admits of states of emergency and regulates their declarations and governance. More precisely, Section 23, which contains 'Basic Rights and Liberties in Situations of Emergency', explicitly enables the government to declare a state of emergency. It adds that during a state of emergency, the government can impose provisional exceptions to basic rights and fundamental liberties:

> Such provisional exceptions to basic rights and liberties that are compatible with Finland's international human rights obligations and that are deemed necessary in the case of an armed attack against Finland or in the event of other situations of emergency, as provided by an Act, which pose a serious threat to the nation may be provided by an Act or by a Government Decree to be issued on the basis of authorisation given in an Act for a special reason and subject to a precisely circumscribed scope of application. The grounds for provisional exceptions shall be laid down by an Act, however.
>
> Government Decrees concerning provisional exceptions shall without delay be submitted to the Parliament for consideration. The Parliament may decide on the validity of the Decrees.

This Section clarifies several important points. First, the situations in which it is deemed necessary to make provisional exceptions to basic human rights, fundamental liberties and freedoms include armed attack or other such emergencies that pose a serious threat to the nation. Second, in all such circumstances, exceptions must be compatible with Finland's international human rights obligations. Third, the constitution permits exceptions to fundamental and basic human rights only if the principles of temporality and necessity are respected in a very strict manner. Fourth, they must be based on an authorisation given in a parliamentary act or by governmental decree, subject to a precisely circumscribed scope of application. Finally, the grounds for provisional exceptions must be laid down by an act and the authorisation of such acts must be circumscribed in scope. It is especially these last two points that are relevant for parliamentary oversight. Requiring that exceptions be laid down by an act enforces the role of the parliament in assessing their scope and rationale.[29]

In interpreting a situation as an emergency, it is important that the parliament be given a role in overseeing it. This ensures that the decision does not rest solely in the hands of the government. Indeed, the way in which emergencies are regulated under Section 23 of the Constitution ensures that the constitutionality of deeming a situation to be an emergency can be assessed. Although Section 23 only mentions explicitly armed conflicts, it maintains an evolutionary character of interpretation. That is, by inserting the phrase 'or in event of other situations of emergency' the legislature intended to expand the instances of states of emergency to more than merely armed conflicts. While such an open-ended list

[29] Salminen and Farzamfar (n 11).

extends the possibility of interpreting other situations as emergencies as well – meaning that the definition or determination of other examples of emergencies is left to parliamentary law – the Constitution of Finland nonetheless sets several relevant boundaries on how the matter is to be regulated by the parliament and parliamentary law. Specifically, this means regulating how the requirement that the threat must 'pose a serious threat to the nation' is to be interpreted. Thus, necessary exceptions could arise either during armed conflicts or due to other serious situations. In this way, the constitutionality of interpreting a situation as an emergency can be controlled.

The parliament's role is the clearest in the obligation established by Section 23 that the grounds for provisional exceptions should be laid down explicitly and clearly in a separate parliamentary act. This means that the grounds and reasons for such exceptions are reviewed by the parliament. All governmental decrees concerning provisional exceptions must be submitted to the parliament for further consideration. As a constitutional rule, the parliament has the authority to decide on the legal validity of these governmental decrees. Despite a certain scarcity of regulation on emergencies at the constitutional level, the constitutional review of decrees upholds the compulsion of legality[30] – deeply rooted in the constitution – by giving no room for unregulated, extra-legal, or extra-constitutional emergency law-making. Thus the constitution establishes that provisional exceptions cannot go beyond what it has explicitly and clearly regulated.[31]

In fact, Section 23 subjects an emergency decree to a stronger parliamentary oversight mechanism than decrees in a normal situation. This means that while a state of emergency might entail granting the executive extraordinary competences, it does not necessarily mean that the legislature's role is weakened. This is evident in the difference between governmental decrees in general and those regulated under Section 23. The issuance of governmental decrees in general is regulated under Section 80 of the Constitution. According to this Section, the president of the republic, the government, and a ministry may issue decrees based on the authorisation given to them in the Constitution or in another act. If there are no specific provisions on who should issue a decree, it is issued by the government. The principles governing the rights and obligations of private individuals and other matters that are legislative in nature are to be governed by the legislative acts of the Parliament. This means that the Constitution includes several reservations regarding the use of parliamentary acts in certain cases; for example, the grounds of the rights and obligations of individuals must be enacted in law.[32] Regarding the decrees created under Section 80 of the Constitution, the Parliament has the possibility to consider only the Sections on which the decree has been issued. In this context, the main restricting element of

[30] Regarding the concept, see D Dyzenhaus, 'The Compulsion of Legality' in VV Ramraj (ed), *Emergencies and the Limits of Legality* (Cambridge University Press, 2008).

[31] Salminen and Farzamfar (n 11).

[32] See, eg, statements of the Constitutional Law Committee of the Parliament, PeVL 26/2013 vp and PeVL 41/2014 vp.

the content of decrees is the requirement of enacting certain issues on the level of parliamentary acts.[33]

In contrast to decrees issued under Section 80 the Constitution, Section 23 concerns the emergency decrees issued only after the declaration of a state of emergency. Requiring a declaration of a state of emergency as a procedure helps control and limit the use of emergency measures.[34] Unlike the ordinary or general decrees issued under Section 80, the decrees issued under Section 23 must be temporary and necessary in nature and subjected to immediate parliamentary review. During its review, the parliament has the power to approve or reject these governmental decrees. This furthers the parliament's role in limiting executive authority during emergencies. Essentially, although the Finnish Constitution allows for some exceptions to constitutional rights, it does not allow official institutions to derogate from their public duties, such as matters related to the relationship between the government, the president of the republic, and the courts. The same applies to the institutional duties of municipalities or other self-governing regional bodies. The constitution does not recognise any other temporary changes during emergencies than those stipulated based on and under Section 23. Thus, the Finnish system of emergency powers presupposes that the parliament and government should function together even during the difficulties of states of emergency.[35]

While Section 23 of the Constitution differs from Section 80 regarding the power to rule by decrees allowing derogation from fundamental rights, it nevertheless requires the grounds for derogations to be set forth explicitly by a parliamentary act. Hence, during states of emergency, the basis for derogation from fundamental rights must be regulated by parliamentary law.[36] To be sure, there are some differences in the wordings of Sections 23 and 80 of the Constitution, by means of which Section 23 allows a slightly greater scope for using governmental decrees during emergencies. However, to balance this power, Section 23 provides the parliament with the right to review all temporary decrees and sets out an obligation for the government to provide the parliament with the possibility to review the decrees immediately after issuing them. According to the Finnish constitution, the parliament decides on the validity of these decrees.[37]

B. The Emergency Powers Act

As mentioned above, Section 23 of the Constitution provides only an indicator for recognising and declaring states of emergency in Finland. In order to limit

[33] Salminen and Farzamfar (n 11).

[34] See Brunila and Salminen (n 4).

[35] Salminen and Farzamfar (n 11). A Jonsson Cornell and J Salminen, 'Emergency Laws in Comparative Constitutional Law – The Case of Sweden and Finland' (2018) 19 *German Law Journal* 219, 241–42.

[36] Salminen and Farzamfar (n 11).

[37] Cornell and Salminen (n 35).

the open-endedness of interpreting this Section, the types of emergencies and the powers of authorities during emergencies are regulated under the parliamentary Emergency Powers Act. On the one hand, this Act shifts the balance of power during emergencies in favour of the executive branch in order to enable swift action. On the other hand, it regulates in detail the powers and actions of the government in emergency situations.[38]

Before going into the substance of the Act itself, the complicated nature of its constitutional basis must be emphasised. While the constitutional basis of the state of emergency is an important value in Finnish legal culture, the one major deviation from this practice in Finnish constitutional law is the fact that the Emergency Powers Act, which regulates exceptions during emergencies, is in a way an exception to the constitutional order. When it was enacted, the Constitutional Law Committee of the Finnish parliament (an *ex-ante* institution of parliamentary control meant to assess the constitutional basis of laws and acts of government) considered the Emergency Powers Act not to be materially in line with the Finnish Constitution, and therefore to be unconstitutional. However, if an act does not declare a constitutional amendment, it can enter into force as an exceptive enactment, which, while being substantially contrary to the constitution, is formally constitutionally valid due to qualified enactment procedures. Since the total revision of the Finnish constitution in 2000, the common constitutional tendency has been to avoid such exceptive enactment, meaning that nowadays, the use of exceptive enactments is very rare. Because the Emergency Powers Act grants a greater possibility for the executive branch to issue decrees during emergencies, and was thus considered to be substantially contrary to the constitution,[39] the constitution was later revisited, in 2011. Section 23 was amended to solve this problematic legal issue. Conversely, it seems that the current Emergency Powers Act is still substantially contrary to the Constitution, even after those amendments made to Section 23, which came into force in March 2012.[40]

Regarding interpreting a situation as an emergency, according to the Emergency Powers Act, the Finnish government, in cooperation with the president, may declare a state of emergency when the criteria for a state of emergency obtain. The current Act defines six types of emergencies that fit the criteria for a crisis gravely threatening the nation. One of these types of emergencies is a widespread, dangerous, life-threatening infectious disease, the gravity of which corresponds to a catastrophe. The Covid-19 pandemic was deemed to fit this definition in 2020. Alongside the selection of criteria laid down in Section 23, the main principles for the use of the Emergency Powers Act are stipulated in the Act itself.[41]

[38] Salminen and Farzamfar (n 11).

[39] J Heikkonen, P Kataja, J Lavapuro, J Salminen and M Turpeinen, 'Valmiuslaki ja perusoikeudet poikkeusoloissa: Valtiosääntöoikeudellinen kokonaisarvio valmiuslain ja perustuslain 23 §:n suhteesta' Valtioneuvoston selvitys- ja tutkimustoiminnan julkaisusarja 64/2018.

[40] ibid.

[41] Salminen and Farzamfar (n 11).

The Act facilitates oversight and control as it also limits and circumscribes emergency measures. According to the Act, under emergency conditions, the authorities may only exercise powers that are necessary for legitimate purposes and proportionate to the objectives pursued. Additionally, the powers may be exercised if and only if the authorities cannot control the situation through their regular public powers. Thus, the use of the emergency powers envisioned by the Act is only possible if it is necessary and proportional, and if the regular powers have proven insufficient. In addition, if a normal parliamentary act is enough for the achievement of the goals of legislation, such a parliamentary act should be used instead, not an act based on Section 23.[42]

Another important aspect of the Emergency Powers Act that serves to limit emergency powers is that it specifies the powers specific to the six different emergencies. In the case of a state of emergency caused by a pandemic, the Act provides only a limited set of additional powers that can be granted to the authorities. These powers are closely purpose-related in comparison with, for example, the extra powers in the cases of a military attack or its aftermath. The Act lays down the possibility to, for example, register and call to work all persons with a medical education, irrespective of where they work. In addition, a pandemic also allows imposing certain limitations on movement within the state.[43]

The role of the Parliament in overseeing emergency measures derives from the fact that a declaration of emergency as such does not entail that all powers mentioned in the Act or allocated within the emergency in question are automatically at the authorities' disposal.[44] Instead, the Act stipulates a procedure according to which the government should first issue a decree stating clearly which powers are needed to handle the emergency. This decree is then subject to parliamentary scrutiny. If the decree is accepted by the parliament, the Government can issue further decrees to apply the adopted powers. All these decrees are reviewed by the parliament *ex-post* their issuance.[45] In addition, the specific powers at disposal, according to the Emergency Powers Act, are dependent on the emergency in question. In the case of a pandemic, the range of powers is rather restricted.

The Emergency Powers Act also empowers the Parliament to limit the government's authority and powers. While the Act does grant new powers to the government upon the declaration of a state of emergency, and while it grants the government authority to decide which powers within the Act to use,

[42] Salminen and Farzamfar (n 11).
[43] Salminen and Farzamfar (n 11).
[44] Brunila and Salminen (n 4) 223.
[45] Lavapuro, Ojanen, and Scheinin (n 3). See also L Kirvesniemi, M Sormunen and T Ojanen, 'Developments in Finnish Constitutional Law' in R Albert, D Landau, P Faraguna and Š Drugda (eds), *2016 Global Review of Constitutional Law* (Boston, I·CONnect-Clough Center, 2017). M Dahlberg, 'Finland-Ex ante constitutionality review of laws relating to the COVID-19 pandemic' (2021) *Public Law* 4. Also see P Johanna Neuvonen, 'The COVID-19 Policymaking under the Auspices of Parliamentary Constitutional Review: The Case of Finland and its Implications' (2020) 6 *European Policy Analysis*.

the use of decrees is regulated and their review is mandated.[46] The Parliament decides whether the decree under review is to apply as such, or whether it is to be repealed in full or in part, and whether it is to remain in force for the period sought or a reduced timeframe. In case the government does not give the parliament the opportunity to review the decree within one week of its being issued, the decree will automatically become void. Governmental decrees may be applied only after the parliament has decided that there is no problem in their application and that they are not to be repealed. Furthermore, all such decrees adopted under the Emergency Powers Act are temporal in nature – although the end of the state of emergency is not legally regulated as such. Decrees issued under the Emergency Powers Act are valid for a maximum of six months. The ending of the emergency entails the end of the decrees and competences under the Act. Furthermore, if the government does use the power to issue decrees during the emergency, all such decrees are subject to parliamentary *ex-post* review as mandated by Section 23 of the Constitution and regulated by the Emergency Powers Act.[47]

Thus the Act establishes the interaction between the Finnish government, the president, and the parliament during states of emergency.[48] In the case of any new legislation on states of emergency based on Section 23, the Act should go separately through the enactment procedures in the parliament. To point out the obvious, in such cases the parliament acts as a legislature in the context of emergencies.

C. The Constitutional Law Committee

While our analysis has focused on the explicit regulation of states of emergency, it is important to mention the special constitutional feature of the Finnish parliamentary oversight mechanisms. The parliamentary oversight during emergencies is linked closely with the peculiar Finnish system of *ex-ante* constitutional review. In Finnish legal culture, one of the main doctrines has been

[46] M Farzamfar and J Salminen, 'The Supervision of Legality by the Finnish Parliamentary Ombudsman during the COVID-19 Pandemic' (2022) 99 *Nordisk Administrativt Tidsskrift* 1, 4.

[47] Salminen and Farzamfar (n 11).

[48] Of course, besides the measures taken in Finland during the state of emergency under this Act, the situation has also been managed by using powers provided for in the legislation applied under normal conditions – including, for example, the Communicable Diseases Act and the Border Guard Act, amongst many other ordinary laws. During the COVID-19 pandemic, over one hundred Governmental proposals for new legislation were issued. During the crisis, ordinary legislation has been amended, partly provisionally. This is particularly the case with the Communicable Diseases Act. In addition, the COVID-19 pandemic has been managed in Finland through guidelines, action plans, recommendations, and decisions issued by local authorities, all of which could be labelled as a softer source of law, see on this E Korkea-Aho and M Scheinin, 'Could You, Would You, Should You? Regulating Cross-Border Travel through COVID-19 Soft Law in Finland' (2021) 12 *The European Journal of Risk Regulation*.

the sovereignty of the parliament,[49] a reason for which the Finnish Parliament has also been given the authority to review the constitutionality of legislation. In this context, the constitutionality of legislation is reviewed by the *ex-ante* parliamentary institution, the Constitutional Law Committee (*perustuslakivaliokunta*) which is a parliamentary committee with a very special function. While it is one of the parliament's committees, it is made up of members of the parliament. It reviews the government's proposals for Acts from a constitutional point of view, and during the legislation process it has the final say regarding the constitutional basis of legislation.[50] It is also in charge of the review of emergency decrees in the parliament. In the Finnish constitutional setting, the Constitutional Law Committee is the key control mechanism for ensuring the constitutionality of legislation.

IV. THE COVID-19 PANDEMIC AND THE FINNISH STATE OF EMERGENCY

The framework we have explicated above was applied in the exceptional conditions of the Covid-19 pandemic. As mentioned, during the pandemic, a state of emergency was declared twice in Finland.[51] Since the World Health Organization (WHO) had already classified Covid-19 a pandemic of seriously dangerous character, it was not problematic to deem that the pandemic threatened the nation in a way that justified declaring a state of emergency.[52] During the pandemic in Finland, the executive branch held a central position in responding to the emergency.[53] The two periods of states of emergency made it possible for the government to claim some of the competences provided by the Emergency Powers Act. However, the Finnish system guarantees a key supervisory role for the parliament in all legislative decision-making.[54] We argue that the parliament was not marginalised in Finland during the Covid-19 emergencies,[55] but functioned in line with the legal framework that had been established in advance. During the two states of emergency announced due to the pandemic, the Finnish parliament functioned and acted rapidly without the need to establish any

[49] Lavapuro, Ojanen and Scheinin (n 3) 507; Husa (n 3) 107, 109; M Suksi, 'Common Roots of Nordic Constitutional Law? Some Observations on Legal-Historical Development and Relations between the Constitutional Systems of Five Nordic Countries' in H Krunke and B Thorarensen (eds), *The Nordic Constitutions – a Comparative and Contextual Study* (Hart Publishing, 2018) 40.

[50] Lavapuro, Ojanen and Scheinin (n 3) 510.

[51] Government Decision (valtioneuvoston päätös) VNK/2020/31.

[52] In addition, several other European States had already declared a state of emergency to respond to the situation. See N Morag (ed), *Impacts of the COVID-19 Pandemic: International Laws, Policies, and Civil Liberties* (Wiley, 2023).

[53] R Niemikari and T Raunio, 'Finland: Balancing Centralized Leadership and Regional Interests' in K Lynggaard, M Dagnis Jensen and M Kluth (eds), *Governments' Responses to the Covid-19 Pandemic in Europe* (Springer International Publishing, 2023) 285; See R Niemikari and T Raunio, 'Centralized Leadership, Ministerial Dominance, and Improvised Instruments: The Governance of COVID in Finland' (2022) 99 *Nordisk Administrativt Tidsskrift* 1.

[54] Salminen and Farzamfar (n 11).

[55] Vedaschi and Graziani (n 8) 1628–29.

additional committees or supervising bodies. For example, the parliament made efforts to secure its functionality by amending its Rules of Procedure to allow Members of Parliament to work remotely.[56]

As pointed out above, while the Finnish government and president can jointly declare a state of emergency based on the Emergency Powers Act, such a declaration does not by itself, without a contribution from the parliament, provide any extra powers for the government.[57] Furthermore, every decree based on the Emergency Powers Act is temporal and needs parliamentary approval. However, the declaration most certainly has very clear social and deep political effects. For example, such declarations often produce, at least in the early phases of an emergency, a 'rally around the flag'-effect, which makes it difficult to oppose governmental measures.[58] This could have resulted in the parliament simply granting the government what it deemed necessary in order to stay out of the way of effective emergency response and not slow it down. However, during the Covid-19 emergencies in Finland, the time limit was used as one of the central elements when considering the proportionality of decrees, and the emergency periods were *shorter* than the Emergency Powers Act would allow.[59] This means that the parliament did not simply approve emergency measures without reservations – a practice that would have marginalised and undermined its role.

As illustrated above, as a compensation for the delegation of powers which can include derogation from rights, the Finnish legal system strengthens the role of the parliament in overseeing the government. This seems to have been the case during the pandemic as well, as the parliament was active in overseeing the government.[60] Indeed, the need to justify restrictions and other reactions, and to evaluate the situation – not only epidemiologically, but also from a wider societal perspective – *increased*. While throughout the pandemic the focus was on the epidemiological facts and health care needs, in retrospect, attention has increasingly been given to other aspects of the crisis as well. This has partly been supported by the parliament and the Constitutional Law Committee, as the latter has demanded an evaluation of the actions taken during the pandemic not only from the narrower point of view of the resources of the health care sector, but also from the perspective of impacts on various special groups in society in general.[61] Thus, the impact assessment of proposed legislation in

[56] Salminen and Farzamfar (n 11). Brunila (n 12) 47–48.

[57] See the report of the Constitutional Law Committee, PeVM 2/2020 vp.

[58] Niemikari and Raunio, 'Centralized Leadership, Ministerial Dominance, and Improvised Instruments' (n 53) 248.

[59] M Scheinin, 'Finland's Success in Combatting COVID-19' in J Grogan and A Donald (eds), *Routledge Handbook of Law and the COVID-19 Pandemic* (Routledge, 2022) 134–35.

[60] ibid 134; Niemikari and Raunio, 'Finland: Balancing Centralized Leadership and Regional Interests' (n 53) 286. In Finnish, see T Brunila, J Salminen and M Värttö, 'Oikeuden Resilienssi Poikkeuksellisissa Oloissa – Perustuslakivaliokunnan Rooli Oikeuden Ylläpitämisessä Covid-19-Pandemian Aikana' [2023] *Lakimies* 1011.

[61] See H Lonka, 'Valmiuslaki Koronapandemian Sääntelystrategiana' (2023) 42 *Hallinnon Tutkimus* 183.

connection with the Covid-19 pandemic has been approached similarly to the regular impact assessment conducted within the law-making process during normal times. This has been partly because of the supervision of the Constitutional Law Committee and its reports and statements,[62] which have underlined, for example, the need to observe restrictions from the perspective of the rights of persons with disabilities and children. However, this requirement also stems from Section 23 of the constitution, which requires that all regulations must be in line with Finnish obligations to the international human rights conventions.[63] Nevertheless, despite resorting to national emergency powers, Finland has not notified international institutions about the human rights provisions from which it has derogated (eg, Article 15 of the European Convention on Human Rights and Article 4 of the International Covenant on Civil and Political Rights).[64]

The oversight role of the Parliament and the Constitutional Law Committee is seen especially in how they insisted on the need for a rationale and justifications regarding the purported necessity of actions taken, and deeper legislative assessment on the effects of these actions.[65] For example, when evaluating the continuation of decrees concerning distance schooling, the Constitutional Law Committee underlined the need for wider evaluation of the effects of these actions.[66] In the same vein, the Committee started to emphasise the need to follow the effects of emergency actions and to terminate the emergency decrees as soon as possible.[67] In addition, the Committee started to increasingly evaluate the overall benefits and costs of restrictions in society, and not only restrictions pertaining to emergencies.[68] During the second state of emergency in Finland, in 2021, the parliament also considered that the wide application of decrees was not needed in the same manner enacted by the government.[69] Concerning the proposed massive restrictions on people's movements, for example, the Constitutional Law Committee found such serious problems that the

[62] Scheinin (n 59) 134.

[63] On limitations to fundamental rights, see the decision of the Chancellor of Justice 1.10.2020 (OKV/61/10/2020) criticising the inadequate analysis of restrictions to fundamental and human rights in Government Decision SM/2020/20 (inadequate consideration of impacts, necessity, alternatives, and requirements imposed by the Schengen Code and Government Decision SM/2020/21 (the citizens' right to leave and enter country, PL 9 §, implied but not explicitly mentioned and similar deficiencies as in the above-mentioned decision)). In this regard, also see the Constitutional Law Committee's assessments in Statements PeVL 7/2021 vp, PeVL 9/2021 vp, PeVL 14/2020 vp, and Report PeVM 11/2020 vp. Concerning the constitutionally problematic governmental propositions, see PeVL 32/2020 vp and PeVL 12/2021 vp (problems of proportionality and indispensability, as the rights and duties were not clearly regulated).

[64] Salminen and Farzamfar (n 11).

[65] See, eg, PeVM 13/2020 vp.

[66] See PeVM 14/2020 vp.

[67] See PeVM 15/2020 vp.

[68] See, eg, PeVM 17/2020 vp.

[69] See PeVM 5/2021 vp.

government finally had to withdraw its plan.[70] It is this last example especially that shows that the parliament did effectively limit the government's emergency measures.

Action has also been taken to ensure that the Parliament is not marginalised. The Constitutional Law Committee has underlined that, prior to issuing decrees on the use of the powers of the Emergency Powers Act, there should be a decision by the parliament on the acceptance of the decree that concerns the powers within the Act planned to be utilised.[71] On several occasions, when reviewing emergency decrees, the Committee has also reiterated the right of the parliament to receive all information needed for legislation and its review.[72] Regarding the legislative or enactment procedures, the Constitutional Law Committee on several occasions clearly declared that the government should respect the procedures of the parliament and plan its own decision-making timetables, so that the parliament might have sufficient time to consider the issues.[73] For future emergencies, the Constitutional Law Committee has pointed out that certain parts of the Emergency Powers Act – especially those regulating the right of the parliament to access information and its possible maneuvers concerning the decrees – should be revisited after the emergency.[74]

Parliamentary oversight and constitutionality control remained active and effective during the pandemic. As pointed out above, the Finnish legal framework strengthens the parliament's capacity to do so during emergencies. Indeed, the Constitutional Law Committee's *ex-ante* constitutional review and the parliament's *ex-post* review of decrees gives the parliament many possibilities to oversee, control and limit the Government's emergency measures, if needed. As the courts are a less relevant part of the review of constitutionality and legality of emergency decrees in Finland, the strong role of the parliament given by the constitution, the Emergency Powers Act, and the legal system is even more justified in ensuring that emergency measures are not disproportional and that they are used strictly for their intended aims. The parliament's success in achieving this task is most visible in reviewing the necessity and scope of emergency decrees based on the Emergency Powers Act.

As we point out below, there are some shortcomings in reaching the parliament's full potential in overseeing the government, such as its lacking a role in declaring a state of emergency. However, while these issues can mainly be addressed by applying principles already inherent to the existing legal framework, there are also drawbacks that pertain to the principles themselves.

[70] See PeVL 12/2021 vp.

[71] See the reports of Constitutional Law Committee, PeVM 2/2020 vp, PeVM 4/2020 vp, PeVM 5/2020 vp and PeVM 6/2020 vp. The report PeVM 8/2020 vp includes a very serious reminder on this issue, pointing out that the action of Government was against the Emergency Powers Act and the constant, new practice of the Constitutional Law Committee.

[72] See, eg, reports PeVM 7/2020 vp and PeVM 8/2020 vp, also PeVM 12/2020 vp.

[73] See, eg, the statement of the Constitutional Law Committee, PeVL 6/2021 vp.

[74] See PeVM 11/2020 vp.

To point out the obvious, the parliament is a fundamentally political entity, and its capacity to act as an overseer of the government is dependent on the willingness of the parliament to do so. While the Parliament was able to limit the scope and time limits of emergency decrees, this was partly due to such a willingness. Perhaps in an emergency that is more politically polarizing (an economic one, say) or one where going against the government would be less politically feasible (a war, most probably),[75] the Parliament would have acted differently. However, at least during the pandemic, the parliament seems to have been unwilling to forgo its role in genuinely trying to oversee and put bounds on the government. Yet it could be pointed out that it seems that the Constitutional Law Committee had a more visible role in doing so than the parliamentary *ex-post* review. Therefore, one could argue that Section 23 of the constitution and the Emergency Powers Act did not establish the *main* mechanisms for parliamentary oversight, as the Constitutional Law Committee – the actions of which are not regulated by these laws – was simply more relevant. Be that as it may, this did not result in the parliament focusing solely on *ex-ante* review. Rather, by requiring also *ex-post* review, the Constitutional Law Committee was complemented by the parliament's capacity to oversee and control the emergency decrees.

V. CONCLUSIONS

One of the key advantages of the Finnish Constitution and its emergency legal framework is that by predicting emergency clauses in law in advance, the Finnish Parliament is permitted the active role of reviewing executive action during emergencies. Both Section 23 of the Constitution and the Emergency Powers Act mandate the parliament to review the grounds and decrees made by the government based on the emergency powers and enables it to dispose of decrees that it deems unnecessary and disproportional to their aims. Against this backdrop, we examined the parliament's powers as exercised during the Covid-19 pandemic in Finland. Our study shows that the parliament carried out regular checks and balances of power and maintained a crucial role during the pandemic in holding executive power to account.

The parliamentary oversight was not without problems, however. According to Korkea-Aho and Scheinin, the parliamentary review failed in the context of soft law; that is, when the government made non-binding recommendations to government officials, as they were not seen as decrees that had to be reviewed.[76] These problems were, however, addressed by other legal actors, such as the Parliamentary Ombudsman.[77] In addition, there were structural problems, such as the parliament's limited role in decisions regarding the declaration and ending

[75] In the context of hybrid threats, see Brunila (n 27).
[76] Korkea-Aho and Scheinin (n 48) 43.
[77] Farzamfar and Salminen (n 46).

of the state of emergency.[78] Nevertheless, while it is true that Finnish party cohesion and discipline make traditionally majority cabinets quite strong against the parliament,[79] and while many scholars have argued that such aspects weaken the capacity of the parliament to audit the executive,[80] our analysis suggests that the parliamentary oversight potential of the constitution was effective during the pandemic. However, this success was not simply a question of legal structures, concerning political power-relations, as has been seen through the gradual politicisation of the constitutional committee.[81] This means that political culture cannot be disregarded in this context.[82]

As underlined by the Venice Commission, 'any legal acts issued by the executive should be subjected to a subsequent parliamentary approval and should cease to produce effects, if they do not secure such approval within a certain period'.[83] Still, during the Covid-19 pandemic, many parliaments within the EU Member States seem to have performed a secondary role, leaving executive power largely unfettered, at least from parliamentary oversight.[84] In contrast to the general trend in pandemic governance, which favoured granting the executive extensive powers and thus marginalising the role of the parliament,[85] in Finland the parliament remained active in facilitating both legislative and constitutional control. We have argued that this is the case not because of mere political good will, but because of the *ex-ante* system of constitutional review and the legal framework that requires governmental decrees to be put to the parliament for review.

[78] Brunila and Salminen (n 4) 229; Scheinin (n 59) 133.

[79] T Raunio and M Wiberg, 'Finland: Polarized Pluralism in the Shadow of a Strong President' in K Strøm, WC Müller and T Bergman (eds), *Delegation and Accountability in Parliamentary Democracies* (Oxford University Press, 2003) 321.

[80] Beetham (n 5) 127; C Friedberg and RY Hazan, *Legislative Oversight* (Center for International Development, 2012) 9.

[81] Husa (n 4) 273; M Pellonpää, 'Perustuslakikontrollista neljässä Euroopan maassa ja Suomessa' (2021) 6 *Lakimies* 934.

[82] Vedaschi and Graziani (n 8) 1644.

[83] Venice Commission, (n 1).

[84] ibid.

[85] Vedaschi and Graziani (n 8) 1614.

14

Review of Covid-19 Measures by the European Court of Human Rights: How to Avoid the 'Fair', the 'Balance' and 'the Fair Balance'

VLADISLAVA STOYANOVA

I. INTRODUCTION

THE COVID-19 CRISIS revealed the breadth of powers that European States have at their disposal. To address the crisis, a panoply of restrictive and intrusive measures was applied – restrictions of movement,[1] denial of family contacts,[2] prohibitions of assemblies[3] and gatherings,[4] imposition of medical interventions such as vaccinations,[5] closure of schools,[6] restriction

[1] *Pešić v Serbia* App no 48973/20 (communicated 5 January 2023); *Bado v Slovakia* App no 23445/21 (communicated 10 July 2023); *Terheş v Romania*, App no 49933/20 decision of 13 April 2021 (inadmissible since the restrictions did not amount to deprivation of liberty in the sense of Article 5 ECHR); *Árus v Romania* App no 39647/21, 30 May 2023 (restriction on freedom of movement due to the obligation to wear a mask in public spaces).

[2] *Michalski v Poland* App no 34180/20 (communicated 17 November 2021) (general ban on family visits introduced in the applicant's prison); *Guhn v Poland* App no 45519/20 (communicated 17 November 2021) (general ban on family visits in prison).

[3] *Szivarvany Misszio Alapitvány v Hungary* App no 32272/21 (communicated 27 Nov 2023) (blanket ban on all public assemblies); *Jambor v Hungary* App no 50723/21 (communicated 27 November 2023); *Jarocki v Poland* App no 39750/20 (communicated 17 November 2021); *Central Unitaria de Traballadores/AS v Spain* App no 49363/20 (communicated 13 October 2021); *Szivárvány Misszió Alaítvány v Hungary* App no 32272/21 (communicated 27 November 2023); *Jámbor v Hungary* App no 50723/21 (communicated 27 November 2023).

[4] *Mégard v France* App no 32647/22 (communicated 19 September 2022); *Figel v Slovakia* App no 12131/21 (communicated 12 December 2022).

[5] *Mittendorfer v Austria* App no 32467/22 (inadmissible 4 July 2023); *Thevenon v France* App no 46061/21 (decision of 13 September 2022).

[6] *M.C.K. and M.H.K.-B. v Germany* App no 26657/22 (communicated 20 December 2022); *Nemytov v Russia* App no 1257/21 (communicated 22 September 2021).

of 'harmful' speech,[7] to name some. These measures resembled nothing close to any restrictions that European societies have experienced after World War II. This makes their legal scrutiny a very important task despite the limited duration of the restrictions and despite the efforts of our societies to move forward so that energy can be redirected towards speedy recovery.

The restrictive measures imposed during the Covid-19 crisis implicate human rights law and in one way or another can be a basis for formulating applications, in the European context, to the European Court of Human Rights (ECtHR). At the time of writing, the Court has already delivered judgments and decisions related to some of the measures under the European Convention on Human Rights (ECHR); while numerous applications are still pending. In light of the pending applications that have not yet been decided or even communicated to the States and the many other cases that will be brought to the Court after the exhaustion of the relevant domestic remedies, there is still uncertainty as to how the Court will approach its role and what substantive human rights law standards it might choose to develop in relation to the Covid-19 crisis.

Yet it is still possible to understand the current approach based on the already delivered judgments and decisions and based on the questions asked by the Court in the communicated cases. Equally important is the already existing leading Grand Chamber judgment on the topic that will be specifically taken note of in the analysis below since it is likely to become a benchmark.[8] This chapter therefore takes account of the judgments, the decisions and the communicated cases since March 2020 up to March 2024, that directly relate to the measures taken during the Covid-19 crisis.[9] To assess them, the analysis is informed by the established standards in the ECtHR case law.

One caveat has to be made immediately. This concerns the distinction between cases *directly* related to the measures as opposed to cases that are only indirectly related. Given the pervasiveness of the measures the States initiated in the beginning of 2020, it can be expected that every sphere of life was affected. In this sense, many cases whose factual basis refers to circumstances arising after March 2020 are likely to include some consideration of the Covid-19 context and the related restrictive measures. My focus however lies on cases where the applicants invoke breaches of obligations, as corelated to a right enshrined in the ECHR, whose content are measures adopted by States and/or claimed

[7] *Jeremejevs v Latvia* App no 44644 (communicated 17 January 2022) (criminal proceedings for posts on social media); *Petrova v Bulgaria* App no 938/21 (communicated 26 August 2022) (the applicant called for protests against the Covid-19 restrictions on her Facebook page, as a result of which a criminal investigation was opened against her); *Avagyan v Russia* App no 36911/20 (communicated on 4 November 2020).

[8] *Communauté Genevoise D'action Syndicale (CGAS) v Switzerland* [GC] App no 21881/20, 27 November 2023.

[9] The Factsheet 'Covid-19 health crisis' was used as a starting point. After that additional searches were conducted in the HUDOC database with Covid-19 as a search word.

to be necessary for responding to the spread of the virus.[10] In this sense, the harm caused by the virus and/or the harm caused by the measures against the spread of the virus,[11] was not simply an aggravating factor in the wider factual substratum of the cases, but the sole or dominant reason for claiming breach of obligations under the ECHR.[12]

Another distinction might be relevant to the efforts to examine the case law. A group of cases can be identified where the harm is directly related to the restrictive measures during the pandemic, but the obligations invoked before the Court are procedural in nature.[13] This group can be distinguished from cases where restrictive measures justified by the States as necessary to prevent the spread of the virus, directly caused limitations of procedural rights, as protected by the Convention. In this latter sense, the harm can be framed as

[10] A case like *Khokhlov v Cyprus* App no 53114/20, 13 June 2023, where the extradition of the applicant was delayed, among other reasons because of the Covid-19 pandemic, and where the Court found a violation of Article 5(4) ECHR, will *not* fall in the category of directly related cases. See also *Feilazoo v Malta* App no. 6865/1911 (ECHR June 2021). A borderline case is perhaps *O. and R. v Slovenia* App no 19938/20, 8 February 2022, where the Court found a violation of Article 6(1) due to very lengthy foster care proceedings. In the Court's view, the restrictions necessitated by the Covid-19 crisis could have understandably had an adverse effect on the processing of the case before the domestic court. However, in the present case the State could not absolve itself, because it could have dealt with it as an urgent case. Here it seems that the Covid-19 measures were only one element causing the delay, albeit an important one. For other cases that do *not* fall within the category of directly related cases, see *Faia v Italy* App no 17222/20 (communicated 5 May 2021) and *Hafeez v the United Kingdom* App no 14198/20 (inadmissible 28 March 2023) where Covid-19 was an aggravating factor. See also *Grgičin v Croatia* App no (inadmissible 12 December 2023); *Kristić v Serbia* App no 35246/21 (ECtHR, 16 December 2021) (extradition to USA).

[11] I use the term 'harm' here in the sense of harmful effects on important interests protected by the rights enshrined in the ECHR. This is without prejudice to the determination whether this harm can be translated into a violation of any specific ECHR right and thus into state responsibility under the ECHR.

[12] Questions can be also raised as to the distinction between sole reason and dominant reason. Examples of cases that fall within the first category are *Ait Oufella v France* App no 51860/20; *E.B. v Serbia* App no 50086/20 (communicated 5 November 2021) and *A.A. v Serbia* App no 50898/20 (communicated 5 November 2021) where the applicants' deprivation of liberty or extension of deprivation of liberty was a direct result of the Covid-19 emergency situation.

[13] An example to this effect is *Piro Planet D.O.D. v Slovenia* App no 34568/22 (communicated 22 May 2023), where the applicant company complained about a ban on selling pyrotechnics, which had been introduced and then prolonged by the Governmental Decrees Concerning COVID-19 Prevention. As a result of the ban, the company suffered a significant decrease in its annual sales revenue. In addition to the right to property, Article 6(1) ECHR was invoked since, as the applicant argued, the Constitutional Court arbitrary rejected its petition for constitutionality review. See also *Galatasaray Sportif Sinau ve Ticari Yatirimlar A.Ş. v Turkey* App no 59957/21 (communicated 21 November 2023), where the harm was the fine imposed on the applicant company (a football club) because it did not observe the Covid-19 measures (admission of more spectators than allowed and violation of mask rules). In this sense, the harm was directly related to the Covid-19 restrictive measures. The obligations arguably breached were procedural (Article 6 ECHR) since the company's claim to challenge the fine was dismissed at the domestic level. See also *Scheffer v Slovakia* App no 16627/21 (communicated 24 January 2023), where the right to property alone and in conjunction with Article 13 (the right to effective remedy) was invoked. See also *Panta Rhesi S.R.O. v Slovakia* App no 38283/21 (communicated 15 May 2023); *Lyžiarsky Klub Baba-Pezinko v Slovakia* App no 34483/21 (communicated 30 May 2023); *Denim Retail S.R.O. v Slovakia* App no 21846/21 (communicated 10 July 2023).

procedural.[14] To the extent that it is possible to isolate them, procedural harm and procedural obligations will not be at the core of this chapter. Undeniably, making all these distinctions between different forms of harm and different obligations might be difficult. It is still, however, useful to make them.

To understand the ECtHR's approach to the Covid-19 measures, this chapter will be structured as follows. Section II will explain that generally the cases expose tensions between important interests, which are not easy to resolve to start with. Such tensions indeed permeate human rights law and, in this sense, there is nothing extraordinary in facing them and trying to address them.[15] Yet there seems to be at least two interrelated distinguishing features. First, a claim is made in the cases that they reveal not simply a tension between general interests and individual interests as enshrined in the ECHR. Rather, there are also tensions (even possible conflicts) between obligations held by States.[16] The second distinguishing feature concerns the invocation of crisis and emergency, which has an impact on how these tensions might be resolved.[17] Having generally explained the complexities that the cases manifest, Section III shows that currently the Court's approach is one of avoidance; namely, the Court evades engagement with the tensions on their merits by declaring the cases inadmissible. In this way, the Court avoids engaging with the difficulties of balancing the competing interests for resolving any tensions. Section IV shows that even if the Court proceeds with reasoning on the merits, it avoids directly assessing whether the balance struck at the national level was 'fair' by invoking a wide margin of appreciation. Section V discusses three factors (severity of the interference; counterbalancing measures; and the temporality of the restrictive measures) that although linked with the margin of appreciation, can be identified in the Court's

[14] An example to this effect is *Kucera v Austria* App no 13810/22 (communicated 14 June 2023), where the applicant claimed a violation of Article 6 ECHR since the domestic court based on the rules for the prevention of the spread of Covid-19, decided to hold an oral hearing in a criminal case via video conference. See also *Pratesi v Italy* App no 28342/21 (communicated 3 April 2023).

[15] L Zucca, *Constitutional Dilemmas* (Oxford University Press, 2007); S Smet, 'Conflicts of Rights in Theoretical and Comparative Perspective' in S Smet and E Brems (eds), *When Human Rights Clash at the European Court of Human Rights* (Oxford University Press, 2017) 1; S Besson, *The Morality of Conflict* (Hart Publishing, 2005) 432; E Brems (ed), *Conflicts between Fundamental Rights* (Intersentia, 2008); V Stoyanova, *Positive Obligations under the European Convention on Human Rights: Within and Beyond Boundaries* (Oxford University Press, 2023).

[16] On the distinction between conflicts and tensions, see J Bomhoff and L Zucca, 'The Tragedy of Ms Evans: Conflicts and Incommensurability of Rights' (2006) 2 *European Constitutional Law Review* 424. V Stoyanova, *Positive Obligations under the European Convention on Human Rights* (Oxford University Press, 2025) 95.

[17] For literature on addressing the tensions in the context of the Covid-19, see K Meßerschmidt, 'COVID-19 Legislation in the Light of the Precautionary Principle' (2020) 8 *Theory and Practice of Legislation* (2020) 267, 287–90; K Lachmayer, 'Democracy, Death and Dying: The Potential and Limits of Legal Rationalisation' in MC Kettemann and K Lachmayer (eds), *Pandemocracy in Europe. Power, Parliaments and People in Times of COVID-19* (Hart Publishing, 2022) 47, 52; P Dąbrowska-Kłosińska, 'The Protection of Human Rights in Pandemics – Reflections on the Past, Present, and Future' (2021) 22 *German Law Journal* (2021) 1028, 1036–37; L Vyhnánek et al, 'The Dynamics of Proportionality: Constitutional Courts and the Review of COVID-19 Regulations' (2024) *German Law Journal* 1.

reasoning on the merits as having an important role in assessing the fairness of the balance struck at national level between competing interests. I will explain that the way these three factors are utilised in the Court's reasoning is problematic since they ultimately undermine the 'fair balance' test as a tool for human rights law reasoning. In this sense, not only does the Court avoid the 'balance' by declaring applications inadmissible (see Section III) and the question about the fairness of the balance struck at national level (see Section IV), but it might also undermine the idea of 'fair balance'. The final section concludes by offering reflections about the implications from the Court's avoidance strategy.

II. TYPICAL TENSIONS AND EXTRAORDINARY CRISES

An overview of the judgments, decisions and pending applications reveals a relatively specific context where applicants invoke the responsibility of States under the ECHR, on competing grounds. In some cases, the applicants argue that the States did not do enough; these are cases where States' positive obligations can be invoked.[18] There is a second group of cases, where the applicants argue that States did too much since the measures were disproportionately intrusive and restrictive; these are the cases where applicants invoke breaches of States' negative obligations under the ECHR.[19] Currently, the second group of cases dominate in terms of the nature of the claims in decisions already issued by the Court and in applications communicated to the respondent States. This means that currently applicants predominantly claim that the measures meant to respond to the Covid-19 crisis were too restrictive and intrusive and thus in violation of States' negative human rights law obligations.

At the time of writing, no violation has been found in the first group of cases. This implies that the Court has not made a pronouncement that a State has failed to fulfil its positive obligations under the ECHR by not sufficiently protecting the lives and physical integrity of persons within its jurisdiction. As to the second group, no

[18] *Le Mailloux v France*, decision 5 November 2020 (inadmissible); *Fenech v Malta* App no 19090/20, 1 March 2022; *Ünsal and Timtik v Turkey* App no 36331/20 (decision of 8 June 2021) (inadmissible since the application is manifestly ill-founded); *Riela v Italy* App no 17378/20, 9 November 2023, para 21; *Maratsis and Others v Greece* App no 30335/20 (communicated 25 February 2021); *Vasilakis and Others v Greece* App no 30379/20 (communicated 25 February 2021); *Vlamis and Others v Greece* App no 29655/20 (committed 16 April 2021), where detainees complain that they were not sufficiently protected during the Covid-19 crisis.

[19] In some context such as prison, where the applicants are under the complete control of the authorities, it might be difficult to make the distinction between positive and negative obligations. See, for example, *Gözütok v Turkey* App no 41412/21 (communicated 20 June 2023). On this distinction, see V Stoyanova, 'Framing Positive Obligations under the ECHR: Mediating between the Abstract and the Concrete' (2023) 23(3) *Human Rights Law Review* 1; J Vorland Wibye, 'Beyond Acts and Omissions – Distinguishing Positive and Negative Duties at the European Court of Human Rights' (2022) *Human Rights Review*; M Klatt, 'Positive Obligations under the European Convention on Human Rights' (2011) *Heidelberg Journal of International Law* 691, 694.

violation has been found either.[20] In *Communauté Genevoise D'action Syndicale (CGAS) v Switzerland*, the Chamber did find a violation of Article 11 (freedom of peaceful assembly);[21] however, this was reversed by the Grand Chamber for reasons that will be explained below. Such a reversal is an important signal from the Court to the effect that it is not willing to review whether and to what extent the restrictive measures were proportionate and thus 'fair'.[22]

In relation to the second group of cases, it is relevant to observe that while the applicants invoke negative obligations as a basis for the alleged breaches, States invoke not only legitimate general interests to limit rights (ie, public health), but also their positive human rights law obligations. This implies that positive obligations are utilised by States to justify the restrictive measures. These utilisations are not rejected by the Court.[23] All of this means that although, as mentioned above, no breach of a positive obligation has yet been found in a concrete case concerning a concrete applicant, the Court has accepted at a very general and abstract level that States had the unspecified positive human rights obligation to, for example, protect life and health under the ECHR during the Covid-19 crisis. Protection of life and health therefore was not 'one possible option available to the States; it is rather an obligation, imposed on them by the Convention.'[24] In *Fenech v Malta*, for example, the Court went to great lengths to outline the positive obligation upon States 'to put in place effective methods of prevention and detection of contagious diseases in prisons'.[25] All of this foregrounds an understanding that there are tensions or even outright conflicts between competing obligations (i.e. the general *unspecified* positive obligation to protect life and health versus the negative obligation upon the State not to take *concrete* measures that are possibly disproportionately intrusive and restrictive in relation to the *specific* applicant).[26]

[20] With the important clarification that it depends how narrowly this group of cases is delimited. In *O and R v Slovenia* App no 19938/20, 8 February 2022, the Court did find a violation of Article 6(1) due to very lengthy foster care proceedings. In *Narbutas v Lithuania* App no 14139/21, 19 December 2023, the Court did find a violation of Article 8 since the information issued by the authorities during the criminal investigation against the applicant, while contributing to a public debate about the purchase of Covid-19 tests, was overall not justifiable. However, in my classification these cases are not directly related.

[21] *Communauté Genevoise D'action Syndicale (CGAS) v Switzerland* App no 21881/20, 15 March 2022.

[22] On proportionality in the context of the ECHR generally, see J Gerards, *General Principles of the European Convention on Human Rights* (Cambridge University Press, 2023) 349.

[23] *Communauté Genevoise D'action Syndicale (CGAS) v Switzerland* App no 21881/20, 15 March 2022, para 84; *Spînu v Romania* App no 29443/20 (11 October 2022) para 63. Such invocations of positive obligations can be traced back to *Vavřička and Others v the Czech Republic* [GC] App no 47621/13, 8 April 2021, para 282. V Stoyanova, 'Positive Obligations as Coercive 'Rights' and Compulsory Vaccination under the European Convention on Human Rights', *International Journal of Constitutional Law* (forthcoming).

[24] Concurring Opinion of Judge Krec, para 4 in *Communauté Genevoise D'action Syndicale (CGAS) v Switzerland* App no 21881/20, 15 March 2022. V Stoyanova, 'Positive Obligations as Coercive 'Rights' and Compulsory Vaccination under the European Convention on Human Rights', *International Journal of Constitutional Law* (forthcoming).

[25] *Fenech v Malta* App no 19090/20, 1 March 2022, paras 127–129. See also *Spînu v Romania*, App no 29443/20, 11 October 2022.

[26] See S Besson, *The Morality of Conflict* (Hart Publishing, 2005) which explains that for there to be an actual tension, the two obligations would have to be framed at the same level of specificity.

While the general interests (ie, protection of public health) that might justify restrictions were undoubtedly legitimate, questions can be raised about the suitability and the necessity of the restrictive measures for actually achieving these general interests.[27] Similar causation questions can be asked about the appropriateness of invoking positive human rights obligations where the object of protection (ie, an individual) was unspecified and unknown. These are challenging questions to address in human rights law, which has more generally justified the Court's deferential approach in applying the tests of suitability and necessity that are relevant for assessing breaches of negative obligations.[28]

As to the invocation of positive obligations, not only are they circumscribed by the test of reasonableness,[29] but if they were to be applied in a specific case, additional factors would circumscribe their content and scope. For example, in *Fenech v Malta* the Court correctly observed that:[30]

> without diminishing the seriousness of this sometimes deadly virus [Covid-19], the Court cannot consider that individuals are a victim of an alleged violation of Article 2 without substantiating that in their own circumstances the acts or omissions of the State have or could have put their life at *real and imminent risk*.

The reality and the imminence of the risk for those who arguably had to be protected, is an important consideration in determining the content and the scope of positive obligations and determining their breach.[31]

The challenges how to apply these tests and who is better placed to apply them seem to be exacerbated at times of crisis and emergencies (actual or perceived),[32] which might justify even more deference from the Court. The following pronouncements by the Court are suggestive in this respect. In

See also V Stoyanova, *Positive Obligations under the European Convention on Human Rights* (Oxford University Press, 2025) 95.

[27] Admittedly, the Court does not generally question the suitability of restrictive measures that might be in breach of negative obligations. B Çali, 'Proving Bad Faith in International Law: Lessons from the Article 18 Case law of the European Court of Human Rights' in G Kajtar, B Çali and M Milanovic (eds), *Secondary Rules of Primary Importance in International Law* (Oxford University Press, 2022). On causation in the context of positive obligations, see V Stoyanova, 'Causation: Why and How for Establishing Breach of Positive Obligations under the European Convention on Human Rights?' in V Stoyanova and D McGrogan (eds), *The Limits of Positive Obligations in Human Rights Law. From Protection to Coercion* (Hart Publishing, forthcoming); V Stoyanova, 'Causation and Breach of Positive Obligations under the ECHR: Correcting the Past, Preventing the Future' in V Stoyanova and M Andenas (eds.), *The Role of the Causal Inquiry under the European Convention on Human Rights* (Cambridge University Press, forthcoming).

[28] E Brems and L Lavrysen, '"Don't Use a Sledgehammer to Crack a Nut": Less Restrictive Means in the Case Law of the European Court of Human Rights' (2015) 15 *Human Rights Law Review* 139.

[29] Stoyanova (n 15). See also I Plakokefalos, 'The Standard of (Un)Reasonableness in Human Rights Positive Obligations' in V Stoyanova and D McGrogan (eds) *The Limits of Positive Obligations in Human Rights Law. From Protection to Coercion* (Hart Publishing, forthcoming).

[30] *Fenech v Malta* App no 19090/20, 1 March 2022, para 104 (emphasis added).

[31] Stoyanova (n 15).

[32] VP Tzevelekos and K Dzehtsiarou, 'Normal as Usual? Human Rights in Times of COVID-19' (2020) 1(2) *European Convention on Human Rights Law Review* 141, 143.

particular, the ECtHR has characterised the specific context of the Covid-19 pandemic as a 'public health emergency.'[33] It has also added that:[34]

> the Covid-19 pandemic is liable to have very serious consequences not just for health, but also for society, the economy, the functioning of the State and life in general, and that the situation should therefore be characterised as an 'exceptional and unforeseeable context'.

The Court has also accepted that 'the authorities were confronted with a novel situation such as a global pandemic – unprecedented in recent decades – as a result of a new strain of coronavirus (called Covid-19) to which they had to react in a timely manner.'[35] In *Bah v the Netherlands*, 'the difficult and unforeseen practical problems with which the State was confronted during the first weeks of the Covid-19 pandemic' had a key role for the Court to conclude that it was not incompatible with Article 5(4) to assess the applicant's detention order without securing his attendance at the hearing in person or by videoconference.[36] The Court has also referred to the 'exceptional circumstances of the Covid-19'.[37]

Admittedly, the deference that the Court has shown so far can be perceived as part of a wider phenomenon: namely the Court's expression of respect for the principle of subsidiarity,[38] which precedes the Covid-19 pandemic and the pandemic-related case law. Yet the above-quoted pronouncements are indicative of even stronger deference. The rejection of many applications as inadmissible supports this indication.

III. AVOIDING THE 'BALANCE'

Most of the current cases are declared inadmissible due to the absence of victim status and/or non-exhaustion of domestic remedies. This section will explain these two grounds.

A. No Actio Popularis

As to the first ground related to the requirement for victim status, the Court has been consistent in saying that it is not its role 'to examine *in abstracto*

[33] *Fenech v Malta* (n 30) para 96.
[34] ibid; *Terheş v Romania* App no 49933/20 (decision 13 April 2021).
[35] *Fenech v Malta* (n 30) para 129.
[36] *Bah v the Netherlands* App no 35751/20 (inadmissible decision 22 June 2021) para 41.
[37] *Perstner v Luxembourg* App no 7446/21, 16 February 2023, para 48.
[38] L Glas, 'The Age of Subsidiarity? The ECtHR's Approach to the Admissibility Requirement that Applicants Raise Their Convention Complaint before Domestic Court' (2023) 41(2) *Netherlands Quarterly of Human Rights* 75, 82.

the compatibility of national legislative or constitutional provisions with the requirements of the Convention.'[39] This relates to the Court's primary objective to provide individual rather than constitutional justice,[40] which is also reflected in the admissibility requirement that the applicant must be a victim of an alleged violation.[41] The latter means that he or she has to be specifically affected. The starting point is therefore that the Court cannot perform a purely abstract review. This expresses the idea that human rights justice is individual-centred. Human rights justice is therefore placed 'not in the abstraction of general situations which law-makers have regard for, but in the concreteness of particular cases, irreducible in their singularity.'[42] In this sense, the Court does not directly review national regulatory frameworks.[43] It can only do so indirectly once these frameworks have affected a concrete individual, who in the proceedings before the Court has standing as a victim.[44] In this respect, the Court has established that:[45]

> In order to claim to be a victim of a violation, a person must be directly affected by the impugned measure: the Convention does not envisage the bringing of an *actio popularis* for the interpretation of the rights it contains or permit individuals to complain about a provision of national law simply because they consider, without having been directly affected by it, that it may contravene the Convention.

It has also clarified that 'in order for applicants to be able to claim victim status, they must produce reasonable and convincing evidence of the likelihood that a violation affecting them personally will occur; mere suspicion or conjecture is insufficient in this respect.'[46]

The requirement for victim status has been applied with some flexibility. An applicant can still be found to fulfil it even 'in the absence of an individual measure of implementation'. In this case, however, the applicant needs to demonstrate that he or she is 'required either to adjust his conduct or risks being prosecuted *or* if he is a member of a class of people who risk being *directly* affected by the

[39] *McCann and Others v The United Kingdom* [GC] App no 18984/91, 27 September 1995 para 153; *Marckx v Belgium* App no 6833/74, 13 June 1979 para 27. For further references, see Partly Concurring, Partly Dissenting Opinion of Judge Pinto de Albuquerque in *Vallianatos and Others v Greece* [GC] App no 29381/08 and 32684/09, 7 November 2013.

[40] On the interplay between these objectives see S Greer, 'Constitutionalizing Adjudication under the European Convention on Human Rights' (2003) 23 *Oxford Journal of Legal Studies* 405.

[41] Article 34 ECHR.

[42] F Tulkens and S Van Drooghenbroeck, 'La Cour de cassation et la Cour européenne des droits de l'homme. Les voies de la banalisation' in *Imperat Lex. Liber Amicorum Pierre Marchal* (Larcier, 2003) 133, cited in F Tulkens, 'Different Standards of Judicial Review. The Nature and Object of the Judgment of the European Court of Human Rights' (2011) 4 *Constitutional Law Review* 31.

[43] Stoyanova (n 15).

[44] J Gerards, 'Abstract and Concrete Reasonableness Review by the European Court of Human Rights' (2020) 1 *European Convention on Human Rights Law Review* 2018, 226.

[45] *Tănase v Moldova* [GC] App no 7/08, 27 April 2010 para 104.

[46] *Zambrano v France* (dec) App no 41994/21, 21 September 2021, para 42; *Le Mailloux v France* (dec) [Committee], App no 18108/20, 5 November 2020, para 11; *Communauté Genevoise D'action Syndicale (CGAS) v Switzerland* [GC] App no 21881/20, 27 November 2023, paras 105–106.

legislation.'[47] It follows that in these two situations an applicant can be a potential victim and his or her application to the Court still accepted as admissible.

However, a direct link needs to be established between the general measures that the applicant complains of, and any potential harm suffered by the specific applicant. The Chamber in *CGAS v Switzerland* concluded that there was such a direct link since the applicant association refrained from organising public meetings to avoid the criminal penalties provided for in Ordinance COVID-19 no. 2. The latter imposed a ban on public events and was amended to the effect that the possibility for exemptions from the ban was removed.[48]

The Grand Chamber disagreed on this point since, according to the ordinance, only individual members could have been criminally sanctioned; any criminal responsibility of the association as such could not be engaged.[49] The Grand Chamber also added that 'there is nothing to suggest that the mere fact of taking administrative steps to organise public events would have amounted to conduct that was likely to be sanctioned.'[50] The Chamber and the Grand Chamber therefore approached the potential victim standard in very different ways. The Chamber's approach was relatively abstract and flexible, with focus on the consequences of the ban (against organising public meetings). In contrast, the Grand Chamber focused on the specific technicalities (i.e., no criminal sanctions on the association as such and no criminal sanctions for taking administrative steps to organise an event as such). Such a formalistic and technical approach allowed the Grand Chamber to ignore the overall context and the consequences (eg, limiting political expression in a democratic society).[51]

In the other inadmissibility decisions issued so far, there was no need to even offer much justification with reference to technicalities. The fact that the restrictive measures were imposed on the entire population as a response to the virus has therefore been a major obstacle to engaging with the cases on their merits.[52]

[47] See generally *Burden v the United Kingdom* [GC] App no 13378/05, paras 33–34; *Communauté Genevoise D'action Syndicale (CGAS) v Switzerland* [GC] App no 21881/20, 27 November 2023, para 115.

[48] *Communauté Genevoise D'action Syndicale (CGAS) v Switzerland* [GC] paras 118–20.

[49] ibid para 112.

[50] ibid para 124.

[51] It can be argued that it is excessively formalistic to say that since the association was not criminally liable, there was no risk of sanctions. Criminal sanctions could have been imposed on the association's representatives and persons participating in the events organised by it. This can be contrasted with the liberal approach to the standing of organisation in the area of climate change, see B Mayer, 'Is Climate Change Mitigation within the Scope of Positive Human Rights Obligations?' in V Stoyanova and D McGrogan (eds), *The Limits of Positive Obligations in Human Rights Law. From Protection to Coercion* (Hart Publishing, forthcoming).

[52] It can be expected that the requirement for a link between the harm alleged by a specific applicant and any omissions by the State would be even more difficult to establish in cases where applicants claim breaches of positive obligations under the ECHR. This difficulty relates to the nature of omissions as a basis for state responsibility. See Stoyanova (n 19). See *Le Mailloux v France* App no 18108/20 (decision of 5 November 2020); *Fenech v Malta*, paras 104 and 107.

Tomáš Lörinc and Others v Slovakia,[53] *Dalibor Magdić v Croatia*,[54] *Piperea v Romania*,[55] *Mittendorfer v Austria*[56] and *Pernechele and Others v Italy*[57] were declared inadmissible since the applicants generally complained about the restrictive measures without being able to show they were harmed in any specific way *different from everybody else*. For example, in the inadmissibility decision in *Dalibor Magdić v Croatia*, the Court reasoned that:[58]

> the applicant complained that the measures in question had breached his freedom of religion but failed to indicate to which religious community he belongs. Likewise, while complaining about the breach of his freedom of assembly, he failed to specify which public gatherings he could not attend because of the measures in question. Similarly, he complained of the breach of his freedom of movement without mentioning where and when he intended to travel but could not because of the impugned measures.

The complete absence of any such individual particulars makes it impossible for the Court to conduct an individual assessment of the applicant's situation. It thus appears that the applicant wishes to complain about the impugned measures in a general manner, contemplating that, as a result of their adoption, his freedoms were automatically violated.[59]

The reasoning was similar in *Pernechele and Others v Italy*, which concerned a complaint by Italian lawyers regarding the requirement for a Covid certificate so that they could access courts and detention centres. They argued that this requirement was in violation of Article 8 ECHR. To declare it inadmissible, the Court observed that:[60]

> the applicants did not submit any information about their situation except for their identity and occupation. They provided no data to show how exactly the impugned measures had affected, or would have been likely to have affected them directly or to target them because of their possible individual characteristics. In particular, the applicants did not indicate whether there had been scheduled hearings that they should have attended during the relevant period or whether they had needed to meet with detained clients in person. Similarly, they did not indicate whether alternative means of participation in hearings or of contact with detainees had been available, for example through videoconferences, telephones calls or in writing. Lastly, five of the six applicants had not attained the age of 50 at the time the application was lodged with the Court. Thus, the vaccination requirement did not apply to them.

In *Mittendorfer v Austria* the applicant also tried to challenge the vaccination mandates. The Court held that 'he has not substantiated in any form how

[53] *Tomáš Lörinc and Others v Slovakia* App no 27877/21, 5 April 2022 (inadmissible).
[54] *Dalibor Magdić v Croatia* App no 17578/20, 5 July 2022, paras 10–12.
[55] *Piperea v Romania* App no 24183/21 inadmissible 5 July 2022.
[56] *Mittendorfer v Austria* (inadmissible 4 July 2023).
[57] *Pernechele and Others v Italy* App no 7222/22 (inadmissible 31 October 2023).
[58] *Dalibor Magdić v Croatia* App no 17578/20, 5 July 2022, paras 10–12.
[59] ibid.
[60] *Pernechele and Others v Italy* App no 7222/22 (31 October 2023) para 13.

the Vaccination Act affected him personally.'[61] An interesting aspect in the reasoning here was the usage of the timeframe of the challenged measures and, more specifically, their temporary nature. In particular, the Court observed that:[62]

> the applicant was neither at risk of being affected by the Vaccination Act when he lodged his application with the Court, given that it had already been suspended by that stage, nor that he will face such a risk in the future, given that the Act has since been repealed.

In light of this reasoning, the mandates as introduced in Austria under the Vaccination Act can barely be challenged by anybody for their compatibility with the ECHR. Given the suspension and the repeal of the mandates, hardly anybody can therefore fulfil the victim requirement. Yet such mandates in themselves constitute an infringement on private life and bodily integrity,[63] whose proportionality should be tested.

Oleg Yuriyovych Makovetskyy v Ukraine is distinct from the previously mentioned cases in that the applicant was actually individually affected in a specific way since he refused to comply with the restrictive measures, as a result of which he was sanctioned.[64] The case concerned the question of whether the administrative-offence proceedings regarding the refusal by the applicant to wear a face mask (part of the measures to control the spread of the virus) were in breach of the applicant's rights under Articles 6 and 7 of the Convention. The intrusive measure itself (ie, the requirement to wear a mask) was therefore not at the heart of the case; rather, the procedural question regarding the fairness of the national proceedings was at the core of the case. In declaring the application inadmissible, the Court first noted the very low amount of the fine imposed on the applicant (4.90 euros at the time). Then it added that:[65]

> the applicant, who was present at the first-instance court hearing, essentially argued that the imposition of pandemic-control measures, including the requirement to wear a face mask and the consequent actions of the police in fining him, had been unlawful. The domestic courts duly examined the applicant's arguments, established that he had committed an administrative offence punishable under the legislation in force and found against him. Accordingly there is no indication that the applicant was prevented in any way from making his case or that the findings of the domestic courts were arbitrary or manifestly unreasonable.

As to Article 7, given the negligible sum of 4.90 euros, it was found that 'the proceedings in question did not involve the determination of a "criminal

[61] *Mittendorfer v Austria* App no 32467/22 (inadmissible 4 July 2023).

[62] ibid.

[63] *Vavřička and Others v the Czech Republic* [GC] App no 47621/13, 8 April 2021, where Article 8 was found breached, but not violated. For a detailed analysis of this case, see V Stoyanova, 'Positive Obligations as Coercive 'Rights' and Compulsory Vaccination under the European Convention on Human Rights', *International Journal of Constitutional Law* (forthcoming).

[64] *Oleg Yuriyovych Makovetskyy v Ukraine*, App no 50824/21, 19 May 2022.

[65] ibid paras 7–8.

charge" within the meaning of Article 6 of the Convention and that this provision accordingly did not apply to those proceedings under its criminal limb.' Article 7 of the Convention therefore could not be regarded as applicable either.[66] A case like *Makovetskyy v Ukraine* therefore indicates that even if the applicants try to invoke procedural harm and procedural obligations, they face serious difficulties.

B. Strict Approach to the Requirement for Exhaustion of Domestic Remedies

Applications have also been declared inadmissible on the basis of the applicants' failure to exhaust domestic remedies. The cases demonstrate the obstacles that applicants encounter when trying to initiate administrative or constitutional proceedings for review of the harms caused by the general restrictive measures adopted by States in respond to Covid-19.[67] In addition, there is an uncertainty as to the availability and effectiveness of domestic remedies for reviewing specifically the various issues raised by the novel and unprecedented situation created with the Covid-19 measures.[68] Relatedly, these difficulties and uncertainties pose challenges as to how flexibly the Court should apply the requirement for exhaustion of domestic remedies. These challenges are further complicated in light of the importance of the principle of subsidiarity.

Similarly to the victim status requirement, the Court has developed certain standards as to the application of the rule for exhaustion of domestic remedies and has noted that 'some degree of flexibility' and no 'excessive formalism' are necessary.[69] Yet, this flexibility has its limits since 'mere doubts as to the effectiveness of a remedy are not a valid reason for an applicant's failure to use it.'[70] In *CGAS v Switzerland* the Grand Chamber reaffirmed that '[t]he existence of mere doubts as to the prospects of success of a particular remedy which is

[66] ibid paras 11–12.

[67] See generally A Vedaschi and C Graziani, 'New Dynamics of the "Post-COVID-19 Era": A Legal Conundrum' (2023) *German Law Journal* 1, 31.

[68] See, eg, *Rus v Romania* App no 2621/21, 9 May 2023 (inadmissible). The core of the applicant's complaint lay in the coronavirus infection he contracted in prison. The Court reasoned by analogy: 'The Government base their plea of non-exhaustion on the fact that a tort action may be brought to determine the medical circumstances and conditions of an infection with the SARS CoV 2 coronavirus, and that some proceedings of this kind are pending before the domestic courts, although no final decision appears to have been handed down in any such proceedings up to the date of the Government's observations.' In declaring the application inadmissible, the Court reasoned that it 'has already held that an action in tort based on ordinary law is an effective remedy for raising grievances arising from a tuberculosis bacillus infection contracted in prison.'

[69] *Communauté Genevoise D'action Syndicale (CGAS) v Switzerland* [GC] App no 21881/20, 27 November 2023, paras 118–20.

[70] *Epözdemir and Beştaş Epözdemir v Turkey* App nos 49425/10 and 51124/10 (decision 22 October 2019); *Milosevic v the Netherlands* App no 77631 (decision 19 March 2002); *Pellegriti v Italy* App no 77363/01 (decision 26 May 2005); *MPP Golub v Ukraine* App no 6778/05, (decision 18 October 2005); *Vučković and Others v Serbia* (preliminary objection) [GC], App no 17153/1, 25 March 2014, paras 74 and 84.

not obviously futile is not a valid reason for failing to exhaust the avenue of redress.'[71] Flexibility could strike against the principle of subsidiarity, leading the Court to show preference in favour of more formalism (focus on technicalities), which facilitates the finding that the application is inadmissible. The public health context and the crisis context have definitely added important nuances as to the scope of flexibility the Court is willing to allow. In *CGAS v Switzerland*, after drawing attention to its 'fundamentally subsidiary role', the Grand Chamber invoked precisely these two contexts in support of its formalistic approach.

As to the public health context, in *CGAS v Switzerland* the Grand Chamber underscored that this context raises the 'complex and sensitive question of the balance to be struck between the various interests at stake for the purpose of verifying the necessity and proportionality of a given restrictive measure'.[72] It added that:[73]

> health care policy matters come within the margin of appreciation of the national authorities, who are best placed to assess priorities, use of resources and social needs. In this field, the Court has already had occasion to state that the margin of appreciation afforded to the States must be a *wide* one.

This makes it 'essential that any balancing has been done beforehand by the domestic courts.'[74]

As to the Covid-19 crisis, the GC in *CGAS v Switzerland* held that it was 'unprecedented and highly sensitive' and of 'exceptional nature.' Therefore, 'it was *all the more important* that the national authorities were first given the opportunity to strike a balance between competing private and public interests or between different rights protected by the Convention.'[75]

These two considerations (ie, the public health context and the context of a crisis) therefore justified a more rigid and formalistic approach to the requirement for the exhaustion of domestic remedies. When applied to the specific applicant in *CGAS v Switzerland*, this rigidity and formalism meant that the applicant was expected to use a remedy when nobody ever was granted an exemption from the ban on public assembly and a request for an exemption had already been dismissed in another case.

Similar formalisms characterised the reasoning in the inadmissibility decision in *Mittendorfer v Austria*, a case where the applicant tried to challenge the vaccination mandates.[76] The implication from declaring the application

[71] *Communauté Genevoise D'action Syndicale (CGAS) v Switzerland* [GC] para 159.
[72] ibid para 161.
[73] ibid para 160 with references to *Hristozov and Others v Bulgaria* App no 47039/11 and 358/12, paras 119 and 124, and *Vavricka* paras 274 and 280.
[74] *Zambrano v France* (dec) para 26; *Communauté Genevoise D'action Syndicale (CGAS) v Switzerland* [GC] para 161.
[75] *Communauté Genevoise D'action Syndicale (CGAS) v Switzerland* [GC] para 163.
[76] *Mittendorfer v Austria* App no 32467/22 (inadmissible 4 July 2023).

inadmissible was that the applicant was expected (as any other future applicant who might try to challenge the Austrian Vaccination Act) to seek domestic remedies despite the existence of a judgment by the Federal Constitutional Court from 23 June 2022 that the Vaccination Act was constitutional and did not violate human rights.[77] The approach in *Thevenon v France* was very similar.[78] This case concerned the question of whether the imposition of a compulsory vaccination on account of the applicant's occupation as a professional firefighter breached his rights under Articles 8 and 14. He was suspended from his job since he refused to take the Covid-19 vaccine. The case was dismissed by the ECtHR as inadmissible since the applicant was expected to have resort to the following domestic remedy: the initiation of a procedure to challenge the suspension order issued by his employer before the French administrative courts. Such an expectation was raised despite the decision of the advisory section of the Conseil d'Etat (the highest administrative court) where the latter had already found that – from a general standpoint – Law No. 2021-1040 was compatible with the French Constitution and the Convention. Yet, the ECtHR demanded that that the applicant should have filed an individual petition to obtain a specific decision on his case.[79]

There are other pending cases, where the restrictive measures have generally been declared constitutional by the domestic courts, and the Court would have to decide whether the particular applicant would still have to seek domestic proceedings to *concretely* challenge the measures in his or her *specific* case.[80] Given the current approach by the Court in *CGAS v Switzerland*, the applicants face an uphill battle.

IV. AVOIDING THE 'FAIR'

Despite the relatively formalist approach taken so far to the admissibility requirements (i.e., victim status and exhaustion of domestic remedies), which

[77] ibid para 33.

[78] *Thevenon v France* App no 46061/21 (decision of 13 September 2022); *Zambrano v France* App no 41994/21 (decision of 7 October 2021).

[79] See also the pending *Pasquinelli and Others v San Marino* App no 24622/22 communicated on 12 December 2022, where by means of judgment no 11 of 2 November 2021, the national Constitutional Court confirmed the legitimacy of the law requiring health care workers to get vaccinated and its compatibility with the San Marino Constitution, the Convention, and other instruments. The Court asked no questions regarding the requirement for exhaustion of domestic remedies.

[80] *Toromag S.R.O. v Slovakia*, App no 41217/20 communicated on 5 December 2020. The case concerns the closure from March to June 2020 of fitness centres, under measures taken by the Public Health Authority of Slovakia as part of the prevention of the spread of Covid-19. The applicants, owners of those centres, complain of the pecuniary damage allegedly suffered, the loss of future income and the loss of clientele. See also *Scheffer v Slovakia* App no 16627/21, communicated 24 January 2023; *Panta Rhei, S.R.O v Slovakia* App no 38283/21, communicated 15 May 2023; *Denim Retain S.R.O. v Slovakia* App no 21846/21, communicated 10 July 2023.

has allowed the Court to avoid the difficult task of balancing, there have been applications declared admissible leading to judgments on the merits, where the Court had to engage with the fairness of the balance already struck at the national level.

Spînu v Romania is one of the few judgments that can give some insights as to the Court's approach on the merits where the proportionality of the restrictive measures was reviewed.[81] It concerned the Romanian authorities' refusal to allow the applicant, a detained member of the Seventh-day Adventist Church, to go to a church in Bucharest to celebrate the Sabbath. Prior to the Covid-19 crisis, he had been allowed by the prison authorities to go to church. After establishing the legality of the restrictive measure and that it pursued a legitimate aim (the protection of public health), the Court reviewed its proportionality. Most importantly, the margin of appreciation afforded to the State was declared to be wide. In particular, the Court considered that:[82]

> the evolution of the health situation and its unpredictability must have posed a certain number of problems for the prison authorities in organizing or monitoring the activities of a religious nature of the detainees. Therefore, it is of the opinion that a *wide margin of appreciation* must be granted to them [...]

This implied more deference and no detailed scrutiny of the restrictive measures. An interesting feature here that deserves to be highlighted is the invocation of 'social solidarity' as an additional justification for the wide margin. Admittedly, it appeared for the first time in *Vavřička and Others v Czech Republic*,[83] where 'social solidarity' was used to rationalise a wide margin and thus the compatibility of an intrusive measure with human rights law. 'Social solidarity' in the specific context of the prison environment meant that the applicant had to accept limitations for the sake of common interests. As the Court clarified,[84]

> the risk of contamination outside the prison and introduction of the virus into the closed environment of this establishment must certainly have had significant weight in the decision of the prison authorities, at a time when prevention measures were focused on the prevention of contact and on isolation or quarantine, among others.

While this reasoning in the specific context of the prison environment (ie, a closed environment where the state authorities have enhanced obligations toward the prisoners), might be easier to accept, it remains to be better understood how the Court will continue to use 'social solidarity' as an argument in justification of restrictive/intrusive measures.

[81] *Spînu v Romania* App no 29443/20 (11 October 2022) para 63.
[82] ibid para 68.
[83] *Vavřička and Others v Czech Republic* [GC] App no 47621/13, 8 April 2021, para 279.
[84] *Spînu v Romania* App no 29443/20 (11 October 2022) para 68.

V. AVOIDING THE 'FAIR BALANCE'?

Despite the wide margin of appreciation that would suggest that the Court would rather steer away from directly balancing individual and general interests, in *Spînu v Romania* certain factors were invoked in the reasoning that are indicative of how 'a fair balance' might be struck.[85] Three such factors can be distinguished: (i) the severity of the interference; (ii) efforts to counterbalance the interference; and (iii) the temporality of the interference. These will be explained below since it is likely that their relevance will be lasting. Of equal importance is the problematic way these factors are utilised in the Court's reasoning since, as I will explain, they ultimately undermine the 'fair balance' test as a tool for human rights law reasoning.

A. Severity of the Interference

As to the severity, the Court noted that the restrictive measures targeted only 'one component of the exercise of his [the applicant's] right to freedom of religion'. This component 'was limited to the applicant's participation in the religious worship of his Church outside the prison.'[86] To explain the low severity of the interference, the Court added that 'religious service was suspended for certain periods at the end of 2020 and the beginning of 2021'.[87] This meant that even if the applicant was allowed to go to service outside of the prison, this would not make much of a difference.

A note of warning, however, needs to be expressed here. The argument is problematic since the consequences of one restriction (ie, suspension of the operation of churches) were used as a justification for the proportionality of another restriction (not allowing the applicant to go to church outside of prison). This is a dangerous path of reasoning because, as already mentioned in the Introduction, the restrictive measures in response to the Covid-19 crisis affected all spheres of our lives and were pervasive. Therefore, cross-referencing for assessing the proportionality of the restrictions is problematic.

B. Counterbalancing Measures

The second factor mentioned in *Spînu v Romania* concerns the State's efforts to counterbalance the interference. The Court admitted that even if alternative

[85] This is reflective of how the Court's reasoning tends to mix substantive arguments and institutional considerations related to the role of subsidiarity. See J Kratochvil, 'The Inflation of the Margin of Appreciation by the European Court of Human Rights' (2017) 29(3) *Netherlands Quarterly of Human Rights* 324.

[86] *Spînu v Romania* App no 29443/20 (11 October 2022) para 66.

[87] ibid para 67.

measures, such as online activities, could not 'fully replace direct participation in religious service', such alternatives were important since they showed that 'the national authorities have made reasonable efforts to counterbalance the restrictions decided during the pandemic.'[88]

Generally, it needs to be first emphasised that the consideration of alternatives is key for any proper proportionality review. This relates to the relevance of the less restrictive means test as part of the proportionality assessment. This test involves an assessment whether alternative less restrictive/intrusive measures could have achieved the legitimate general aim (here, public health) as pursued by the State. The test means that when States restrict rights, they should search for restrictive measures that are more protective of individual interests as enshrined in the right.[89] *Spînu v Romania*, however, reveals a reversal of the test: the question made relevant in the reasoning was whether the applicant could use alternatives that were more restrictive of his interests (ie, freedom of religion) and more protective of the general interest (public health).

Admittedly, the less restrictive means test is not consistently applied in the Court's case law.[90] In some of the communicated cases where applicants argued breach of negative obligations because of the restrictive measures during the Covid-19 crisis, the Court asked whether the national authorities had envisaged or considered any less severe measures to achieve the aim pursued;[91] in other communicated cases, such questions are not asked.[92] The application of this test is also directly linked with the scope of the margin of appreciation: the wider the margin, the less likely the Court is to search for alternative, less intrusive measures. As established by the Grand Chamber in *Vavřička and Others v the Czech Republic*,[93] in the area of healthcare policies the margin is wide. *Spînu v Romania*, however, indicates not simply a wide margin and thus no scrutiny of alternatives that are more protective of the right, but a reversal of the test.

[88] ibid para 69.

[89] Brems and Lavrysen (n 28).

[90] ibid. The GC refused to ask questions about the availability of less restrictive/intrusive means in *Vavřička and Others v Czech Republic* [GC] App no 47621/13, 8 April 2021, a refusal criticised by Judge Wojtyczek in his dissenting opinion.

[91] *Pešić v Serbia* App no 48973/20 (communicated 5 January 2023); *Bado v Slovakia* App no 23445/21 (communicated 23445/21) about restrictions of freedom of movement; *Central Unitaria de Traballadores/AS v Spain* App no 49363/20 communicated 13 October 2021 where the Court did ask 'Would less stringent measures have achieved the same or a comparable result?' See also *E.B. v Serbia* App no 50086/20 (communicated 5 November 2021) and *A.A. v Serbia* App no 50898/20 (communicated 5 November 2021).

[92] In *Szivarvany Misszio Alapitvany v Hungary* App no 32272/21 communicated 27 Nov 2023 (freedom of peaceful assembly – blanket ban on public assemblies), the Court did *not* pose a question about less restrictive means. Similarly, in *Sandor Jambor v Hungary* App no 50723/21, communicated 27 November 2023, where the applicant complained about the general prohibition on peaceful assemblies, no question was posed about whether there were any less restrictive means.

[93] *Vavřička and Others v the Czech Republic* [GC] App no 47621/13, 8 April 2021, para 274.

C. The Role of Temporality

The third factor mentioned in *Spînu v Romania* concerns the temporality of the interference, and in particular the limited duration of the restrictions and their one-off nature. The Court noted that 'the applicant's complaint relates to a one-off situation' and not to a 'continuing situation'.[94] In the Court's reasoning, the temporary nature of the limitation was linked to 'the unpredictable and unprecedented nature of the health crisis.'[95]

Indeed, a temporary restriction can imply lesser harm to the important interests protected by human rights, which is a pertinent consideration in any proportionality assessment. However, a note of warning is also due. In particular, one-off measures characterised by an unprecedented level of intrusiveness, even if temporary, can in the long term change the society's *baseline perceptions* as to what a State can acceptably do. In addition, such one-off measures might be mere *improvisations*. The qualification of the one-off measures as mere improvisations can be revealed when the measures are looked at in their totally, which allows the exposure of inconsistencies. Laudably, the Chamber in *CGAS v Switzerland* explicitly uncovered the inconsistency. In particular, there was a prohibition on public assemblies and demonstrations outdoors, whereas the physical presence of employees in offices and factories was not restricted in any way. The exposure of inconsistencies is possible when comparisons start being made between the activities that were banned and those that were not. The inclusion of such comparisons is possible only if the Court were to choose to more closely examine the measures, in this way also providing a guidance to national courts and national decision makers. At this stage of the Court's practice such guidance in absent.

VI. CONCLUSION

The objective of this chapter was to understand the ECtHR's approach to the measures taken by States during the Covid-19 crisis. The approach can be assessed as one of avoidance. Although the admissibility requirements (victim status and exhaustion of domestic remedies) are linked with the essence of the preservation of human rights,[96] these requirements are applied strictly, leading to the rejection of applications as inadmissible. More generally, these rejections (and more the requirement for the applicant to be individually and specifically affected in order to claim victim status) demonstrate the limits of human rights

[94] *Spînu v Romania* App no 29443/20 (11 October 2022), para 70.

[95] ibid. See also *Fenech v Malta*, para 130: 'This process is still ongoing, and it is in that light that the Court must not lose sight of the challenges being posed by the constant evolution of the Covid-19 pandemic.'

[96] Joint Dissenting Opinion in *Communauté Genevoise D'action Syndicale (CGAS) v Switzerland* [GC] App no 21881/20, 27 November 2023, para 2.

law to respond to structural and systemic measures. More problematically, the Court has so far refrained from developing emergency/crisis *acquis* to better guide national decision-makers in reviewing Covid-19 measures. It has avoided developing standards that can be perceived as deterrents.[97] By walking the path of avoidance, the Court risks making itself irrelevant. It has allowed States to improvise and such improvisations seem to be accepted given their temporary nature. The Court's reasoning itself also reveals aspects of very questionable improvisations. In particular, the reversal of the less intrusive means test and the cross-referencing between different restrictive measures for assessing their proportionality, were identified and described in this chapter.

[97] As Tzevelekos and Dzehtsiarou have argued, 'the "shadow" of the Court should always be in the mind of national decision-makers and judges.' VP Tzevelekos and K Dzehtsiarou, 'Normal as Usual? Human Rights in Times of covid-19' (2020) 1 *European Human Rights Law Review* 141, 144.

Index

Aarhus Convention 194–5, 200, 203, 233, 236
Abbot, Carolyn 194
absolutist approach/accommodations model of constitutionality 8, 84–5, 96–7
access to justice 13, 194–5, 233–7
accountability 9, 23, 43, 195
  Canada's Emergencies Act 101–2, 105–6, 116, 118
  climate emergency 193, 195
  Denmark, crisis rhetoric during Covid-19 pandemic in 7, 23–4, 26, 29–32
  executive 105, 106, 266
  Finland, parliamentary oversight of Covid-19 measures in 13, 266
  general emergency clause, proposal for a 67
  legal accountability 24, 29, 31, 117
  political accountability 29, 31, 117
  proportionality 43
  public participation 193, 195
Ackerman, Burke 14–15
actio popularis 287, 288–93
ad hoc instruments 123, 126, 127–31, 134, 138–40, 144, 146–7
advance preparation *see* preparation
ageing population crisis 156
Alexy, Robert 44, 47
Anderson, Ben 187–8
anticipatory action *see* preparation
Association Agreements 150, 152–4
asylum seekers *see* migration crises
authorisation of measures
  Canada's Emergencies Act 102, 105, 109, 113–16
  Covid-19 pandemic 265–74
  executive 3–4, 102, 265–74
  Finland, parliamentary oversight of Covid-19 measures in 265–74
  judiciary 58
  migration crises 135, 168
  parliaments 58, 105, 265–74
  rule of law 113
  Sweden's migration courts' response to Temporary Act 2016 11
balancing interests
  Covid-19 pandemic 252–6, 258, 260–1
  European Green Deal (EGD) 13, 228–32
  executive 265–6, 271
  fair balance test 284–5, 295–9
  Finland, parliamentary oversight of Covid-19 measures in 265–6, 271
  horizontal balance 10, 132, 136–7
  institutional balance, principle of 131, 132–3, 136–7, 143–4, 147
  migration crises 132–7, 138, 143–4, 147
  proportionality 52–3
  redistribution of power 133–4
  vertical balance 10–11, 132–5, 136
Baltic countries and migration 128, 129
Belarus-EU border crisis 2021 128, 129
***Better Lawmaking* programme** 142–3, 145, 228–9, 230
Better Regulation Agenda 202, 228–30
border controls
  Covid-19 pandemic 241–2, 244–6, 251–2
  informalisation of management of external borders 132, 134
  internal controls 241–2, 244–6, 251–2
  migration 10, 141–2, 161
  precautionary principle 241–2, 244–6, 251–2
  proportionality 241–2, 244–6, 251–2
  Schengen Borders Code (SBC) 125–6, 130, 135, 138–9, 144, 244–6, 251–2
business-as-usual model 8, 83–4, 86–7, 89, 91, 93, 95–7, 207

Campesi, Giuseppe 127, 135
Canada's Emergencies Act 15, 99–120
  accountability 101–2, 105–6, 116, 118
  after-the-fact inquiries, requirement for 105, 118–19
  British Columbia 103
  categories of emergency 103–5
    international emergencies 104, 105
    public order emergencies 104–5, 107, 117
    public welfare emergencies 103–4
    war emergencies 102, 104

centralisation 99, 100–2, 119
Charter of Rights and Freedoms 106
civil liberties 106, 113
climate emergency 106, 107, 110, 116
committees, commissions, and inquiries 105, 117–19
Covid-19 pandemic 99–101
 declaration of a public order emergency 100
 Freedom Convoy 99–101, 104–5, 106, 109–12, 118
 Ukraine, Russia's invasion of 108
 vaccinations for cross-border truckers 99
cumulative impact of emergencies 108
declarations of emergency 100, 102–5, 108
delegation of powers 106, 113
design 101
division of powers between provincial and federal governments 105
economic emergencies 107–8
emergency, definition of 103–4, 107, 109–11, 117
emergency management cycle as closed loop reinforcing the status quo 107, 111–14, 117
framing 111–12
Freedom Convoy 99–101, 104–5, 106, 109–12
 border crossings, targeting 100
 freezing orders 100
 inquiry 118
 law enforcement, overwhelming 100
 right-wing populist movements 110, 118
 vaccinations for cross-border truckers 99
 Yellow Vest Movement 110
freezing orders 100
future, legislating for the 107–8
institutional competence and capacity, overestimates of 107, 108–9, 112
interdisciplinary disaster studies scholarship 101, 106–7, 109, 111
interjurisdictional coordination 101, 105
international emergencies 104, 105
internment 102, 105
judicial oversight 102, 105–6, 117, 119
last resort, as a tool of 106
life, health and safety, threats to 103–4
limitations and imperfections 101, 106–12, 118–19
misinformation and disinformation 118
Parliament
 declarations of emergency, ratification or veto of 105, 117
 institutional competence and capacity, overestimates of 107, 108–9, 112
 future, legislating for the 107–8
 Parliamentary Review Committee 117–18
 rule of law 115
 supremacy of 104
past experiences, limitations of reliance on 107–8
public justification, as 113–15, 116, 119
public order emergencies 104–5, 107–8, 110, 117
public welfare emergencies 103–4
right-wing populist movements 110, 118
rule of law 100–1, 103, 106, 112–19
scope of powers 104–5
Sendai Framework on Disaster Risk Reduction, implementation of 103
terrorism 102, 104
threshold for emergency 104, 107, 109–10
transparency 102, 117
triggering emergencies, institutions as 108–9
Ukraine, Russia's invasion of 108
urgent, critical and temporary, situations must be 104
vaccinations 99
war emergencies 102, 104–5
War Measures Act 102
Cannon, Terry 111
categories of emergency 102–5, 107, 117
Central and Eastern European countries, accession to UK of 156
centralisation 72–4, 99, 100–2, 119, 366
CGAS v Switzerland 282, 286, 290–1, 293–5, 299
Charter of Fundamental Rights of the EU (CFREU)
 Covid-19 pandemic 28, 241, 243, 244, 248, 253–4
 derogation clause, absence of a general 77
 European Green Deal (EGD) 218, 220–1, 228–9, 232
 future generations, rights of 218, 220–1
 general supranational emergency clause, proposal for a 76–7
 interpretation 220–1
 migration crises 142, 145

precautionary principle 241, 243, 244, 248, 253–4
privacy 28
proportionality 241, 243, 244, 248, 253–4
children, rights of 229–30, 233
Citizens' Rights Directive (CRD) 242–56, 259–60
civil liberties 103, 113, 246
Civil Protection Mechanism (EU) 124, 190–1
civil society 193, 197, 200, 235
climate emergency *see also* **climate emergency and public participation; European Green Deal (EGD)**
access to information 186
activism of judges 36–7
anticipatory action 187–8
Canada's Emergencies Act 106, 107, 110, 116
Civil Protection Mechanism (EU) 190–1
constitutional framework 4–5, 82, 190, 192
Covid-19 pandemic 26
crisis and emergency, connection between 187–8
Czech Republic 12, 38–9, 53, 58
declarations 6, 189, 191
definition 191
democracy 14, 186
EU legal order 187–92
European Parliament 189, 193, 197
exception, state of 187, 188–92
executive, expansion of powers of 190
framing 186–91
France 12, 39–40, 41, 43, 53
Germany 12, 40, 42–3, 47, 53, 56–7
Hungary 12, 38–9, 40
national versus global issues 56
net-zero 199, 216
neutrality 197, 199–200, 205, 207, 210, 212, 214, 216–20, 226
Nordic countries 82
polycrisis, as 185
procedural guarantees 192
proportionality 12, 28–9, 36–43, 47, 53–4, 56–8
reactive framing 186, 189–91
renewable energy 186
rule of law 5, 189
separation of powers 191
strategic framing 186, 188–90, 191–2
Switzerland by ECtHR, criticism of 35
temporary measures 191–2
time 186, 190–2, 197–8, 203–5
Treaties 186
triggering a state of emergency 192
urgency, levels of 14, 186
climate emergency and public participation 185–206
Aarhus Convention 194–5, 200, 203
access to justice 194–5
accountability 193, 195
civil society 193, 197, 200
CJEU, case law of 195
collective carbon numbers, achieving 199
Commission 196–7, 199–201
consultation 194, 201
Council of EU, indirect representation of governments by 193
deadlines 197–8
decision-making 185–7, 190, 192–6, 198–200, 202–6
democracy 192–6, 204–6
EU constitutional law 192–206
EU environmental law 192–206
European Citizens' Initiative (ECI) 194
European Climate Law (ECL) 197–201, 203
European Climate Pact (ECP) 200
European Council, indirect representation through Heads of State and governments in 193
European Green Deal 196–7
European Parliament 193, 197
expertise 196–9, 204
framing 205
fundamental rights 192
future generations, rights of 197
Governance Regulation 201, 202–3
greenhouse gas emissions (GHG) 197
individual behaviour change 200
informal engagement 201
information sharing 199–200
institutions 193, 198, 201, 204
interpretation 195
IPCC 196, 198
long-term policy perspective 197
marginalised communities 205
NGOs 194–5, 198, 203
renewables acceleration areas 201–3
repositioning participation 199–201
secondary law 195–6
social behaviour change 200

stakeholder consultation 201
targets 196–9, 201, 205, 206
time for participation 203–5
transparency 193, 201
urgency of action 196–203, 205
Commission
Better Lawmaking programme 228–9
centralisation 74
climate emergency 196–7, 199–201
consultation 234–5
Covid-19 pandemic 248–9, 252
Crisis Regulation 144–5
declarations of states of emergency 70, 74
delegation 75–6
European Citizens' Initiative (ECI) 194
European Green Deal (EGD) 208, 209, 212, 216–17, 219, 221, 223, 227–30, 233–5
European Parliament 74–5
executive powers 63
general emergency clause, proposal for a 74–6
migration crises 130–1, 136, 140, 145, 155, 157–9
oil crisis in the 1970s 155, 157–9
precautionary principle 248–9, 252
proportionality 248–9, 252
public participation 196–7, 199–201
risk assessments 67
Union Civil Protection Mechanism (UCPM) 68
commissions, committees, and inquiries
Canada's Emergencies Act 105, 117–19
Denmark, crisis rhetoric during Covid-19 pandemic in 23, 27
Finland, parliamentary oversight of Covid-19 measures in 266, 273–5
Common European Asylum System (CEAS) 125, 129, 134, 141
competences
allocation 11–12, 64–5, 72
climate emergency 186, 190
European Green Deal (EGD) 215
exclusive 72, 76
general 4, 11, 124
general emergency clause, proposal for a 63–5, 68, 72, 76, 78
migration crises 124, 137, 138, 150, 155–6, 162
national competences 155–6
national security 72
oil crisis in the 1970s 155–6, 162
shared 65, 159
supportive competences 190
Competitiveness Compass 208
constitutional accommodation model 8, 84–5, 96–7
constitutional law 9–14, 38
aptness of constitutional legal orders 4, 5
climate emergency 4–5, 82, 190, 192
Covid-19 pandemic 7, 13, 17–33, 263–4, 267, 268–78
Denmark, Covid-19 pandemic in 7, 17–33
emergency constitutionalism 9–10
EU constitutional law 192–206
EU emergency law 10–12
extra-legal models 83, 84, 85
Finland 13, 263–4, 267, 268–78
general emergency clause, proposal for a 70–7
migration crises 3, 4, 11, 123–47
scrutiny/oversight, who does the 12–13
who decides 9–12
constitutional necessity, doctrine/principle of 84–91, 93–7
constitutional proportionality review 35–59
accountability 43
activism of judges 36–7, 55
balancing interests 52–3
climate emergency 12, 28–9, 36–43, 47, 53–4, 56–8
collective versus individual, prioritising 57–9
concurrent legitimacies 52–5
concurrent perspectives 56–9
constitutionality of measures 4, 7, 8, 38, 43, 55, 263, 268–9, 274, 277
Covid-19 pandemic 36–7, 55–7, 285, 294, 296, 297–300
Czech Republic 12, 46, 58
Finland 272, 275, 277
France 12, 41–2, 45
Germany 12, 42, 48
scientific evidence 44, 55
Czech Republic 12, 37–9, 41, 43, 46, 48–9, 52–5, 58
discretion 36–7
European Convention on Human Rights 36, 52, 285, 294, 296, 297–300
facts, freedom through 44–51
Finland, parliamentary oversight of Covid-19 measures in 272, 275, 277

France 12, 37–43, 45, 47–9, 53, 57–8
freedom of judges 36–59
facts, freedom through 44–51
legislator, constraining the 36, 37
new objectives or interests, development of 41
priority of one interest over another 41, 43
reinforcement of the scope of norms 38–40
standards, invalidating the interpretation by legislator of 41
theory, freedom limited by 51–9
uncontrolled standards as justification of the law 40–3
usual legal tools 38–51
fundamental rights 36, 39, 43, 46–7, 52, 58
future generations, rights of 42–3, 47, 53, 57
Germany 12, 37, 40, 42–3, 47–9, 53, 56–7
Hungary 12, 37–43, 45–6, 49–51, 55
identity-based argumentation, review of 49–51
impact of measures, limited 12, 47, 56, 59
intensification of emergencies 37, 53, 58
interests versus majority will 52–3
interpretation 37, 39, 41, 43, 49, 50, 52, 55, 58
ITLOS 36
legitimacy
concurrent legitimacies 52–5
popular 52
long-term interests, prioritising 53, 59
margin of appreciation 254, 259
migration crises 12, 37, 38, 47–51, 57
national versus global issues 56–7
new principles, recognising 38
normal times 35, 37
objective rights into subjective rights, turning 38, 41
parliaments, constraining 36, 37
political decisions, emergencies as 35–6, 39
priority of one interest over another 41, 43, 52–3, 57–9
reinforcement of the scope or norms 38–40
rule of law 12, 54
scientific conformity 45–7, 55
scientific evidence, review of 44–9, 54–5
scientific reliability 45, 47–9
short-term interests, prioritising 53, 59
temporary departures from law 36
theory, freedom limited by 51–9
truth versus majority will 54–5
uncontrolled standards as justification of the law 40–3
urgency 35–6
consultation 170, 172, 181, 194, 201, 223, 233–6
corporate social responsibility (CSR) 212
Council of the EU 63, 75, 136, 140, 144–5, 155–9, 164, 193, 220, 227
Court of Justice (CJEU), case law of
burden of proof 258–9, 260
climate emergency 195
controlled discretion, model of 13–14, 243, 260
Covid-19 pandemic 13–14, 242–60
European Green Deal (EGD) 236–7
externalisation measures 146
family reunification, income requirement for 173–6, 180–1
future generations, rights of 220–1
general emergency clause, proposal for a 77
legal certainty 145
lex specialis 139–40
Nordic Info case 242–56, 259–60
precautionary principle 13–14, 242–60
preliminary rulings procedure, role of national courts in 181, 258–9
private and family life, right to respect for 173–4
proportionality 13–14, 242–60
public participation 195
Relocations Decisions 139–40
Sweden's migration courts' response to Temporary Act 2016 173–6, 180–1
Covid-19 pandemic *see also* **Covid-19 pandemic and parliamentary oversight in Finland; Covid-19 pandemic and precautionary and proportionality principles; Covid-19 pandemic measures by ECtHR, review of**
Asylum Procedure Directive 138–9
Canada's Emergencies Act 99–101, 104–5, 106, 109–12, 118
constitutionality of executive measures 3, 4
Czech Republic 12, 46, 58
European Green Deal (EGD) 215
financial assistance 10
Finland 81–2, 92–3, 97–8

fragmentation of EU law 79
France 12, 41–2, 45
Freedom Convoy (Canada) 99–101, 104–5, 106, 109–12, 118
fundamental rights 46, 243, 253–4, 257, 260–1
general emergency clause, proposal for a 64–7, 71–3, 78–9
Germany 12, 42, 48
judicial review 243, 258, 296, 298
justification of measures 42
national versus global issues 56
Norway 81–2, 95–6, 97–8
oversight/scrutiny 13, 256, 263–79, 282
proportionality 12, 36–7, 41–2, 44–6, 48, 55–8
public health emergencies of international importance (PHEIC), declarations of 70–1
recovery instrument 67
rule of law 5
scientific evidence 44, 55
supranational emergencies 71–3, 78
SURE Regulation 66–7
Sweden 6, 81–2, 87–8, 97–8
Ukraine, Russia's invasion of 108
unilateral actions as undermining EU integration 73
vaccinations mandates 45–6, 99, 291–2, 294–5

Covid-19 pandemic and parliamentary oversight in Finland 263–79
accountability of executive 13, 266
advance preparation 265, 267, 274–5
armed conflicts 268–9
authorisation 265–74
balance of power, shift in 265–6, 271
centralisation 266
checks and balances 266, 278
committees, commissions, and parliamentary inquiries 266, 273–5
Constitution 13, 263–4, 267, 268–78
declarations of state of emergencies 268–72
legislative acts, constitutionality of 263–4, 274
limits on executive powers 266–7, 269–72
new 263
Constitutional Law Committee, *ex ante* review by 273–4, 275–8
declarations of state of emergencies 263, 265–6, 267–75, 278–9
constitutional *de jure* states 265
extra-constitutional *de facto* states 265
delegation 266, 267, 275
democratic legitimacy 265–6
derogations 275–6
Emergency Powers Act 13, 263–4, 267, 270–3, 274–5, 277
ex ante review 273–4, 275–9
executive 13, 263–79
balance of power, shift in 265–6, 271
delegation 266, 267, 275
limits 266–7, 269–73, 277
exemptions/exceptions 264, 266, 268–71, 273, 277
fundamental rights 265, 267, 268, 270, 275–6
impact assessments 275–6
interpretation 268–71
justifications for actions 266
legislative acts, constitutionality of 263–4, 274
limits on executive power 266–7, 269–73, 277
necessity, principle of 268, 277
objectives of decrees 267
parliamentary governance structure, change to a 263–4
Parliamentary Ombudsman 278
political culture 264, 279
proportionality 272, 275, 277
regulation 267–74
remote working by MPs 275
rule of law 264, 266
separation of powers 266
soft law 278
sovereignty of parliament 273–4
sunset clauses 266
temporality, principle of 268, 273, 275, 278
termination of states of emergency 265–6
triggering a state of emergency 263
types of emergency 271–2

Covid-19 pandemic measures and precautionary and proportionality principles 241–61
balancing (substantive) test 252–6, 258, 260 –1
border controls 241–2, 244–6, 251–2
Charter of Fundamental Rights of the EU (CFREU) 241, 243, 244, 248, 253–4

Citizens' Rights Directive 242–56, 259–60
CJEU, case law of 13–14, 242–60
  burden of proof 258–9, 260
  controlled discretion, model of 13–14, 243
  Nordic Info case 242–56, 259–60
  preliminary rulings procedure, role of national courts in 258–9
Commission 248–9, 252
controlled discretion, model of 13–14, 243, 260
derogations 242, 259
discretion 242–61
  consistency, lack of 14
  controlled 13–14, 243, 260
  emergency discretion, concept of 256–9, 260
  Nordic Info case 242–56, 259–60
  precautionary principle and emergency discretion 247–53, 257
  structuration of proportionality in emergency discretion 252–6, 257, 260
  unified model, lack of 14
EFTA Court, case law of 13–14, 249, 254, 260–1
emergency discretion and precautionary principle 247–53
free movement of persons 242–56, 259–60
fundamental rights 243, 253–4, 257, 260–1
internal border controls 241–2, 244–6, 251–2
interpretation 243–8, 251–2, 258–61
judicial review 243
less restrictive means test 252
margin of appreciation 254, 259
national regulations 241–52
necessity test 252–3
non-discrimination principle 246–7
Nordic Info case 242–56, 259–60
  Citizens' Rights Directive 242–56, 259–60
  discretion 242–56, 259–60
  travel restrictions 242–56, 259–60
public health, public policy, public order, and public security 246, 255, 260
public policy 245–6, 251–2
rule of law 14, 242–3, 247, 255–60
safeguards
  procedural 14, 247, 252, 255–6, 258–60
  substantive 14, 247, 252–4, 256–7, 260
Schengen Border Code (SBC) 244–6, 251–2
scientific uncertainty and precautionary principle 249
solidarity 241
structuration of proportionality in emergency discretion 252–6, 257, 260
travel restrictions 241, 242–56, 259–60
  Citizens' Rights Directive 242–56, 259–60
  free movement of persons 242–56, 259–60
Treaties 241–3, 248–9, 255
urgency 242–60
Covid-19 pandemic measures by ECtHR, review of 281–300
  acquis, no development of an emergency/crisis 12, 282, 300
  actio popularis 287, 288–93
  avoidance strategy 284–5
  causation 287
  CGAS v Switzerland 282, 286, 290–1, 293–5, 299
  counterbalancing measures 284–5, 297–8
  deferential approach 287–8, 296
  direct link between general measures and potential harm 290–1
  directly related cases and indirectly related cases, difference between 282–3
  discrimination 295
  effective remedy, right to an 293
  exhaustion of domestic remedies 288, 293–5, 299
  fair balance test 284–5, 295–9
  fair hearing, right to a 292–3
  flexibility 289–90, 293–4
  formalism 293–6
  freedom of peaceful assembly 286, 290
  general interests 286–7
  imminence of risk 287
  improvisations 299–300
  inadmissibility 284–5, 288–95
    avoidance of balance by declarations of inadmissibility 284–5
    exhaustion of domestic remedies 288, 293–6, 299
    fair balance test 284–5, 295–9
    formalism 293–6
    victim status, lack of 287, 288–93, 295–6, 299
  less restrictive measures test 298, 300
  liberty and security, right to 288

margin of appreciation 284–5, 296, 297–8
counterbalancing measures 284–5, 297–8
fair balance test 284–5, 296, 297
severity of the interference 284–5, 297
temporality of restrictive measures 284–5, 297
necessity test 287, 294
negative obligations 285–7, 298
physical integrity and lives of people, protection of 285–6
positive obligations 285–7
private and family life, right to respect for 291–2, 295
procedural rights 283–4, 292–3
proportionality 285, 294, 296, 297–300
public health emergency, characterisation of Covid-19 pandemic as a 288
public interest 294
reasonableness test 287
restrictive and intrusive, claims that measures were 285–6, 289–300
retrospectivity 292–3
severity of the interference 284–5, 297
sole or dominant reason for claims, where Covid-19 pandemic was the 282–3
subsidiarity 288, 293–4
suitability test 287
technicalities 290, 294
temporality of restrictive measures 284–5, 284–5, 297, 299–300
typical tensions and extraordinary crises 285–8
vaccination mandates 291–2, 294–5
victim status, lack of 287, 288–93, 295–6, 299
direct link between general measures and potential harm 289–91
flexibility 289–90
inadmissibility 287, 288–93, 295–6, 299

crises *see also* **crisis rhetoric during Covid-19 pandemic in Denmark**
crisis, definition of
Denmark, crisis rhetoric during Covid-19 pandemic in 20
oil crisis in the 1970s 150, 160
Crisis Regulation 128–30, 138–9, 143–5
crisification of EU policy-making 123, 146
emergency, connection with 187–8
polycrises 185

crisis rhetoric during Covid-19 pandemic in Denmark 17–33
2022 political programme 17
accidents, disasters and war, management of 19
accountability 7, 23–4, 26, 29–32
asylum seekers, illegal separation of married 32
burning platform argument 18, 29
centralisation of political decision-making 22–3
civil servants 30, 32
climate emergency 26
committees 23, 27
Constitution 7, 17–33
legal basis for deviation 19–20, 30
unwritten constitutional principle with binding effect, deviation as 19–20
violation 19–20, 29–31, 33
courts
executive's partial suspension of 7, 13, 23
rapid legislative procedure 22, 27
Supreme Court, decisions on violation of Constitution by 31
crisis, definition of 20
decision-making, centralisation of political 22–3
defence minister and head of Military Intelligence Service, handling of accusations against 24–6
election 2022 24–9
European Convention on Human Rights 28–9, 33
exceptions 21–2, 27, 32
executive 7, 19, 24–6, 31–2
centralisation of political decision-making 22–3
courts, partial suspension of 7, 13, 23
legal bases for actions 21, 28–9
majority government 24–6, 31–2
Parliament, checks by 13
facial recognition technology for use by police, introduction of 28–9
court, authorization by a 28
gang violence 28–9
Justitia think tank, criticism by 28–9
legal basis 28–9
privacy 28–9
freedom of assembly 22
fundamental rights 22, 28–30

gang violence 28–9
impeachment 24, 31–2
institutions, trust in public 30, 32
interpretation 22, 27
labelling 7, 30, 32
legal bases for actions 21–2, 28–9, 90
legality, principle of 22, 27, 33
majority governments 24–6, 31–2
Military Intelligence Service, handling of accusations against head of 24–6
Ministry of Defence, acts issued by 19
Ministry for Emergency Situations, introduction of 19
minks, culling of 21, 23–4, 32
  accountability 24, 32
  legal basis, lack of 21
  Mink Commission 21, 24
Nazi occupation 19–20
Nordic ConReason project 31
ordinary legislative procedure, exceptions to 21–2, 23, 26–7, 32
Parliament
  executive, checks on 13
  open, as remaining 23
  rapid legislative procedure 22, 27, 29–30
post-pandemic crisis rhetoric during and after the 2022 election 24–9
Prime Minister, votes of no confidence in the 31
rapid legislative procedure 22, 23, 26–7, 29–33, 89
  accountability 29–31
  clarity and consistency, lack of 22, 27, 33
  co-responsibility of Parliament with executive 30
  legality, principle of 22, 27, 33
  Parliament 22, 27, 29–30
  sunset clauses 27
  use after Covid-19 pandemic 22, 26–7
Rechtsstaat 22, 27, 32–3
resignations 31
restraint of courts 30–1
rule of law 22, 27, 29–30, 32
Second World War, violation of Constitution during 19–20
separation of powers 23, 27, 33
spill-over effects 22, 26–7
Standing Orders 21–3, 26–7, 29–32, 89
  exceptions 21–2, 27, 32
  rapid procedure 22, 27
  states of emergency 20–1, 23, 29
  sunset clauses 27
  transparency 23, 26
  urgency, matters of 22
  unwritten constitutional principle with binding effect, deviation from Constitution as an 19–20
crisis, definition of 123–4, 126
Crisis Regulation 128–30, 138–9, 143–5
  derogations 145
  force majeure 129, 143
  impact assessments 143
  Recommendation on an EU mechanism for preparedness and management of crises
  130
  situations of crisis 128, 129
  third-country nationals or non-state actors, instrumentalisation by 129, 145
Czech Republic
  climate emergency 12, 38–9, 53, 58
  Constitutional Court 43, 48–9, 53, 54–5
  Covid-19 pandemic 12, 46, 58
  fundamental rights 46
  future generations, rights of 43
  healthy environment as a public good 39, 41, 43
  proportionality review 12, 37–9, 41, 43, 46, 48–9, 52–5, 58
  rationality 46, 54, 58
  scientific conformity 46, 58
  scientific evidence 54–5
  scientific reliability 48–9

de Witte, Bruno 10, 63, 123, 192
decision-making 3–4, 9–12
  centralisation of political decision-making 22–3
  climate emergency 185–7, 190, 192–6, 198–200, 202–6
  collective decision-making 9, 11
  democracy 192–5, 233–7
  Denmark, crisis rhetoric during Covid-19 pandemic in 22–3
  European Green Deal (EGD) 236
  political decisions, emergencies as 35–6, 39
  public participation 185–7, 190, 192–6, 198–200, 202–6
  Sweden's migration courts' response to Temporary Act 2016 170, 179–81

declarations of states of emergency
Canada's Emergencies Act 100, 102–5, 108, 117
climate emergency 14, 186
conditions 7
Covid-19 pandemic 100, 268–72
European Green Deal (EGD) 215–16
Finland 92, 263, 265–6, 267–75, 278–9
general emergency clause, proposal for a 65, 70–1, 74–5
parliament, ratification or vetoes by 105, 117
prerogatives of member states 65
Deforestation Regulation 234
delegation of power 7, 75–6, 106, 113, 266, 267, 275
democracy
accountability 195
Council of the EU 193
democratic deficit 54
European Council 193
European Green Deal (EGD) 13, 215, 223, 229, 233–7
European Parliament 144, 193
Finland, parliamentary oversight of Covid-19 measures in 265–6
legitimacy 144, 196, 265–6
migration crises 137, 150, 160–1, 164
oversight/scrutiny 3, 6, 11, 137, 236, 265–6
public participation 192–5, 204–6, 235
representative democracy 193, 233
short-term approaches 160–1, 164
Denmark 88–90 *see also* **crisis rhetoric during Covid-19 pandemic in Denmark**
business-as-usual/legality/absolutist model 89, 96
constitutional accommodation, model of 96
Constitutional Act of Denmark 88–9
constitutional necessity, doctrine/principle of 88–90, 96–7
Covid-19 pandemic 81–2, 89, 97–8
legislative accommodation model 89, 96
derogations from legislation
Asylum Procedure Directive 131
Charter of Fundamental Rights of the EU (CFREU) 77
clarity 13
climate emergency 40
constitutional necessity, doctrine/principle of 88–9
Covid-19 pandemic 242, 259, 275–6
Crisis Regulation 145
Finland, parliamentary oversight of Covid-19 measures in 275–6
fundamental rights 142, 275–6
general emergency clause, proposal for a 74
migration crises 126, 127, 131, 138, 140, 142–3, 145–7
misuse 13
precautionary principle 242, 259, 275–6
proportionality 242, 259, 275–6
Relocations Decisions 140
Returns Decisions 150
review, measures as subject to regular, independent 13
temporary measures 13, 138
Dermine, Paul 11
DiCarlo, Rosemary A 208
disaster, definition of 67
discretion
controlled discretion, model of 13–14, 243, 260
Covid-19 pandemic 13–14, 242–61
emergency discretion, concept of 256–9, 260
executive 112
migration crises 130
Nordic Info case 242–56, 259–60
precautionary principle 13–14, 242–61
proportionality 13–14, 36–7, 242–61
rule of law 256–9
structuration of proportionality in emergency discretion 252–6, 257, 260
discrimination 153–4, 155, 156, 246–7, 295
do no harm/do no significant harm principle 210, 214, 217–18, 221, 227–9, 232
dualism 167–8, 171
duration of states of emergency 4, 12, 75, 143, 265–6, 299
Dworkin, Ronald 257
Dyzenhaus, David 12, 113–15, 119

economic growth 152–9, 297, 212
EESC (European Economic and Social Committee) 209, 211, 223–4, 227, 229–30, 233–5
effective remedy, right to an 293

EFTA (European Free Trade Area) Court, case law of 13–14, 249, 254, 260–1
Emergencies Act (Canada) *see* **Canada's Emergencies Act**
emergency, definition of 4, 6–9
Canada's Emergencies Act 103–4, 107, 109–11, 117
elasticity of concept 5–9
migration crises 123–4, 126
normalcy, line between an emergency and 109–10
emergency management cycles as enforcing the status quo 107, 111–12, 118
Emergency Support Instrument (ESI) 124
employment *see also* **EU labour migration law, history of; oil crisis in the 1970s and EU labour migration policy**
European Green Deal (EGD) 211, 224
policies 224
unemployment 155–7, 159
energy *see also* **oil crisis in the 1970s and EU labour migration policy**
efficiency and affordability 211
European Green Deal (EGD) 211–12, 215–16
renewable energy 186, 201–3, 216, 226
transition 212
Ukraine, Russia's invasion of 212, 215–16
equality and non-discrimination 153–4, 155, 156, 246–7, 295
Ericsson, Angelica 258
EU Agency for Migration (EUAA) 135
EU labour migration law, history of 150–4, 164
1950s and 1960s 150, 151–3, 157
1970s 154
1980s and 1990s 150
Action Programme in Favour of Migrant Workers and their Families 154
archival documents 150
Association Agreements 150, 152–4
bilateral agreements 150
economic growth 152–4, 157
free movement of workers 151–4
guest-workers 151
institutions 150, 153–4
non-Community workers 151–4
non-discrimination 153–4
rights of migrant workers 154
short-term workers 151
soft law 150, 153
working conditions 153
European Citizens' Initiative (ECI) 194, 235–6
European Civil Protection Tool 68
European Climate Pact (ECP) 200
European Commission *see* **Commission**
European Convention on Human Rights (ECHR) *see also* **Covid-19 pandemic measures by ECtHR, review of**
accession of EU 261
constitutional court, ECtHR acting as a 35
Denmark, crisis rhetoric during Covid-19 pandemic in 22, 28–9, 33
European Green Deal (EGD) 237
liberty and security, right to 288
life, right to 39, 142
private and family life, right to respect for 28–9, 33, 141–2, 167, 170–1, 173–81, 291–2, 295
proportionality 36, 52
Sweden's migration courts' response to Temporary Act 2016 166–8, 171–81
European Council 134–5, 136–7, 144, 193, 209
European Environment Agency (EEA) 207, 209
European Green Deal (EGD) 207–37
Aarhus Regulation 233, 236
access to justice 13, 233–7
balance of interests and rights 13, 228–32
Better Regulation Agenda 228–30
business as usual paradigm 207
Charter of Fundamental Rights of the EU (CFREU) 218, 220–1, 228–9, 232
children, rights of 229–30
CJEU, case law of 236–7
Commission 208, 209, 212, 216–17, 219, 221, 223, 227–30, 233–5
Competitiveness Compass 208
conciliation 232
consultation 223, 233–6
Covid-19 pandemic 215
decarbonisation 208, 210
declarations of states of emergency 215–16
Deforestation Regulation 234
democracy 13, 215, 223, 229, 233–7

do no harm/do no significant harm principle 210, 214, 217–18, 221, 227–9, 232
economic growth 207, 212
EESC 209, 211, 223–4, 227, 229–30, 233–5
employment policies 224
energy 211–12, 215–16
environmental justice 13, 211, 223–8, 232–3, 237
environmental organisations, role of 236
European Citizens' Initiative (ECI) 235–6
European Parliament 208, 210, 212–14, 218, 230, 235
extraterritoriality 217
fair ecological transformation of EU's socio-economic system 210–12
finance and costs 209, 211–12, 217, 223, 225–7
fundamental rights 231–2, 237
future generations, rights of 208, 210, 211, 214, 218–23, 229
impact assessments 228–32
indigenous people, rights of 234–5
institutions 225, 228, 230–1, 235, 237
integration 225, 227, 228, 234, 237
interpretation 214, 220–2, 225, 237
leave no one behind principle 207, 210–11, 214–15, 217–18, 224, 227–9, 235
marginalised communities 226, 233–5
normative dynamic 212–14
poverty 212, 224, 226, 229
precautionary principle 219, 221
proportionality 229, 231–2
protests 213
provisional measures 215
public interest 216, 228, 236
public participation 196–7
radioactive waste 219–20
refugees, formal recognition of climate 234
renewable energy 216, 226
rule of law 215, 237
social justice 13, 208, 210, 213, 223–8, 232–3, 237
spatiotemporal dimensions, legal considerations of the 214–23, 227
strategic legal framework for a just ecological transition 223–37
sustainability trajectory, ambivalence of 213–14, 237
temporary measures 215–16
urgent legal action 215–16, 227, 230
vulnerability 13, 208–12, 213–29, 232–7
young people, role of 233–4

European Ombudsman (EO) 236

European Parliament (EP) 63–6
climate emergency 189, 193, 197
Council of the EU 75
democracy 144, 193
European Council, President attending meetings of 144
European Green Deal (EGD) 208, 210, 213–14, 218, 230, 235
general emergency clause, proposal for a 64–6, 70–1, 74–8
migration crises 136, 137, 143, 144–5
public participation 193, 197

European Pillar of Social Rights (EPSR) 211, 224, 226

European Semester 224

exception, state of 3, 36, 64, 189
climate emergency 187, 188–92
Denmark, crisis rhetoric during Covid-19 pandemic in 21–2, 27, 32
Finland, parliamentary oversight of Covid-19 measures in 264, 266, 268–71, 273, 277

executive
accountability 105, 106
authorisation of measures 3–4, 102, 265–74
Canada's Emergencies Act 105, 106, 112–14, 117
centralisation of political decision-making 22–3
climate emergency 190
Commission 63
Council of the EU 63
Covid-19 pandemic 3, 4, 242, 257
decision-making 3, 11
delegation of powers 106, 113, 266, 267, 275
Denmark, crisis rhetoric during Covid-19 pandemic in 7, 13, 19, 22–6, 28–9, 31–2
division of powers 105, 137
expansion of powers 190
Finland, parliamentary oversight of Covid-19 measures in 13, 263–79
legal bases for actions 21, 28–9
precautionary principle 242, 257
proportionality 242, 257
Sweden's migration courts' response to Temporary Act 2016 11, 169–71

exhaustion of domestic remedies 288, 293–5, 299
expertise 196–9, 204
externalisation measures for migration and asylum 127, 131–2, 134
CJEU, lack of control by 146
informalisation of management of external borders 132, 134, 146
third countries, deals with 131–2, 134, 146
extra-legal measures models of emergency powers 83, 84, 85

facial recognition technology for use by police, introduction of 28–9
Faigman, David L 47
fair balance test 284–5, 295–9
fair hearing, right to a 292–3
family reunification
application of the Act 172–9, 180
CJEU, case law of 173–6, 180–1
Family Reunification Directive 167, 170, 173–9
income requirement 169–70, 172–80
limits 169–79
private and family life, right to respect for 170–1, 173–81
student loans as acceptable income 177–8
Sweden's migration courts' response to Temporary Act 2016 169–79
Farano, Alessi 55
Ferejohn, John 4
Finland 90–3 *see also* **Covid-19 pandemic and parliamentary oversight in Finland**
anticipatory statutorification, principle of 91
business-as-usual/legality/absolutist model 91, 93, 96
categories of emergency 91
Constitution 90–3, 96–7
constitutional necessity, doctrine/principle of 91, 93
Covid-19 pandemic 81–2, 92–3, 97–8
declarations of state of emergency 92
Emergency Powers Act 90–2
human rights, limits on 96
legislative accommodation model 96
structural model of constitutional accommodation 96
temporary legislation, adoption of 93
textual model of constitutional accommodation 91, 93, 96–7
Fischer, Frank 187
Fit for 55 legislative package 197
flexibility 79, 289–90, 293–4
food supply and food security 124, 208–9
force majeure 129, 143
formalism 12, 290, 293–6
fragmentation of EU law 11, 63, 79
framing 7, 73–4
Canada's Emergencies Act 103 111–12
climate emergency 186–91, 205
powers theory, framing of 73, 74
public participation 205
reactive framing 186, 189–91
strategic framing 186, 188–90, 191–2
France
age assessments for migrants 47–8
climate emergency 12, 39–40, 41, 43, 53
Environmental Charter in preamble of the Constitution 39–40, 53
environmental protection, constitutional value of 39
future generations, rights of 53
Constitutional Council 39, 43, 45, 47–9, 53, 57–8, 222
Covid-19 pandemic 12, 41–2, 45
crime of solidarity, constitutionality of 38, 49
future generations, rights of 53
identity-based argumentation 49
liberty, equality, fraternity 49
interpretation 39, 41, 49
migration crises 12, 38, 47–8, 49
age assessments for migrants 47–8
crime of solidarity, constitutionality of 38, 49
non-regression, principle of 40
preparatory works 42–3, 45
priority of one interest over another 57–8
proportionality 12, 37–43, 45, 47–9, 53, 57–8
terrorist attacks in 2015 10
Yellow Vest Movement 110
free movement of persons 11, 242–56, 259–60
free movement of workers 151–4, 158, 162
Freedom Convoy (Canada) 99–101, 104–5, 106, 109–12, 118
freedom of assembly 22, 254, 286, 290
freedom of establishment 254
freedom of expression 86

Friberg, Anna 116
Frontex 135
fundamental/human rights *see also* **Charter of Fundamental Rights of the EU; European Convention on Human Rights (ECHR); future generations, rights of**
Canada's Emergencies Act 106, 113
civil liberties 103, 113, 246
climate emergency 192
Covid-19 pandemic 46, 243, 253–4, 257, 260–1
Denmark, crisis rhetoric during Covid-19 pandemic in 22, 28–30
derogations 142
European Green Deal (EGD) 231–2, 237
executive 257
Finland 96, 265, 267, 268, 270, 275–6
freedom of assembly 22, 254, 286, 290
freedom of expression 86
Hungary 43
impact assessments 13, 143, 145, 147
inhuman or degrading treatment 141–2
life, right to 39, 142
migration 131, 141–7, 149, 154, 162–3
national security 141–2
Nordic countries, emergency models in 98
oil crisis in the 1970s 149, 162–3
precautionary principle 243, 253–4, 257, 260–1
private and family life, right to respect for 141–2
proportionality 36, 39, 43, 46–7, 52, 58, 243, 253–4, 257, 260–1
public participation 192
sincere cooperation, principle of 145
social rights 153, 205, 211, 224, 226
suspension 141
future generations, rights of
CJEU, case law of 220–1
domestic courts, case law of 221–2
European Green Deal (EGD) 208, 210, 211, 214, 218–23, 229
France 53
Germany 42–3, 47, 57
impact assessments 229
proportionality 42–3, 47, 53, 57
public participation 197
solidarity 211, 218, 220
vulnerability 218–23
general principles of EU law 145, 147
general supranational emergency clause, proposal for a 63–79
accountability 67
activation of the clause, circumstances which justify 11, 71–2
affected State's principle 72
centralised emergency management 72–4
Charter of Fundamental Rights of the EU (CFREU) 76–7
CJEU, judicial control by 77
Commission 70, 74–6
competences 63–5, 68, 72, 76, 78
constitutional issues 70–7
Covid-19 pandemic 64–7, 71–3, 78–9
declarations of state of emergencies 65, 70–1, 74–5
delegation of powers 75–6
derogation clauses in EU Treaties 74
European Parliament 64–6, 70–1, 74–8
flexibility clause, reactivation of 79
fragmentation of EU law 11, 63, 79
framing of powers theory 73, 74
improper implementation, controls and remedies in cases of 77
institutions 65, 74–8
interpretation 71, 73, 76, 78
last-resort mechanism, as 72, 76
legal bases 65, 66–9, 70, 78
legality, principle of 76
national security 72–4
ordinary revision procedure 64–5
prerogatives of member states 65, 68, 72–4
primary law 11, 63–79
priority measures 67
solidarity clause 65, 69, 72–3
sovereignty 64, 73–4
spill-over effects 71–2
supranational constitutional framework, context of the 74–7
supranational emergencies 71–4, 77–8
transparency 67
generational equity *see* **future generations, rights of**
Germany
accountability 43
Basic Law 40, 42–3, 48–9, 222
climate emergency 12, 40, 47, 56–7
Climate Change Act, invalidation of the 43
Federal Constitutional Court 40, 56–7

fundamental national objective, environmental protection as a 40
future generations, rights of 42–3, 47, 57
global emergency, as 56–7
Covid-19 pandemic 12, 42, 48
Federal Constitutional Court 40, 46–7, 56–7, 222
future generations, rights of 42–3, 47, 57
migration crises 12, 50
priority of one interest over another 53
proportionality 12, 37, 40, 42–3, 47–9, 53, 56–7
scientific conformity 46–7
scientific reliability 48
good administration, principle of 255
government *see* **executive**
Greece
living conditions of refugees 125, 141–2
migration crises 128, 129, 135, 141–2
relocation of asylum seekers 128
Green Deal *see* **European Green Deal (EGD)**
Grogan, Joelle 7
Gross, Oren 8, 83–4
Guterres, António 208–9, 214

High Representative of the Union for Foreign Affairs and Security Policy 209
Hilson, Chris 198
human rights *see* **fundamental/human rights**
Hungary
climate emergency 12, 38–9, 40
Constitutional Court 42, 49–51
constitutional identity, referendum on 50
Covid-19 pandemic 12, 43, 45–6
fundamental rights 43
healthy environment, right to a 39, 40, 41
life, right to 39
non-derogation, principle of 40
non-regression, principle of 40
subjective right, as 39
identity-based argumentation 49–50, 55
interpretation 43, 50, 55
migration crises 12, 49–51
CJEU decisions, limits on 50
community members, identity of 50, 55
identity-based argumentation 49–51
relocation of asylum seekers 49–50
scientific conformity 45–6
proportionality 12, 37–43, 45–6, 49–51, 55
truth versus majority will 55

identity-based argumentation, review of 49–51
immigration *see* **migration crises**
impact assessments 143, 145, 147, 201–2, 228–32, 275–6
impeachment 24, 31–2
indigenous people, rights of 234–5
individual behaviour change 200
information sharing 186, 199–200
inhuman or degrading treatment 141–2
inquiries *see* **commissions, committees, and inquiries**
institutions *see also* **particular institutions**
balance 65, 75, 78, 131, 132–3, 136–7, 143–4, 147
Canada's Emergencies Act 107, 108–9, 112
climate emergency 193, 198, 201, 204
complex environments 11
Council of the EU 63, 75, 136, 140, 144–5, 155–9, 164, 193, 220, 227
Denmark, crisis rhetoric during Covid-19 pandemic in 30, 32
division of labour 137
European Green Deal (EGD) 225, 228, 230–1, 235, 237
failure 162–3
fundamental rights 142–3
general emergency clause, proposal for a 65, 74–8
interplay between institutions 11
migration crises 125, 131–3, 136–7, 142–4, 147, 150, 153–4, 162–3
notification, duty of 144
public participation 193, 198, 201, 204
supranational constitutional framework 74–7
triggering other emergencies, competence and capacity as 108–9
trust 30, 32
Integrated Political Crisis Response Arrangements (EU) 124
integration
civic integration 174
European Green Deal (EGD) 225, 227, 228, 234, 237
migration 149, 151, 159, 160, 162–4
oil crisis in the 1970s 149, 151, 159, 160, 162–4
Sweden's migration courts' response to Temporary Act 2016 170, 173–4, 179

intensification of emergencies 37, 53, 58
interdisciplinary disaster studies scholarship 101, 106–7, 109, 111
interests versus majority will 52–3
inter-governmentalism 134–5, 138, 143–4, 147
Interinstitutional Agreement on Better Law-making 142–3, 145, 230
international emergencies 104, 105
international law 8–9, 167, 174
international obligations, compatibility of measures with 168, 170–80
internment 102, 105
InvestEU Just Transition programme 226

Jasanoff, Sheila 107
judicial review *see also* **constitutional proportionality review; Covid-19 pandemic measures by ECtHR, review of**
- activism 36–7, 55
- Canada's Emergencies Act 102, 105–6, 117, 119
- consequentialism 44
- constitutional model 9
- Covid-19 pandemic 243, 258, 296, 298
- deferential approach 12, 287–8, 296
- Denmark, crisis rhetoric during Covid-19 pandemic in 7, 13, 22–3, 27, 30–1, 90
- facts, freedom through 44–51
- general emergency clause, proposal for a 69
- identity-based argumentation, review of 49–51
- migration crises 131
- precautionary principle 243
- proportionality 243
- restraint 30, 31, 36, 263
- Return Directive 131
- theory, freedom limited by 51–9
- usual legal tools 38–51

Just Transition Fund 211, 226
justice
- access to justice 13, 194–5, 233–7
- environmental justice 211, 225–7, 232–3
- social justice 13, 208, 210, 213, 223–8, 232–3, 237

Klatt, Matthias 47
Korkea-Aho, Emilia 278
Koselleck, Reinhart 160
Kuvolesi, Kati 201

labelling 7, 30, 32
last-resort mechanisms 69, 72, 76
leave no one behind principle 207, 210–11, 214–15, 217–18, 224, 227–9, 235
Lee, Maria 194
legal bases for actions 8–9
- Denmark, crisis rhetoric during Covid-19 pandemic in 21–2, 28–9, 90
- general emergency clause, proposal for a 65, 66–9, 70, 78
- Single Market Emergency Instrument (SMEI) 124

legal certainty 13, 139, 145, 146, 147, 255–6
legal realism 167
legality, principle of 22, 27, 33, 76, 264
legislation *see also* **Canada's Emergencies Act; derogations from legislation; general supranational emergency clause, proposal for a; Treaties**
- ad hoc instruments 128–9, 134
- constitutional status, granting legislative principles 38
- Denmark
  - ordinary legislative procedure, exceptions to 21–2, 23, 26–7, 32
  - rapid legislative procedure 22, 23, 26–7, 29–33, 89
  - Standing Orders 21–3, 26–7, 29–32, 89
- emergency clauses 127, 131, 134–5, 138–9, 144, 146–7
- Finland, Emergency Powers Act in 13, 263–4, 267, 270–3, 274–5, 277
- Fit for 55 legislative package 197
- future, legislating for the 107–8
- legislative accommodation model 87, 96–7
- migration crises 123–47
- primary law 11, 63–79, 123–34, 136–7, 139–40, 144–6
- rapid legislative procedure in Denmark 22, 23, 26–7, 29–33, 89
- secondary law 63, 123–31, 133, 138–45, 152, 195–6

legislative accommodation model 87, 89, 95–7
legislatures *see* **parliaments**
lex specialis 8, 131, 138, 139–40, 255
liberty and security, right to 288
life, right to 39, 142
Loevy, Karin 165, 181
long-term perspectives 53, 59, 151, 156, 160–1, 163–4, 197
loyal cooperation, principle of 131, 133

Macron, Emmanuel 35
majority will 52–5
margin of appreciation
counterbalancing measures 284–5, 297–8
Covid-19 pandemic 254, 259, 284–5, 296, 297–8
fair balance test 284–5, 296, 297
private and family life, right to respect for 174
severity of the interference 284–5, 297
temporality of restrictive measures 284–5, 297
marginalised communities 110, 205, 226, 233–5
Martín Rodríguez, Pablo 135
Meister, Moritz 47
Mendes, Joana 257
migration crises 12, 123–47 *see also* **oil crisis in the 1970s and EU labour migration policy**
2015 crisis 127, 136, 141, 149
ad hoc instruments 123, 126, 127–31, 134, 138–40, 144, 146–7
legislative measures 128–9, 134
non-legislative measures 128, 130
ratione materiae, ratione personae and *ratione temporis* 139
age assessments for migrants 47–8
Agenda on Migration 2015 127
Asylum Procedure Directive 130, 131, 138–9
balance of powers 132–7, 138
horizontal balance 10, 132, 136–7
institutional balance, principle of 131, 132–3, 136–7, 143–4, 147
vertical balance 10–11, 132–5, 136
Baltic countries 128, 129
Belarus-EU border crisis 2021 128, 129
binding and non-binding instruments 127
border control 10, 141–2, 161
classification of emergency mechanisms 127
climate emergency 234
collective interests versus individual interests 57–9
Commission 130–1, 136, 140, 145
competences 124, 137, 138
constitutional implications of emergency measures 3, 4, 11, 123–47
Council of the EU 136, 140, 144–5
crisification of EU policy-making 123, 146
crisis, definition of 123–4, 126
Crisis Regulation 128–30, 138–9, 143–5
democratic foundations of decisions 137
derogations from ordinary legislation 126, 127, 131, 138, 140, 142–3, 145–7
distortive effects of emergency measures 143–6
Dublin Regulation 138, 141
emergency clauses in legislation 127, 131, 134–5, 138–9, 144, 146–7
emergency, definition of 123–4, 126
EU Agency for Migration (EUAA) 135
European Council 134–5, 136–7, 144
European Parliament 136, 137, 143, 144–5
externalisation measures 127, 131–2, 134, 144, 146
France 12, 38, 47–8, 49
fundamental rights 131, 141–6
Greece 128, 129, 135, 141–2
Hungary 12, 49–51
identity-based argumentation 49
informalisation of management of external borders 132, 134
institutions 125, 131, 132–3, 136–7, 142–4, 147
instrumentalisation by third-country nationals or non-state actors 128, 129, 145
inter-governmentalism 134–5, 138, 143–4, 147
international events, large-scale or high-profile 130
interpretation 123, 134, 140–1
judicial review 131
legal certainty 139, 145, 146, 147
legislative measures 123–47
derogations from ordinary legislation 126, 127, 131, 138, 143, 145–6
emergency clauses in legislation 127, 131, 134–5, 138–9
migratory pressure, impact of 138–41
legitimate expectations 145
lex specialis 131, 138, 139–40
living conditions 125, 141–2
loyal cooperation, principle of 131, 133
mass influxes 126, 128–9, 130
national security 128, 130, 135, 140–2, 145
necessity, situations of 123–4, 126, 136, 146
notification, duty of 144
oversight/scrutiny 133, 137, 153
primary law 123–34, 136–7, 139–40, 144–6
proportionality 12, 37, 38, 47–51, 57

public interest 141
public order, threats to 130, 135, 140, 142
public policy, serious threats to 126
Recommendation on an EU mechanism for preparedness and management of crises 130
Relocations Decisions 130, 134, 136, 139–40
Return Directive 130–1
rule of law 5, 144
safeguard clauses of TFEU 124
Schengen Area 127, 134, 141
Schengen Borders Code 126, 130, 135, 138–9, 144
secondary law 123–4, 126, 128–31, 133, 138–45
separation of powers 137
serious organised crime, threats from 130
sincere cooperation, principle of 133, 136, 144–5, 147
Single Market Emergency Instrument (SMEI) 11, 124
situations of crisis 128, 129, 138
soft law 124, 130, 146
temporary measures 126, 127–8
Temporary Protection Directive (TPD) 128, 139, 140–1, 144, 146
terrorist attacks 123, 130
third countries 131–2, 134, 146
Treaties 123–8, 130–2, 134, 136–7, 139–40, 144–6
typology of emergency response mechanisms 126–32
Ukraine, Russia's invasion of 128, 140, 146
undocumented migrants, helping 38, 49
unilateral responses, prevention of 125, 138, 139

minks in Denmark, culling of 21, 23–4, 32, 90
misinformation and disinformation 118
monocentric position 167–9, 170, 172, 176–9
mutual defence clause 10

national security 25, 72–4, 128, 130, 135, 140–2, 145
Natura 2000 sites 202
Nazi regime 19–20
necessity, principle of
constitutional necessity, doctrine/principle of 84–91, 93, 96–7
Covid-19 pandemic 252–3, 287, 294
Finland, parliamentary oversight of Covid-19 measures in 268, 277
migration crises 123–4, 126, 136, 146
precautionary principle 252–3
proportionality 252–3

New Pact on Migration and Asylum 125, 128, 143
New Zealand, declarations of emergency in 103
Ní Aoláin, Fionnuala 8, 84
non-governmental organisations (NGOs) 194–5, 198, 203, 236
Nordic ConReason project 31
Nordic countries, emergency models of the 9, 81–98
anticipatory statutorification, principle of 87, 91
business-as-usual/legality/absolutist model 83–4, 86–7, 89, 91, 93, 96–7
climate emergency 82
combination of models, use of a 85
constitutional accommodation, model of 84–6, 96–7
constitutional necessity, doctrine/principle of 84–90, 91, 93, 96–7
Covid-19 pandemic 81–2, 87–9, 92–3, 97–8
Denmark 81–2, 88–90, 96–8
exceptionalism 30–1
extra-legal models 83, 84, 85
Finland 90–3, 96–8
structural model of constitutional accommodation 96
temporary legislation, adoption of 93
textual model of constitutional accommodation 91, 93, 96–7
fundamental rights 96, 98
legislative accommodation model 87, 89, 96, 97
Norway 93–8
structural model of constitutional accommodation 96
Sweden 85–8, 96
textual model of constitutional accommodation 91, 93, 96–7
theoretical frameworks of emergency models 82–5, 96
types of emergency situations, different models in different 9
war emergencies and peacetime emergencies, difference between 86–8, 96

***Nordic Info* case** 242–56, 259–60
normalcy, times of 35, 37, 109–10, 166, 179, 181
Norway 93–6
business-as-usual/legality/absolutist model 95–6
Constitution 93–4
constitutional necessity, unwritten doctrine/ principle of 94–5, 96–7
Covid-19 pandemic 81–2, 95–6, 97–8
Infection Control Act 1994 95
Health Preparedness Act 2000 95
Norwegian Corona Commission 95
temporary legislation 95–6
extraordinary circumstances 93–4
legislative accommodation, model of 95, 96
sectoral legislation or specific laws 95
structural model of constitutional accommodation 96
textual model of constitutional accommodation 96

oath 210, 212, 221, 228
oil crisis in the 1970s and EU labour migration policy 7, 149–64
border closures 161
Commission 155, 157–9
common and shared concern 162
common approach
after the oil crisis 155–9, 164
before the oil crisis 151–4, 164
competences 155–6, 159, 162
Council of the EU 155–9, 164
crisis, concept of 150, 160
demographics, changes in 157
economic growth 155–9
equal opportunities 155
free movement of workers 158, 162
historical analysis 149–50
institutional failure 162–3
integration 149, 151, 159, 160, 162–4
long-term approaches 151, 156, 160–1, 163–4
national bans on migrant workers 161
non-Community workers 159
political instability 156
populism 161, 164
residence rights 158
restrictive measures 156
rights of migrants 149, 162–3
rule of law 163
sectoral legislation 158, 161
short-term approaches 150, 151, 155–64
Single Permit Directive 163
students, admission of 157
timeframes of crisis 159–63
ubiquity, unpredictability and durability, problems of 160
unemployment 155–7, 159
xenophobia and racism 156
old and new-type of crises 6
Orbán, Viktor 51
Orlove, Ben 185–6
oversight/scrutiny 4, 6–7 *see also* **judicial review**
Canada's Emergencies Act 105, 109, 115, 117
Covid-19 pandemic 13, 256, 263–79, 282
Crisis Regulation 143
democracy 3, 6, 11, 137, 236, 265–6
European Green Deal (EGD) 216
European Parliament 144
Finland, parliamentary oversight of Covid-19 pandemic in 13, 263–79
fundamental rights 6
migration crises 133, 137, 153
national policies 70
parliaments 7, 12–13, 105, 117, 144, 263–79
rule of law 6, 14
who does the scrutinising 4, 12–13

Pact on Migration and Asylum 125, 128, 143
parliaments *see also* **European Parliament** (**EP**)
accountability of national parliaments 193
authorisation of measures 58, 105, 265–74
Canada's Emergencies Act 105, 107–9, 112, 115, 117–18
courts, executive's partial suspension of 13
committees 117–18
Covid-19 pandemic 13, 263–79
declarations of emergency, ratification or veto of 105, 117
Denmark, crisis rhetoric during Covid-19 pandemic in 13, 22–3, 27, 29–30
Finland 13, 263–79
future, legislating for the 107–8
oversight/scrutiny 7, 12–13, 105, 117, 144, 263–79
proportionality 36, 37
supremacy 76, 104, 273–4
Sweden's migration courts' response to Temporary Act 2016 178–9

participation *see* **climate emergency and public participation**
Pasquino, Pasquale 4
Patterson, James 188, 191
Peers, Steve 139
Perrow, Charles 108
political polarisation 191
polycentric position 167–9, 170, 172–6, 178–81, 198
populism 110, 118, 161, 164
poverty 212, 224, 226, 229
precautionary principle 219, 221 *see also* **Covid-19 pandemic and precautionary and proportionality principles**
preparation
 anticipatory statutorification, principle of 87, 91
 business-as-usual model 97
 Canada's Emergencies Act 102, 107–8
 climate emergency 187–8
 Covid-19 pandemic 267, 274–5
 Denmark 19, 95
 Finland 91, 265, 267, 274–5
 general emergency clause, proposal for 67
 migration crises 143
 preparatory works 27, 167–8, 172, 174, 176–80
 public participation 194, 204
 reaction, emergency as 190–1
 Recommendation on an EU mechanism for preparedness and management of crises 130
primary law 11, 63–79, 123–34, 136–7, 139–40, 144–6
priorities
 collective versus individual, prioritising 57–9
 general emergency clause, proposal for a 67
 long-term interests, prioritising 53, 59
 proportionality 41, 43, 52–3, 57–9
 short-term interests, prioritising 53, 59
privacy 28–9
private and family life, right to respect for 141–2, 167, 170–1, 173–81, 291–2, 295
procedure *see also* **climate emergency and public participation**
 Aarhus Convention 194–5
 climate emergency 192
 Covid-19 pandemic 283–4, 292–3
 ECtHR, case law of 283–4, 292–3
 rule of law 14, 247, 255–6, 258–60
 safeguards 4, 14, 247, 252, 255–6, 258–60
proportionality *see also* **constitutional proportionality review; Covid-19 pandemic and precautionary and proportionality principles**
 European Green Deal (EGD) 229, 231–2
 private and family life, right to respect for 177
public health emergencies of international importance (PHEIC), declarations of 70–1
public interest 52, 141, 179, 216, 228, 236, 294
public order 72, 104–5, 107–8, 110, 117, 130, 135, 140, 142
public participation *see* **climate emergency and public participation**
public policy 115, 126, 130, 236, 245–6, 251–2, 255, 260
public welfare emergencies 103–4

radioactive waste 219–20
Rapid Border Intervention in the Aegean Sea Region 135
Rechtsstaat 22, 27, 32–3
Recovery and Resilience Facility (RRF) 229
relativist/extra-legal measures approach to constitutionality 7, 8
Relocations Decisions 130, 134, 136, 139–40
renewable energy 186, 201–3, 216, 226
residence rights 152, 154, 158, 169, 171
retrospectivity 292–3
Return Directive 130–1
rhetoric *see* **crisis rhetoric during Covid-19 pandemic in Denmark**
Rivers, Julian 36–7
Rodriguez, Pablo Martín 8–9
Roma inclusion 234
rule of law 3, 255–7
 access to a court, right of 255
 Canada's Emergencies Act 100–1, 103, 106, 112–19
 climate emergency 5, 189
 Covid-19 pandemic 5, 242–3, 247, 255–60
 Denmark, crisis rhetoric during Covid-19 pandemic in 22, 27, 29–30, 32
 discretion 256–9
 European Green Deal (EGD) 215, 237
 Finland, parliamentary oversight of Covid-19 measures in 264, 266

judicial review 12, 54
legal certainty, principle of 255–6
limited governance/power, theory of 257
migration 5, 144, 163
oil crisis in the 1970s 163
oversight/scrutiny 6, 14
precautionary principle 242–3, 247, 255–60
procedural safeguards 14, 247, 255–6, 258–60
proportionality 12, 242–3, 247, 255–60
public justification, as 113–15, 116
scaffolding 116–19, 120, 243, 260
short-term approaches 163
substantive safeguards 14, 247, 256–7, 260
Sweden's migration courts' response to Temporary Act 2016 169
vagueness 156
Runciman, David 150, 159–64
Russia *see* **Ukraine, Russia's invasion of**

safety valves, proposal for 170–1, 174–7
Scheinin, Martin 278
Schengen Area 127, 134, 141, 241
Schengen Borders Code (SBC) 125–6, 130, 135, 138–9, 144, 244–6, 251–2
scientific conformity 45–7, 55
scientific evidence, review of 44–9, 54–5
scientific reliability 45, 47–9
scientific uncertainty 249
Schmitt, Carl 7–8, 35, 64, 73, 83
Schütze, Robert 144
scrutiny *see* **oversight/scrutiny**
Second World War, Nazi occupation of Denmark during 19–20
secondary law 63, 123–31, 133, 138–45, 152, 195–6
Sendai Framework on Disaster Risk Reduction, implementation of 103
separation of powers 23, 27, 33, 105, 137, 266
serious organised crime, threats from 130
short-term approaches 53, 59, 150, 151, 155–64
sincere cooperation, principle of 73, 133, 136, 144–5, 147
Single Market Emergency Instrument (SMEI) 11, 124
Single Permit Directive 163
social behaviour change 200
Social Climate Fund 211, 226
social exclusion 212
social justice 13, 208, 210, 213, 223–8, 232–3, 237
social rights 153, 205, 211, 224, 226
socio-ecological Oath/Green Oath 210, 212, 221, 228
soft law 124, 130, 146, 150, 153, 278
solidarity 10, 155, 241
Civil Protection Mechanism (EU) 191
climate emergency 56
Covid-19 pandemic 241
France, crime of solidarity in 38, 49
general emergency clause, proposal for a 65, 69, 72–3
Solidarity Fund (EU) 124
sovereignty 45, 56, 64, 73–4, 76, 104, 273–4
spill-over effects 22, 26–7, 71–2
Stability and Growth Pact (SGP) 224
Stacey, Jocelyn 6, 35, 54, 189
states of emergency 7, 265–6 *see also* **declarations of states of emergency**
definition 20
Denmark, crisis rhetoric during Covid-19 pandemic in 20–1, 23, 29
derogations 242
duration 4, 12, 75, 143, 265–6, 299
termination of states of emergencies 4, 265–6
triggering 192
Støjberg, Inger 32
strategy framing 186, 188–90, 191–2
Streeck, Wolfgang 161
structural model of constitutional accommodation 96
subsidiarity 76, 229, 233, 288, 293–4
Sulyok, Tamás 51
sunset clauses 27, 266
supranationalism *see* **general supranational emergency clause, proposal for a** 63
Sustainable Development Goals (SDGs) 197, 224, 227, 228–9
Sweden 85–8 *see also* **Sweden's migration courts' response to Temporary Act 2016**
Act of Succession of 1810 (SO) 86
anticipatory statutorification, principle of 87
business-as-usual/legality/absolutist model 86–7, 96
Constitution 86
constitutional accommodation model 86, 96

constitutional necessity, doctrine/principle of 86–7
Covid-19 pandemic 6, 81–2, 87–8, 97–8
Freedom of the Press Act 1949 86
Fundamental Law on Freedom of Expression 1991 86
Instrument of Government (RF) 86
legislative accommodation model 87, 96
social trust, social distancing upheld by 6
temporary legislation 88
voluntary measures 6
war emergencies and peacetime emergencies, difference between 86–8, 96
Sweden's migration courts' response to Temporary Act 2016 165–81
2015 crisis 165, 169, 178–9
Aliens Act 169, 171
background 169–70
civic integration 169, 174
CJEU, case law of
family reunification, income requirement for 173–6, 180–1
preliminary references, reluctance to make 181
consultation 170, 172, 181
decision-making of Swedish courts 170, 179–81
dualism 167–8, 171
European Convention on Human Rights 166–8, 171–81
Europeanisation of Swedish law 166–81
legal literature, theories in 166–9
monocentric position 167–9, 170, 172, 176–9
polycentric position 167–9, 170, 172–6, 178–80
transparency 168
evidence-based studies, need for 166, 180
executive 11, 169–71
extension of Act 169
family reunification
application of the Act 172–9, 180
CJEU, case law of 173–6, 180–1
Family Reunification Directive 167, 170, 173–9
income requirement 169–70, 172–80
limits 169–79
private and family life, right to respect for 170–1, 173–81
student loans as acceptable income 177–8
indeterminacy of law 166
integration 170, 173–4, 179
international obligations, compatibility with 168, 170–80
interpretation 167–8, 171–2, 175–7, 179–80
legislator, fidelity to the 178–9
legislative process 170–2, 180
Migration Court of Appeal 169, 176–7
monocentric position 167–9, 170, 172, 176–8
normalcy, decision-making in times of 166, 179, 181
polycentric position 167–9, 170, 172–6, 178–81
preparatory works 167–8, 172, 174, 176–80
private and family life, right to respect for 167, 170–1, 173–81
residence permits 169, 171
respite, objective of 178–9
role of Swedish courts 170
safety valves, proposal for 170–1, 174–7
self-sufficiency 170, 175
Swedish Migration Agency, appeals of decisions of 169
transparency 168–9
workload 180
Switzerland's lack of action on climate emergency, criticism of 35

targets on climate emergency 196–9, 201, 205, 206
temporary measures *see* **time/temporality**
Temporary Protection Directive (TPD) 126, 128, 139, 140–1, 144, 146
termination of states of emergencies 4, 265–6
terrorism 10, 14, 19–20, 69, 94, 104, 123, 130
Tesauro, Giuseppe 78–9
textual model of constitutional accommodation 91, 93, 96–7
third countries
Crisis Regulation 129, 145
externalisation measures 131–2, 134, 136
migration crises 131–2, 134, 146
thresholds for emergency 104, 107, 109–10
Thunberg, Greta 116
time/temporality *see also* **Sweden's migration courts to Temporary Act 2016, response of**
Aarhus Convention 203
Asylum Procedure Directive 131

climate emergency 186, 190–2, 197–8, 203–5
Covid-19 pandemic 284–5, 284–5, 297, 299–300
Denmark, crisis rhetoric during Covid-19 pandemic in 19, 27
duration of states of emergency 12, 75, 143, 299
European Green Deal (EGD) 215–16
exceptions 268, 273
fair balance test 297
Finland, parliamentary oversight of Covid-19 measures in 268, 273, 275, 278
framing 190
legal certainty 13
margin of appreciation 284–5, 297
migration 126, 127–8, 159–63
oil crisis in the 1970s 159–63
proportionality 12, 36
public participation 197–8, 203–5
sunset clauses 27, 266
Sweden 88
Temporary Protection Directive (TPD) 126, 128, 139, 140–1, 144, 146
termination of states of emergencies 4, 265–6
Timmermans, Frans 213
Tocqueville, Alexis de 160–1
transparency 7, 236, 266
accountability 26
Canada's Emergencies Act 102, 117
climate emergency 193, 201
Denmark, crisis rhetoric during Covid-19 pandemic in 23, 26
general emergency clause, proposal for a 67
migration crises 137
public participation 193, 201
Sweden's migration courts' response to Temporary Act 2016 168–9
travel restrictions during Covid-19 pandemic 241, 242–56, 259–60
Treaties *see also* **general supranational emergency clause, proposal for a**
climate emergency 186, 193
Covid-19 pandemic 241–3, 248–9, 255
crisis, definition of 123–4
emergency, definition of 123–4
European Parliament 63
migration crises 123–8, 130–2, 134, 136–7, 139–40, 144–6
safeguard clauses 124
triggering emergency responses
Canada's Emergencies Act 107–9
climate emergency 187, 191–2, 196
constitutional law 9
Covid-19 pandemic 263
general emergency clause, proposal for a 64, 71
migration crises 134, 145
Nordic countries 81, 92
Trócsnáyi, László 51
truth versus majority will 54–5
Tushnet, Mark 83
types of emergency *see* **categories of emergency**

Ukraine, Russia's invasion of 17, 26, 43, 58, 74
Covid-19 pandemic 108
decision-making 10
energy 212, 215–16
European Green Deal (EGD) 212, 215–16
migration crises 128, 140, 146
Temporary Protection Directive (TPD) 128, 140, 146
vulnerability 215–16
Union Civil Protection Mechanism (UCPM) 63, 67–8
United Nations (UN) 70, 209
urgency of action 14–15
Canada's Emergencies Act 104
climate emergency 14, 186, 196–203, 205
Covid-19 pandemic 242–60
Denmark, rapid legislative procedure in 22
European Green Deal (EGD) 215–16, 227, 230
precautionary principle 242–60
proportionality 35–6, 242–60
public participation 196–203, 205
renewables acceleration areas 201–3

vaccination mandates 45–6, 99, 291–2, 294–5
Venice Commission 76, 265, 279
victim status before ECtHR 287, 288–93, 299
direct link between general measures and potential harm 289–91
flexibility 289–90
inadmissibility 287, 288–93, 295–6, 299
positive obligations 287, 288
vaccination mandates 291–2

von der Leyen, Ursula 78, 129, 208, 214, 218
vulnerability 13, 208–12, 213–29, 232–7

war and armed conflicts 6, 77 *see also* **Ukraine, Russia's invasion of**
Canada 102, 104–5
Covid-19 pandemic 268–9
Denmark, Nazi occupation of 19–20
economic growth 151, 153
Finland 90, 268–9
internment 102
peace agreements 5
peacetime emergencies and war emergencies, difference between 86–8, 96
Second World War, Nazi occupation of Denmark during 19–20
Sweden 86–8, 94, 96
terrorism 102
Weis, Lael K 38
WHO (World Health Organization) 70–1, 244, 247
Wilson, Andrew 185–6

xenophobia and racism 156

Yellow Vest Movement 110
young people, role of 233–4

Zemskova, Anna 9
Zwitter, Andrej 3

www.ingramcontent.com/pod-product-compliance
Ingram Content Group UK Ltd.
Pitfield, Milton Keynes, MK11 3LW, UK
UKHW020238290926
15470UKWH00002B/608

9 781509 993321